In the Collected Studies Series:

C. J. BISHKO
Studies in Medieval Spanish Frontier History

PETER LINEHAN
Spanish Church and Society, 1150-1300

JOSEPH F. O'CALLAGHAN
The Spanish Military Order of Calatrava and its Affiliates

JEAN GAUTIER DALCHÉ
Economie et société dans les pays de la Couronne de Castille

C. R. BOXER
From Lisbon to Goa, 1500-1750
Studies in Portuguese Maritime Enterprise

DAVID HERLIHY
The Social History of Italy and Western Europe, 700-1500

DAVID HERLIHY
Cities and Society in Medieval Italy

LÉON-ROBERT MÉNAGER
Hommes et institutions de l'Italie normande

PIERRE RICHÉ
Instruction et vie religieuse dans le Haut Moyen Age

JACQUES DUBOIS
Histoire monastique en France au XIIe siècle

RAYMONDE FOREVILLE
Gouvernement et vie de l'Eglise au Moyen-Age

BRYCE LYON
Studies of Western European Medieval Institutions

DONALD E. QUELLER
Medieval Diplomacy and the Fourth Crusade

REINHARD ELZE
Päpste-Kaiser-Könige und die mittelalterliche Heerschaftssymbolik

CHRISTOPHER R. CHENEY
The Papacy and England, 12th-14th Centuries

YVES DOSSAT
Eglise et hérésie en France au XIIIe siècle

Spanish and Portuguese
Monastic History
600–1300

Charles Julian Bishko

Spanish and Portuguese Monastic History 600–1300

VARIORUM REPRINTS
London 1984

British Library CIP data

Bishko, Charles Julian
Spanish and Portuguese monastic history, 600-1300. – (Collected studies series; CS188)
1. Monasticism and religious orders – Spain – Middle Ages, 600-1500 2. Spain – Church history – Medieval period, 600-1500 3. Monasticism and religious orders – Portugal – Middle Ages, 600-1500
4. Portugal – Church history – Medieval period, 600-15(
I. Title
271'.0094601 BX2682

ISBN 0-86078-136-4

Published in Great Britain by Variorum Reprints
20 Pembridge Mews London W11 3EQ

Printed in Great Britain by Galliard (Printers) Ltd
Great Yarmouth Norfolk

VARIORUM REPRINT CS188

CONTENTS

Preface		i–iv
I	The Pactual Tradition in Hispanic Monasticism *London: Variorum Reprints, 1984*	1–43
II	The Date and Nature of the Spanish *Consensoria Monachorum* *American Journal of Philology, LXIX. Baltimore, Maryland, 1948*	377–395
	Additional Note	396A–399A
III	Gallegan Pactual Monasticism in the Repopulation of Castile *Estudios dedicados a Menéndez Pidal, vol. II. Madrid, 1951*	513–531
	Additional Note	532A–536A
IV	Portuguese Pactual Monasticism in the Eleventh Century: The Case of São Salvador de Vacariça *Estudos de História de Portugal, vol. I – sécs. X-XV. Homenagem a A. H. de Oliveira Marques. Lisbon: Editorial Estampa, Lda., 1982*	139–154

V Spanish Abbots and the Visigothic Councils of Toledo 139–150

Humanistic Studies in Honor of John Calvin Metcalf. University of Virginia Studies, vol. I. Charlottesville, Virginia, 1941

Additional Note 151A–152A

VI The Abbey of Dueñas and the Cult of St Isidore of Chios in the County of Castile (10th-11th Centuries) 345–364

Homenaje a Fray Justo Pérez de Urbel, OSB, vol. II. Abadía de Silos, 1977

VII The Liturgical Context of Fernando I's Last Days According to the So-Called "Historia Silense" 47–59

Hispania Sacra XVII-XVIII. Madrid-Barcelona, 1964-65 = Miscelánea en Memoria de Dom Mario Férotin, 1914-1964. Barcelona, 1965

VIII Liturgical Intercession at Cluny for the King-Emperors of Leon 53–76

Studia Monastica III. Abadía de Montserrat, 1961

Additional Note 77A–82A

IX Count Henrique of Portugal, Cluny, and the Antecedents of the Pacto Sucessório 155–188

Revista Portuguesa de História XIII. Coimbra, 1971

Additional Note 189A–190A

X	The Spanish Journey of Abbot Ponce of Cluny	311–319
	Ricerche di Storia Religiosa I (Studi in Onore di Giorgio La Piana). Rome, 1957	
	Additional Note	320A–321A
XI	The Cluniac Priories of Galicia and Portugal: Their Acquisition and Administration, 1075-c.1230	305–356
	Studia Monastica VII. Abadía de Montserrat, 1965	
	Additional Note	357A–358A
XII	Peter the Venerable's Journey to Spain	163–175
	Studia Anselmiana XL (Petrus Venerabilis 1156-1956). Rome, 1956	
XIII	Peter the Venerable's Traverse of Spain: Some Further Observations	1–13
	London: Variorum Reprints, 1984	
Index		1–7

This volume contains a total of 336 pages

To my wife
Lucretia Ramsey Bishko
who, as always,
shared unstintingly
in the making
of these papers.

PREFACE

Medieval Spanish and Portuguese monastic history is religious history; it is social and economic history; it is the history of the rise, survival, diffusion and operation of ideas, institutions, spirituality, culture. To the myopia that results from its study as a narrowly ecclesiastical discipline corresponds an impoverished comprehension of the forces of social, structural and intellectual change below the Pyrenees which afflicts those who ignore the monastic factor or underestimate its profoundly creative role in Iberian history – a role that commences in the Romano-Suevo-Visigothic epoch, extends with increasing force down through the long, formative centuries of the Reconquista, and reaches its resounding climax in the still imperfectly investigated movement of the Observancia and other powerful monastic revivals of the Later Middle Ages and the Siglo de Oro. Furthermore, to a degree by no means always appreciated, the narrative and documentary materials relating to Luso-Hispanic monasticism, particularly before the twelfth century, cast a revealing light (often unobtainable from other sources) upon the history, institutions, lines of cultural innovation and circulation, and factors of growth in secular no less than in religious life – a light focused, moreover, at the vital local and regional levels where medieval society can be most meaningfully assessed.

It is with these general considerations in mind that in the essays here collected I have long sought to explore neglected or manifestly misapprehended problems central to reconstructing the course of Iberian monastic evolution, not by any means for the Middle Ages as a whole but at three critical stages of its earlier history. Of the thirteen studies included in this volume, ranging in date of preparation from 1941 to 1983, two (I, XIII) appear in print for the first time, although a preliminary version of Study I can be found in *Classical Folia* XXVII (1973), 173-185, under the title "Hispanic Monastic Pactualism: The Controversy Continues."

Studies I-IV scrutinize the genesis and remarkable persistence of the peculiarly indigenous tradition of Iberian pactual cenobitism from late Visigothic times to its eventual confluence, in the course of the monastic colonization of the Castilian, Riojan and Luso-Gallegan frontier lands, with the new Carolingian Benedictinism entering western Spain from Aquitaine and Catalonia in the ninth and tenth centuries. The resultant synthesis, as yet far too little acknowledged, of Hispanic and trans-Pyrenean monastic practices and liturgy I have also treated in "Salvus of Albelda and Frontier Monasticism in Tenth-Century Navarre," a paper first published in 1948 in *Speculum* XXIII and subsequently reprinted in my *Studies in Medieval Spanish Frontier History* (Variorum Reprints: London, 1982).

Studies V-VII examine the often misinterpreted monastic factor in the celebrated Visigothic councils of Toledo, the impact of Byzantine and Carolingian currents upon a key proto-Benedictine monastic foundation of King Alfonso III, and the Hispanic Rite setting of the Leonese-Castilian king-emperor Fernando I's death as one essential key to determining the composition of the anonymous *Historia Silense.*

Finally, six studies (VIII-XIII) treat major issues in the "Europeanizing" penetration of Cluny into Spain and Portugal between the eleventh and thirteenth centuries. These seek to clarify the geography and chronology of the Burgundian monastic dependencies in the Peninsula; the administration of these possessions by the mother abbey; and the significant political as well as ecclesiastical implications of Ibero-Cluniac expansion and alliance for the history of the Hispanic Empire of the king-emperors of Leon-Castile and the separatist ambitions of the counts of Portugal, implications especially evident in the direct personal interventions and visitations of the abbots of Cluny. On these topics should also be consulted my closely related papers "Fernando I and the Origins of the Leonese-Castilian Alliance with Cluny," first published in Spanish in Buenos Aires (*Cuadernos de Historia de España,* XLVII-XLVIII, 1968; XLIX-L, 1969; revised English version in the Variorum volume just cited), and "A Hispano-Cluniac Benefactor in the Epoch of Navarro-Aragonese Separation: Fortún Garcés Cajal and the Founding of San Adrián de Vadoluengo (Sangüesa), 1133-1145," scheduled to appear in the forthcoming *Homenaje* to Prof. Claudio Sánchez Albornoz.

In the Additional Notes, and in Studies I and XIII, I have tried to take due cognizance of the current growing literature in the field, especially the major contributions by Pérez de Urbel, Orlandis, Linage Conde, Díaz y Díaz, Mattoso, Segl, Reilly, and others. This has compelled me to reconsider various positions I had assumed or defended on controversial issues; but while I am fully aware of the extent to which the historiography of the last several decades has extended and enriched our understanding of medieval Spanish and Portuguese cenobitism, and cheerfully acknowledge the debt I owe to my commentators for occasional corrections in matters of detail, I have not found it necessary to revise in any essential respect the fundamental theses argued in these pages. If my views do something to stimulate in the rising new generation of Iberianists a greater awareness of the many unresolved complexities of the monastic constituent in the formation of medieval Spain and Portugal, they will have served a useful purpose.

Over the years I have accumulated numerous obligations, only a few of which can be given individual mention. The collections of the Harvard University Libraries, the Library of Congress, the Catholic University of America and (above all) my own University of Virginia have been indispensable, while I owe many past favors to friends and colleagues, and to the staffs of the Archivo Histórico Nacional, the Real Academia de la Historia, and the Biblioteca Nacional, all of Madrid. Acknowledgement is gratefully made of the financial support of these researches by the Frederick Sheldon Fund of Harvard University and by two agencies of the University of Virginia, the Wilson Gee Institute for Research in the Social Sciences and the University Research Committee. For permission to reproduce various of these papers I would cordially thank the Johns Hopkins University Press, Baltimore, Md. (II), the Jefatura de Publicaciones, Consejo Superior de Investigaciones Científicas, Madrid (III, VI); Editorial Estampa, Lda., Lisbon (IV), The University of Virginia, Charlottesville, Va. (V), the Abbey of Santo Domingo de Silos (Burgos) (VI), the Editorial Board of *Revista Portuguesa de Historia*, Coimbra (IX), Dom Josep Massot OSB, editor of *Studia Monastica*, Abbey of Montserrat (VIII, XI), and to the Biblioteca Pontificio Ateneo S. Anselmo, Rome (XII).

Particularly appreciated in the publication of this collection have been the counsel and cooperation of Mr. John Smedley of Variorum Reprints.

Chiefly, I would pay heartfelt and necessarily inadequate tribute to my wife, Lucretia Caroline Ramsey Bishko, whose learning and constructive criticism have so frequently enriched the preparation of these studies, and to whom in collected form they are affectionately dedicated.

CHARLES JULIAN BISHKO

University of Virginia
July 1983

I

THE PACTUAL TRADITION IN HISPANIC MONASTICISM

The historical development of Hispanic monasticism in the Early Middle Ages can no longer be envisaged as the relatively simple, straightforward story it appeared in the 17th century to its first major chroniclers, Prudencio de Sandoval, Antonio de Yepes and Gregorio de Argaiz.[1] In recent decades the need has become increasingly urgent to advance beyond the older simplistic accounts and to perceive that in the last century of Roman Hispania, under the Suevic and Visigothic monarchies, and in the first four hundred years of the Reconquista, the Iberian Peninsula in this as in other fields displays marked regional diversities, striking originality of institutions, and a tenacious adherence to indigenous patterns that until the days of the Leonese-Castilian king-emperors Fernando I and Alfonso VI set it apart from the main stream of ultra-Pyrenean, typically 'European', cenobitic evolution.

In the traditional conception there existed below the Pyrenees down to the eventual triumph of full Benedictinism a single vigorous ascetic movement, thoroughly orthodox by proto-monastic standards, which could be studied in the canons of the Romano-Visigothic councils, the *ordines* of the Hispanic Rite, the eclectically used *codices regularum* of both eastern and western Rules (to which those of Sts Leander and Isidore of Seville and of St Fructuosus of Braga came to be added), and the *Vitae sanctorum* and ascetic writings produced by the Suevic and Visigothic Churches.[2] To be sure, the point at which the autochthonous cenobitism succumbed to the code of Monte Cassino was disputed. Many, especially the older, scholars sought to fix the date as early as possible, on the assumption that well before 711 the great majority of peninsular abbeys were already authentically Benedictine. Others, more soundly,

[1] Prudencio de Sandoval, *Primera parte de las fundaciones de los monasterios del glorioso padre San Benito* (Madrid, 1601); Antonio de Yepes, *Coronica general de la Orden de San Benito* (Irache, 1609–1621; abridged ed. by J. Pérez de Urbel, *Crónica general de la Orden de San Benito*, Madrid, 1959–60. Biblioteca de autores españoles, vols. 123–5); Gregorio de Argaiz, *La soledad laureada por San Benito y sus hijos en las iglesias de España* (Madrid, 1675). [This study is a revised, much expanded version of my paper "Hispanic Monastic Pactualism: The Controversy Continues," in *Classical Folia*, XXVII (1973), 173–85.]

[2] See, on the subject in general, Antonio de Siles, "Investigaciones históricas sobre el origen y progresos del monacato español," *Memorias de la Real Academia de la Historia*, VII (1832), 47–578 (dated but especially useful for the older bibliography); J. Pérez de Urbel, *Los monjes españoles en la Edad Media* (Madrid, 1933–4); *idem*, "Los monjes españoles en los tres primeros siglos de la Reconquista," *Bol. r. Acad. hist.*, CI (1932), 21–113; Anscari Mundó, "Il monachesimo nella Penisola iberica fino al sec. VII," in *El monachesimo nell'alto medioevo e la formazione della civiltà occidentale, Settimane di studio del Centro Italiano di Studi sull'Alto Medioevo, Spoleto*, IV (1957), 73–108 (discussion, 109–17); Maur Cocheril, *Études sur le monachisme en Espagne et au Portugal* (Lisbon, 1966); Antonio Linage Conde, *Los orígenes del monacato benedictino en la Península ibérica* (León, 1973) (with extensive bibliography); J. R. Sánchez, "Guía para el estudio del monacato medieval en la Península ibérica, 1959–1979," *Cistercium*, XXXI (1979), 193–220.

pointed to the abundant evidence showing that the indigenous non-Benedictine tradition of the late Visigothic period not only survived the disaster of the Islamic invasion but long flourished in both Muslim and Christian Spain, until its archaic spirituality and observances inevitably and without noticeable resistance gave way to the exclusive observance of the *Regula Benedicti* (henceforth *RB*) as universally established above the Pyrenees.

This latter view, still widely current, is by no means wholly mistaken or superseded; but at two vital points it requires drastic correction. One of these, on which the following pages will touch only marginally, is the belief in a relatively early Hispanic reception of *RB*, for it is now certain from the pioneer essays of Antonio de Siles (1832) and Dom Beda Plaine (1899), the authoritative works of Dom Justo Pérez de Urbel, and the recent major investigations of José Mattoso and Antonio Linage Conde, that before 711 no true Benedictine communities existed anywhere in the Peninsula, although the Rule itself apparently circulated there in the 7th century.[3] Spain and Portugal constitute in fact one of the last major subdivisions of early medieval Europe to abandon the *regula mixta* of the *codices regularum* for the sole observance of the Montecassinese code; and whatever the precise roles we ultimately assign in this transformation to the Carolingian reformism of Benedict of Aniane, the latter's enthusiastic Catalan partisans, the influence of the Cluniacs under Sancho el Mayor, Fernando *el Magno* and Alfonso VI, and the Franco-Hispanic or *afrancesado* bishops of the 11th century, it now has to be recognized that west of the Hispanic Mark the Benedictine victory was a slow, stubbornly resisted process which profoundly affected, along very diverse chronological and regional lines, the religious and cultural history of the Alta Reconquista.

The other aspect of the subject, no less complex and even more controversial, bears upon the question whether the indigenous cenobitism was not itself deeply divided for centuries, both before and after 711, between two contrasting and in part hostile traditions, one of orthodox type, similar in spirituality and institutional organization to that characteristic of the pre-Benedictine West, the other a constitutionally quite different movement, originally Galaico-Portuguese in provenance, which came to be deeply rooted in central and western Iberia during the first centuries of the Reconquista and which can be described, for comparative purposes and without theological implications, as heterodox. This second peninsular ascetic tradition, along with the thesis of the remarkable duality of Hispanic cenobitism prior to the ultimate establishment of Benedictinism, is the subject of the slim but authentically pathbreaking volume published in 1907 at Stuttgart by Dom Ildefons Herwegen of Maria Laach Abbey, then still a young student but already displaying the talents and scholarship he was later to devote as abbot to historical science and the modern liturgical movement. The work, entitled *Das Pactum des hl. Fruktuosus von Braga: ein Beitrag zur Geschichte des suevischwestgotischen Mönchtums und seines Rechtes*, was reprinted in 1965 and remains one of the truly fundamental contributions to the study of early medieval Luso-Hispanic monastic history,[4] although in recent

[3] Siles, *op. cit.*; Beda Plaine, *La Regla de San Benito y su introducción en España* (originally published in *Soluciones católicas*, 1899; separately issued, 35 pp., Valencia, 1900); Pérez de Urbel, *opp. citt.*; *idem*, *El condado de Castilla* (Madrid, 1969), I, 326–37; José Mattoso, *Le monachisme ibérique et Cluny: les monastères du diocèse de Porto de l'an mille à 1200* (Louvain, 1968), 112–34; Linage Conde, *Origenes*, I, 61–86 (valuable survey of the 'estado de la cuestión'), 275–88; *idem*, "La difusión de la Regula Benedicti en la Península ibérica," *Regulae Benedicti studia*, I (Hildesheim, 1972), 297–325.

[4] Stuttgart, 1907 (*Kirchenrechtliche Abhandlungen*, 40); reprinted by Verlag P. Schippers, Amsterdam, 1965. To be cited henceforth as 'Herwegen'. On this learned future abbot of Maria

years its contentions have been increasingly challenged and have become the subject of lively debate.

What the German Benedictine modestly styled a *Beitrag* has in fact resulted in a renewed scrutiny of long known monastic writings and other documentation of the Visigothic and post-Visigothic eras, a search for new or previously neglected texts, and, above all, a major effort to resolve the complex problematics of the genesis, lines of diffusion and comparative significance of the two rival pre-Benedictine Hispanic traditions, the orthodox Visigothic and the Luso-Gallegan heterodox. Since some leading authorities deny the very existence of this duality before or after 711, this has given rise to sharply conflicting interpretations and drawn into the discussion such Spanish and Portuguese specialists as Pérez de Urbel, Mário Martins, Anscari Mundó, Manuel Díaz y Díaz, José Orlandis, Ramón Abadal i de Vinyals, Antonio Linage Conde, José Mattoso, and others, and from outside Iberian soil Maur Cocheril, Claude Barlow, and the present writer.

The controversy has done much to enrich and deepen our whole understanding of early Hispanic monachism, but it is fair to say that on the central issues no notable degree of consensus has yet been reached. The following pages propose to consider, therefore, although inevitably much more summarily than the many complexities of the theme make desirable, the chief points in dispute; to defend the validity of certain of Herwegen's more fundamental contentions; and to call attention to some hitherto ignored or misunderstood aspects of the Luso-Gallegan tradition that are central to its correct understanding both before and after the year 711. Such a survey, if it does not bring the warring camps closer together, may at least encourage renewed investigation into the authentic role of the pactual tradition in the monastic history of the Hispanic Middle Ages.

I

We shall commence by reviewing the major issues raised in the historiography of the subject between 1907 and the present.

In his book Herwegen depicts the Hispanic monastic pactum as a written juridical act of threefold purpose: as *Gründungsformel*, it recorded the foundation of the ascetic society (of men or women or, as commonly in the peninsular adhesion to paleo-monastic practice, of both); as *Professformel*, it contained the formal commitment of the religious to the ascetic life; and as *Wahlinstrument*, it declared their choice of governor, the abbot or abbess.[5] Unlike the individual profession act which in the orthodox tradition the monk submitted at his reception with the pledge of *stabilitas*, *conuersio morum*, and *obedientia* without reservation (in a manner which, according to Herwegen, St Benedict saw as analogous to the unilateral oath taken by the Roman army recruit enlisting for military service),[6] the pactual profession was a communal

Laach (1874–1946), see H. A. Reinold, "Herwegen, Ildefons," *The New Catholic Encyclopedia* (New York, 1967), VI, 1087; E. von Severus, "Herwegen, Ildefons," *Lexikon für Theologie und Kirche*, 2nd ed. (Freiburg, 1960), 284–5.

[5] Herwegen, 24–50.

[6] *RB* 58, 10–23, ed. Rudolph Hanslik, *Benedicti Regula* (*Corpus scriptorum ecclesiasticorum latinorum*, LXXV; Vienna, 1960); Herwegen, 29–31; Christine Mohrmann denies to this and to the five other occurrences in *RB* of the terms *militare, militia*, any genuine military meaning, even in the paleomonastic sense of combat against demons, and deflates the connotation of these terms

instrument, contained in a single diploma which all the religious jointly subscribed, with the names of those subsequently received being added as occasion arose. Addressed to a named abbot or abbess, it created a specifically personal bond: the monks made a binding submission (*traditio*) of their persons to their superior but at the same time retained the extraordinary right in carefully stipulated circumstances to reject the abbatial authority when this was exercised arbitrarily or unjustly. For this inherently conditional relationship Herwegen found the model in the political oath (*Untertaneneid*) which he believed the Visigoths took at the coronation of their king, when they promised fidelity only so long as he ruled equitably under law.[7] Thus, the Luso-Gallegan monastic pactum, as its very phraseology confirmed, embodied the substitution of Germanic juridical concepts for the Roman law principles of normal monasticism, and brought into being a peculiarly bilateral or synallagmatic contractual cenobial polity, in sharp contrast with that founded upon the canonical monarchical abbatiate.[8]

The oldest, and after 711 most widely adopted, form of the pactum appeared to be that appended as a model formula to the terminal chapter (20) of the *Regula (monastica) communis* (henceforth *RCom*), a work traditionally ascribed to the metropolitan St Fructuosus of Braga-Dumio (653/4-ca. 665), which Herwegen identified as in fact a collection of decrees promulgated by Luso-Gallegan abbatial synods that met under the presidency of this monk-prelate (*episcopus sub regula*).[9] It was possible therefore to assign the introduction of the Germanicized collective profession instrument to this notable propagator of the ascetic gospel in the Iberian northwest in the middle 7th century, when *Gallaecia* as in the Roman and Suevic epochs still extended well below the river Miño to the northern bank of the Duero.

Furthermore, since pactualism was to survive after 711 as a prominent feature of the Hispanic cenobitism of the Alta Reconquista, it was possible to trace its evolution through extant specimens and the rubrics of the monastic *ordines* of the Hispanic Rite. From published and manuscript sources Herwegen was in fact able to assemble six pactual texts—five associated with known communities, the sixth the model formula

---

to synonymity with the civil phrase *seruitus Dei*: "La langue de saint Benoît," in *Sancti Benedicti Regula monachorum*, ed. Philibert Schmitz (rev. ed., Maredsous, 1955), 28–31; reprinted in her *Études sur le latin des chrétiens*, II, Rome, 1961, 337–9). She does not however explore for *RB* 58 the general parallel of *promissio* (i.e., *professio*) and the Roman military oath, which Herwegen favors, and to which, as we shall see, St Isidore makes explicit allusion in his *Regula monachorum* 4, 2. On the Benedictine profession act as, unlike the Hispanic pactum, not a *Vertrag* but a *Rechtgeschäft eigener Natur*, see the monographs of I. Herwegen, *Studien zur benediktinischen Professformel* and M. Rothenhaüsler, *Zur Aufnahmeordnung der Regula s. Benedicti* in *Beiträge zur Geschichte des alten Mönchtums und des Benediktinerordens*, III (Münster i. W., 1912).

[7] Herwegen, 28, 34–5.

[8] This remarkable Hispanic experiment has escaped the notice of Dom David Knowles in his informative little volume, *From Pachomius to Ignatius: A Study in the Constitutional History of the Religious Orders* (Oxford, 1966).

[9] There is no modern critical edition of *RCom*. The text in Holstenius-Brockie, *Codex regularum* (Augsburg, 1759), I, 208–19, which actually dates from 1661, is reprinted in J. P. Migne, *Patrologiae cursus completus. Series latina* (Paris, 1844–55) (henceforth *PL*), 87, cols. 1109–30; and, with some minor corrections and a Castilian translation by Julio Campos Ruiz in *Santos padres españoles*, ed. Vicente Blanco García, J. Campo Ruiz and I. Roca Melia (Madrid, 1971. Biblioteca de autores cristianos), II, 163–211. A useful introduction accompanies the English translation by Claude Barlow in *Iberian Fathers*, II (*The Fathers of the Church*, v. 63; Washington, 1969), 176–209 (and cf. 145–54). Herwegen, 1–4, reproduces the pactum from Holstenius-Brockie, and discusses the nature of *RCom* on 53–60. See also Claude Barlow, "The Latin Texts of the Regulae of Fructuosus of Braga," *Bracara Augusta*, XI–XII (1960–61), 15–18.

Mabillon had secured from a lost codex of St-Honorat de Lérins;[10] and by classifying these in three categories according to the extent of their linguistic, prescriptive and juridical divergence from the prototypal 'Fructuosan' pactum (henceforth *RComP*) he was able to chart the successive stages of approximation to Benedictine norms until in the course of the 11th century the then long anachronistic usage disappeared before the full acceptance below the Pyrenees of orthodox Benedictinism.[11]

Herwegen's book, although only slowly recognized in Spain and Portugal, met there with general favor, so that from the 1930s such authoritative historical accounts of early medieval Hispanic monasticism as those of García Villada, Pérez de Urbel and Mário Martins fully accepted its conclusions.[12] Then, in 1951, I myself, on the basis of additional pacta unknown or inaccessible in 1907 to Herwegen, published in the *Estudios dedicados a Menéndez Pidal* a paper entitled "Gallegan Monastic Pactualism in the Repopulation of Castile". This undertook to interpret the history of pactualism not from Herwegen's exclusively juridico-institutional viewpoint but in terms of its place in the frontier colonization of Castile and the Rioja between the ninth and eleventh centuries.[13] I called attention to the fact that after 711 the heterodox tradition could be documented only from two widely separated subdivisions of medieval Spain, the Galaico-Portuguese west and the Castello-Riojan east, with no discoverable traces occurring in the Cantabrians-to-Duero heartland of the Asturo-Leonese state, among the Mozarabic abbeys of Islamic Spania, or in the new foundations transplanted to León and Castile by refugee monks from the Muslim south. On Herwegen's premise, which I accepted, of the Gallegan origin of pactual monasticism, the extant pacta of the Galaico-Portuguese west, although few in number, seemed to offer no special problem; but to account for the surprising emergence of the heterodox tradition beyond León in the multiplying foundations of Castile and the Rioja, I conjectured that when, as the chronicles tell us, Alfonso I (739–757) evacuated the inhabitants of Braga, Lugo, Astorga and other Luso-Gallegan districts, monks familiar with the pactual polity must have carried it eastwards to Liébana, Asturias de Trasmiera and Bardulia, i.e., the birthplaces of Castile. From these districts their successors would have spread it in a variety of forms, including the Lérins or (as I preferred to call it) Burgalese Formula, southwards into the new foundations of the late ninth and tenth centuries below Burgos and in the Rioja. On the whole, my contentions were in harmony with Herwegen's primarily institutional exposition; but for the first time they related pactualism to the general historical problem of Reconquest expansion, posited a key role for the Gallegan monastic element in the making of primitive Castile, and called attention to a little appreciated phenomenon, a synthesis of pactual monasticism and Carolingian Reform Benedictinism that was widespread in the colonial monastic foundations of Castile and trans-Ebro Navarre during the Early Reconquest.

[10] Herwegen's collection, based upon specimens previously gathered by his master Ulrich Stutz (cf. the latter's *Vorwort* in Herwegen, vii–x, on the origin of the whole pactual project) and including one previously unknown example, the pactum of the abbess Eufrasia, nevertheless overlooked some four or five pacta then available in Spanish and Portuguese editions; cf. the pertinent bibliographical notices in Bishko, "Gallegan Pactual Monasticism in the Repopulation of Castile," *Estudios dedicados a Menéndez Pidal*, II (Madrid, 1951), Study III in this volume.

[11] Herwegen, 36–49.

[12] Z. García Villada, *Historia eclesiástica de España* (Madrid, 1929–1936), II, 1, 291–8; Pérez de Urbel, *Monjes españoles*, I, 438–50; II, 372–5; Mário Martins, "O monacato de S. Frutuoso de Braga," *Biblos*, XXVI (1950), 315–412. For surveys and recent bibliography, see Linage Conde, *Orígenes*, I, 291–342; C. J. Bishko, "Pactos monásticos", in *Diccionario de historia eclesiástica de España* (Madrid, 1972–75), III, 1858; and, especially, J. G. Freire and G. Rocca, "Patto", in *Dizionario degli istituti di perfezione*, ed. G. Pelliccia and G. Rocca, VI (Roma, 1980), cols. 1292–1294.

[13] "Gallegan Pactual Monasticism" (Study III in this volume).

Since 1951, however, the views of both Herwegen and myself have come under sharp attack. In 1956 that able student of early western monasticism, Anscari Mundó, in a paper presented to the IV Settimana at Spoleto of the Centro Italiano di Studi sull'Alto Medioevo,[14] took strong exception to the thesis that pactualism originated in seventh-century Galicia, arguing that, on the contrary, before 711 all Hispanic monasticism was pactual, since as early as the commencement of the fourth century canon 13 of the Council of Elvira, in speaking of women taking the veil in public ceremony, alludes to their *pactum uirginitatis.*[15] This could be demonstrated even more convincingly from that type of pactum which Herwegen had denominated the Formula of Lérins and placed in his third group as of ostensibly late composition and, in its markedly pro-abbatial quasi-Benedictine unilaterality, radically furthest removed from the compact of the *Regula communis*. According to Mundó, this text in fact antedated that of Galicia, being ascribable, if not to the hand of St Isidore of Seville himself, at least to the heavily pactual *ambiente* of Visigothic Andalusia in the first third of the seventh century. In this light, the 'Fructuosan' pactum would represent simply a Gallegan adaptation of an institutional form everywhere employed in Romano-Visigothic cenobitism, a regional variant of Romano-Visigothic monastic pan-pactualism. In 1954–5 this hypothesis appeared to find further corroboration from the claim of Abadal i de Vinyals to have discovered pactualism of Visigothic origin among the newly planted Catalan abbeys of the Spanish Mark in the ninth century.[16]

Then in 1963 there commenced a much more comprehensive and formidable assault upon what might be called the Herwegen-Bishko position, launched this time by the leading authority in the field of pre-12th-century Spanish monastic history, Dom Justo Pérez de Urbel, author of the standard *Los monjes españoles de la Edad Media*, and of numerous other works on early medieval Hispanic cenobitism and on the rise of Castile. In four different articles appearing between 1963 and 1971 in the journals *Revista portuguesa de história*, *Bracara Augusta*, *Ciudad de Dios* and *Yermo* (the latter three for the most part repeating or amplifying points presented in the first of the four),[17] Fray Justo flatly rejected Herwegen's and my views, presenting a case in which he stressed three principal counter-arguments, as follows:

(1) all pre-711 Hispanic monasticism was pactual, as Mundó contends, and as can be firmly established from canon 13 of Elvira; St Leander's reference in his so-called *Regula* to the *pactum cum Christo* of his sister, the nun Florentina;[18] the Isidorian, or at least Baetic, provenance of the Formula of Lérins; the model profession act (*pactum uel placitum*) included as no. 45 in the *Formulae Visigothicae*

---

[14] "Monachesimo", 105–6.

[15] *PL* 84, col. 303: *Concilios visigóticos e hispano-romanos*, ed. José Vives (Barcelona-Madrid, 1963), 4.

[16] Ramon d'Abadal i de Vinyals, "Com neix i com creix un gran monestir pirinenc abans de l'any mil: Eixalada-Cuixà," *Analecta montserratensia*, VIII (1954–5), 125–337, reprinted in his *Dels Visigots als Catalans*, I (Barcelona, 1969), 377–484, at 370–1, 384–5 (unfortunately this edition lacks the indispensable appendix of 119 documents attached to the original publication).

[17] J. Pérez de Urbel, "Vida y caminos del Pacto de San Fructuoso," *Revista portuguesa de história*, VII (1963), 377–97; "Carácter y supervivencia del pacto de San Fructuoso," *Bracara* Augusta, XXII (1968), 226–42; "El monaquismo castellano en el período posterior a San Fructuoso," *Ciudad de Dios*, CLXXI (1968), 882–910; "Los monasterios castellanos de la reconquista," *Yermo*, VIII (1970), 99–110. Cf. also his *El Condado de Castilla*, III, 326–30.

[18] S. Leandri Hispalensis, *De institutione uirginum et contemptu mundi*, ed. Ángel Custodio Vega (El Escorial, 1948), c. 31 (p. 126); not c. 21, as in Pérez de Urbel, "Vida y caminos," 381, n. 7).

edited by Zeumer;[19] the variant pactum known as the *Consensoria monachorum*;[20] the pactual rubrics found in the *Liber ordinum* of the Hispanic (or Mozarabic) Rite;[21] and of course *RComP*.

(2) the type of pactum associated with St Fructuosus and Galicia must be seen as an institutional innovation brought to the Iberian northwest in the mid-7th century by this converted Visigothic noble who had previously been indoctrinated in the monastic life at Palencia, i.e, outside Galicia and in the region extending from Valladolid to Burgos and Soria that is known to have been heavily settled by the Goths at the time of the conquest. Fructuosan pactual monasticism must therefore reflect the strongly Germanic juridical, social and political mores of Visigothic abbeys and *conuersi* in the latter heartland of Castile; and this explains why, when St Fructuosus subsequently introduced this Visigothic system into the Romano-Suevic society of Galicia, he met with only limited success in overcoming the stiff opposition of the *pseudomonachi* and priests recorded in *RCom* 1–2.

(3) the efflorescence of pactualism in the Castilian-Riojan east of the 9th and 10th centuries can be attributed, not to any hypothetical transplant from Galicia, but to the presence in primitive Castile of Visigothic pactual monks from the region between Valladolid and Soria, who had fled straight north before the Islamic invasion and taken refuge in Santander, Liébana and Bardulia. From here after 711 the pactum moved vertically southwards along with the new monastic foundations of the Castilian frontier *repoblación* below Burgos and in the Rioja, while largely unsuccessful efforts were also made by Castilian churchmen to plant it once again in the Galicia and Portugal of the Alta Reconquista, from which it had long disappeared.

In these three propositions Fray Justo can be said to champion a distinctly Visigothic-Castilian revisionism that even more than Mundó's pre-711 pan-pactualism stands in radical contradiction to the conclusions reached by Herwegen and me. It is a thesis that, although accepted by Fernández Conde in his monograph on the Asturian Church,[22] has failed to persuade Mattoso, who believes in an unbroken descent of Portuguese pactualism from the abbeys of St Fructuosus; or Orlandis, who cites but does not follow Pérez de Urbel in his several studies of the 'Congregación dumiense'; or Sá Bravo in this writer's introductory discourse to his two tomes on Gallegan monachism.[23] Above all, it is flatly rejected by Linage Conde who, in reconstructing the process of Benedictine displacement of the old Hispanic cenobitism, found himself necessarily compelled to reckon with the genesis and stubborn persistence of the pactual tradition. This eminent scholar aligns himself firmly against the doctrines of both Pérez de Urbel and Mundó, accepting Herwegen's case for the pactum as a

[19] *Monumenta Germaniae historica, Leges*, V, *Formulae merowingici et karolini aevi*, ed. K. Zeumer (Hannover, 1886), 595.

[20] On this species of pactum, see Herwegen, 71–9; and my "The Date and Nature of the Spanish *Consensoria monachorum*," *American Journal of Philology*, LXIX (1948), 377–92 (Study II in this volume).

[21] Cf. Herwegen, 39–49.

[22] Francisco J. Fernández Conde, *La Iglesia de Asturias en la alta Edad Media* (Oviedo, 1972), 104 ff., especially 111, note 131.

[23] J. Mattoso, "Sobrevivência do monaquismo frutuosiano em Portugal durante a Reconquista," *Bracara Augusta*, XXII (1968), 42–54; *idem*, *Monachisme ibérique*, 113–20; José Orlandis, "Las congregaciones monásticas en la tradición suevo-gótica," *Anuario de estudios medievales*, I (1964), 97–119; *idem*, "El elemento germánico en la Iglesia española del siglo VII," *ibid.*, III (1966), 27–64; "El movimiento ascético de S. Fructuoso y la Congregación monástica dumiense," *Bracara Augusta*, XXII (1968), 81–91 (studies reprinted in his *Estudios sobre instituciones monásticas medievales*, Pamplona, 1971); Hipólito de Sá Bravo, *El monacato en Galicia* (La Coruña, 1972), I, 50–6.

Luso-Gallegan creation, although he is rightly sceptical of assigning its actual authorship to St Fructuosus himself; and on the transmission of the pactual tradition after 711 from Galicia to the cenobia of primitive Castile, as on the identification of the Burgalese Formula, he adopts the views I expressed in 1951.[24]

As for myself, I am convinced that Fray Justo's earnest campaign to depict the Hispanic monastic pactum as of extra-Gallegan Gothic provenance and to explain its emergence in the Alta Reconquista as the exclusive achievement of Castilian monks, is totally misguided. All three of his contentions, as summarized above, appear to me to incorporate basic confusions that make it impossible to determine the true place of the pactual tradition in Luso-Hispanic cenobitic history both before 711 and in the later *repoblación* of Galicia-Portugal and Castile-Rioja during the first centuries of the Reconquista. And since the revisionist doctrine, although questioned, has not yet been subjected to critical examination, it is imperative to marshal the principal objections against acceptance of the pan-pactual and Visigothic-Castilian hypotheses of both Pérez de Urbel and Mundó.

II

Let me first challenge emphatically the claims of Mundó and Pérez de Urbel that before 711 all Hispanic cenobitism was constitutionally pactual. This generalization, as Linage Conde has also observed,[25] stems from failure to observe a simple semantic distinction. True enough, our monastic sources for Romano-Visigothic cenobitism commonly employ *pactum* or its synonymous alternative *placitum* for what outside the Peninsula would be called *professio* or *petitio*; but in canon 13 of Elvira and St Leander's *De institutione uirginum*, precisely as in St Isidore's *Regula monachorum* (henceforth *RI*) 4, 2,[26] these terms designate only the normal individual profession of orthodox monastic usage.

When Isidore parallels the abandonment of civil life for the ascetic society to enlistment in the Roman army, he notes that military recruits are not enrolled for service "nisi ante in tabulis conferantur",[27] and this reference to official *tabulae* or muster lists might be taken to correspond to the placing of the names of *conuersi* in a collective profession pact—a point, however, not made by either Mundó or Pérez de Urbel, despite their views on the Isidorian authorship of the Burgalese Formula. Yet it is certain that in this passage Isidore's language in fact connotes only an individual *professio*, for at the same time he also declares that "omnis conuersus non est recipiendus in monasterio nisi prius ipse scripto se spoponderit permansurum . . . nisi prius professione uerbi aut scripti teneantur [conuersi], in numerum societatemque seruorum Christi transire non possunt." Here the *scriptum* or *professio uerbi aut scripti*

---

[24] *Orígenes*, 1, 291–342. Linage Conde, in my judgment mistakenly, places the *Consensoria monachorum* in the 8th rather than the mid-7th-century (I, 263–6), and revises somewhat my catalogue of the pacta of the Reconquista by distinguishing (not altogether convincingly) the 'impropios' from those he regards as authentic (I, 329–35); but on the paramount issues of pactual history he is anti-revisionist.

[25] *Orígenes*, I, 291–304; cf. Herwegen, 61–4.

[26] Pending the much anticipated publication of Prof. Díaz y Díaz's critical edition of *RI*, the text followed here is that of Holstenius-Brockie as reprinted in *PL* 83, cols. 867–94. Meanwhile, cf. M. Díaz y Díaz, "Aspectos de la tradición de la *Regula Isidori*," *Studia monastica*, V (1963), 27–57.

[27] *RI* 4, 2.

can only mean an individual oral or written promise of *stabilitas* and submission of person, in diplomatic form doubtless something comparable to No. 45 of the *Formulae Visigothicae*, where the promise is to be made directly by the *conuersus* to the bishop, a point not made explicit in the Isidorian code.[28] It is highly significant that this formula, the very existence of which refutes the proponents of Visigothic pan-pactualism, was known to the composer of *RComP*, as Herwegen observes;[29] and that while incorporating into his collective text its provisions on recovery of *fugitiui*, he deliberately discarded its clauses on individual profession and submission to the diocesan ordinary. Formula 45, finally, is especially conclusive since it forms part of a collection of legal instruments assembled by a Cordobese notary between 613 and 621,[30] and thus circulated in the very same epoch and province that produced the Isidorian *Regula* itself.

As a principal basis of their pan-pactual theory, Mundó and Pérez de Urbel seek to prove that certain pactual or quasi-pactual testimonies dating from the earlier centuries of the Reconquista actually originated before 711 in regions of the Visigothic kingdom other than Galicia. In this connection they adduce, as traceable to an Isidorian *ambiente* in 7th-century Andalusia, the distinctive type of pactum in the form of a model instrument which was published in 1703 by Mabillon.[31] This came from a now lost 'codex Liriensis vetustissimus', which that scholar believed was associated with the abbey of St-Honorat de Lérins and is now known to have been preserved as late as 1679 at Narbonne. This is the pactum which Herwegen, who reprints it from Mabillon, christened the Formula of Lérins, which I style the Formula of Burgos or Burgalese Formula, and of which Díaz y Díaz has provided a more accurate text.[32] Mundó, relying on the fact that in the codex it stood just before the index and chapters of *RI*, and on Mabillon's misleading statement that the Isidorian code was here prefaced by the dedicatory inscription *sanctis fratribus in cenobio Honorianensi constitutis* that is found in certain MSS of the interpolated version,[33] concluded that both pact and Rule were of the same Isidorian provenance and perhaps were originally designed for the use of a 7th-century Andalusian monastery located not far from Seville at Fregenal de la Sierra, in modern Extremadura.[34]

These deductions, despite their endorsement by Pérez de Urbel, appear unacceptable. If the mere prefixing of a pactum to *RI* warrants identifying St Isidore as its composer, then we should also have to assign to him, against all probability, the *Consensoria monachorum* (henceforth *CM*) which stands in several Hispanic *codices regularum* as c. 25 of his Rule, although this collective covenant directly contradicts (precisely as does that of the Lérins codex) the Saint's explicit requirement in *RI* 4, 2 (cf. *supra*) of the orthodox individual profession act, and indeed is so radically collective and egalitarian a document as to have induced Dom Donatien De Bruyne in 1909 to wrench it from its actual mid-7th-century Gallegan context and attribute it to heretical Priscillianist circles of the 5th century.[35] In any event, whatever the significance of the codicological inscription certain MSS of *RI* preserve to a *cenobium Honorianense*—and this is most unlikely to designate a house at Fregenal and may

[28] Zeumer, *Formulae*, 595, note 4.

[29] Herwegen, 25.

[30] Zeumer, *op. cit.*, 573–4.

[31] *Annales ordinis sancti Benedicti*, I (Paris, 1703), 363; reproduced in Herwegen, 23.

[32] M. Díaz y Díaz, "El manuscrito de Lérins de la *Regula Isidori*," *Studia monastica*, VII (1965), 369–82, at 373–4.

[33] Díaz y Díaz, "*Aspectos*," 28–9, 40–6.

[34] "Monachesimo," 105–6.

[35] Cf. Bishko, "The Date and Nature of the Spanish *Consensoria Monachorum*," *American Journal of Philology*, LXIX (1948), 377–95 (Study II in this volume).

possibly refer, as Meyvaert has suggested, only to St-Honorat de Lérins—it is now certain that this toponym did not occur in the lost codex[36] and therefore cannot be attached to the pactual Formula.

We now possess much better understanding of the nature of the vanished Lerinensian MS than Mabillon provides or was available to Herwegen, thanks to recent intense interest in the Narbonne-Spanish family (Φ) of codices of the interpolated *RB*, since its folia had included also a version of the *H* text of the code of Monte Cassino.[37] The information furnished by Paul Meyvaert from his examination in the Bibliothèque Nationale of the very notes (*H4*) taken in 1679 by the Maurist Dom Claude Estiennot that were used by Mabillon as a base for his remarks and publication of the Formula, has made it possible for Díaz y Díaz to formulate several hypotheses as to the origin and date of the MS. For the present inquiry the most relevant of these is that it must have been a *codex regularum*, written in Visigothic letter, and resembling in content the oldest portions of Escorialensis a.I.13, the collection of Rules copied by the nun Leodegundia in Castile at the commencement of the 10th century. This might seem to suggest a similar date for the Lérins codex; in fact Díaz y Díaz, drawing on paleographical clues contained in the Estiennot notes, proposes the late 8th or early 9th century, a time when many other Hispanic MSS are known to have crossed the Pyrenees into the monastic centers of southern Gaul.[38] This in turn would impose for the composition of the Formula a *terminus ante quem* of ca. 800 and indeed for all practical purposes throw it back into the Visigothic era, thus serving to corroborate—particularly if the codex is regarded as an extra-Gallegan production—the Mundó-Pérez de Urbel position on pan-pactualism before 711.

But is so early an allocation for the Lérins codex justifiable? Without challenging the acknowledged paleographical and codicological expertise of Díaz y Díaz in these matters, I believe that no definitive conclusion can be achieved without also taking into account other factors, historical and juridical, that tend strongly to place the Burgalese Formula in the late 9th or 10th century, i.e., a century or more after the era proposed by the Spanish scholar. It is worth noting that Benedict of Aniane, so well provided in southern Aquitaine ca. 800 with Hispanic monastic Rules and related ascetic texts, including some of quite restricted circulation, such as the *De genere monachorum* of the Vierzan monk Valerius (ca. 685), displays no knowledge whatever of this Formula, as he does of *RComP* and *CM*, in his *Codex regularum* and *Concordia regularum*; and this makes it highly probable that it was not yet in use below the Pyrenees.[39] Herwegen places this Formula in his third class as furthest removed from *RComP* in terms of general abandonment of the exact language of the latter, approximation to the norm of the Benedictine *professio*, and above all the non-contractual, unilateral submission (*traditio*) of the monks (still acting as a body, however) to their elected abbot.[40] All this

---

[36] Díaz y Díaz, *Manuscrito de Lérins*, 371.

[37] For the important new material on the codicology of the Burgalese Formula, see Paul Meyvaert, "Towards a History of the Textual Transmission of the *Regula S. Benedicti*," *Scriptorium*, XVII (1963), 83–110, at 90–5; Díaz y Díaz, "Manuscrito de Lérins"; *Benedicti regula*, ed. Rudolphus Hanslik (*Corpus scriptorum ecclesiasticorum latinorum*, LXXV; Vienna, 1960), lv–lviii; Cf. also, on the Benedictine side, Adalbert de Vogüé and Jean Neufville, *La Règle de Saint Benoît*, I (Paris, 1972), 342–4.

[38] "Manuscrito," 380–2.

[39] It is also worth observing that there is no discoverable trace of this text in the very complete collection of diplomas published by Antonio C. Floriano, *Diplomática española del periodo astur* (Oviedo, 1959–61), which runs from 718 to 910.

[40] Herwegen, 35.

in his opinion, as in mine, points to a stage of pactualism posterior to that found in the first and second juridical groups.

Particularly indicative of a date later than ca. 800 is the testimony of the actually used specimens of the Formula which I encountered when searching the diplomatic collections, archival and published, for my study of 1951 on the diffusion of Gallegan pactualism in Castile (Study III in this volume). These were four in number, all connected with Castilian or Riojan monasteries of the 10th century: San Pedro y San Pablo *in ualle qui uocitur Azadina* (921), San Juan de Tabladillo (931), San Julián de Villagonzalo Pedernales (959), and San Martín de Modúbar (975).[41] While the site of the first of these abbeys is uncertain, despite Pérez de Urbel's highly questionable identification of it with San Pedro de Cardeña,[42] it can certainly be placed in Castile or the Rioja; the other three can all be seen as lying to the south of Burgos, in the *suburbium* of that ancient Castilian town, and as products of the monastic colonization that accompanied the *repoblación* of this entire *comarca* in the 10th century—hence my proposal that the Formula be called Burgalese rather than the historically meaningless 'of Lérins'. Such popularity is firm evidence that this juridically late type of pactum was circulating in the communities of women as well as of men at this time between Burgos and the Duero and as far east as the Rioja. In none of these four cases could an exclusive observance of *RI* be supposed, while in two, Tabladillo and Modúbar, that of *RB* was visible in their documentation.

Thus, the historical and juridical signs all indicate that the Burgalese Formula was a product of the Castilian frontier of the late 9th or early 10th century, a chronology which is at least a century later than that conjectured by Díaz y Díaz but does not seem to present any insuperable paleographical problems and has the merit of coinciding with the production of the *codex regularum* of Leodegundia.[43] It can therefore in all probability be seen as a new, relatively late, phase in the evolution of the Hispanic pactual tradition, the creation of that confluence of paleo-pactual and Carolingian Benedictine observances which precedes the mono-regular adoption of *RB* in the Castello-Riojan zone of this epoch. In short, I here exchange position with Mundó, Pírez de Urbel and Díaz y Díaz: they champion a Visigothic solution prior to 711, I a Castilian one but of ca. 900, which can now also appeal to the conclusions reached by Linage Conde.[44]

A second unconvincing witness on behalf of alleged Visigothic pan-pactualism is to be found in the more or less casual suggestion of Ramon Abadal i de Vinyals that certain Catalan monastic charters, specifically those drawn up by the monks at the establishment of such new abbeys as Sant Vicenç de Gerri (807), San Esteban de Servàs (833), Sant Andreu de Eixalada (854) and Sant Germà de Cuixà (879), resemble the terminal pactum of *RCom*. Abadal did not undertake to prove that these *pergaminos* were based upon a Visigothic model or to explain how the supposed Gallegan prototype or the 'Regla de sant Frutuós' (i.e., *RCom*), which he believed these monks may well have observed, reached the Tarraconensis before 711, or at any rate by 800;

[41] A fifth example, which in 1951 I listed as of 950 from 'San Martín' (i.e., San Prudencio) de Laturce, and which was preserved in the now dispersed Conde de Mora collection of the Archivo Historico Nacional, has since turned out to be a diploma not of this class at all; cf. the additional note to Study III in this volume.

[42] First defended in his "La conquista de la Rioja y su colonización espiritual en el siglo X," *Estudios dedicados a Menéndez Pidal*, I (Madrid, 1950), 515–8.

[43] On the date and character of this celebrated MS, which contains the pact of Sabaricus, see Díaz y Díaz's brilliant study, "El códice monástico de Leodegundia (Escorial a. I. 13)," *Ciudad de Dios*, CLXXXI (1968), 567–87.

[44] *Orígenes*, I, 325–8.

but his remarks encouraged Fray Justo to posit a pactual background in the Hispanic Mark dating from the days of the Toletan monarchy.[45]

A most effective rebuttal of Abadal's unwise adhesion to the untenable doctrine of Visigothic pan-pactualism and consequent misinterpretation of the Catalan foundational charters, was published in 1977 by Dr Linage Conde, who agrees entirely with my own scepticism regarding the survival in 9th-century Catalonia of a pactualism comparable to that found in Galicia by ca. 675.[46] Meanwhile, three years previously, Abadal's case for a pactual presence in the northeast had been given much further supportive elaboration by A. García Sanz in a substantial paper which throws useful light on various juridico-institutional features of 9th-century cenobitism in the Hispanic Mark but which fails to convince by reason of its basic confusions.[47] Although rightly rejecting Abadal's appeal to a 'Fructuosan' solution, García Sanz accepts without question Mundó's fallacious attribution of pactualism to all Visigothic monasteries, including those he imagines devoted to mono-regular use of the Isidorian Rule. At the same time he strangely makes no effort to ascertain whether the monastic *ambiente* of the Tarraconensis and Septimania before 711 provides any evidence of his hypothetical Visigothic substratum for Pyrenean pactualism in the 9th century; nor does he consider the possibly Aquitanian descent of his foundational charters. In any case, his argument rests too largely upon questionable exegesis of the monastic and liturgical meaning of 'pactum' within the context of its broad employment in Visigothic secular and canon law.

This is not the occasion to undertake the needed detailed refutation of the pactual theses of the Catalan school. For the moment let it suffice to remark that it cannot be said that their validity is confirmed by the diplomas adduced. These texts, drawn up by groups of founding monks with their abbots, appear to use 'pactum' in its conventional Romano-Visigothic sense of any sort of legal agreement between contracting parties, whether lay or religious; they stipulate no synallagmatic exchange of rights and obligations between abbot and subjects; and in phraseology, ascetic ideology, and constitutional and disciplinary aspects they plainly have nothing in common with the authentic Gallegan pactum. These are documents that, while undoubtedly meriting further study as examples of collective *Eigenklöster* in which the *patroni* are the founding monks themselves, display no visible relationship with the pactual texts of Galicia or Castile, not even with such an instrument of roughly parallel purpose as *CM*, where once again the divergence in language and institutional content is so complete as to underscore the totally different origin and character of the Catalan foundation acts.

A much more formidable case can be made for a third of Pérez de Urbel's contentions, namely, that the appearance of the pactum in the monastic *ordines* of the Hispanic (or Mozarabic) Rite proves its general adoption in the Visigothic epoch. For if these texts contained in our extant liturgical codices of the 11th and 12th centuries descend directly from the observance of the Romano-Visigothic Church—and Férotin,

[45] Abadal, "Com neix," 125ff. and Apèndix, núms. 9, 61; also but without documents, *Dels visigots*, 377–84. *Idem*, "La vida monàstica després de l'expulsió dels sarraïns," *Studia monastica*, III (1967), 165–77; also, *Dels visigots*, 365–76. Pérez de Urbel, "*Vida y caminos*," 383.

[46] Bishko, "Gallegan Pactual Monasticism," 514 (Study III in this volume); Linage Conde, *Orígenes*, I, 328; *idem*, "¿Pactualismo en Cataluña?," *Yermo*, XV (1977), 45–60.

[47] A. García Sanz, "Els pactes monàstics a la pre-Catalunya del segle IX," *Studia monastica*, XVI (1974), 7–44. Cf. Abadal's influence upon M. Riu, "El monasterio de Santa María de Alaón y su patrimonio en el siglo IX," in *Homenaje a Don José María Lacarra de Miguel* (Zaragoza, 1977), I, 63–85, at 83–4.

Herwegen and Fray Justo are in agreement that the monastic sections of this Rite antedate 711[48]—then it would seem necessary to acknowledge that well before the overthrow of the Toletan state the collective-contractual profession instrument was in use throughout the Peninsula and not exclusively in Galicia. This is a crucial question that cannot be dismissed, as Linage Conde tends to suggest at various points,[49] as largely relating to merely verbal reminiscences of regional origin. What has to be decided is whether our relatively late MSS of the Rite preserve unchanged the ancient monastic uses of Visigothic cenobitism or whether the *ordines* have been interpolated or adapted to suit the circumstances of the post-Visigothic Church in the four centuries before total peninsular acceptance of *RB* and the Roman ordinal.

Many years ago I argued—and am still of this opinion—for the textual fluidity after 711 of at least the monastic sections of the Hispanic *Liber ordinum*,[50] a thesis that has received support from so acknowledged an authority on this Rite as Dom Louis Brou,[51] but has yet to result in the long overdue abandonment of the traditional belief in the immutability of the 'Mozarabic' liturgy from Roman times on. As usual, the texts obstruct easy generalization, compelling us to distinguish first of all between the prescriptions intended for women being admitted to the religious life and those applicable exclusively to men. Of the several *ordines* concerned with the profession of women, the two of direct pertinence here are *XXII. Ordo uel benedictio ad uelandas Deo uotas* and *XXVIIII. Ordo conuersorum conuersarumque.*[52] These prescribe the conduct of the ceremony by a bishop or priest, and make no mention either in text or rubric of a profession instrument, whether individual or collective. In contrast, the final section of *ordo XXVIIII*, which unlike the earlier segments that are specifically intended for both sexes ("tam uiris quam feminis") deals only with the passage of the male *conuersus* from novitiate to final reception, explicitly requires enrollment by the abbot in the community's pactum: "monacus uero in cenobio, quum hunc predictum ordinem primitus susceperit, ita ut stabilitatem professionis sue per adnotationem sui nominis firmet, hic ordo seruabitur: Postquam enim *Ad accendentes* communicauerit, tota iam explicita missa, accedit in choro ad abbatem, et roborato proprio nomine in p a c t i o n i s libello per manum abbatis,[53] suscipiunt eum deducendum ad altare presbiter et diaconus." Then, following the versicle *Suscipe me, Domine*, and the Gloria and Kyrie, the monk "posito super altare testamenti libello, prosternit se ante altare", while the priest prays *Suscipe queso, Domine*, etc.

---

[48] Dom Marius Férotin, ed., *Le* Liber Ordinum *en usage dans l'Église wisigothique et mozarabe d'Espagne du cinquième au onzième siècle*, Monumenta ecclesiae liturgica, V (Paris, 1904), xxi; Herwegen, 40; Pérez de Urhel, "Vida y caminos," 10.

[49] See his generally hasty and inconclusive treatment of liturgical pactualism in *Orígenes*, I, 335–6; II, 769–70.

[50] "Salvus of Albelda and Frontier Monasticism in Tenth-Century Navarre," *Speculum*, XXIII (1948), 559–90, at 578–82, and note 97. Reprinted in my *Studies in Medieval Spanish Frontier History* (London, 1980), Study I.

[51] See the reference to private correspondence on this subject in Hieronymus Frank, "Untersuchungen zur Geschichte der benediktinischen Professliturgie im frühen Mittelalter," *Studien und Mitteilungen zur Geschichte des Benediktiner-Ordens und seine Zweige*, LXIII (1951), 102–4.

[52] Férotin, *Lib. ord.*, cols. 64–6, 82–6.

[53] The text here probably should be corrected to read: "roborato proprio nomine in pactionis libello [uel] per manum abbatis," to judge by the comparable passage in the pactual reception of a *soror* in c. 26 of the *Libellus a regula sancti Benedicti substractus*: "ut nomen eius adnotetur com nominibus earum, accepta igitur licentia si potuerit ipsa scribere nomen suum scribet, si uero non potuerit alia subrogata persona eum adnotabit" (A. Linage Conde, *Una regla monástica riojana feminina del siglo X: El "Libellus a regula sancti Benedicti subtractus"* (Salamanca, 1973), 64–5, and cf. 119ff. on this passage; Bishko, *Salvus of Albelda*, 572.

To this inclusion in the masculine rite of a pactum that is manifestly communal, a *libellus* in which the subscription of each *conuersus* is inserted at his reception, and which contrasts with the absence of any similar provision in the case of nuns, there is an exact parallel in the rubrics of the *ordines* for the consecration (*ordinatio*) of abbesses and abbots. In the former case, *XXIII. Ordo ad ordinandam abbatissam*, the officiating bishop presents the abbess with the *Liber regule* (observe use of singular) and the *baculum* of her office; no mention is made of the pactum.[54] But in *Ordo XVIII. Ordo in ordinatione abbatis*, the bishop first bestows the symbolic *staminia*, *pedules* and *sucelli*; then the abbot-consecrand delivers to him "placitum suum tam pro se quam pro subditis de honestate uite regularis"; and only then does the bishop present him with the *baculum* and *Liber regularum* (observe use of plural).[55]

There are several major questions here. First, how to explain the silence of these *ordines* regarding the pactum in the case of women? and is this a telling argument against the claims for pan-pactualism before 711? Férotin, the editor of the *Liber ordinum*, whom Herwegen follows on this subject, believed that down to the 11th century the Hispanic Church maintained for the profession of nuns and consecration of abbesses a closer adhesion to Roman law principles and forms than was true in the case of the rubrics for men, where he allowed for the work of revisers under Visigothic influence in the 7th century.[56] This might seem to imply that the pactum remained unknown in communities of women. But against this is the abundant evidence of the pacta surviving from communities of female religious, such as that of Eufrasia from San Mamés de Ura (930) or of Urraca from San Julián de Villagonzalo de Pedernales (959);[57] the many subscriptions of women to the pacta of double communities, as in the cases of the Argilegus pactum from San Pedro y San Pablo de Naroba (818) or the Sabaricus pactum from an unknown Castilian cenobium (*ante* 931);[58] and, as conclusive proof of specifically liturgical character, the Rule for nuns produced in the Rioja between 950 and 962, the *Libellus a regula sancti Benedicti subtractus* of Abbot Salvus of San Martín de Albelda, which contains a reception rite providing for the insertion (*adnotatio*) of the nun's name in the community's pactum by herself, or, if she is illiterate, by the abbess.[59]

If the otherwise inexplicable absence of pactual references from the feminine rites of the *Liber ordinum* is thus one clear sign of late textual change, the contamination of the same texts by *RB* points to the same conclusion. Férotin, Herwegen and others admit that the monastic *ordines* of the Hispanic liturgy have undergone Benedictinization in language and procedure,[60] but unlike these older scholars, with our much superior understanding of the manner of penetration into ultra-Catalan Spain of the code of Monte Cassino, we can now advance this phenomenon from the 7th century to the late 9th and the two following centuries. It thus becomes plain that in their extant form the rubrics governing the profession of women and consecration of abbesses (the prayers are another matter) represent rubrical revisions made in this later period when, in conformity no doubt with episcopal promotion of *RB* in communities of women, the old pactual references which

[54] *Lib. ord.*, cols. 66–8.

[55] *Lib. ord.*, cols. 57–60.

[56] Férotin, *Lib. ord.*, notes to cols. 57–68, 80–2; cf. Herwegen, who states this firmly, 48.

[57] Herwegen, 11–14, 22.

[58] Floriano, *Diplomática española*, I, 146–51 (no. 27); Herwegen, 6–10; and cf. Donatien De Bruyne, "Les signataires du pacte de Sabaricus," *Rev. bénédictine*, XXVIII (1911), 80–6.

[59] Cf. *supra*, note 53.

[60] Férotin, *Lib. ord.*, notes to cols. 80, 57–9; Herwegen, however, tends to minimize the degree of Benedictinization in note 1 on 45; Linage Conde, *Orígenes*, II, 769–70.

the texts must once have contained were purged from the Castilian and Riojan ordinals in favor of the individual profession act and its liturgical submission according to the orthodox Benedictine pattern. The mono-regular exclusivism suggested in the feminine *Ordo XXIII*, which cites the *Liber regule* as against the *Liber regularum* of the masculine *Ordo XVIII*, provides further corroboration of this same trend, just as does the very appearance in the mid-tenth-century of the Salvan *Libellus*, where despite the retention of pactualism the Benedictine concept of mono-regular observance has triumphed over the *codex regularum*.

All this looks as if we have good reason to suppose that the *ordines* relating to women earlier contained much the same provisions relating to the communal pactum and its submission to abbot or bishop as is found in those for men; and this brings us inevitably to the key question, the dating of the introduction of pactualism into the Hispanic liturgy. Here for lack of codicological material we are compelled to proceed by inference. We have no *Libri ordinum* copied in Asturias, León or Mozarabic Spania, regions where in my view the pactual tradition never replaced the Visigothic; or, regrettably, for Galicia-Portugal, where it did, especially above the river Miño, and where rubrics similar to those of the masculine ones of the Castello-Riojan liturgical codices might be expected.

We are left then with three possibilities:

(a) the Castello-Riojan pactual rubrics for *conuersi* and abbots, as formerly also for *deouotae* and *abbatissae*, derive in unbroken descent from a peninsular pactual tradition which before 711 found expression in all the liturgical books of the national Toletan Rite. Against this is the testimony of the non-liturgical sources to the a-pactual character of Visigothic monasticism outside Galicia, and the total lack of pacta or pactual allusions in the diplomatic documentation of Asturias-León, Navarre above the Ebro, and the Hispanic Mark.

or (b) the pactualism of the *ordines* dates from the 7th century but stems from interpolated redactions which were made in the liturgical MSS of Visigothic Galicia alone by St Fructuosus or his immediate successors; subsequently, these texts, like the pactum itself, were carried by refugee monks from the environs of Braga to extreme eastern Asturias and primitive Castile. This is a possible solution but probably counter-indicated by the absence in the masculine rubrics of other expectable 7th-century Gallegan symptoms—e.g., interest in the *episcopus sub regula*—and by the emphasis placed upon the authority of the bishop as such, particularly in the consecration of abbots.

or (c) the pactual rubrics, but not the actual texts of the *ordines*, contain Castello-Riojan interpolations dating from the centuries of the Alta Reconquista, and these attest the intrusion into the originally non-pactual Visigothic *Liber ordinum* of the dominant monastic observance of the region from which our extant codices come, Castile and the Rioja. Presumably, the same would be true of Galicia-Portugal for which we lack comparable MSS. It is this third alternative that I find the most persuasive, in view of the demonstrable fluidity of the liturgical books after 711, the ubiquity of pactualism in the Castello-Riojan zone, and the copying in this same region of our late codices of the *Liber ordinum*.

On some such basis I would envisage the following sequence in the history of the rubrics of the Hispanic monastic *ordines*: (i) before 711, no pactual content, except possibly in Galicia; (ii) after 711, a pactualization of both masculine and feminine rubrics, due either to early Gallegan influence or, more probably, to the effects of the Castilian adhesion to pactualism between the 8th and 10th centuries; (iii) the elimination of the pactum, probably in the late 10th or early 11th centuries, under episcopal and Benedictine pressure, from the rites relating to female religious; (iv) the survival of pactualism in the masculine rubrics of the ordinals of 11th and 12th century Castile and La Rioja.

Whatever the validity of this reconstruction, it can at least be insisted at this point that, in themselves and without adequate demonstration of their immutability before and after 711, the extant liturgical books cannot be used to prove the pactual character of all Visigothic monasticism. The solution must be sought on other grounds, and here we can draw upon the plentiful positive testimony that places the genesis of the pactual tradition in Visigothic Galicia, and its subsequent survival to ca. 1100 in the Galaico-Portuguese and Castello-Riojan borderlands of the Asturo-Leonese kingdom.

III

It is one of the chief defects of the thesis of Visigothic pan-pactualism that it fails to explain why this heterodox species of cenobitic constitutionalism should ever have arisen before 711 in the Iberian peninsula or allegedly have found there such primacy over orthodox monastic practice. To be sure, Pérez de Urbel adduces the Visigoths, but since he apparently does not mean to contradict Mundó's Romano-Baetic premise, it must be that he assumes for the northern meseta a radically Germanicized version of a pactual polity already existent to the south. All of this lies largely, as we have observed, in the realms of fantasy and speculation. What our documentation decisively affirms is, first, that in Galicia alone, and there only after ca. 650, did there emerge not merely one but several varieties of collective profession and foundation instrument—the so-called 'Fructuosan' pactum, the *Consensoria monachorum*, and the *conditio sacramenti* or *iuramentum* of *RCom* 1; and, secondly, that pactualism is found nowhere outside of Galicia until the first centuries of the Reconquista, when it appears also in Castile and the Rioja as well as finding new life in Galicia itself and comital Portugal.

It is indeed impossible to take seriously Pérez de Urbel's claim that in its 'Fructuosan' form the Hispanic pactual tradition stems from otherwise unknown and undocumentable cenobia supposedly existing before 711 in the zone of heavy Visigothic settlement between Valladolid and Soria.[61] This affirmation rests solely on the inference that (i) because many early Castilian houses of the Reconquista were pactual, they must have had direct Visigothic antecedents in the same area; and (ii) because the *RComP* (ostensibly) employs linguistic and legal concepts that are recognizably Germanic, it can only have been developed to meet the needs of markedly non-Romanized communities among the northern Visigoths that were the immediate forerunners of those of primitive Castile. As against Herwegen's premise, that since the pactum first appears within the Galaico-Minhotan boundaries of the fallen kingdom of the Sueves (indubitably Germans, indeed far less Romanized ones than the Visigoths), its origins were Suevic or broadly speaking, Suevo-Visigothic,[62] Fray Justo emphasizes that St Fructuosus (whom he regards as responsible for the introduction of pactualism into Galicia) must have brought the heterodox observance with him from Palencia, in the heavily Germanicized district of the *Campi Gothici*, the original area of his

61 "Vida y caminos," 392–3; "Carácter y supervivencia," 232–6, 241–2.

62 Herwegen, 51–60.

indoctrination in the ascetic life.[63] This would mean that Gallegan pactualism began with the Saint's initial Bierzan foundation of Santos Justo y Pastor de Compludo and thence spread into other monasteries of the province established by him or under his influence.

Any such assumptions however are definitely refuted by the fact that no pactual formula is mentioned in or attached to the *Regula monachorum* (henceforth *RFr*) which Fructuosus composed for his Complutensian proto-abbey (ca. 630–35, as I believe). While this Rule in c. 22 mentions a *pactum* in connection with reception, this designates, as Herwegen long ago showed, the conventional individual profession act; and Linage Conde, who justly notes the rigid adherence to the spirituality and practices of oriental monasticism characteristic of this code, has also reached the same conclusion.[64] Thus, if we can justifiably associate the Saint at all with the emergence of the pactual tradition in Galicia, it can only be on the extremely dubious premise that he was responsible for the very latest chapters of the final redaction of *RCom*, where the true collective contract finds mention for the first time (c. 18 *ad finem*), and is also, in model form, appended to c. 20 as *RComP*.[65] If so, we can at best suppose that he encountered in Galicia an already existent pactualism, or there became himself its inventor; but on neither assumption can he be proved to have transported it with him from the Visigothic east.

But to explain the Gallegan break with orthodox monastic organizational principles, it is necessary above all to advance beyond the superficial recourse to Romanist vs. Germanicist genetics so dear to 19th-century historical thought, and to examine the forces and conditions affecting monastic life in Galicia in the century antecedent to the Islamic invasion. Since I have in preparation a comprehensive re-interpretation of the monastic apostolate of St Fructuosus, and the bitter conflict of monasticism and episcopate in the province out of which the pactual tradition arose, it is possible here only to summarize certain principal conclusions to which this inquiry has led me.

At the start we must again pay tribute to Herwegen for insisting that the pactual problem cannot be solved in isolation from two other distinctive components of the monasticism of Visigothic Galicia which it subsumes and which are linked to it in the chapters of *RCom*: the monk-bishop or *episcopus sub regula*; and the governing and legislating body of abbots and (surely also) abbesses, known as the Sancta Communis

---

[63] Pérez de Urbel, "Vida y caminos," 391–2; "Carácter y supervivencia," 231–2. For the career of St Fructuosus of Braga it will suffice to cite those titles which provide further bibliography: Frances Clare Nock, *The Vita Sancti Fructuosi: Text with a Translation, Introduction, and Commentary* (Catholic University of America, *Studies in Mediaeval History*, New Series, VII; Washington, 1946); M. Díaz y Díaz, "Fructueux de Braga (saint)," *Dictionnaire de Spiritualité*, V (Paris, 1964), cols. 1541–6; and the two meaty volumes of *Bracara Augusta*, XXI (1967) and XXII (1968), which contain the numerous papers presented in 1966 at Braga to the Congresso de Estudos da Comemoração do XIII Centenário da Morte de S. Frutuoso. The best edition of the *Vita* is by M. Díaz y Díaz, *La vida de San Fructuoso de Braga* (Braga, 1974).

[64] Herwegen, 65–70; Linage Conde, *Orígenes*, I, 298–300; *idem*, "En torno a la Regula Monachorum y a sus relaciones con otras Reglas monásticas," *Brac. Aug.*, XXI (1967), 123–63. Text of *RFr* in Holstenius-Brockie, *Codex regularum*, I, 201–7; reprinted, *PL* 87, cols. 1099–110.

[65] The Fructuosan composition of *RCom*, although supported by several early MSS and traditionally accepted, can at best be defended only for a nuclear core of chapters in the primitive redaction, as I hope to establish. The scepticism I have expressed regarding the authorship of this extraordinary Rule has been endorsed by Díaz y Díaz: cf. his "La cultura de la España visigótica del siglo VII," in *Caratteri del secolo VII in Occidente, Settimane di studio del Centro Italiano di Studi sull'Alto Medioevo, Spoleto*, V (1958), t. II, 836, note 66. Cf. also Linage Conde, *Orígenes*, I, 234–5.

Regula. Thus, not one, but a triad, of inter-related Gallegan peculiarities requires to be explained, and the origins of these are neither identical nor chronologically concomitant.

Herwegen identified the *episcopus sub regula* as the prelate we find ruling conjointly the monastic see of Dumio and the metropolitan church of Braga; and since 1907 it has been debated whether this combination of monastic and episcopal offices reached Spain through contacts with the Celtic Christianity of Britain, Ireland and Brittany or else came directly from its original homeland in the Byzantine East.[66] On the first assumption, much has been made of the presence in northeastern Galicia by at least 572 of the Celtic see of Britonia (near Mondoñedo), which is described in the 6th-century Suevic *Parochiale*, edited and analyzed by David, as *ecclesia Britoniae cum monasterio Maximi*.[67] Yet a monastery affiliated with a bishopric, perhaps even as closely as in the case of the Anglo-Saxon cathedral abbeys, is not the impression we receive of the *monasterium Dumiense*, where there is no hint of the typical Celtic subordination of episcopal to abbatial authority; where the bishop, so far as our texts allow us to speak, never called himself abbot; and where the diocese was plainly based not on a tribal or other secular territorial circumscription but, being completely devoid of *parochiae*, was comprised solely of the monastic domain and its resident *familia*.[68] While the head of the see of Britonia consistently and conventionally styles himself in conciliar subscriptions *episcopus ecclesiae Britoniae*,[69] the monk-prelate of Dumio is known to others and appears in the acta as *episcopus monasterii Dumiensis*, a significant structural distinction, uniquely applied in the history of the Suevic and Visigothic Churches to a prelate living under the monastic observance as *episcopus sub regula* (the other phrase attached to him), but in no sense *sub abbate*. In any event, the remote Celtic center at Britonia, normally isolated from the Bracaran *comarca* except for the rare provincial synods, is most unlikely to have exerted upon either Dumio or Braga the decisive influence that the defenders of the Celtic thesis have ascribed to it.

A more promising direction in which to seek the root of this oldest of the three inter-related components of the original pactual tradition is the Byzantine East. For this solution the key figure is the Pannonian monk Martin, the Apostle to the Sueves, an accomplished scholar in Greek as well as Latin, who before arriving in Galicia ca. 550 had sojourned in the monasteries of the Holy Land.[70] St Martin's advent

---

[66] On the Celtic diocese of Britonia and its possible influence upon the abbey-see of Dumio, see Pierre David, *Études historiques sur la Galice et le Portugal du VIe au XIIe siècle* (Lisbon-Paris, 1947), 57–64; José Orlandis, "Congregaciones monásticas," 105–8 (sympathetic to a Britonian origin for the *episcopus sub regula*); Nora K. Chadwick, *The Age of the Saints in the Early Celtic Church* (London, 1961), 58–9; *idem*, *Early Brittany* (Cardiff, 1969), 267–9, 271 (unduly inclined towards a Celtic origin for the Gallegan Church as a whole); E. A. Thompson, "Britonia," in *Christianity in Britain, 300–700*, ed. M. W. Barley and R. P. C. Hanson (Leicester, 1968), 201–5 (healthily sceptical on grounds of the Catholic character of the bishopric). On this and the larger problem of Hispanic ties with the Celtic north, cf. the monograph of continuing illumination by Jocelyn Hillgarth, "Visigothic Spain and Early Christian Ireland," *Proceeding of the Royal Irish Academy*, LXII, Section C, no. 6 (1962), 167–94. On the problem in perspective, see Gerhard Ladner, *The Idea of Reform: Its Impact on Christian Thought and Action in the Age of the Fathers* (Cambridge, Mass., 1959), 393–400.

[67] Pierre David, "L'organisation ecclésiastique du royaume suève au temps de saint Martin de Braga," in his *Études historiques*, 44, 57–64.

[68] Cf. the *Parochiale*, VI. 1 (David, p. 38): "Ad Dumio familia servorum," where no list of parochial *ecclesiae* follows as with the other sees. See also Orlandis, "Congregaciones monásticas," 103–5.

[69] David, 60.

[70] In addition to the edition of Martin's works by Claude W. Barlow, *Martini episcopi Bracarensis opera omnia* (New Haven, 1950), my review of this volume in *American Journal of*

coincides so closely with the years when the Eastern Empire of Justinian, already controlling much of southern Hispania, would have been eager to attract the then still Arian Sueves into a Catholic alliance against the common Visigothic foe at Toledo, that it is difficult not to assess this apostolate as somehow connected with Constantinople.[71] Certainly it was as a Byzantine monk that St Martin made Dumio an abbey-see along lines possibly familiar in the eastern Mediterranean homelands of monasticism; and who, after becoming metropolitan of Braga in the converted Suevic Church ca. 569, kept both bishoprics in his hands and set the pattern of the double see under a monk-prelate that was to be continued by his successors down to 585–6, when Leovigild's conquest of Galicia and the gothicization of the Suevic Church effected by this king and his son Reccared led to the complete separation of Dumio from the metropolitical capital.[72]

For pactual history it is crucial that when, some three-quarters of a century later, St Fructuosus became monk-bishop of Dumio (653/4) and metropolitan of Braga (656), he revived the old Martinian union of the two sees and once again connected the leadership of the Gallegan Church with the abbey-see which was now the cult center of the Suevic Apostle.[73] No less important, he seems to have sought to spread the combination of monastic and episcopal offices to certain other abbeys of his own foundation;[74] and there is some reason to think that when King Wamba, a decade after the death of Fructuosus, sought to introduce this same concept into the neighboring province of Lusitania, and thus in 681 earned the fierce condemnation of the bishops of XII Toledo,[75] he was promoting a monasticized as against a secular episcopate. In such terms alone can we understand the major role *RComP* assigns to the *episcopus qui sub regula uiuit* in the disciplining of abbots, an *episcopus* who

---

Philology, LXXIV (1953), 183–6, and this same scholar's introduction to v. I of *The Iberian Fathers*, 3–16, see the substantial article, with basic bibliography, of P. Avelino de Jesus da Costa, "Martinho de Dume ou Bracarense" in *Dicionário de história de Portugal*, II (Lisbon, 1965), 957–9; and the papers presented at the International Congress held at Braga in 1950 on the XIV Centenário da chegada de S. Martinho de Dume a Península Ibérica and published in *Bracara Augusta*, V–VIII (1954–7).

[71] On the general subject, cf. Paul Goubert, "Byzance et l'Espagne wisigothique," *Études byzantines*, II–IV (Paris, 1944–6): Walter Goffart, "Byzantine Policy in the West under Tiberius II and Maurice: the Pretenders Hermenegild and Gundovald, 579–585," *Traditio*, XIII (1957), 73–118; J. N. Hillgarth, "Coins and Chronicles: Propaganda in Sixth-Century Spain and the Byzantine Background," *Historia*, XV (1966), 483–508. Much remains to be learned, however, on the Byzantine antecedents of Martinian ecclesiastical and monastic organization. See in general the Actas do Colóquio Bracarense de Estudos Suévico-Bizantinos, published in *Bracara Augusta*, IX–X (1958–9), XI–XII (1960–1).

[72] E. A. Thompson, *The Goths in Spain* (Oxford, 1969), 86–90.

[73] David, *Études*, 215, insists that Martin of Braga, admittedly a fervent devotee of St Martin of Tours (another monk-prelate), enjoyed no public cult himself before the 12th century; but this seems open to question as running counter to (i) the hagiological language of the *Aliud decretum* of X Toledo: "testamentum gloriosae memoriae sancti Martini ecclesiae Bracarensis episcopi" (ed. Vives, 322); and (ii) the sanctity with which we can surmise Fructuosus and his sucessors would have surrounded the tomb at Dumio of the Suevic evangelizer whose *ecclesia sub regula* from 653/4 on was the cornerstone of their drive to monasticize the Gallegan hierarchy and clergy. On the prime importance for Dumio and Martin of Braga of the latter's Turonensian namesake, cf. the unjustly neglected article of Dom A. Lambert, "La fête de l''Ordinatio sancti Martini': ses origines, sa doctrine, dans la liturgie wisigothique," *Rev. Mabillon*, XXVI (1936), 1–27.

[74] See my brief preliminary statement, "*Episcopus sub regula* or *episcopi sub regula*? St Fructuosus and the Monasticized Episcopate in the Peninsular West," *Bracara Augusta*, XXI (1967), 63–4.

[75] Canon 4 (ed. Vives, 389–92).

was not, as Herwegen thought, exclusively associated with Dumio-Braga but could be found elsewhere in the province in abbey-sees of Dumian type.[76]

Another principal element in the Fructuosan system is the Sancta Communis Regula, the supreme assembly of abbots and abbesses which stood at the head of the federation of cenobia established by Fructuosus and his disciples, and other houses attracted to the organization, and which under the presidency of the monk-metropolitan of Braga promulgated ordinances of general application to all the member communities.[77] Orlandis believes that this supreme body descends from an abbatial synod of the Martinian era,[78] thus (I would stress) constituting like the reunion of Braga and Dumio further evidence of Fructuosus' deliberate emulation of his great prececessor of the Suevic era. Whether or not this is so, the important thing is that at some point after 656 the Sancta Communis Regula must have been consulted on the adoption of the pactual constitution and have given its consent to this heterodox polity, a step that would seem to have been taken some years after the death (ca. 665) of Fructuosus, who cannot therefore have been the author of *RComP*. In other words, although the pactum appears in c. 17 of *RCom* as something already well established, and is not introduced as are some other fundamental decisions with the quasi-conciliar formula *Placuit sanctae communi regulae*,[79] it must be viewed as the product of learned discussion and formal legislative action by an educated monastic leadership, not as an illiterate barbarization of the Roman legal principles of orthodox cenobitism. Once this is appreciated, we can move away from sterile debate over the supposed victory of Germanicism and undertake to identify the true forces moving the Fructuosan monastic federation, with its monasticized episcopate and synodal government, towards the creation of the pactual constitution that has been so variously explained by its modern interpreters.

Two paramount features of Gallegan monastic life in the second half of the 7th century are central to any such investigation. One is the powerful wave of popular enthusiasm for the ascetic gospel generated in the province by the charismatic preaching and example of Fructuosus, an almost too successful apostolate, since the rapid multiplication of converts and monasteries, and the widespread pressures for a monasticized clergy, exceeded the capacity of the Fructuosan leadership to control this response or imbue it, except imperfectly, with genuine understanding of proto-cenobitic spirituality and organization. The new movement seems to have appealed particularly to one vital sector of the provincial society, the owners of the small and medium-sized *uillulae* and *uillae* that dotted the Galaico-Minhotan countryside.[80] Together with their wives, children and the conscripted slaves (*serui*) of their domains who were constrained to take up the ascetic life, these rural proprietors were unmistakably the principal source of potential *conuersi* and benefactors for all the monasteries of Galicia, especially in view of the legal inability of the unfree peasantry to become monks without patronal approval or compulsion. These men must be carefully distinguished from the *principes terrae*, the magnates whom the authors of *RCom* regard with hostile eyes,[81] and also from the group of Visigothic royal officials

[76] Cf. note 74.

[77] Herwegen, 55–60; Orlandis, Congregaciones monásticas, 98–103.

[78] Orlandis, "Congregaciones monásticas," *loc. cit; idem*, "Movimiento ascético," 84.

[79] *RCom* 6, 15.

[80] Cf. *RCom* 1. On the structures of land use, proprietorship and rural settlement in Romano-Suevo-Visigothic Galicia, see especially Orlando Ribeiro, "Portugal," in *Geografía de España y Portugal*, ed. Manuel Terán, V (Barcelona, 1955), 74–81, 96–7, 172–3; Pierre Birot, *Le Portugal: étude de géographie rurale* (Paris, 1950), 63–88, 191–5.

[81] Cf. cc. 1–2, and probably also c. 20.

and aristocratic ladies who in Fructuosus' own lifetime were drawn from Toledo and elsewhere by his renown and to whom his *Vita* pays transparently excessive attention.[82] The small proprietors in contrast were men of overwhelmingly Celtic, Roman and Suevic stock, not Visigoths, for in the century since Leovigild's conquest of the Suevic kingdom in 585 there had been no perceptible Visigothic migration to the northwest.[83] They came from a rural world in which individual rights tended to be attached to the land, which itself, although in individual hands, was so subject to deeply embedded familial rights of inheritance as to be not easily alienable, in the full Roman sense, even to God and his saints. The result, so contrary to the monastic ideal of poverty, can be seen in the strong sense of ownership, inseparable from the contribution the *conuersi* made at their reception, that survived among these proprietarian monks. This is the outlook that finds its fullest expression in the violent individualism, weak abbatiate and inherent instability of two distinctive types of heterodox monastic communities, other than the 'Fructuosan', that find reflection in the documents of the age. These are, first, the ascetic societies condemned in *RCom* 1 as "falso nomine monasteria", which were organized by such rural proprietors as *uicini* on the basis of a *sacramenti conditio* or *iuramentum*; and, secondly, those based upon the radically contractual and egalitarian *Consensoria monachorum*, a far more heterodox constitution than *RComP*, yet one that finds acceptance in the *codices regularum* in attachment to the Basilian or Isidorian Rules.[84] These proprietarian monasteries, to be cited henceforth as respectively vicinal and consensorial, should be looked upon, as we have suggested, as a kind of *monasterio propio* where the founding monks were in effect the resident *patroni*.

There can be no doubt that the very existence and widespread popularity of these middle-class, proprietarian, contractualist monasteries made them formidable competitors to the houses under the Sancta Communis Regula, while at the same time threatening to draw these towards similar modification and secularization of paleo-monastic patterns. The violent assault contained in *RCom* 1 upon such *pseudo-monasteria* is proof enough; but we are fortunate to have also an informative contemporary source that allows us to gauge the impact of vicinalism and consensorialism, the little sketch of Gallegan monastic history written, probably ca. 685, by the Bierzan abbot Valerius.[85] In the MSS this text bears the title *De genere monachorum* (*DGM*) but this looks like an early scribal error for *De septimo genere monachorum*, since the evident aim is to extend St Isidore of Seville's catalogue of the six different kinds of

[82] *Vita*, cc. 3, 8, 14–15.

[83] This is of course an entirely different (if related) question from that of the settlement of refugee Goths in Galicia after the catastrophe of the Islamic invasion, which has been discussed by, *inter alios*, Ramon d'Abadal i de Vinyals, "A propos du legs visigothique en Espagne," *Caratteri del secolo VII in Occidente, Settimane di studio, Spoleto*, V (1958), II, 541–88 (also "El llegat visigòtic a Hispània," *Dels visigots als catalans*, I, 95–133); and especially by Claudio Sánchez Albornoz, "Tradición y derecho visigodos en León y Castilla," *Cuad. hist. España*, XXIX–XXX (1959), 244–65 (also in his *Investigaciones y documentos sobre las instituciones hispanas*, Santiago de Chile, 1970, 114–31); *idem*, *Despoblación y repoblación del valle del Duero* (Buenos Aires, 1966). On the general problems created for early medieval monasticism by prevailing secular concepts of property, see the penetrating study by Dom Michael P. Blecker, "Roman Law and 'Consilium' in the *Regula Magistri* and the *Rule* of St Benedict," *Speculum*, XLVII (1972), 1–28.

[84] Cf. my "*Consensoria monachorum*," Study II in this volume.

[85] The 17th-century edition of Ménard, reprinted by Flórez (E. Flórez and M. Risco, *España Sagrada* [Madrid, 1747–1879], henceforth *E.S.*), *E.S.*, XVI, 387–90, and Migne, *PL* 87, cols. 437–9; and also that of Ramón Fernández Pousa, ed., *San Valerio. Obras* (Madrid, 1944), 138–41, have been superseded by the text (with introduction) of M. Díaz y Díaz, "Sobre el tratado *De genere monachorum* de Valerio del Bierzo," in his *Anecdota wisigothica* I (*Acta Salmanticensia, Filosofía y Letras*, XII, 2;Salamanca, 1958), 49–61.

monks by adding a seventh—"peius prioribus"—to be found in the Galicia of the writer's own day.[86] Here we learn that after Fructuosus's death the abbeys associated with his name were so hard hit by failure to attract new recruits that they were compelled to conscript into their ranks children and the less able-bodied adults from their own patrimonial *familiae*; and that in consequence these monasteries had become filled with compulsory converts who lacked all true vocation for the ascetic life and used their now elevated position to acquire material wealth—the same charge, incidentally, *RCom* 1–2 brings against the vicinal *pseudomonasteria*. Valerius, to be sure, characteristically inclines throughout his works to rhetorical exaggeration and violent denunciation, and it is just possible that he is speaking here only of the Bierzo rather than of all Galicia, so that his dismal picture must be received with due caution. Yet what he says confirms other signs that within two decades after its founder's death, the Fructuosan federation did face a critical shortage of *conuersi* due in large part to the flow of small proprietor postulants to the vicinal and consensorial cenobia and the flight of *fugitiui* whom these and other non-Fructuosan houses sheltered against their rightful abbots.

The second paramount factor behind the rise of 'Fructuosan' pactualism, no less decisive, is the disruptive conflict from mid-century on between the monasteries presided over by the monk-metropolitans of Dumio-Braga, and the Gallegan secular hierarchy and clergy, who sought to foster their own non-Fructuosan cenobitism by encouraging not only the vicinal but also the presbyteral abbeys vehemently condemned in *RCom*. In the initial stages of this poorly studied struggle St Fructuosus himself plainly played the leading role, as any scrutiny of the dramatic circumstances under which, with the powerful backing of King Recceswinth, he came to replace the bishop Riccimir at Dumio (653/4) and the metropolitan Potamius at Braga (656), quickly reveals.[87] The intense hostility these episodes attest between the reformist, monasticizing Fructuosan wing of the Gallegan Church and its secular, anti-Fructuosan counterpart unquestionably continued to the end of the Visigothic monarchy, and has left numerous traces in our sources, not least in the language of *RCom*, which uses the startling term (c. 20) *nostra ecclesia* to distinguish its supporters from the monks and clergy loyal to the secular episcopate, while it accuses the vicinal communities of being responsible for *haeresis et schisma et grandis per monasteria controuersia*. The same deep resentment towards the opposing camp underlies the savage attack in *RCom* 2 upon presbyteral monasteries, i.e., the apparently numerous cenobia created by *presbyteri saeculares*, who transformed their parish churches into tiny monasteries where the rector, assuming the office of abbot, could claim to be *sub regula*. This metamorphosis *RCom* assails as an insincere means of appeasing popular demand for a monastic ministry, adopted in order to assure the continuance of the charities of the faithful.

In all these instances the immediate target appears as monastic; but beyond this the real enemy is unmistakably the Gallegan secular Church, its bishops and clerics, and their influential allies, the *principes terrae* or high nobles. Just how this conflict fits into the larger picture of ecclesiastical and political breakdown throughout Visigothic Spain in its final apocalyptic decades has yet to be determined; but it certainly offers an illuminating regional instance of one kind of internal trouble that preceded the end.

In this strife-torn *ambiente* of intra-monastic and secular-regular polarization in later 7th-century Galicia, how are we to understand the adoption by the federated monasteries of the Sancta Communis Regula of the 'Fructuosan' pactum? Two

---

[86] Díaz y Díaz, *op. cit.*, 50.

[87] See the two *decreta* appended to the acts of the Council of X Toledo (*Concilios visigóticos*, ed. Vives, 319–24).

intimately dependent lines of explanation suggest themselves. From at least 656, when its leader came into possession of the supreme ecclesiastical office in the province, the Fructuosan cenobitic movement would have been under compulsion to find an alternative to the secular bishop in the exercise of authority, as defined by the canons of Chalcedon and IV Toledo, over his diocesan monasteries, while at the same time avoiding the danger, acute under 7th-century conditions, that complete exemption from external control might result in serious abuses and tyrannical rule on the part of abbots. If the provincial authority of the monk-metropolitan of Dumio-Braga, the synods of the Sancta Communis Regula, and the local *episcopi sub regula* were available, these were hardly sufficient: the first two were too exalted, too remote, for handling local issues; the *sub regula* bishops probably too few and of impugnable status. The alternative was to re-formulate the monastic polity structurally so as to insure a firm degree of limitation upon the abbot by securing in advance his written acceptance of a constitutional-contractual relationship with his *subditi* as regards the rights and duties of each. To safeguard this compact the monks were therefore allowed to initiate external intervention against abbatial despotism, that is, they were given the right to appeal to other monasteries or, alternatively, to an *episcopus sub regula* acting conjointly with the *catholicus ecclesiae defensor comes*—an illuminating example of the cooperation of Fructuosan and royal agencies. In either case, the *episcopus saecularis* is excluded; in the 7th century the monasteries of the pactual tradition stand completely outside the normal episcopal visitation and installation of abbots.

This is one side of the story; the other is the increasing pressure from the rival forms of monasticism that by ca. 675–85 confronted the Sancta Communis Regula with the urgent necessity of moving beyond the ruinous dependence upon conscription of the children and physically handicapped adults of the patrimonies to some formula that would attract the numerous *conuersi* emerging from the lower landowning strata of provincial society. For this purpose also the contractual polity was a sheer necessity, for the multiplication of vicinal and consensorial communities proved the widespread popularity among these classes of such adaptations of monastic orthodoxy to the indigenous mores as favored looser organizational structure and relaxation of the sternly rigorist discipline of the Fructuosan *Regula monachorum*. In this light the 'Fructuosan' pactum, which has been assessed by Herwegen and other modern students primarily in terms of its departure from traditional norms, looks very much like an attempt to meet the enemy half way, a compromise between two extremes which it successfully avoided: an orthodox cenobitism inseparable from secular episcopal control and exploitation, and an egalitarian vicinalism with its weak abbatiate and inescapable instability.

Was this an ill-advised surrender to expediency, a debasement of paleomonastic spirituality and an acceptance of barbarizing forms of social and juridical association in an only superficially coated-over Germanic *Genossenschaft*? I do not believe so. Certainly Herwegen's emphasis, manifestly first suggested to him by his teacher Stutz,[88] upon the basic Germanism of *RComP* and its post-711 adaptations, demands much more qualified definition than it has yet received, although scepticism on this point has been growing.[89] Nor can credence be given to the claim that the model for the

[88] For Stutz's initial (and predictable) assessment of the pactum as the product of primitive Germanic legalism 'wegen ihres stark germanischen Gepräge,' a view that must have influenced his Benedictine pupil, see his *Vorwort* to Herwegen, vii–ix.

[89] The Germanic theory continues to flourish in, e.g., García Villada, *Historia eclesiástica*, II, 1, 295–6; Henri Leclercq, "Pacte," *Dictionnaire d'archéologie chrétienne et de liturgie*, XIII, 1 (Paris, 1937), cols. 232–6; Martins, "Monacato de S. Frutuoso," 341–4; Pérez de Urbel, *Monjes españoles*, I, 446; *idem*, "Vida y caminos" (1963), 13–14; *idem*, "Carácter y supervivencia" (1968), 229–31; Alfredo Esteves, "O germanismo de S. Frutuoso na profissão monástica do século VII," *Bracara Augusta*, XXI (1967), 258–76.

Gallegan pactum is to be found in the oath the Visigoths took to a new king, pledging him an obedience conditional upon his ruling justly and under law; this hypothesis of Herwegen, although endorsed by Martins, Pérez de Urbel and Esteves, among others, offers at best a remote analogy to the pactual abbey.[90] Since 1907 more sophisticated studies of the Toletan constitution have made clear the relative insignificance of this oath, its late appearance (mid-7th century) and strongly Roman and ecclesiastical origin, while they discount the extent to which Germanic *Widerstandsrechte* were based upon contractual assumptions.[91] Furthermore, as P. D. King observes, there is no counterpart in the political sphere to the monks' appeal against arbitrary rule to the regular bishop and count.

Still, it is evident that in vicinalism and contractualism, at least, we behold monasticism conforming itself to the dominant mores of the Gallegan countryside in the 7th century. The precise nature of this background remains, however, to be determined. The landowning classes below the high provincial nobility were a mixed society of Celtic, Roman and Suevic elements, of whose law and institutions we know painfully little as yet. Many complex questions urgently call for exploration before the roots of Gallegan monastic contractualism can be uncovered. To evaluate the allegedly Germanic phraseology and assumptions of *RComP*, we badly need a thorough study by specialists of the vocabulary, syntax and mentality of the whole range of literary and diplomatic texts produced in the Galaico-Portuguese region between the 5th and 11th centuries. That familial concepts of property were so strong that they affected not only vicinalism and consensorialism but also drove *RCom* 18 to prohibit, in extraordinary fashion, all benefactions by *conuersi* to the monastery of their reception, is plain enough. But what incomprehension of corporative organization, and of personal and collective monastic ideals of poverty, underlies the instability of the houses of *uicini* and *consentientes*? Surely, if we are to seek analogies, we should look to the forces that in the Spain of this period were finding expression in the relations between *commendati* and their *patronus* or, at a somewhat later date, between the members of the medieval *benefactoria* or *behetría*, particularly in the form known as the *incommuniatio* or *incomuniação* that is found in the Luso-Gallegan homeland of the pactum.[92]

But, to conclude this portion of our inquiry, what we must keep in mind is the underlying orthodoxy of the 'Fructuosan' pactum, the authentic basis of its circulation under the drastically changed conditions of the Alta Reconquista. We can see this in its protection of *stabilitas*, obedience, discipline, and properly directed abbatial power in contrast with the latitudinarian permissiveness which the Gallegan secular episcopate

---

[90] Herwegen, 27–30.

[91] On the Visigothic oath, the best recent treatment, which cites Herwegen's pactual analogy (although omitting its author's name) is P. D. King, *Law and Society in the Visigothic Kingdom* (Cambridge, 1972), 39–51, especially 46, note 2. See also, with mention of Herwegen, Fritz Kern, *Gottesgnadentum und Widerstandsrechte im früheren Mittelalter* (Leipzig, 1914; 2nd ed. Münster-Cologne, 1954), Appendix XVI; and in the English version by S. B. Chrimes, *Kingship and Law in the Middle Ages* (Oxford, 1939), the translator's Introduction, xvii–xxii. On the Visigothic kings' relations with their nobles, see also José Orlandis, *El poder real y la sucesión al trono en la monarquía visigoda* (*Estudios visigóticos*, III; Rome, 1962); Dietrich C. Adel, *Kirche und Königtum im Westgotenreich* (Sigmaringen, 1971). Actually, in view of the patronal-commendatory implications of monastic pactualism, an investigation of proto-feudal and seigneurial structures would be a more fruitful line of approach than the monarchical.

[92] Cf. Henrique de Gama Barros, *Historia da administração pública em Portugal nos séculos XII a XV*, ed. Torquato de Sousa Soares (Lisboa, 1945–54), VI, 349–59; VII, 218–34; Claudio Sánchez Albornoz, "Las behetrías," *Anuario de historia del derecho español*, I (1924), 196–240; also in his *Estudios sobre las instituciones medievales españolas* (México, 1965), 47–88.

was willing to allow in the monasteries of *uicini* and *consentientes.* If the pactum bestows anti-abbatial *Widerstandsrechte*, yet the pactual abbot remains a strong governor, capable of imposing corporal punishment and of pursuing deserters with the full cooperation of *comites*, *iudices* and *saiones*. His monks make to him a *traditio* of their persons, but while they retain the right to challenge his arbitrary behavior, they cannot do so as individuals but only through action by the community as a whole. The pactual treaty was not, as with its more extreme rivals, a partnership of monks (*Genossenschaftsvertrag*), but a covenant between the corporate community of *subditi* and its constitutional monarch (*Gesamtuntertanenvertrag*). Finally, and above all, in the panorama of western and Iberian monasticism, it was a local solution to problems peculiarly Gallegan; and its success is to be judged not alone by what it accomplished in the final decades of the Visigothic province but even more by its tenacious survival after 711, when during the long difficult centuries of monastic recovery it enjoyed a central place in the religious life of two of the most institutionally and culturally fruitful regions of medieval Christian Iberia, Galicia-Portugal and Castile-Rioja.

IV

At this point, before turning to the pactualism of the Alta Reconquista, there needs to be considered one largely ignored feature of 'Fructuosan' instrument of the 7th century upon which the comparable diplomas of succeeding centuries throw considerable light. Both *RComP* and its various more or less closely related adaptations after 711 have been studied by Herwegen and later students in terms of strictly monachal acts, addressed by the *subditi* to their abbot and terminating with their subscriptions. But what provision did the system make for what would seem to be no less juridically necessary in a bilateral contract, the abbot's own promise to serve under the terms stipulated? Herwegen apparently assumed that such an abbatial commitment was implicit in his texts and therefore never sought to explain why the abbot's own name normally does not appear among the subscribants to what he saw as primarily a foundational charter.

This is a difficulty that disappears once we perceive that, by the commencement of the 9th century at least, evidence survives to show that the 'Fructuosan' pactum from the very beginning actually consisted of not one, but two, distinct yet inseparably linked parts or subpacta: one the well-known covenant of the monks, the *pactum monachorum*; the other, the abbot's own declaration, a *pactum abbatis* or *abbatiale.* Taken together, both texts constitute what we may call the double, or, preferably, so as to avoid all confusion with double monasteries and double *traditiones*, the binary pactum.

The principal characteristics of such a combined instrument can most readily be isolated in the early, exceptionally complete case of the Liébanese abbey of San Pedro y San Pablo de Naroba, one of the oldest known eastern centers of the transplanted Gallegan pactualism of the Alta Reconquista. The extant pactual *pergamino* preserved from this house was first drawn up in 818 and remained in use through the terms of three successive abbots down to ca. 825–35. An unusually large document of some 42.5 × 35 cms., it survives in a copy of the 12th century, so carefully made in a good Visigothic hand as to give the strong impression of being a faithful, almost photographic, facsimile of the lost original.[93] What we have here in fact are not merely two but five associated texts, all unknown to Herwegen and first published in 1944 by Sánchez Albornoz and a year later by Pérez de Urbel. Of these only one, which stands first in the series, is the *pactum monachorum* by which the monks and nuns of this double community promise to observe the ascetic life under the abbot Argilegus; as might be expected in such an act only a century removed from those circulating in the monasteries of Visigothic Galicia, this follows relatively closely the language and provisions of *RComP*, although with certain highly informative adaptations and omissions.

At the close of the monachal pactum the date "sub die pridie kalendas martias discurrente era DCCCLVI" is carefully recorded; but this is not followed, as might be expected, by the subscriptions of the religious. Instead, after a short space, there commences in the name of the abbot Argilegus a "confirmatio uel compromissio" by which the community's governor bestows upon it various of his properties. This is to all intents and purposes the abbatial counterpart to the self-submission of the monks, the *pactum abbatis* under which by implication Argilegus assumes office in accordance with the stipulations made in the monachal pactum; although undated it must have been drawn up at the same time as the latter. Then follows in the *pergamino* a third text, also without date but evidently issued simultaneously with its two predecessors, which takes the form of a donation made "in hunc pacto uel traditione" by the abbot's kinsman Sisbertus, who bestows upon Naroba and its religious one-fourth of his landed properties and movables. This charter, although confirming other testimony to the familial character of the structure and primitive endowment of the abbey, is of secondary interest; more important is the fact that following its eschatocol we finally reach the subscriptions of the twelve monks and nuns who composed the *subter notati* of the *pactum monachorum*, each cast in the form "in hoc pacto manu mea (*Sig.*) feci". This terminal list of names constitutes the bond that ties together the first and second pieces, the *pacta* or strictly *subpacta*, i.e., the two fundamental, inseparable parts of the full synallagmatic contract that is the legal basis of the new monastic society.

The two undated remaining pieces of the Naroban *pergamino* must have been composed between 825 and 835, following Argilegus' death at some point in that decade. One of these, the fourth text of the entire pentad, is the *pactum abbatiale* of the second abbot, Arias, who calls himself Argilegus' *cognatus* and makes a "traditio uel confirmatio" to the house similar to that of his predecessor in 818. In this case, however, in addition to the cession of lands, there is also an explicit *traditio* of his person ("trado me et omnia mea ereditate") by the abbot to the monastery and the *fratres*. The subscriptions of the latter follow, thirteen in number, all masculine, and each following the formula "in hoc pacto manu mea (*Sig.*) feci". Finally, no. 5 of the series contains a *traditio* of his person and goods by Arias' nephew Adefonsus, directed this time both to the monastery "et tibi tio et abbati meo Ariani". This text, validated in the words "in hoc pacto manu mea (*Sig.*) feci et coram testibus roborabi", continues with the subscriptions of four other religious, all masculine, and in each case except the last employing the same phrase, "in hoc pacto manu mea (*Sig.*) feci".

[93] Madrid, Archivo Histórico National (henceforth AHN), Clero, San Julian de Samos leg. 794, no. 116; publ. by Sánchez Albornoz, "Serie de documentos inéditos del reino de Asturias," *Cuad. hist. España*, I–II (1944), 334–7; and in his *Investigaciones y documentos*, 165–6 (no. III); Pérez de Urbel, *Historia del condado de Castilla* (Madrid, 1945), III, 1044–7 (no. 12); Floriano, *Diplomática*, I, 146–51 (no. 27). The *Tumbo Nuevo* of Lugo (AHN), fols. 336–8 contains two 18th-century copies, with the additional information that the original was then in the "Archivo del Monasterio de Sta Fee de la Ciudad de Toledo de SS.[ss] Commendadoras del Orden de Santiago"; it must have been an archival error of the 19th century that placed this Liébanese text among the documents of Samos in the AHN.

It is not necessary to relate here the specific history of the Naroban monastery to this group of pactual texts, the underlying Gallegan character of which in the 9th century is so strongly indicated by the relative fidelity of the *pactum monachorum* to *RComP*; but certain points of broad interest for the pactual tradition as a whole should be noted. One has to do with the procedure followed in the pactual monasteries after an abbot's demise. Herwegen thought that with each new abbot the monastic pactum, which he regarded as an *Abtwahlinstrument* as well as a *Professformel*, had to be drawn up anew. Here however we have proof that this was not necessarily so; it was in fact not the initial perpetual commitment of the monks to the ascetic life that required reformulation, but the assumption of office by one abbot succeeding another as the second of the contracting parties (in the case of Santos Pedro y Pablo, Arias after Argilegus). The subscriptions following the Arias *privilegio*, all different from those terminating the Argilegus triad, indicate that names already attached to the original binary pactum carried over without repetition into the regime of the next abbot, while those of *conuersi* admitted after the latter's succession were attached to his abbatial pactum, manifestly on the assumption that these monks, although committing themselves to precisely the same *traditio* and promises as in the foundational monachal pactum, should make their profession to the abbot ruling at the time. The four additional names placed "in hoc pacto" after the diploma of Adefonsus may also imply that in due course this nephew of Arias assumed the abbatiate, or conceivably they may have been added before Abbot Arias's death in the only space available.

From the Naroban pentad, as from other cases presently to be cited, it is evident also that at least after 711 (and no doubt before) the pactual system was frequently associated with familially possessed or endowed *monasterios propios* where a dynastic abbatial succession based upon consanguinity within the founding clan was normal and maintained by the readiness of an abbot's kinsman to take over his office either from outside the community (as apparently with Arias), or from within the ranks of the abbey's monks (as possibly with Adefonsus). In neither case can there have been any free election by the religious; under such circumstances Herwegen's *Abtwahlinstrument* would have been no more than the legal expression of a predetermined choice.[94] Note should also be taken here of the early transformation of San Pedro y San Pablo from a double into a masculine community, possibly a sign of episcopal intervention.

There are other conclusions to be drawn concerning the binary pactum, but before attempting to do so it will be useful to list all the examples discovered in a preliminary search, so as to make clear that the procedure at Naroba is typical of the pactual tradition in both Galicia-Portugal and Castile-Rioja. Certain of the entries that follow have long been known to students of Asturo-Leonese diplomatics; but their true nature has been concealed, either by later medieval copyists who inscribed the monastic and abbatial subpacta in the *tumbos* as successive, separately rubricked documents (despite their probably original normal occurrence in a single *pergamino* or *pactionis libellus*), or by the similar practice of modern editors.

I shall catalogue these pacta chronologically by house, since the location and date of the pactual monastery is historically more pertinent than the abbot's name; but those involving successive rulers of the same community will be entered separately for

[94] The close association of pactualism with the familial *Eigenklöster* of the period manifestly demands further study, as does the nature of the control exercised by *patroni* over such foundations. Cf. the diploma of 928 in which the founders Alvarus and Sabita of the double, and almost certainly pactual, monastery of San Clodio "in territorio Castellae uilla Emeiheris discurrente riuuolo Auiae" (San Clodio de Ribeiro, prov. Orense, ayunt. de Leiro, on the río Avia below Osera) define this authority at length (A. Manrique, *Cisterciensium Annales*, III, Lyons, 1649, 128–30, *sub anno* 1182; cf. *E. S.*, XVIII, 30–1).

purposes of reference. Future scrutiny of the precise origins of these monasteries and of the provenance of their founding fathers can be expected to throw light upon the lines of pactual diffusion.

Provisional List of Identifiable Binary Pacta

1. 818, 28 February. San Pedro y San Pablo de Naroba (Liébana; modern prov. Santander, at or near Venta de Naroba, a few kms. south of Potes). Extant binary pactum with his monks of the abbot Argilegus; discussed immediately above.

2. Ca. 825–35. San Pedro y San Pablo de Naroba. Extant binary pactum of Abbot Arias with his monks; discussed immediately above.

3. 856? 876? Santa Eulalia de Búbal (Galicia; where the road running north from Orense to Chantada crosses the río Búbal).[95] The binary covenant from this house, preserved in the *Tumbo de Celanova* and first published by Emilio Sáez, consists of: the "placitum uel pactum" addressed to the abbot-presbyter Absalom by five religious, including one woman and three clerics, a text belonging to an entirely different tradition from that of *RComP* and looking very much like what we might expect to have been used in the small presbyteral monasteries of the late Visigothic Galicia depicted in so unfavorable a spiritual (but not, be it noted, constitutional) light in *RCom* 2. Between the monachal pactum and the subscriptions of the members of the community stands, exactly as in the Naroban binary instrument, the *pactum abbatiale* of Abbot Absalom himself, surrendering his person, and his share in the monastery and its books and *ornamenta*, together with all his lands and livestock, to "uobis fratribus meis" and the monastery of Santa Eulalia. This second part of the text includes at the end the words "qui in hanc placitum uel pactum regule roboratus fuerit" and Absalom's own subscription "in hac placitum regule quem fratribus meis trado et mihi placuit." Then, once again as in the case of the Argilegus binary act, there now follow the names of the religious, who subscribe in the form "in hac (*or* hoc) placitum regule . . . manu mea (*Sig.*)", thus serving to bind together the two juridically inseparable halves of the full binary pactum.

4. 871, 5 June: Santa María de Mezonzo (Galicia; p. j. de Arzúa, ayunt. de Vilasantar, northeast of Santiago in the upper valley of the río Tambre).[96] The *Tumbo de Celanova* contains for this house in immediate juxtaposition: (i) fols. 24r–24v, the *pactum abbatiale* of the abbot Fulgaredus, in which, along with his brother, the

[95] *Tumbo de Celanova* (AHN), fols. 151v, col. 2–152r, col. 2. Text in Emilio Sáez, "Documentos gallegos inéditos del período asturiano," *Anuario de historia del derecho español*, XVIII (1947), 417–9 (no. 6); Floriano, *Diplomática*, I, 267–70 (no. 62). Sáez (417, note 19) rightly rejects as mistaken the date 826 given in the *Tumbo*, on the grounds that the abbot Absalom and the cleric Ansemundis who figure in the pactum also appear in a presumably correctly dated document of 879 (Saéz, 422, no. 10). But Saéz' proposed restoration (which Floriano adopts) of an *x aspada* in the date 'era DCCCªLªXIIIIª', which yields A. D. 856, requires a minimal abbatiate for Absalom of 23 years and a lengthy co-existence of abbot and presbyter. I am therefore inclined to think that the mistake may lie in the copyist's misreading of a fourth 'C' as an 'X'; correction to 'era DCCCCªXIIII', i.e., A. D. 876, would bring the two documents into more convincing conjuncture.

[96] *Tumbo de Celanova*, fols. 24r–25r. Published by Antonio López Ferreiro, *Historia de la Santa A. M. Iglesia de Santiago de Compostela* (Santiago, 1898–1901), II, Apéndices, 20–1 (no. IX), 22–3 (no. X); Floriano, *Diplomática española*, II, 70–73 (no. 101), 73–6 (no. 102). Cf. Maximino Arias, "Los monasterios de benedictinos de Galicia," *Studia monastica*, VIII (1966), 35–69, at 51; Sá Bravo, *Monacato en Galicia*, I, 343–7.

presbyter Pedro, and his sister, the *deouota* Berildi, he bestows various possessions upon the monastery; and (ii) fols. 24ᵛ–25ʳ, the "pactum simul et placitum" addressed to Abbot Fulgaredus by his subject monks and nuns, which does not follow except for certain verbal reminiscences the pattern of *RComP*. Together the two acts comprise the binary pactum and were probably incorporated in a single original *pergamino*.

5. Ca. 900 (?). Santa María de Mezonzo. The binary pactum of the abbot Vimara, apparently Fulgaredus' successor, which is cited in 955 by Vimara's nephew, the abbot Gudesindus of this house, in a diploma of the *Tumbo de San Salvador de Sobrado*.[97] This text contains our most explicit depiction of the actual drafting and function of a binary pactum: "Defunctusque ipse Fulcaredus abba et frater eius Petrus presbyter reliquerunt eam (i.e., the church-monastery) ad suprinos uel fratres suos atque sorores secundum in pactum resonant. isti sunt Ildefonsus presbyter, Iubandus presbyter, Fromaldus presbyter, Petrus presbyter, Uisterla diaconus, Sisamirus diaconus uel ceteri fratres atque sorores ibidem commanentes et stantes in ipsum iam prefatum locum absque abbate. Et accessit illis spontanea uoluntas ut eligerent sibi ipsos Uimaram abbatem qui de illorum erat progenie et neptus ipsius Reterici abbatis. Et iterum Uimara abbas fecit suum pactum in eius nomine et tradiderunt se ei et omnia illorum secundum eis regula docuit et in eorum testamento resonat. Et fuerunt omnes a seculo migrati in eius iure et reliquerunt ei omnia sua secundum pactum rouorauerant. Defunctus uero ipse Uimara abbas reliquit ipsam uillam et ipsam ecclesiam simul et pactos atque testamentos et cartas uel omnia sua possidenda ad suprinum suum Gundesindum abbatem, etc."

6. 907, 18 March. Santiago 'de Mortalones' (?) (Galicia, prov. Lugo).[98] Binary pactum between the presbyter Sisericus and the "fratres uel sorores" of this house. This consists of an abbatial *traditio* of self ("trado corpus meum") and property to the community, followed by the corresponding corporative *traditio* of the religious (none of whose subscriptions survive), which commences: "Et nos omnes qui sumus in loco isto tecum congregati . . . tibi abbati nostro tradimus propria uoluntate nostram omnino facultatem . . . simul et nostras personas, etc." The monachal section towards its end recalls the language of *RComP*, although it does not approach this model closely.

7. 930, 27 January. San Mamés de Ura (Castile, prov. Burgos, p. j. Lerma; to the south of the capital on the río Ura, the modern Mataviejas, a southern affluent of the Arlanza).[99] The only extant binary pactum so far known involving an abbess, it contains (i) the pactum of the nuns (in all probability this was a community of women exclusively) which is addressed to "domna et matre nostra Eufrasia", and as of adapted *RComP* type was assigned by Herwegen to his second group; (ii) the corresponding *pactum abbatissae* in the form of a *traditio* of herself and her possessions to God and San Mamés made by the abbess Eufrasia: "et hinc sancte regule consensi, trado me et

---

[97] *Cartulario de Sobrado*, I, no. CX. Published by López Ferreiro, *op. cit.*, II, Apéndices, 151–4 (no. LXVI).

[98] Published in part from *Escritura 210* of the *Tumbo de San Julián de Samos* by Plácido Arias, *Historia del real Monasterio de Samos* (Santiago de Compostela, 1950), 463 (Apénd. II), and cf. 44–6; and in more complete form by M. Rubén García Alvarez, "Más documentos gallegos inéditos del período asturiano," *Boletín del Instituto de Estudios Asturianos*, XIX (1965), 37–8 (no. 6), and cf. also 15. The Latin toponym should perhaps be read 'Mortalanes'. The identification of this house with Santiago de Bardaos (prov. Lugo, p. j. Sarria, ayunt y. feligr. de San Juan de Bardaos), as proposed by García Alvarez (37, note 91), seems to me unlikely.

[99] Text in Herwegen, 11–14; L. Serrano, *Cartulario de San Pedro de Arlanza* (Madrid, 1925), 26–9 (no. VIII); Pérez de Urbel, *Hist. cond. Cast.*, III, 1098–9 (no. 115).

me ipsam corpus simul et animam meam Deo et sancte Mametis cum omni rebus meis quiquid michi accidit de parentum meorum hereditate"; and (iii) a donation of 27 January 930 in which the *condes* Fernán González and Sancha bestow upon San Mamés their church of Santa Eugenia in the valley of the río Ura, with all its appurtenances. Herwegen (p. 15), noting the absence of subscriptions after (i) and regarding (ii) and (iii) as completely separate diplomas, denies that the date given in the comital donation was also that of (i). But the fact is, (i) and (ii) belong inseparably together as components of a binary pactum, to which, either at the foundation of the house or at an installation of a new abbess, the *condes* of Castile attached their dated benefaction, almost certainly issued at the same time as one of these contingencies. It is true that in the 18th-century copy now at Silos the subscriptions have been omitted from all three pieces, even those of the witnesses to that of the *condes*; but that these texts were originally contained in a single *pergamino*, which remained in use as the constitutional basis of the nunnery, is strongly indicated by the fact that subsequently King Sancho I of León (956–965) and Count Fernán González (920–970) added their confirmations; and these are followed by more subscriptions including those of the abbess María, and of a nun Auria who declares "in hoc pacto manu mea signum † feci".[100]

8. 1045, 21 September. São Salvador de Vacariça (Portugal; Beira Litoral, concelho of Mealhada, some 20 kms. due north of Coimbra).[101] Three diplomas, found at different points in the *Livro Preto* of the see of Coimbra but all of identical date and rightly printed together by Herculano, belong to this solitary known Portuguese binary pactum. Although formulated between the monks of Vacariça and their abbot Tudeildus, in language and juridical content it actually represents the pactualism found at this abbot's more northern house of São Salvador de Leça (near Porto), itself a product of the Galaico-Portuguese pactual movement of the 9th and 10th centuries; see Study IV in this volume for full discussion of this interesting case. Many of the questions these documents raise have been ably treated by Mattoso.[102]

The foregoing series of binary pacta, however incomplete, should suffice to establish the basic twofold content of the pactum of Gallegan type, a characteristic that in all probability dates from its genesis in the second half of the 7th century, to judge from the general conservatism of phraseology and contractual content that marks the evolution of the pactual tradition, the relatively early occurrence (9th century) of specimens from both Castile and Galicia-Portugal, and the fairly high proportion of binary cases in the total corpus of extant or traceable monastic pacta. From the very emergence of the pactual tradition in the northwest such an arrangement would have been a logical necessity, since in contrast with the *consensus*, *sacramenti conditio* or *iuramentum* of the consensorial-vicinal societies, the pactual house based itself on a treaty between the *subditi* as a corporate group and their powerful abbot-*patronus*. It is true that *RCom* does not provide at its close a formula for the abbot as it does for the monks (*RComP*). This lack is readily comprehensible when we perceive that the *abbatiale* did not attempt to re-state the terms of association found in the *monachale*,

---

[100] Text in *Libro de Regla o Cartulario de la antigua abadía de Santillana del Mar*, ed. Eduardo Jusué (Madrid, 1912), 31–5 (nos. XXVIII–XXIX). Herwegen (16–18) gives only the monachal pactum, which he reproduces from Francisco de Berganza, *Antigüedades de España propugnadas en las noticias de sus reyes y condes de Castilla la Vieja* (Madrid, 1719–21), 1, 300–2.

[101] *Portugaliae monumenta historica*, Diplomata et Chartae, I (Lisboa, 1867), 209–11 (rubricked under no. CCCXLII as, respectively, *Pacti cartula*, *Carta dimissionis*, *Carta pacti uel placiti*).

[102] *Monachisme ibérique*, 12–14, 331–2.

but was simply a formal transfer to the corporate community of its ruler's person and possessions, which required no more than the standard *carta traditionis et donationis*.

The paramount question raised by the binary pactum is the meaning of its central element, the reciprocal or double *traditio*, by which the monks, acting as a *corpus* (since, as we have noted, the monastic contract is between the community and its head), and the abbot place themselves in turn in each other's power. If the *confirmatio uel compromissio* of Argilegus in 818 does not mention the *traditio sui* of this abbot, that of his successor Arias explicitly does; and we may safely assume that this usage was common in not only Naroba but other early pactual houses of Liébana, Asturias de Trasmiera and Bardulia. For Galicia the example of Santa Eulalia de Búbal (ca. 876?) proves that the binary instrument circulated in this region also, certainly after 711. Nor need we hesitate to recognize that it is once more the binary pactum that is the subject of the rubric of *Ordo XVIII* of the *Liber ordinum*,[103] which requires the abbot at his consecration to deliver to the presiding bishop the "placitum suum tam pro se quam pro subditis de honestate uite regularis", even if the episcopal intervention in this rite may indicate an interpolation in the liturgical text after 711, when the secular bishop succeeded in imposing his authority on pactual circles. Neither for abbot nor monks, moreover, did the reciprocal *traditio* signify the simple *traditio animae* to God, normal in orthodox observance, but a genuine *traditio corporis* which entailed for the monks permanent personal subjection to the abbatial *patrocinium*, and for the abbot a corresponding subjection to the power of his united subjects. How are we to understand this curious relationship of mutual subordination?

In his extensive monograph dealing with Hispanic ecclesiastical *familiaritas* in the Middle Ages, José Orlandis touches only marginally on this problem,[104] since his focus is primarily fixed upon laics attached to churches and monasteries who remain laymen, such as *donadeos*, *clientes*, *commendati*, and the like; and he does little to examine those drawn into the religious life as *conuersi* by the kind of *adscriptio cellae*—or, more strictly, *potestati abbatiali*—practised in late Visigothic Galicia.[105] Yet it is this latter peculiar type of *traditio* that is linked to the pactual system; and there can be little doubt that if the widespread *instabilitas* of *conuersi* in the monasticism of the province was partly responsible for its introduction, a principal reason was the incorporation by ca. 675 into the abbeys of the Sancta Communis Regula of large numbers of unwilling or very imperfectly converted laics—the children and physically handicapped adults of the patrimonies whose conscription was deplored by Valerius in the *DGM*, the whole families of men, women and children depicted in *RCom* 6,[106] the old men and penitent criminals of *RCom* 8 and 19. There is no mistaking the fact that the abbot's rights of punishment and of pursuit and recovery of fugitives bulk very large in *RComP*; and we know that the flight of *mancipia* was a major social preoccupation of the Visigothic code in the 7th century, reflected in the numerous severe laws on such runaways.[107] If ecclesiastical practice required manumission of slaves as a prerequisite to their entering the monastic life, it is no less true that both the

---

[103] Cf. text at note 55, above.

[104] José Orlandis, "'Traditio corporis et animae'. La 'familiaritas' en las iglesias y monasterios españoles de la Alta Edad Media," *An. hist. derech. esp.*, XXIV (1954), 95–279, especially 112–24.

[105] It is noteworthy that adscription of *serui* was not peculiar to the Fructuosan monasteries but was also to be found from their very foundation in those of the *uicini* of *RCom* 1.

[106] See José Orlandis, "Los monasterios familiares en España durante la Alta Edad Media," *An. hist. derech. esp.*, XXVI (1956), 5–46, at 14–17; *idem*, "Los monasterios dúplices españoles en la Alta Edad Media," *An. hist. derech. esp.*, XXX (1960), 49–88, at 63–5.

[107] See the valuable recent treatment of this subject in King, *Law and Society in the Visigothic Kingdom*, 159–89.

Hispanic Councils and secular legislation recognized that emancipation of *serui* was definitely *sub modo*, not only revocable but imposing upon the *liberti* a permanent obligation of *obsequium* and services to their patron.[108] A *traditio corporis* could also of course be voluntary; but in either case it is evident, as the texts themselves repeatedly affirm, that under the pactual concept of the *conditio religiosa* all *conuersi* became the personal *subditi* of the abbatial *pater-patronus*. This is a status of individual subordination and helplessness utterly different from that of the *consentientes* and *uicini* of the egalitarian—and therefore highly unstable—rival communities, one very far from that retention of personal freedom and individual rights that Herwegen attributed to his idealized, allegedly Germanic, pactual society.

As for the other, the abbatial, side of the binary *traditio*, we have already seen that, once the monasteries of the Fructuosan federation had rejected the normal canonical visitation and disciplinary rights of the secular bishop over the cenobia of his diocese, it was indispensable for them to find an alternative, local mechanism for proceeding against abuses of power by an abbot or abbess, and that this took the form of entrusting to the monastic community as a whole the right to reprove its governor and, if necessary, to select the external agents who would cooperate in his correction or removal.

In short, whatever influences of Germanic, Roman or canon law we may wish to attribute to the language, form and content of the Gallegan pactum with its reciprocal *traditio*, these were at best secondary elements in its inspiration. The truly decisive factor was the necessity faced by the Sancta Communis Regula of enforcing *stabilitas* and *obedientia* among unwilling or restless *conuersi*. This meant insistence upon a strong abbatiate; but since the latter, freed from the hated authority of the secular bishop, posed its own threat, the community's governor was made subject under the binary pactum to the cenobitic body politic, the ever present guarantor against tyranny or arbitrary contravention of the *regulae patrum*.

V

Whatever views we cherish regarding the genesis and diffusion of monastic pactualism in the Visigothic era, we are nevertheless obliged to account for its survival and expansion after 711 in two, and only two, widely separated subdivisions of the Asturo-Leonese kingdom, the Galaico-Portuguese west and the Castello-Riojan east. Each of these regions imposes its own problems; we shall commence with those of the much more poorly recognized Atlantic zone.

For Pérez de Urbel, pactualism appears so insignificant a factor in the monastic colonization of Galicia and Portugal between the 8th and 11th centuries that he can dismiss the few instances known to him as either chance archaic survivals of Visigothic-Mozarabic transmission (which, he believes, would account for the pactum of Vacariça of 1045), or as the result of deliberate but largely unsuccessful efforts to introduce the system into the northwest from Castile (i.e., the case of Mezonzo, which Fray Justo links to the promotional activity of Bishop Sisnando I of Compostela, ca. 869–ca. 920,

[108] See, with particular reference to *liberti* of churches and monasteries, Toledo III (589), c. 6; Seville I (590), cc. 1–2; Seville II (619), c. 8; Toledo IV (633), cc. 67–74; Toledo VI (638), cc. 9–10; Toledo IX (655), cc. 11–16; Mérida (666), cc. 20–21; Zaragoza III (691), c. 4. On the secular legislation, cf. King, *loc. cit.*; Aleksandr R. Korsunskii, *Gotskaia Ispania* (Moscow, 1969), 100–42, and Spanish summary, 306–7.

originally a monk of Liébana).[109] In the Benedictine scholar's own words: "los monasterios [gallegos] pueden contarse por millares; los pactos son únicamente cuatro ... No hay motivo para considerar a Galicia como una tierra pactual."[110]

This judgment, which must be pronounced indefensible, derives from my own erroneous statement in 1951, that from the only four (as I then supposed) cases of western *pacta monachorum* there could be inferred an extremely restricted circulation of this instrument after 711 in the land of its birth.[111] Since 1951, however, although no new pacta as such have come to light, it has become increasingly manifest that the diplomas of the monastic houses of Galicia, and to a perceptibly lesser extent, of Portugal, contain a number of direct references to pacta now lost or still awaiting rescue from the archives; and that these prove extensive use of the old constitutional contract in many abbeys or their dependencies, including such famous centers as San Salvador de Celanova, San Salvador de Sobrado,[112] San Julián de Samos, San Esteban de Ribas de Sil, São Salvador de Guimarães, and others. Thus the view to which I gave circulation in 1951 must be totally reversed: it can now be averred that the pactual tradition was virtually as firmly established in Galicia as in Castile, although in view of the non-pactual strains in the earlier monastic history of the northwest I am not prepared to follow Dom Maximino Arias in his sweeping generalization that all pre-Benedictine Gallegan monasticism was pactual.[113]

The evidence for the revisionist position is best presented in the form of a preliminary catalogue of Galaico-Portuguese cenobia with which extant or firmly attested lost pacta can be associated; and it will be useful to incorporate in it at the same time the key diplomatic passages that confirm this observance and often illumine its place in the history of the house in question.

Provisional List of Gallegan and Portuguese Pacta

1. ca. 850–875. Santa Leocadia de Castañeda (prov. León, in the Bierzo, south of Villamartín on the left bank of the Upper Sil).[114] Attested as pactual by the restoration charter of Bishop Gennadius of Astorga (8 January 916): "fuit a sanctis et electis patribus Valentino et Moysi abbatibus coenobio constructo a quibus et loca

[109] "Vida y caminos," 378, 392–6; "Carácter y supervivencia," 233, 238–9, 242.

[110] "Carácter y supervivencia," 235. Of the four houses in question, Búbal, Mezonzo, Vacariça and the unidentifiable one from which the pactum of Sabaricus comes, the last must now be assigned to Castile; see Díaz y Díaz, *Códice monástico de Leodegundia*, 569–71; and Section VI, following.

[111] "Gallegan Pactual Monasticism," 516–7 (Study III, in this volume).

[112] Although I have omitted this originally double house from the preliminary list below, San Salvador de Sobrado was almost certainly pactual, to judge from the (possibly ambiguous) reference to its "pactos et testamentos" in Ramiro III's real privilegio of 18 July 978 (*Tumbo de Sobrado*, AHN Clero, Cód. 1068, I, fols. 39^{r-v}; L. Barrau-Dihigo, "Chartes royales léonaises, 912–1037," *Rev. hispanique*, X, 1903, 417–9, no. xxvii); the acquisition in 966 of the certainly pactual house of Santa María de Mezonzo (fols. 63–67^{v}; cf. list following, no. 2); and the strongly archaic quasi-pactual phraseology of the earliest documents of this *Tumbo* from 952 on. If none of these signs is decisive, they at least indicate the extreme improbability of Pérez de Urbel's conjecture that the pactualism of this *comarca* commences only with the Liébanese bishop of Compostela, Sisnando I.

[113] "Monasterios benedictinos en Galicia," 49–52.

[114] On the troubled early history of Castañeda, and for the full text of the *privilegio* of 916, cf. *E. S.*, XVI, 53–4, 426–9; and especially the excellent study of Augusto Quintana Prieto, "El monasterio berciano de Santa Leocadia de Castañeda," *Studia monastica*, VI (1964), 39–93.

prius fuit cepta, et uixerunt ibidem tamdiu illis uita comes fuit . . . sicut et alia loca quae ab eis excepta sancti Cipriani, ubi dicunt Farum, etiam et ibi reconditae sunt sanctae Marinae reliquiae in Vugueza. Post fundationem itaque sanctorum patrum cecidit eadem loca sancta in diusisione uaria per fratrum negligentiam. Tum aliquanti ex fratribus per superbiam furarunt pactum seu testamentum et tradiderunt ipsum Indisclo episcopo; at ille curam suam gerens non priorum optimorum fratrum nec coenobii uitam sequens, ut potuit, cuncta contraxit sibi in episcopio habens. Post mortem tamen ejus Ranulfus episcopus subcedens, inuentum testamentum quem ille suus decesor reliquerat ad negligentiam, adduxit illud in secularia causa, etc."[115]

2. 856? 876? Santa Eulalia de Búbal. The extent binary pactum of the abbot-presbyter Absalom. No. 3, above; cf. note 95 on the more probable later date.

3. 871. Santa María de Mezonzo. The extant binary pactum of the abbot Fulgaredus. No. 4, above.

4. 898. San Verísimo de Arcos de Furco (*feligresía*, prov. Pontevedra, ayunt. Baños de Cuntis, to the northeast of Villagarcía and below the río Ulla).[116] Fragmentary terminus of a monachal pactum addressed to the abbot Adulfus, which, besides an incomplete promise of submission and the date, records six *traditiones* of men and women in such form as: "Tructesindus pr(e)s(byter) hanc pactum uel placitum a me factum manu mea . . . Fradegunda deouota uobis abbati meo domino Addaulfo sicut me iam dudum uobis et ecclesie sancti Verissimi tradidi cum omnia mea . . . trado et manu mea titulum placiti et pacti subscribo."

5. 904, 24 May. San Martín de Rosende (prov. Lugo, p. j. and ayunt.Sarria, in the valley of the Miño between Páramo and Barbadelo).[117] Pactum of Abbot Visclafredus, mentioned in his extensive donation to this house, with the implication that he was continuing the practice of his predecessors Abbots Natalis, Visclamundus and T(r)asimirus: "in uilla que dicitur Ranosindi . . . confero ibidem ad ecclesie uestre . . . omne familie ecclesiam de omne parentum uel aborum meorum uel de priorum abbatorum nostrorum domni Natalis abba, domni Uisclamondi abba, domni Tasmiri et aliis plurimis qui in pactum recule sunt testati post partem ecclesie nostre sancte (p. 31) . . . Siquis tamen ab hoc cenobii uel pactum regule discipline . . . uagaberit, sit exoneratus ab omni dono ecclesie sancte, etc. (p. 33) . . . (. . .)rious presbiter in hoc pactum recule ubi me trado cum omnia ad ecclesiam . . . (. . . fredus presbiter in pactum) recule ubi me trado cum omnia mea (*Sig.*) (p. 34)." The subscriptions of the religious here have the form of *traditiones*, which implies that this text is juridically part of a binary pactum; there is no corresponding *traditio* of himself by Visclafredus, but there may originally have been a *libellus pactionis* containing the *pacta abbatialia* of the three predecessors with whom Visclafredus was associating himself, and the foundational *pactum monachorum*.

6. 907, 18 March. Santiago 'de Mortalones' (prov. Lugo, near Samos). The binary pactum of Abbot Sisericus and his religious. No. 6, above.

---

[115] *E. S.*, XVI, 426–9; Quintana Prieto, 82–4 (no. II).

[116] A. López Ferreiro, *Iglesia de Santiago*, II, 268–70, and Apéndices, 42–3 (no. XXIII); Floriano, *Diplomática*, I, 396–7 (no. VIII); Linage Conde, *Orígenes*, III, 60 (no. 103); Sá Bravo, *Monacato en Galicia*, I, 52, 56.

[117] The charter, preserved in copies of the early 11th (AHN, Clero, San Julián de Samos, carpeta 1.239, no. 3) and 18th centuries (BN, Madrid, MSS, Cód. 18.387, fols. 260^v–261^r), was first published by M. Rubén García Alvarez, "Más documentos gallegos," 20–36 (no. 5); cf. also 14–15. L. Sánchez Belda, *Documentos reales de la Edad Media referentes a Galicia* (Madrid, 1953), 40 (no. 36), dates this *privilegio* "[910–924]" and ascribes it to the monastery of San Martín and Santa Marina de Barbadelo.

7. 916, 1 September. San Ciprián de Pinza (prov. Orense, just south of the capital at modern San Ciprián de Viana del Bollo).[118] Pactum cited by the founder and probable first abbot, the presbyter Julian, in his charter of donation: "et donationem decerno ut quidquid sacerdos uel religiososque Deo [in] hunc locum per pactum et placidum Regule dicati an pauperibus se tradiderunt deserbiendum sub manu abbatis uel senioris, sit illis hec omnia comuniter, etc."

8. 921, 12 October. San Esteban de Ribas de Sil (prov. Orense, some 15 kms. northeast of the capital, on the south bank of the Sil).[119] This abbey's pactual character is inferrable from the fact that the approval given its restoration by the *real privilegio* of Ordoño II of this date was granted at the joint request of Count Gutier Menéndez (the father of San Rosendo of Celanova and Mondoñedo) and of the first abbot Franquila, who in 936 was also to found San Salvador de Celanova as a pactual house (cf. no. 15, below).

9. 922. 1 August. San Julián de Samos (prov. Lugo, p. j. Sarria, ayunt. Samos).[120] The *real privilegio* of this date of Ordoño II may be open to suspicion as to the accuracy of its chronicle of the early history of the abbey, but at least its redactor was familiar with the existence there of the pactum, which is noticed at two points: "post obitum uero eius [Ophilonis abbatis] iterum uero fratres qui usque nunc conmorantes fuerunt ac si pertranseuntes ob quod omnes ipsos testamentos pactos uel dotes monasterii eglesie eiusdem non inuenerunt, eo quod ut arbitramus deperierunt aut illi eos furauerunt, etc."; and farther on, "omnia trado . . . et donatione decerno ut quisquis sacerdos uel religiosorumque Deo in hunc locum per pactum uel placidum regule ditati an pauperes se tradiderint deseruiendum sub manu abbatis uel senioris sint illis hec omnia supra(dicta) comunia, etc."

10. *ante* 927. Santa María de Loyo (prov. Lugo, close to the capital, between the rivers Loyo and Miño).[121] Pactum of Abbot Quintila, cited in the historical *expositio* of the episcopal and abbatial charter of restoration of this house, dated 23 December 927: "quidam uir religiosus et Deo deuotus, nomine Quintilane abbate, adprehendit

[118] Text from AHN, Clero, Cód. 992, *Privilegios de Astorga*, copied by Carlos Portero (1753), fols. 268^{v}–273^{r}, from the *Tumbo Negro de Astorga*, doc. no. 388; also Cód. 970, *Privilegios de Astorga*, copied by Jerónimo de Chirivoga (1735), fols. 74^{r}–75^{v}. The date in Portero of Era DCCCCI (863) is obviously in error; Chirivoga reads Era DCCCCL (912); but Flórez, who also used the original *Tumbo* (*E. S.*, XVI, 64), gives the year as 916.

[119] Text of *real privilegio* of Ordoño II in Yepes, *Coronica*, V, 450^{r-v}. See also *E. S.*, XVII, 16–20; Emilio Sáez, "Los ascendientes de San Rosendo," *Hispania*, VIII (1948), 31, note 58. Sá Bravo, *Monacato de Galicia*, II, 57–67.

[120] Text in *E. S.*, XIV, 367–73 (Apénd. III); cf. Plácido Arias, *Historia del real monasterio de Samos* (Santiago de Compostela, 1950), 51–5. Ofilón, abbot from 856 to 872, according to Arias, *op. cit.*, 39–42, was a refugee monk from Córdoba; the period between his death and the accession of Sabaricus (900–907) is particularly obscure. The whole question of pactualism at San Julián de Samos, a house perhaps twice colonized by monks of the Mozarabic observance from Spania, calls for more thorough investigation. Particular attention needs to be paid not only to the early Samonensian diplomas (the authenticity of which Sánchez Albornoz defends against Barrau-Dihigo's scepticism; see Cl. Sánchez Albornoz, "Documentos de Samos de los reyes de Asturias," *Cuad hist. Esp.*, IV, 1946, 147–60; reprinted in his *Miscelánea de estudios históricos*, León, 1970, 255–70), but also to the complementary documentation of San Julián's dependencies and of the many neighboring monasteries in the Gallegan comarca so strongly affected by the pactual tradition.

[121] Text from *Tumbo de Celanova*, fols. 62^{r}, col. 1–62^{v}, col. 2, in *E. S.*, XVIII, 326–9; E. Sáez, "Notas y documentos sobre Sancho Ordoñez rey de Galicia," *Cuad. hist. Esp.*, XI (1949), 82–6 (doc. no. 4); cf. Flórez, *E. S.*, *vol. cit.*, 96–7; Sánchez Belda, *Docs. reales referentes a Galicia*, 51 (no. 38).

locum antiquum monasterii olim nomine fundatum... et collegit in eodem contionem religiosorum regulari sub tramite degentium... quibus sub federe pacti cunctis manentibus diuinitum euenit consilium, etc."

11. 903? 928? Santa Eulalia "in uilla domini Didaci" (on the Miño within the *suburbium* of Lugo).[122] The pactum is mentioned in the charter by which the deacon Vermudus gives this house various *uillas*: "habeant fratres et sorores cleros atque domesticos qui in uita sancta perseuerauerint post pacto ipsius ecclesie."

12. 947, 7 August. Santa Marina de Paradela (prov. La Coruña, p. j. Estrada, on the río Ulla).[123] A private act of the presbyter Letimius, addressed to the *fratres et sorores* of this monastery, which styles itself "pactum uel placitum". The imperfectly legible phraseology, as reproduced by López Ferreiro, recalls *RComP*: "pro salute animarum nostrarum qualiter iuste et pie, caste et sobrie uiuamus in hoc seculo et quidquid annuntiare uel imperare iusseris pro salute anime nostre humiliter adimpleamus, nihil nobis proprium uindicantes sed omnia quicquid uisi sumus abere, etc."

13. *ante* 955. Santa María de Mezonzo. Pactum of Abbot Vimara, probably of the same type as that of Fulgaredus (no. 2, above), as mentioned in the diploma of 955 of Abbot Gundesindus. Binary pactual list, above, no. 5.

14. *ante* 959. San Salvador de Celanova (prov. Orense, p. j. Celanova, ca. 22 kms. due south of the provincial capital).[124] Pactum of the abbot San Rosendo, later bishop of Mondoñedo (presumably modeled after that of his predecessor Franquila, the first abbot of this house founded in 936); mentioned in the agreement on rents made in 959 between Goia, Videla, Vico, Rudila and Oveco, and their children, and Abbot Rosendo: "ista uilla sanctę Eolalie de testam[en]tos sancti Petri de Lemos unde uos fratres hereditarios habeatis et traditos in pactos regule in monasterio Cellenoue, etc."

15. 959. São Salvador de Guimarães (prov. Minho, to the southeast of Braga).[125] Pactum cited in the foundation charter by which the Portuguese noblewoman Dona Mumadona Dias bestows numerous *vilas*, lands and other goods upon those who "in hunc locum sub manu abbatis et census regule fuerint Domino seruientes et in pactum roborati."

---

[122] *Tumbo Nuevo de Lugo* (AHN, fols. 43r–44v). The reference to King Alfonso as son of Ramiro (!) apparently means that the copyist's ligature in the date is intended for an *x aspada*, i.e., DCCCCXLI (903), which places this *pergamino* under Alfonso III. Alternatively, if read as DCCCLXVI (928), the ruler would be Alfonso IV.

[123] A. López Ferreiro, *Hist. Iglesia de Santiago*, II, Apéndices, 127–32 (no. LVIII); commentary, 304–5.

[124] *Tumbo de Celanova*, fols. 153r, cols. 1–2. On San Rosendo and the early history of this famous abbey, see above all, while awaiting publication of his *San Rosendo y los orígenes del monasterio de Celanova*, the studies by Emilio Sáez: "El monasterio de Santa María de Ribeira," *Hispania*, IV (1944), 3–27, 163–210; "Notas al episcopologio minduniense del siglo X," *ibid.*, VI (1946), 3–79 (especially 6–9); "Los ascendientes de San Rosendo," *ibid.*, VIII (1948), 3–76, 179–233 (also separately). Cf. for the older bibliography, F. Pérez, "Celanova," *Dict. hist. géog. ecclés.*, XII (Paris, 1953), cols. 48–50; Sá Bravo, *Monacato en Galicia*, II, 123–39.

[125] *Portugaliae monumenta historica, Dipl. et chart.*, I (Lisboa, 1867), 44–8 at 45 (no. LXXVI). Cf. J. Mattoso, "Sobrevivência," 45; *idem*, *Monachisme ibérique*, 114. On the monastery, see Luiz Gonzaga de Azevedo, *História de Portugal*, II (Lisboa, 1939), 99–101; and on its foundress and her familial ties, Avelino de Jesus da Costa, "Mumadona Dias," *Dic. de hist. de Port.*, III (1968), 121; José Mattoso, "A nobreza rural portuense nos séculos XI e XII," *Anuario de estudios medievales*, VI (1969), 465–520; *idem*, *As famílias condais portucalenses dos séculos X e XI* (Porto, 1970), 46–7; *idem*, "A nobreza portucalense dos seculos IX a XI," *Do tempo y da história*, III (1970), 35–50.

16. ca. 977. San Salvador de Celanova. Pactum of the abbot Manila, mentioned in a diploma of 1002[126] which refers to the last year of San Rosendo's life (977): "Ipse (Rudesindus) prius per se in manibus eius pro patre spiritale accepit et post eum reliqua turba fratrum et omnium monachorum sub dicionem pactum regule abbatem domnum Manillanem constituit atque elegit."

17. 1045. São Salvador de Vacariça. Extant binary pactum of the abbot Tudeildus. Binary list, above, no. 9.

The preceding catalogue can surely be enlarged by more extended search of the archives and printed materials, but it will serve to make patent the emphatic diffusion in the northwest of the pactual tradition. If we take into account the probability of similar usage in the dependencies and neighboring communities of the houses listed, it looks as if by the middle 9th century, at the very time the pactum was enjoying widespread reception in the new foundations of an expanding primitive Castile, it found equal popularity in the monastic *repoblación* of Galicia and, in some degree also, across the Miño in Portugal.

This is a phenomenon hardly explicable in terms of uninterrupted direct descent from the ancient Fructuosan cenobia of Visigothic Galicia. Without venturing here into the still unresolved debate over continuity or discontinuity of settlement in the westernmost districts of the 'desierto del Duero', with which the names of Herculano, Pierre David, Sánchez Albornoz, da Costa and others are linked,[127] we can deduce with some confidence that the Galaico-Portuguese pactualism visible to us from the second half of the 9th century stems most immediately from centers located not around Dumio and Braga but in the extreme north and northeast *comarcas* of Galicia close to the borders of the kingdom of Asturias. Here its presence is most plausibly explained as being due to monks and nuns from both sides of the Miño who found refuge there, either at the time of the first Islamic irruption or, more probably, ca. 740–50, during Alfonso I's evacuation of the inhabitants of Entre-Douro-e-Minho. The impression we receive is of an early nucleus in the basin of the upper Sil and in the Bierzo, with a subsequent spread westward and southwestward along the valleys of the Tambre, the Búbal, the lower Sil, and the Miño itself.

Across the Miño, however, and as far south as Coimbra and the banks of the Mondego, the picture is much less clear, despite the two pioneering studies of Prof. Mattoso—his essay on the survival of the 'Fructuosan' tradition in Portugal after 711, and the admirable volume on the abbeys of the diocese of Porto between 1000 and 1200, the era of transition from pre-Benedictine to Benedictine observance.[128] In both these works he contends that the Portuguese cenobitism of the Alta Reconquista, which the diplomas (somewhat limited in number before 1000, relatively abundant thereafter) show as extremely conservative in vocabulary, ideology and institutions, was the direct, authentic continuation of the late 7th-century pactual tradition of

[126] *Tumbo de Celanova*, fols. 94r–95r.

[127] See Alexandre Herculano, *História de Portugal*, 9th ed. (Lisboa, s. a.), VI, 7–54, especially 32–51; Alberto Sampaio, "As villas do Norte de Portugal," in his *Estudos históricos e económicos* (Porto, 1923), I, 3–254; Pierre David, *Études historiques sur la Galice et le Portugal*, 169–256; Avelino de Jesus da Costa, *O bispo D. Pedro e a organização da diocese de Braga* (Coimbra, 1959), I, 139–70 (with valuable critique of previous views); Sánchez Albornoz, *Despoblación y repoblación del Valle del Duero*, especially 215ff.

[128] "Sobrevivência do monaquismo frutuosiano em Portugal durante a Reconquista," *Bracara Augusta*, XXII (1968), 42–54; *Le monachisme ibérique et Cluny: les monastères du diocèse de Porto de l'an mille à 1200* (Louvain, 1968), especially 112–20.

Galicia. In Study IV in this volume, this line of reasoning is rejected on several grounds; and in particular because the one surviving Portuguese pactum, that of the abbot Tudeildus from the Mondego Valley house of São Salvador de Vacariça in 1045, can be identified as in fact a fortuitous reproduction of the one actually used at this same abbot's more northern monastery of São Salvador de Leça. Furthermore, the latter house, like the also pactual center of São Salvador de Guimarães in the diocese of Braga, was no merely moribund institutional survival from the 7th-century world of Luso-Gallegan 'Fructuosanism', but part and parcel of the powerful new wave of pactual foundations which in the late 9th and 10th centuries accompanied the monastic *repoblación* of Galicia, Minho, Castile and the Rioja. In short, everything indicates that the Portuguese pactual tradition of the Alta Reconquista, with the sole explicable and ephemeral exception of Vacariça in 1045, did not cross the Duero or—contrary to Mattoso—ever establish itself as far south in the County of Portugal as Beira Litoral or the valley of the Mondego.

VI

For reconstructing the history of the pactual tradition in the ancient County of Castile and of its projection across the upper Ebro into the Rioja, the materials have been much better known, and it is not necessary to reproduce here my catalogue of 1951 of Castello-Riojan pacta of 'Fructuosan', i.e., *RComP* type and of those based upon the Burgalese Formula. No further Castilian or Riojan pacta have come to light since that date, nor do the diplomas of this zone provide the illuminating references to pacta that made possible the Gallegan list above. Linage Conde has questioned the authenticity of several of my inclusions in the eastern group;[129] but there are two more important corrections that need to be made. One is the elimination of the supposed pactum of San Prudencio de Laturce, which has turned out not to be a pactual text at all, and must be dropped from consideration (see the additional note to Study III in this volume).

A second imperative is the addition to the Castello-Riojan series of the well-known monachal pactum of Sabaricus, which stands at the present commencement of Escorialensis a. I. 13, a codex which Professor Díaz y Díaz has now shown was written by the nun Leodegundia not in Galicia, as so long believed, but in Castile between 925 and 931.[130] In its present state the *codex regularum* Escorialensis a. I. 13 begins abruptly on what is now fol. 1^r in the midst of the pactum with the words "et secundum editum apostolorum, etc.", which in *RComP* belong to the first expository sentence after the initial creed; and Díaz y Díaz has established from analysis of this signature of the MS that there were two preceding folia which have now disappeared.[131] It is therefore a reasonable conjecture that these folia contained more than the brief creed, and commenced with the *pactum abbatis* of Sabaricus, i.e., the *traditio* of himself and his possessions to the unknown community. Herwegen, analyzing the juridical components of the extant part of the Sabaricus text, placed it in his first group where indeed it was the solitary exemplar.[132] We can now go beyond this assessment and

[129] *Orígenes*, I, 329–32.
[130] "El códice monástico de Leodegundia," *Ciudad de Dios*, CLXXXI (1968), 569–72, 580–2.
[131] *Ibid.*, 572–5.
[132] Herwegen, 32–3.

recognize that at the head of this *Liber regularum* there may originally have stood a full binary pactum of which only the monachal half remains.

Since the Sabaricus text is an exceptionally interesting one by reason of its closeness in language and content to the prototypal *RComP*, the discovery of its eastern rather than Galaico-Portuguese provenance makes it possible for the first time to place it in the historical context of the other similar Castilian pacta from the new cenobia that were being planted below Burgos in the 9th and 10th centuries. What is evident also is that the monachal pactum of Sabaricus belongs with the three specimens, all of them unknown to Herwegen; those from Castile, of Rodanius of San Pedro de Tejada (855) and of Arciselus of Santa María de Sotovellanos (1045); and the related Portuguese instrument of Tudeildus from São Salvador de Vacariça (1045). It can also be seen that in their section on conspiracy these texts, and that of Sabaricus, all coincide in presenting a different version from that of *RComP*.[133] It must now be noticed that at several other points the three Castilian instruments of Rodanius, Sabaricus and Arciselus display certain common departures from the text of both *RComP* and Tudeildus.

For one thing, *RComP*, referring to the expulsion of irredeemable offenders, orders: "deposita ueste monasterii, indutus quod in introitu exutus est scissum, notabili cum confusione a coenobio expellatur"; but with minor variations the Castilian trio read: "deposita ueste monasterii, indutus aliquod scisum laycale captans densissimas tenebras nocte cum confusione et nota a cenobio excomunicatus euellatur."[134] Again, where *RComP* threatens excommunication against anyone offering protection from his abbot to a fugitive monk: "si aliquis eum defendere uoluerit episcopus uel eius qui sequitur ordo aut laicus", the later reading has become: "si aliquid eum defendere uoluerit aut presbyter aut monachus aut quilibet layci."[135] Finally, in the crucial matter of appeal by the monks to external intervention, *RComP* provides the procedure commented upon at such length by Herwegen: "habeamus et nos potestatem cetera monasteria commonere aut certe episcopum qui sub regula uiuit uel catholicum ecclesiae defensorem comitem et aduocare ad nostram collationem ut coram ipsis te corripias." Here the Castilian texts all modify this to something like: "tunc habeamus et nos potestatem de altera monasteria abbates de conlatione nostra inuitare et quoram eos te corripias."[136] Especially do the last two of these variations from the prototype, in their abandonment of the *episcopus sub regula* and of the extinct comital administrative machinery of the Visigothic era, and their drastically changed attitude towards the secular episcopate, reflect the new ecclesiastical circumstances of the Alta Reconquista.

More important is the manner in which the Sabaricus pactum, by its omissions from *RComP* and by its verbal agreements with the Rodanius and Arciselus texts, is stamped as a member of that branch of the Gallegan tradition in Castile and the

---

[133] See Bishko, "Portuguese Pactual Monasticism" (Study IV in this volume).

[134] This and the following two passages are reproduced as they appear in the Sabaricus pactum (Herwegen, 7–8); but I shall give in the notes the readings of that of Rodanius (Pérez de Urbel, *Hist. del Cond. de Cast.*, III, 1058–60), from which the unpublished version of Arciselus presumably differs little or not at all (*ibid.*, 1325). On the expulsion procedure, the Rodanius instrument has: "depositus ueste monasterii, indutus aliquis sissum laicale, captas densissimas tenebras, nocte cum confussione et nocturna cenobio excomunicatus euellatur."

[135] Rodanius: "si quid eum defendere uoluerit aut presbiter aut monachus aut quislibet persona."

[136] Rodanius: 'habeamus et nos potestatem de altera monasteria abbates de collationem nostram inuitare, et coram cos et corripere."

Rioja which represents a far more conservative adhesion to the language and basic contractual principles of the prototype than is true of Herwegen's second group. It is likely therefore that all three descend from a formula not too far removed from *RComP*, one which commenced its eastern circulation in the early stages of proto-Castilian pactualism, perhaps around Valpuesta or in Asturias de Trasmiera, and thence descended without further editorial revision to the Castilian foundations springing up around and below Burgos in the 9th and 10th centuries. The ascription of Escorialensis a I. 13 to 926–931 does not, of course, do more than provide an *ante quem* for the promulgation of the Sabaricus instrument, and the latter may belong anywhere in the half century that separates this codex from the pactum of Rodanius of 855. We may at any rate conjecture with some assurance that the unknown abbey over which Abbot Sabaricus presided may well have been located in the *terra predilecta* of the Castilian pactual tradition below Burgos, perhaps not far from the environs of Tejada or Sotovellanos; and that this community, unlike many others, held itself aloof from the Benedictine and Smaragdan unilateralism then infiltrating this region, and sedulously preserved in its observance the binary pactum and *Liber regularum* which Leodegundia so faithfully copied during the reign of Alfonso IV.

The Sabaricus pactum thus belongs to a well attested line of pactual transmission in Castile which is clearly distinguishable from two others, that of the heterogeneous congeries of texts that represent much more radical departures from the language and content of *RComP*, and that of the Burgalese Formula. From this standpoint, it can therefore be said that Herwegen's triple classification on verbal and juridical grounds remains valid for Castile and the Rioja at least, if not for Galicia and Portugal. Of course, this is not the only, or even the most important, level on which all this documentation can be exploited. Each of the three branches of the Castilian tradition calls for closer study in terms of the historical setting of each known pactual house and the broad movement of monastic colonization that accompanied the advance of the Castilian Reconquest between the 9th and 11th centuries. And beyond these questions lie the two larger ones of the initial introduction of the Gallegan system into the eastern zone and the circumstances of its eventual disappearance before the rising tide of Benedictinism. I shall deal very summarily with both these topics before terminating the present inquiry.

So far as the controversial issue of the origins of the pactual tradition in Castile is concerned, the problem is that of determining how in the early 8th century this distinctive form of Luso-Gallegan monastic constitutionalism, previously unknown in the area (or anywhere else in Visigothic Spain outside the northwest) was introduced into the oldest Castilian monasteries of the Alta Reconquista. Here I would continue to defend against the indigenous Visigothic hypothesis of Pérez de Urbel the solution which in 1951 I proposed on the basis of the Chronicle of Alfonso III. This is, that when ca. 740–750 King Alfonso I of Asturias, as the Chronicle affirms, transplanted to other parts of his kingdom the dwellers around Braga, Porto, Lugo, Astorga, etc., some of these were re-settled in Santander, Asturias de Santillana and de Trasmiera, and Liébana; and that among these emigrés were pactual monks who now planted their pactual system in the northern districts from which there proceeded the eventual monastic *repoblación* south towards Burgos, the Duero and the Riojan Ebro. Conceivably, at some other point in the 8th century pactualism could have leaped over Asturias proper and León, which remained faithful to the orthodox Visigothic observance, to reach new communities being founded in Liébana and around Valpuesta; but on what occasion and at whose instigation? Pérez de Urbel complains that the toponymy, and specifically the hagiotoponymy, of early Castile fails to reveal traces of Gallegan settlement; but in view of both the lack of toponymic studies for comital Castile (as lamented by Sánchez Albornoz in his *Despoblación y repoblación del Valle del Duero*),[137] and the difficulty of distinguishing in this area possible Suevo-Gallegan from other Germanic placenames, this contention carries little weight.

In the same way that the primal plantation of the pactual tradition in Castile and the Rioja can be ascribed to Luso-Gallegan migrants, so its eventual disappearance before the commencement of the 12th century can be seen as due to still another external cultural intervention, the penetration into these regions from southern France and Catalonia of Carolingian and post-Carolingian Reform Benedictinism. This phenomenon has now been treated *in extenso* in the valuable work of Linage Conde on the retarded victory of Benedictinism below the Pyrenees, which devotes particular attention to the mono-regular use of *RB* and the circulation of the *Expositio* (or, as the Hispanic MSS entitle it, *Explanatio*) of Smaragdus of Saint-Mihiel-sur-Meuse, which embedded the code of Monte Cassino in a full Carolingian commentary. In my opinion, however, neither this able scholar nor Pérez de Urbel, who has also dealt with this subject, pay sufficient attention to the long, highly interesting process of amalgamation or synthesis so characteristic of Castilian and Riojan cenobitism from the later 9th century on.[138]

It is a fact of paramount importance that for two centuries the pactual tradition in Castile and the Rioja (and presumably in Galicia and Portugal also, although parallel investigation there is as yet entirely lacking), was able, despite the strong European pressures towards monastic conformity, to maintain a compromise in which its two most central elements, collective profession and the contractual relationship between community and abbot, were preserved in the communities of men and of women and in the many double houses containing both. This is remarkable, as we have observed, not only as a phase in Hispanic monastic evolution, but also as an early medieval instance of those significant occasions when the Iberian Peninsula has been forced to adjust its autochthonous institutions and ideas to powerful Europeanizing forces from without.

What is needed above all in this quarter is, first, a comparative study of the different ways in which, and times when, *RB* was gradually accepted in the pactual and non-pactual zones. Equally imperative is intensive analysis of the inter-penetration of pactual, non-pactual and Benedictine terms, concepts and usages in the extant sources of mixed character, such as the monastic *ordines* of the Hispanic Rite, where the precise degree of Benedictinization of the pactual rubrics and liturgical text requires careful study.

A prime text here is the remarkable Riojan Nuns' Rule of ca. 950–960 preserved among the *codices Aemilianenses* of the Real Academia de la Historia, the *Libellus a Regula sancti Benedicti subtractus*, which in 1948 I first identified, analyzed, and ascribed to the pen of the scholarly abbot Salvus of San Martín de Albelda, near Nájera.[139] This work was subsequently given its *editio princeps* by Linage Conde in

---

[137] Pérez de Urbel, "Carácter y supervivencias," 234–5; Sánchez Albornoz, 311 ff.

[138] See Linage Conde, *Orígenes*, II, 854–60; Pérez de Urbel, "La conquista de la Rioja y su colonización espiritual en el siglo X," *Estudios dedicados a Menéndez Pidal*, I (Madrid, 1950), 522–31; *idem*, "Vida y caminos," 24; *idem*, "Carácter y supervivencia," 240–1 (largely concerned to minimize the significance of the pactual-Benedictine synthesis); *idem*, *El condado de Castilla*, I, 334–6; *idem*, "Monasterios castellanos de la Reconquista," 108–10.

[139] C. J. Bishko, "Salvus of Albelda and Frontier Monasticism in Tenth-Century Navarre," *Speculum*, XXIII (1948), 559–90; reprinted in *idem*, *Studies in Medieval Spanish Frontier History* (London, 1980), No. I, and Addenda, p. 1. J. M. Lacarra, *Historia política del Reino de Navarra* (Pamplona, 1972), I, 173–4.

1973, along with a richly informative commentary.[140] He however rejects (in my judgment, quite mistakenly) my thesis of Salvan authorship, and also fails to recognize the Rule's particular historical value as testimony to the vitality of the pactual tradition in the face of the powerful wave of Carolingian Reform Benedictinism sweeping Europe in the 10th century. To be sure, the *Libellus* consists mainly of extracts from *RB* and the *Expositio* of Smaragdus, but in certain key chapters it retains from Galaico-Castilian pactualism a pactual reception *ordo* and the ancient Hispanic *horarium*—proving it beyond question a product of the synthesis of indigenous and Carolingian Benedictine elements that is the most striking characteristic of Castello-Riojan (and doubtless Galaico-Portuguese) monasticism of the 10th century.

Above all, the Castilian-Riojan pacta themselves reflect this same admixture, which was, in a real sense, no mere recalcitrant traditionalism, but a veritable expression of the Castilian creative genius. They allow us to follow the transition in the 10th and 11th centuries from pure Gallegan contractualism to the kind of quasi-Benedictine unilateralism which is found in the Burgalese Formula, and which directly preceded the abandonment of the collective for the orthodox individual profession act. From one 10th-century Castilian abbey there survives testimony of what must have been a fairly widespread practice on the road to Cassinensian orthodoxy: San Juan de Tabladillo, presumably from its foundation, but certainly by 924, was a true Benedictine house; yet in 931 it is found addressing a collective promise of profession and obedience to its abbot Stefanus, couched in terms of the Burgalese Formula.[141] There is, then, in liturgy, in customs, in profession acts, abundant reflection of the synthesis of pactualism and Benedictinism that was long maintained in the eastern, as no doubt also in the Galaico-Portuguese, territories of the old heterodox observance.

Where then at the moment does the debate over the pactual tradition in Hispanic monasticism stand?—no idle wrangle, since its subject matter relates to central themes in the organization of Suevo-Visigothic Galicia on the eve of the Muslim invasion, the rise and fall of pre-Benedictine peninsular monachism, and the formation of the societies and structuring of Galicia, Portugal and historic Castile in the centuries of the Alta Reconquista. With all due allowance for subsequent scholarship and the urgency of further study in depth of the many issues involved, Herwegen's case for the specifically Galaico-Portuguese genesis of the Hispanic pactual tradition remains unshaken by the doctrines of pan-Visigothicism and proto-Castilianism. We are still confronted by the duality of an orthodox pre-Benedictine, Visigothic monasticism, familiar to St Isidore of Seville and his contemporaries, and the collective contractualism which was developed in the Galicia of the late 7th century and became the

[140] A. Linage Conde, *Una regla monástica riojana femenina del siglo X: EL "Libellus a Regula sancti Benedicti subtractus"* (Salamanca, 1973); see also his *Orígenes*, II, 802–20. Over against Linage's unconvincing proposal of other redactors of the text can be set (i) the extreme improbability of two such Nuns' Rules appearing in the same Riojan milieu of the mid-tenth century, and (ii) the positive testimony of Salvus' disciple, the Albeldensian scribe Vigila, who in his *Vita Salvi abbatis* not only approximates the actual title by describing his master's work as "sacris uirginibus regularem libellum" but further implies its Benedictine base when he characterizes it as "eloquio nitidum et rei ueritate prespicuum", words strongly reminiscent of those St Gregory uses of *RB*: "discretione praecipuam, sermone luculentam" (*Dial.*, II, 36). The very production of this Rule subsumes the rise of a Benedictine-inspired hostility towards the *regula mixta* of the old Hispanic observance. So too the strictly unilateral Burgalese Formula, in silently departing from the prescription of *Ordo* XVIII that the abbot submit to the bishop "placitum suum tam pro se quam pro subditis", implies a rejection of the binary pactum—thus constituting still another testimony to the amalgamation of the two traditions on a Benedictine base.

[141] Cf. Serrano, *Cartulario de San Pedro de Arlanza*, 14–17 (no. IV), 29–30 (no. IX).

dominant observance in the two great, crucial zones of the Reconquista for three centuries after 711, Galicia-Portugal and Castile-Rioja. To recognize this, and to assess its significance for the indigenous resistance to Benedictinism, is the indispensable preliminary to understanding the conditions encountered by the Cluniacs in their penetration of central and western Iberia. It is no less a key to the monastic policies pursued by the king-emperors Fernando I and Alfonso VI in their transformation of the old Leonese-Castilian-Gallegan state into that imperial Hispania which incarnates so many definitive changes in the religious as well as the secular life of the Luso-Hispanic peoples.

II

THE DATE AND NATURE OF THE SPANISH *CONSENSORIA MONACHORUM*.[1]

In the fourth volume of his *Geschichte der römischen Literatur* (2nd ed., 1914) M. Schanz briefly discusses under the Late Latin literature of Spanish Priscillianism the so-called *Regula Consensoria Monachorum*.[2] This short work, the correct title of which is *Consensoria Monachorum* (henceforth abbreviated as *CM*), takes the form of an agreement among a group of individuals seeking to establish a monastic community. It defines the terms of association, the admission of new members and the secession of old ones, the abbot's powers, and the preservation of the community and its movable wealth in the event of violent assault from without. Although certain late medieval MSS and the earliest printed editions ascribe the text to St. Augustine,[3] L. Holstenius rightly rubricked it *incerti auctoris* in his 1661 *Codex Regularum Monasticarum*.[4] No attempt at identification, however, was made until 1907, when I. Herwegen published his important study of the monastic *pactum*, that uniquely Spanish written contract between abbot and monks under which, in the territories of Galicia, Asturias, Castile, and the Navarrese Rioja, the strongly authoritarian abbatiate of orthodox cenobitism was radically modified in favor of a constitutional monastic polity emphasizing the monks' rights, even to rebellion, against their abbot.[5] Impressed by certain quasi-pactual features of the *CM*,

[1] For assistance in the course of this study, grateful acknowledgment is made to the authorities of the Biblioteca del Escorial; the Frederick Sheldon Fund, Harvard University; the Institute for Research in the Social Sciences, University of Virginia; and the Research Committee, University of Virginia.

[2] *Handbuch der klassischen Altertumswissenschaft*, ed. I. von Müller, VIII, iv, 1, p. 384.

[3] P. Schroeder, "Die Augustinerchorherrenregel. Entstehung, kritischer Text und Einführung der Regel," *Archiv für Urkundenforschung*, IX (1926), p. 273.

[4] References are to the 1759 Vienna edition of Holstenius, by M. Brockie, which prints the *CM* text, t. I, pp. 136-7. With minor revisions, this is the text reproduced in J. P. Migne, *Patrologiae Latinae Cursus Completus* (Paris, 1844-64), LXVI, cols. 993-6.

[5] Dom Ildefons Herwegen, *Das* Pactum *des hl. Fruktuosus von Braga* (Stuttgart, 1907; *Kirchenrechtliche Abhandlungen*, ed. U. Stutz, Heft 40), pp. 71-9.

Herwegen (pp. 71-9) very tentatively asserted the work might well emanate from the same general region and period which, as he ably demonstrated, produced the *pactum*, i. e., the old Roman-Visigothic province of Callaecia, Gallaecia, or Galicia, soon after 650. This proposal, however, was immediately and forcefully assailed by D. DeBruyne, who argued that its reference to the Germanic invasions of Roman Spain and its use of a pre-Hieronymian Bible necessarily dated the *CM* no later than the fifth century, while peculiarities of content and terminology proved it to be a monastic Rule used by communities of heretical Priscillianist monks.[6]

Since 1908 DeBruyne's conclusions have been almost unanimously accepted among students of Hispano-Latin literature and Spanish ecclesiastical history,[7] the only exceptions being the already cited Schanz, who finds them "ohne durchschlagende Gründe," and Ángel Custodio Vega, the latest editor of the text, for whom the Priscillianist evidence particularly seems inconclusive.[8] It is the aim of the present paper to attack this current identification and, after refuting DeBruyne, to prove that the *CM*, as Herwegen suggested, is a type of non-Priscillianist Galician monastic *pactum* of the later seventh century.

1. *The charge of Priscillianism.* DeBruyne's case for the *CM's*

[6] Dom Donatien DeBruyne, "La *Regula Consensoria.* Une règle des moines priscillianistes," *Revue Bénédictine,* XXV (1908), pp. 83-8. DeBruyne's Priscillianist theory apparently derives from a remark of U. Berlière, *Rev. Bénéd.*, XXIV (1907), p. 41*. Although Herwegen took occasion to reply to other strictures of DeBruyne upon *Das* Pactum (e. g., *Rev. Bénéd.*, XXIX [1912], pp. 97-8), he tacitly accepted the demolition of his *CM* hypothesis.

[7] E. g., O. Bardenhewer, *Geschichte der altkirchlichen Literatur* (Freiburg i. B., 1902-32), III, p. 412; U. Moricca, *Storia della Letteratura Latina Cristiana* (Turin, 1928-), II, 1, p. 594; Pascual Galindo, "Literatura hispano-latina. Escritores cristianos," in R. Menéndez Pidal (ed.), *Historia de España. II. España Romana* (Madrid, 1935), p. 557; H. Leclercq, "Cénobitisme," *Dictionnaire d'Archéologie Chrétienne et de Liturgie*, II, 2 (Paris, 1910), cols. 3220-1; Z. García Villada, *Historia Eclesiástica de España* (Madrid, 1929-), I, 2, p. 141; J. Pérez de Urbel, *Los Monjes Españoles en la Edad Media* (Madrid, 1933-4), I, pp. 158-162.

[8] *La Regla de San Agustín* (El Escorial, 1933), p. 7. I have not seen B. Garnelo, "Datos históricos acerca de la Regla de San Agustín," *Archivo Augustiniano,* XXXVIII (1932), pp. 364-97, which includes a brief treatment of the *CM*, presumably based on DeBruyne.

Priscillianist origin is by no means strong. The work's promulgation by the monks themselves rather than by a monastic legislator, its sharp curtailment of the abbot's powers, and its marked interest in the monastic temporal, which is strangely viewed as the collective possession of the *consentientes*, all testify to a certain unorthodoxy, but this no more proves the *CM* Priscillianist than his mortality proves Socrates a hare. The first feature is abnormal only if the *CM* is assumed to be a Rule, which, as we shall see, it is not; the second recalls the non-monarchical abbatiate of the *pactum*, which, however unorthodox, is certainly not Priscillianist; and as for the third, it may be pointed out that Priscillianism was at least as hostile as orthodox monasticism to the possession of material goods by avowed ascetics.[9] Again, the single citation of a probably apocryphal scripture (c. iii: *amicum noli*, etc.), which DeBruyne relates to the known Priscillianist addiction to this type of literature, likewise carries little weight, for, down to the tenth century at least, Spanish writings of unimpeachable orthodoxy cite uncanonical prophetic and exhortatory tracts as if they possessed Biblical authority.[10]

Hardly more convincing is DeBruyne's claim that the strong fear of doctrinal contamination from without (c. v.: *aut si quis ab aliquo doctrinam audierit, praeter quam in monasterio consecutus est, ab eo cui se credidit hanc aut non suscipiat aut eam non subtrahat doctori* [i. e., *abbati*]) is directed against orthodoxy. This really cuts both ways: orthodox monks in a Priscillianist milieu might well so seek to protect themselves against circumambient heresy. But the correct interpretation of this passage is surely not a doctrinal one, for in monastic circles *doctrina* commonly means not tenet of faith but ascetic practice.[11]

[9] Cf., *inter alios*, E.-Ch. Babut, *Priscillien et le Priscillianisme* (Paris, 1909), pp. 84-5; 135.

[10] E. g., *Regula Monastica Communis*, c. xii: *omnis detractor eradicabitur* (Holstenius-Brockie, *Cod. Reg. Mon.*, I, 214, where its ascription to "Gal. 7" is equivalent to dating it on the Greek Kalends); Z. García Villada, *Crónica de Alfonso III* (Madrid, 1918), pp. 60-1: *in vanum currit*, etc.; and an 864 charter of the cathedral church of Santa María de Valpuesta, beginning *inquirite dominum*, etc. (L. Barrau-Dihigo, "Chartes de l'église de Valpuesta du ixe au xie siècle," *Rev. Hispanique*, VII [1900], pp. 297-9).

[11] Cf. St. Benedict, *Reg. Monach.*, c. lxxiii: *sunt* doctrinae *sanctorum patrum quarum* observatio *perducat hominem ad celsitudinem perfectionis* (ed. C. Butler [Freiburg i. B., 1927], p. 131).

To cite only Spanish examples, the council of VII Toledo in 646 (c. v) declares of itinerant anchorites: *in monasteriis omnimodo deputentur ut illic sancti ordinis meditantes* doctrinam *primum possint discere quae sunt a patribus instituta . . . atque tunc demum si* doctrinae *et sancti operis fructu exstiterint fecundati, ad summam virtutis properent.*[12] In XI Toledo (675) abbots are warned against tolerating any departure from traditional liturgical usage (c. iii); a violator is to be punished: *et necessariam officiorum* doctrinam *studiose addiscat.*[13] The *Regula SS. Pauli et Stephani Abbatum* parallels the *CM* passage closely, when it says (c. xiv): *nec ab adveniente hospite sine iussu prioris quidquam talium rerum aliquis audeat meditari, ne peregrinis varietatum* doctrinis *et quodammodo diliramentorum suavitatibus irretiti, simplicitatis et veritatis maturitatem fastidiant.*[14] That *doctrina* in *CM*, c. v, has the same meaning as in the foregoing instances is confirmed by the context: the monk believes (*se credidit*) the transmitter of the *doctrina*, but the *doctrina* itself is not so much believed as followed or observed (*consecutus est*). Monastic usage, moreover, is a subject upon which abbots might properly pass judgment; matters of faith would be more naturally referred to sacerdotal or episcopal authorities.

DeBruyne's final proof of Priscillianist origin is the *CM*'s use of *doctor* as equivalent to *abbas* (c. v), which he regards as unique in monastic history. The title *doctor* is known to have been applied by the Priscillianists to members of their ascetic governing élite, and its assumption by individuals was expressly forbidden in Spain by the anti-Priscillianist council of Saragossa in 380 (c. vii).[15] But to identify the Priscillianist *doctor*, whose charismatic authority would in all likelihood make him a highly autocratic official,[16] with the weak *primus inter pares* of the *CM*, hardly seems logical. Besides, early monastic literature both within and outside Spain frequently refers to the teaching functions of the abbot;[17] and evidence exists to show that, whatever

[12] Migne, *Patr. Lat.*, LXXXIV, col. 408.

[13] *Ibid.*, col. 459.

[14] *Patr. Lat.*, LXVI, cols. 953-4.

[15] *Patr. Lat.*, LXXXIV, col. 316.

[16] Cf. A. Puech, "Les origines du priscillianisme," *Bull. d'Ancienne Littérature et d'Archéologie Chrétienne*, II (1912), pp. 176-7.

[17] E. g., *Reg. Iª. SS. Patrum*, c. xvi (Holst.-Brockie, I, p. 14; *Patr.*

its original heretical connotation, *doctor* eventually came to be used technically in Visigothic Spain to mean a ruler of monks, whether an abbot or (with reference to episcopal control over diocesan monasteries) a bishop. The *Regula Orientalis* of Vigilius, apparently written in Gaul in the early fifth century, and widely used in Spain, refers to the abbot (c. i) as *doctor et pater.*[18] Two metrical Latin epitaphs of the *Anthologia Hispana* illustrate, it would seem, the episcopal application. One, that of the metropolitan bishop John of Tarragona (d. 519-20), speaks of him as *rector* doctorq(ue) *prefuisti monacis et populis.*[19] The other, the epitaph of the bishop Justinian of Valencia (*ca.* 546), reads in part: *pius preclarus* doctor *alacer facundus* / . . . / *virgines institue(n)s monacos(que) gu⟨bernans⟩.*[20] The early tenth century Escorial MS Lat. a. I. 13, containing much pre-711 Galician material, speaks, in an as yet unidentified text, of penitents who remain *sub potestate iudicis aut* doctoris *vel abbatis.*[21] Other examples might be cited from unpublished tenth and eleventh century Spanish charters in which Hispano-Visigothic ecclesiastical terminology is conservatively retained.[22]

Lat., CIII, cols. 440-1); S. Orsiesius, *Doctrina de Inst. Monach.*, c. xxv (A. Boon-L. Th. Lefort, *Pachomiana Latina* [Louvain, 1932], p. 126); S. Fructuosus, *Reg. Monach.*, c. xx (*Patr. Lat.*, LXXXVII, col. 1108).

[18] Holst.-Brockie, I, p. 61; *Patr. Lat.*, CIII, col. 477; cf. Boon-Lefort, *op. cit.*, pp. 42-4.

[19] José Vives, *Inscripciones Cristianas de la España Romana y Visigoda* (Barcelona, 1942), pp. 83-4 (no. 277); G. B. de Rossi, *Inscriptiones Christianae Urbis Romae* (Rome, 1857-8), II, 1, p. 294; E. Hübner, *Inscriptionum Hispaniae Christianarum Supplementum* (Berlin, 1900), p. 84 (no. 413). Vives is doubtless right in confining *doctor* in these two inscriptions to episcopal monastic jurisdiction and denying its equivalence to *abbas*; but since Visigothic bishops were commonly recruited from the abbatiate, an implied reference to the fact that John and Justinian had earlier served as abbots need not be altogether ruled out.

[20] Vives, p. 85 (no. 279); de Rossi, p. 293; Hübner, no. 409.

[21] Fol. 52r; cf. G. Antolín, "Un 'codex regularum' del siglo IX," *Ciudad de Dios*, LXXV (1908), p. 316.

[22] 970: doctori *Sigerrici abbati* (L. Barrau-Dihigo, "Notes et documents sur l'histoire du royaume de Leon. I. Chartes royales léonaises," *Revue Hispanique*, X [1903], p. 399); *ca.* 980: . . . *abba siue* doctor *albel(d)ensis* (Madrid, Archivo Histórico Nacional, Clero, *Libro de Pergaminos de San Juan de la Peña*, I [MS 442], priv. 12-R; date restored on prosopographical grounds); 1087: *pelagius abba* doctor

Lastly, DeBruyne fails to explain the sanctions clause of the *CM*'s initial chapter: *in domino ergo iure observationis et legis nos teneamus,* etc. *Observatio* here means *observatio monastica,* i. e., the canonical obligations of the monastic vows; while *lex* has reference to the *lex civilis,* i. e., to secular enforcement in Late Roman and post-Roman law of the *conditio monastica,* as well as of the contract as such. Either we must assume, contrary to all probability, that the state in Galicia, whether Late Roman, Suevic, or Visigothic, was expected to enforce a heretical covenant which could have no validity in its courts following the Emperor Maximus' official proscription of Priscillianism (384), a ban never revoked under Suevic or Visigothic law, so far as we know; or, as is far more probable, the *CM* was a covenant not among heretics but among orthodox monks, binding in the *ius utriusque fori.* In the latter case, the charge of Priscillianism loses its last remaining support.

2. *The Germanic invasions.* Since Priscillianism, as the canons of the council of II Braga (572) show, survived in Galicia until late in the sixth century, DeBruyne uses other evidence to prove the *CM*'s fifth century origin, although its alleged heretical character naturally strengthened the case for an early date. From cc. vii-viii it appears that the *CM* monastery was frequently (*ut fieri solet*) menaced with destruction by *incursio repentina aut hostilitas.* In c. vii the monks promise that, if forced to flee for this reason, they will reassemble about the abbot and restore to him whatever monastic chattels they have been able to rescue at the time of attack. For DeBruyne, these mysterious assaults fix 500 A. D. as the *CM*'s *terminus ante quem,* for he explains them as due to the fifth century Germanic invasions of Roman Spain, at a time when the province of Gallaecia was repeatedly harassed by marauding bands of Alans, Asdingian Vandals, and Sueves. This interpretation would be more convincing if the context did not equally permit the destroyers to be the hostile Arabs or Berbers of the eighth century,[23] or, assuming the *CM* Priscillianist, orthodox extirpators of heretical

monacorum (Arch. Hist. Nac., Clero, *Tumbo de San Salvador de Celanova* [MS 986 B], fol. 41v).

[23] L. Barrau-Dihigo, "Recherches sur l'histoire politique du royaume asturien (718-910)," *Rev. Hisp.*, LII (1921), pp. 106-45, 150-7, and especially pp. 250-60 and 348-52 on monastic establishments in frontier territory still subject to hostile invasion.

monachism. But the true significance of these passages is clarified by other Galician references to destructive attacks upon monastic communities. The *Regula Monastica Communis,* written in the province *ca.* 660-675, speaks in several places of attacks upon abbeys by kinsmen seeking to recover property granted a house by some relative at the time of his monastic profession.[24] So, in c. i, it describes the frequency with which monks of what it calls false monasteries encompass the ruin of their communities: *quod si aliqua ex illis imbecillitas apparuerit, propinquos, quos in saeculo reliquerunt, cum gladiis et fustibus ac minis sibi adiutores adducunt, et qualiter haec disrumpant in prima dudum conversatione excogitant.* Such armed violence, however, was equally feared by more orthodox communities, for in c. xiv the *Reg. Mon. Com.* notes the necessity of expelling a monk who *contra seniorem vel fratres in facie perstiterit, et cum propinquis se vindicare maluerit*; and a little later it adds (c. xviii): *comperimus per minus cauta monasteria qui cum facultaticulis suis ingressi sunt, postea tepefactos cum grandi exprobratione repetere et saeculum quod relinquerant, ut canes ad vomitum, revocare; et cum propinquis quod monasteria contulerant hoc extorquere et iudices saeculares requirere et cum senioribus*[25] *monasteria dissipare.* So, too, in the *pactum* appended to this Rule, the monk pledges the abbot that he will not *contra regulam occulte cum parentibus germanis filiis cognatis vel propinquis aut certe cum fratre secum habitante consilium de absente supradicto patre nostro inierit.* Other examples might be cited, but these will suffice to prove that cc. vii-viii of the *CM* refer not to such major political catastrophes as the Germanic or Muslim invasions, but to attacks of hostile kinsmen whose hopes of landed inheritance and other wealth lay in destroying the monastery and recovering their relative's portion of its temporal. This background of familial property concepts and of hostility toward Roman modes of alienation of goods illumines the *CM*'s insistence upon the temporal as permanently transferred to communal ownership. It reveals that this latter doctrine was designed to meet the needs of an environment in which monastic poverty and divine proprietorship of ecclesiastical goods were but dimly understood and little respected. All of which points not to the

[24] Holst.-Brockie, I, pp. 208-19; *Patr. Lat.,* LXXXVII, cols. 1109-30.
[25] Perhaps read *saionibus,* with Herwegen, p. 3, n. 1.

Roman fifth, but the Visigothic seventh, century as the period of the *CM*'s composition.

3. *The Biblical citations.* In DeBruyne's judgment, the *CM*'s fifth century origin is decisively proved by its use of an Old Latin rendering of the Scriptures, since by 500 the Vulgate was well established in the Iberian peninsula.[26] Of the fourteen Biblical citations one, as already seen, is probably apocryphal: *amicum noli,* etc. (c. iii); a second is too brief or free a paraphrase to be significant: *unum,* etc. (c. i); two are the same in OL and Vulg.: *habentes,* etc. (c. i; Acts 2, 44 or 4, 32) and *pacifici,* etc. (c. iv; Ecclus. 6, 6); and the remaining ten unquestionably contain a high proportion of OL readings, chiefly from *a, b, c,* and several African versions, above all, *k.* DeBruyne assumes (hence apparently Schanz's doubts, *loc. cit.*) that by the sixth century the Vulg. had either displaced or so corrupted OL Biblical MSS in Galicia that a work so predominantly OL in its citations as the *CM* could not have been written. Yet everything we know of the history of the Spanish Bible well into the Middle Ages testifies to the remarkable longevity of the OL and the retarded triumph of the Vulg. This applies with especial force to so relatively isolated and remote a province as Galicia. Berger and Dom Quentin have shown that even down to the eleventh century Spanish Biblical texts fall into four main categories: OL Bibles; Vulg. Bibles containing whole books in OL; Vulg. books peppered with OL readings, and even occasionally provided with OL marginal glosses; and Vulg. Bibles, although as DeBruyne himself notes, "on devait chercher longtemps avant de trouver [en Espagne] une Vulgate pure."[27] Peninsular Biblical citations, therefore, ordinarily display an admixture of OL and Vulg. readings, something a more careful analysis may show to be true of the *CM,* since two of its citations could be from the Vulg. and among the other ten there are some possibly distinctively Vulg. readings.

[26] On the OL in Spain, cf., *passim,* Samuel Berger, *Histoire de la Vulgate* (Paris, 1893); F. C. Burkitt, *The Old Latin and the Itala* (Cambridge, 1896; *Texts and Studies,* IV, 3); F. Stummer, *Einführung in die lateinische Bibel* (Paderborn, 1928); and D. DeBruyne, "Étude sur les origines de la Vulgate en Espagne," *Rev. Bénéd.,* XXI (1914-19), pp. 373-401.

[27] Berger, pp. 8-28; H. Quentin, *Mémoire sur l'Établissement du Texte de la Vulgate, Ière partie: Octateuque* (Rome-Paris, 1922), chap. VI; DeBruyne, *Rev. Bénéd.,* XXV (1908), p. 88.

In short, the strong probability exists of OL Bibles surviving in Galicia at least to 711, above all in the rural milieu from which the *CM* evidently springs. This argument DeBruyne partially anticipates by calling attention to the difference in the Biblical versions used in the seventh century Galician *Regula Monachorum* of Fructuosus of Braga and the *Regula Monastica Communis*.[28] The degree of "hieronymianization" of these two works in the unsatisfactory printed editions is uncertain, but in any case the four brief citations of the *Reg. Monach.* prove nothing. The some thirty-four citations of the *Reg. Mon. Com.*, however, reflect a highly mixed Bible, almost as much OL as Vulg., and with the same affinities as the *CM* to *a*, *b*, *c*, and the African group. The higher content here of Vulg. readings as compared with *CM* is explicable geographically as well as chronologically. It is just what might be expected in a literary work emanating from Braga, the chief cultural and ecclesiastical center; undoubtedly the rate of occurrence of OL readings and OL Biblical MSS would rise as one moved out from the provincial capital.

Until we get some much needed chronological and regional studies of OL-Vulg. interaction in Spain, we can only generalize with caution, but it seems reasonable to conclude that setting the fifth century as the arbitrary terminus of OL circulation in Galicia is hazardous, if not downright erroneous. This is particularly true if it can be shown that all the other evidence strongly points to a seventh century date for the *CM*, as examination of the text and its transmission will soon make clear.

If the *CM* is neither Priscillianist nor necessarily of the fifth century, then Herwegen's proposed identification as a type of later seventh century Galician monastic *pactum* merits the critical examination it has not yet received. Of first importance in this connection is the neglected evidence of the manuscript tradition. Three early medieval collections of monastic Rules preserve the *CM* text: (1) Munich Hof- und Staatsbibliothek Lat. 28118, saec. ix (*M*), the great Codex Trevirensis from the St. Maximinus abbey at Trier, containing the *Codex Regularum* of the Carolingian monastic reformer St. Benedict of Aniane (d. 821);[29] (2) Escorial Lat. a. I. 13, fols. 50^{v}, col. 2-51^{v}, col. 2,

[28] Holst.-Brockie, I, pp. 201-219; *Patr. Lat.*, LXXXVII, cols. 1099-1130.

[29] O. Seebass, "Über das Regelbuch Benedikts von Aniane," *Zeitschrift*

saec. x ineunte (*B*), copied by Leodegundia for the Galician nunnery of Bobadilla, near Samos, prov. Lugo;[30] and (3) Escorial Lat. s. III. 32, fols. 66ʳ-67ᵛ, saec. ix (*E*), of northwest or north-central Spanish provenance.[31] In addition, the rubric of a lost text survives in London Brit. Mus. Addit. MS 30055, fol. 223ʳ, saec. x (*L*), a *codex regularum* from the archive of the monastery of San Pedro de Cardeña, near Burgos in Old Castile.[32]

According to Seebass and Plenkers, Holstenius' printed text, which Migne reproduces with slight revision, is probably based upon a 1467 Cologne MS (Stadtbibliothek theol. 231) that is an accurate copy of *M*.[33] Ángel C. Vega's 1933 edition is the first to use the important Escorial codices, but it regrettably fails to publish the majority of their variant readings, tending to conceal the fact that the Holstenius-Brockie-Migne text con-

für Kirchengeschichte, XV (1894-5), pp. 244-60; H. Plenkers, *Untersuchungen zur Überlieferungsgeschichte der ältesten lateinischen Mönchsregeln* (Munich, 1906; *Quellen und Untersuchungen zur lateinischen Philologie des Mittelalters,* Bd. I, Hft. 3), pp. 4-8. On Benedict of Aniane and his *Codex*, cf. P. Schmitz, "Benoît d'Aniane," *Dictionnaire d'Histoire et de Géographie Ecclésiastique,* VIII (Paris, 1935), pp. 177-88 (with good bibliography).

[30] G. Antolín, "Historia y descripción de un 'codex regularum' del siglo IX," *Ciudad de Dios,* LXXV (1908), pp. 23-33, 304-316, 460-71, 637-49; LXXVI (1908), pp. 310-323, 457-70; LXXVII (1908), pp. 48-56, 131-6 [also separately, Madrid, 1908]; *idem, Catálogo de los Códices Latinos de la Real Biblioteca del Escorial* (Madrid, 1910-23), I, pp. 21-25. For the date, cf., most recently, A. Millares Carlo, *Nuevos Estudios de Paleografía Española* (Mexico City, 1941), pp. 106-7.

[31] Antolín, *Catálogo,* IV, pp. 82-5.

[32] W. M. Whitehill, "Un códice visigótico de San Pedro de Cardeña (British Museum, Additional ms. 30055)," *Boletín de la Academia de la Historia,* CVII (1935), pp. 513-14. The survival of still another early *CM* text in Paris Bibl. Nat. Lat. 10876, saec. x, is suggested by Gerou's reference to the *Regula S. Isidori* as there containing 25 titles (note that in *B* and *L* the *CM* appears as c. xxv of this *regula*); but L. Delisle's description of this MS, giving the Isidorian *explicit* and the rubrics of two short appended pieces (*Reg. S. Pachomii,* c. lxxvii; *Conc. Hispal. II,* c. xi) seems to rule out this possibility. Cf. Delisle, "Notices sur les manuscrits disparus de la bibliothèque de Tours pendant la première moitié du xixᵉ siècle," *Notices et Extraits des Manuscrits de la Bibliothèque Nationale,* XXI, 1 (1884), pp. 246-7; *Catalogue Général des Manuscrits des Bibliothèques Publiques de France. Départements,* XXXVII, 1 (ed. M. G. Collon; Paris, 1900), pp. 493-4.

[33] Plenkers, *loc. cit.*

tains numerous errors. Vega's text also rests primarily upon *M*, so that the need for a new critical edition is evident. Collation of all three MSS, the results of which can only be briefly summarized here, establishes several important points hitherto overlooked. The most obvious is the just mentioned weakness of *M*, which is corrected not infrequently by the agreement of *B* and *E*. More striking, however, is the fact of the general agreement between *M* and *E* as against *B*, a divergence marked enough to justify the conclusion that there exist two fairly distinguishable versions of the text. This double tradition is established by the following major variant readings:

M and *E*: communi definitione decrevimus apud nos, ab ullo, quod et (a *E*) nobis scriptum est, teneamus et in eo usque in finem permaneamus quoniam (c. i); vestimento, vestiemini, quaerite, opponentur (adponentur *E*) (c. ii); qui prior est, amicum noli cito comprobare (c. iii); indicet (*om. E*) abbati (c. iv); haec quae scripta sunt (hec conscriptum est *E*) (c. v); adversus alterum (abbatem *E*) altercatus fuerit semel sed (altercatus emendet se *E*) secundum evangelium (c. vi); abbatem, festinare debebunt, ullo modo poterunt (poterint *E*) separari quos divina charitas (karitas *E*) sociavit quia cautum (c. vii); superius, proprie (cui per *E*) retinere, cogitaverit (c. viii); propter, cauta qui (c. ix).

B: degretum est apud nos, ab ullis, quod a nobis ceptum est, teneamus quoniam; uestitum, utimini, querite primum, adicietur; qui preęst, amicum noli cito conprobare aut si cito conprobaberis noli cito reprobare; renuntiet abbati; hęc conscriptio; aduersus aliut altercatus fuerit emendet secundum euangelium; abbatem eorum, festinare debent, ullo metu poterint separari cautum; iam superius, cum ipso retinere, contigerit; non propter, cauta quia.

Some of *B*'s variants from *M* and *E* are explicable as scribal omissions or alterations (e. g., in c. ii *utimini* and *adicie(n)tur* are Vulg. substitutions for the original OL), and at certain points its text is less clear than that of *M* and *E*. Nevertheless, there are indications that in some respects *B* stands closer than either *M* or *E* to a lost archetype. The apocryphal citation of c. iii, which no scribe would be likely to supplement, appears in fuller form; the *altercatio* passage (c. vi) avoids the confusing readings of both *M* and *E*, which disagree here; and the logical *non propter . . . stabiles* of c. ix is found only in *B*. All these variants, although they do not affect the meaning of the text in any serious sense, suffice to establish two different traditions.

No less significant is the fact that this double textual tradition is reinforced by the MSS in another way. All four MSS attach the *CM* closely to a monastic Rule. In *M* and *E* the work immediately follows the *Regula S. Basilii*, under the rubric *incipit consensoria monachorum.*[34] In *B* and *L* it stands as an additional twenty-fifth chapter of the *Regula S. Isidori* (in *B* simply rubricked *c. xxv;* in *L* as *c. xxv. incipit conscensoria monachorum*). From this it may be inferred that before passing into the *codices regularum* each of these Rules must have circulated independently in MSS containing only the Rule and the attached *CM*. This testimony to what may be called Basilian and Isidorian lines of transmission takes on even greater interest when it is discovered to parallel exactly the double descent of the text. *M* and *E*, textually in basic agreement, both belong to the Basilian line; *B* (unfortunately the *L* text is lost), to the Isidorian.

All this throws much needed light upon the origins and nature of the *CM*. It confirms its Spanish and, specifically, Galician, provenance, first proposed by Herwegen but never proved, even by DeBruyne. Three of the known MSS are now seen to be Spanish (*B* from Galicia, *L* from Castile, *E* from the same general area); and it could be shown without much difficulty, although this is not the place to undertake it, that all the early medieval Spanish *codices regularum* (and a number of these are known) derive from one or more late seventh century Galician collections of monastic Rules. The same is true of Benedict of Aniane's *Codex Regularum*, which *M* preserves; this contains an undue proportion of Galician material, some of it not otherwise preserved, even in Galician MSS (e. g., the complete *Regula Monastica Communis*, the *Regula SS. Pauli et Stephani Abbatum*, and the *De Genere Monachorum* of the abbot Valerius), and it seems very likely that the great leader of the Carolingian Benedictine Reform drew heavily, and perhaps directly, upon the rich literary tradition of seventh century Galician monasticism.[35]

[34] Benedict of Aniane places the *CM* after the Benedictine Rule, but for its post-Basilian position in *M*, see Plenkers, p. 8.

[35] According to Vega (pp. 27, 30), *M* is of Spanish provenance.

Furthermore, the collocation of the *CM* in Basilian or Isidorian MSS assists in determining its date, for it is possible to discover within reasonable limits when the *Regula S. Isidori* reached Galicia. Isidore did not write his Rule until the period of his metropolitanate, 620-636; and Fructuosus of Braga, author *ca.* 635 of the first Galician monastic Rule, shows no knowledge of it, although he draws freely upon such other monastic sources as Cassian, Pachomius, Jerome *ad Eustochium,* and the *De Ordine Monachorum.* On the other hand, the Galician *Regula Monastica Communis,* which appeared *ca.* 660-675, definitely cites the Isidorian Rule.[36] The latter thus seems to have reached Galicia soon after 650. The Basilian Rule cannot be traced in this fashion, but it was not used by Fructuosus and probably reached Galicia at much the same time as the *Reg. S. Isid.* To be sure, it is not enough to know that the *CM* could not have circulated in Galicia, as an appendix to the Isidorian and Basilian Rules, before *ca.* 650, since conceivably it could have done so earlier as an independent document. But if, as seems inherently likely, it was written to supplement a monastic Rule, and if, as the MSS indicate, it was normally used with either the Basilian or Isidorian *regulae,* then the probability is that it dates from about the same period as the Galician advent of these Rules, namely *ca.* 650-675.

That the *CM* was intended to accompany a Rule and be used with it, exactly as the so-called Fructuosan *pactum* was designed for use with, and was attached in the MSS to the terminus of, the *Regula Monastica Communis,* seems certain. Rule the *CM* emphatically is not, nor is it so entitled except in late non-Spanish MSS and the printed editions. It contains none of the prescriptions on daily régime, diet, clothing, labor, prayer, etc., indispensable to monastic Rules. The significant fact that, as in the Fructuosan *pactum,* the monks affix their signatures to it,

[36] *Reg. Mon. Com.,* c. ix: *et patrum exempla . . . lignarius fuit* is based on *Reg. S. Isid.,* c. v, 2: *nam patriarchae . . . officium gessit.* This passage originally comes from St. Augustine, *De Opere Monachorum,* c. xiii: *si Iudaeos dixerint . . . faber fuit* (ed. J. Zycha, *Corpus Script. Eccles. Lat.* [Vienna, 1900], p. 555); but the language shows it reached the *Reg. Mon. Com.* through Isidore. For a clue to the advent and popularity of Isidore's writings in Galician monastic circles *ca.* 675, cf. the prologue to the *Vita S. Fructuosi* (ed. by F. C. Nock, *The* Vita Sancti Fructuosi [Washington, 1946; *Cath. Univ. of America Studies in Mediaeval History,* N. S., VII], pp. 86-9).

proves beyond all cavil its true character as a formal legal instrument. Style and terminology supply further evidence. The *CM*'s opening formulae closely resemble the juridical language of the Visigothic ecclesiastical synods, as can be seen by comparing its initial *communi definitione decrevimus (degretum est apud nos B) . . . residentibus nobis in monasterio . . . omnibus placuit* with *consensu communi decrevimus* (council of II Seville [619], c. xi); *communi definitione decrevimus . . . communi decreto sancimus* (IX Toledo [655], *praef.* and c. ix); *patribus residentibus* (XIII Toledo [683]); *nobis residentibus . . . patribus residentibus* (XVII Toledo [694]).[37] *Omnibus placuit* is a common commencement of conciliar decrees. This legal terminology is in keeping with the fact that in c. viii the *CM* expressly calls itself a *pactum*. This is in the passage prohibiting seizure of the monastic temporal by any of the *consentientes* on the grounds that this *per pactum ad omnes pertinet*; and it would be absurd to posit any other agreement on common ownership than cc. iv and viii of the *CM* itself. Five other terms occur in the MSS to describe the text: *definitio* (c. i: *M, E*); *conscriptio* (c. v: *B*); *liber* (c. ix); *sermo* (c. ix: *E*, which terminates: *finit hic sermo*); and the titular *consensoria monachorum*. *Conscriptio* is fairly neutral, and *sermo* is evidently a later scribal rubric; but *definitio* recalls the synonymous use of *definitio* and *pactum* (or *placitum*) in the *Leges Visigothorum* (e. g., II, 5, 8: *placitum sive definitio*; III, 1, 4: *pacta vel definitiones*).[38] The phrase *in isto libro* preceding the monks' subscriptions can be paralleled in the Mozarabic liturgy by the use of *libellum* to designate the monastic *pactum*.[39] Given the original terminal position of the *CM* in MSS of the Basilian or Isidorian Rules, however, it seems possible to take *liber* here as referring to the whole *liber regulae*, with the Rule and consensorial *pactum* taken together. The term *consensoria* is a ἅπαξ λεγόμενον, found only in the *CM*, and the *Thesaurus Linguae Latinae* (IV, 390, *s. v. cōnsēnsōrius, -a -um*), misled by the printed editions, erroneously regards it as an adjective, with *regula* understood.

[37] *Patr. Lat.*, LXXXIV, cols. 598, 433, 437, 487, 551, 552.

[38] Ed. K. Zeumer, *Monumenta Germaniae Historica, Leges*, I, 1 (Hanover-Leipzig, 1902), pp. 109, 126, and index, *s. v. definitio, pactum.*

[39] M. Férotin, *Le* Liber Ordinum *en Usage dans l'Église Wisigothique et Mozarabe d'Espagne* (Paris, 1904; *Monumenta Ecclesiae Liturgica*, V), col. 86.

If anything is understood it is really *definitio* or the like, but the probability is that the word is a noun, not an adjective (cf. similar Late Latin first declension feminines as *tractoria, completuria, tonsuriae*).[40] The employment of *consensoria* rather than *pactum* in the title reflects the juridical distinction between the *CM* and the *Reg. Mon. Com. pactum*: the latter is a bilateral contract between two parties, the abbot and the corporate body of monks, while the *CM*, in which each *consentiens* is a contracting party, resembles more closely the Roman *societas omnium bonorum.* Notwithstanding this difference, the *CM* from the monastic standpoint is essentially a *pactum,* i. e., a written and subscribed covenant for the foundation, governance, and enlargement of a monastic society.

At this point it becomes necessary to defend the unity of the text against DeBruyne's captious effort (pp. 83-4) to split it into two different redactions, one terminating with the sentence *iugiter* (*igitur* MSS) *haec,* etc. of c. v, and the other, of perceptibly later date, extending through to the conclusion.[41] DeBruyne holds that (1) *iugiter haec,* etc. logically conclude an original form of the text; (2) the two mentions of property (cc. iv, viii) would have been united in a document written at one time, and c. viii could only have been added later after non-observance of c. iv; (3) disunity and incoherence are proved by the phrase *quod superius diximus* (c. viii), which has no application to anything whatsoever in the text. Actually, however, the words *iugiter haec,* etc. conclude and emphasize the immediately preceding directives on property and withdrawal, and could never have been followed by the signatures of the *consentientes,* as c. ix is. The separate treatment of property is accounted for by the fact that c. iv deals with it under normal conditions, c. viii with its preservation under abnormal conditions, i. e., after the monastery's destruction, as anticipated in c. vii. The phrase *quod superius* (*iam superius B*) *diximus* naturally and logically applies to the *causa necessitatis* theme of cc. vii and possibly iv. DeBruyne himself admits the text is "tout entière conçue dans le même esprit et peut-être aussi

[40] C. D. Du Cange, *Glossarium Mediae et Infimae Latinitatis* (Niort, 1883-7), VIII, p. 144; Férotin, *op. cit.*, index, *s. v. completuria, tonsurie.*

[41] Berlière (*Rev. Bénéd.*, XXV [1908], p. 72) also had his doubts concerning this partition of the text, which was first suggested by Herwegen, p. 72.

dans le même style." In short, the logic of the text surpasses that of the hypercritical attempt to dichotomize it.

Recognition of its unity and its pactual character considerably advances the problem of the *CM*'s chronological allocation. It is DeBruyne's greatest weakness that he wholly neglects to determine the work's logical place in the historical and institutional evolution of Galician monasticism.[42] His major premises, that in fifth century Galicia (as nowhere else in Spain) Priscillianist anchoritism developed full-fledged monastic communities, that two centuries before orthodox monastic Rules were written in Spain Galician Priscillianism had produced one, and that the peculiarities of this Rule could be explained by its heretical background, are all of them historically unwarrantable assumptions. The truth is, cenobitism, as opposed to the asceticism of isolated individual ascetics or that of small unorganized groups, cannot be proved to have existed in Galicia before *ca.* 550, when with royal support it was introduced into the Suevic kingdom by the eastern monk Martin of Braga. Martin founded the *monasterium Dumiense* near Braga, and perhaps some other houses, presumably organizing them along normal oriental lines; but his cenobitism made little headway, and it was not until the following century, with Fructuosus of Braga (*ca.* 615/20—*ca.* 660), that a widespread, popular monastic movement swept over the province. By *ca.* 660, furthermore, for reasons that cannot be entered into here, Galician monasticism was abandoning certain basic institutions of orthodox monasticism and embarking upon a singular period of radical experimentation in the organization and government of the monastic community. The individual *professio* charter was replaced, or at least supplemented, by the group covenant-profession, variously called *pactum, sacramentum,* or *iuramenta* (*Reg. Mon. Com.*, cc. i, xviii); and this brought with it free election of abbots, as against the episcopal appointment normal to Visigothic monasticism and sanctioned in c. li of the council of IV Toledo (633), and diminution in varying degree of the abbot's authority. It entailed also a marked rise of chronic internal controversy among the now more or less

[42] On Galician monasticism before 711, see Herwegen; Pérez de Urbel, *Monjes Españoles,* I, pp. 183-93; 377-450; and C. J. Bishko, "Spanish monasticism in the Visigothic period," *Harvard University, Summaries of Ph. D. Theses, 1937* (Cambridge, 1938), pp. 126-9.

equalitarian monks, weakening of the monastic ideal of *stabilitas*, and frequent withdrawals from monasteries by dissatisfied monks (*Reg. Mon. Com.*, cc. i, ii, xviii and xx, and the *pactum*). Furthermore, although perhaps due as much to contemporary property concepts as to internal weakness, all these Galician houses suffered from violent attacks by kinsfolk of disgruntled monks, often resulting in a monastery's destruction and the loss of its temporal (*Reg. Mon. Com.*, cc. i and xviii, and the *pactum*).

Into this world of contractual, equalitarian, unstable, and potentially short-lived monastic communities of post-650 the *CM* fits perfectly. It is, like the Fructuosan *pactum* and the *Reg. Mon. Com.*, c. i, *sacramentum* or *iuramenta*, a group *professio*; and like them it incorporates a tradition of non-episcopal institution of abbots, weakened abbatial authority, internal disorders, chronic secessions, and familial attacks. Just where the consensorial community stands with relation to these other types of Galician monastery is less clear. It was Herwegen's proposal that the *CM* might be the *pactum* of the type of monastery attacked in *Reg. Mon. Com.*, c. i; but there are certain objections to this otherwise attractive identification. The difference in title is of some importance, even though the *Reg. Mon. Com.* might contemptuously stigmatize a *consensoria monachorum* as a mere *sacramentum* or *iuramenta*. The *CM*'s silence about the wives, children, and serfs taken into the *Reg. Mon. Com.*, c. i, monasteries by the landowners who established them, is noteworthy; such houses would have to be double monasteries, and certain questions of servile manumission *sub modo* would arise. These are problems their covenant might logically be expected to treat. Again, the *CM*'s preservation in collections of Rules almost certainly put together in the late seventh century by monks of the *Reg. Mon. Com.* tradition indicates amicable relations between the latter and consensorial monachism, not the acrid hostility of *Reg. Mon. Com.*, c. i. Nor do we gain much by associating the *CM* with the presbyteral monasteries also denounced by the *Reg. Mon. Com.* in c. ii, for these were not of group origin and undoubtedly had in their presbyter-abbots stronger rulers than the consensorial *doctor*.

A more fruitful line of inquiry into the precise connections of the *CM* is suggested by the two short texts that follow it in

MS Escorial Lat. a. I. 13, fols. 51ᵛ-52ʳ. These have been published by Antolín under the titles (*De caritate fraterna*) and (*De poenitentia?*).[43] The first of these, rubricked in the MS as c. xxvi of the *Reg. S. Isid.*, is an impassioned plea for the abandonment of internal disputes in monastic houses, the unknown author arguing that those who have given up family, home, and wealth ought not to allow personal quarrels and animosities to destroy communal harmony. The second piece, without rubric or, more probably, included under the preceding rubric, deals with penitential discipline in cases of murder, adultery, and perjury. It insists that penance for such sins is to be determined by the bishop, not the priest; presents a list (*censum penitentie*) of seven money commutations (in *solidi*); and declares penitents are to remain under the authority of a judge or abbot, depending obviously on whether or not they have entered monasteries (cf. *Reg. Mon. Com.*, c. xix: *Quid in monasterio debeant observare qui peccata graviora in saeculo commiserint*). Both these texts have significant links with the *CM* and probably come from the same locale. The appeal for internal concord strikes at a major *CM* problem; and the use of *doctor* for *abbas*, as noted above, parallels *CM*, c. v. The Biblical citations are mixed OL-Vulg., with a perceptibly stronger Vulg. inclination than the *CM*, although this may be due partly to the hieronymizing tendencies of *B*. There is even an apparently apocryphal citation, beginning *non poterat loqui*, in the first piece. Until we know something about the origin of the probably Irish-inspired Galician penitential system, the establishment of which in the province hardly antedates 650, the chronological data of these two texts cannot be fully exploited. But if they do have the same provenance as the *CM*, they prove that the houses using the latter were closely associated with the episcopate and the parochial system, which in turn shows that such houses, maintaining relations with what the *Reg. Mon. Com.* (cc. i-ii) would call an *episcopus saecularis*, stood outside the limits of the *Reg. Mon. Com.* monastic federation of Fructuosan and allied houses in the so-called *sancta communis regula*.

Further study of Galician monasticism in the latter half of the seventh century will be needed before all the institutional

[43] *Ciudad de Dios*, LXXV (1908), pp. 314-16.

problems, and the precise monastic, ecclesiastical, and secular connections of the *CM* can be fully understood. For the present, it need only be concluded that the current identification is completely misleading; and that the work properly belongs in the Late Visigothic period of Galician literature, between 650 and 711. So understood, it constitutes a new and important source for the history of Spanish monasticism on the eve of the Muslim invasion.

University of Virginia.

ADDITIONAL NOTE

While no one, as Estatal and Verheijen remark,[1] any longer dreams of defending the old conception of the *CM* as the *Regula prima* of St Augustine, the confusion and uncertainty surrounding the character, date and provenance of this text have not yet been altogether dispelled. Two errors in particular that I sought to correct in 1948 continue in circulation: (i) the classification as a monastic rule, a terminology dating from at least the time of Benedict of Aniane and subsequently promoted by various medieval and modern editors who mistook this little monastic piece for a composition of the bishop of Hippo; and (ii) the ascription to a Priscillianist milieu, the thesis of DeBruyne. De Vogüé in his authoritative *Règle de Saint Benoît*, to cite a recent example, still classifies the *CM* among the some thirty monastic Rules emanating from the old Latin cenobitism.[2] Ayuso in the *Prolegómenos* volume of his projected edition of the *Vetus Latina Hispana*, where he summarizes without comment the views of DeBruyne and myself on the *CM*, rubrics it as an "anónimo priscillianista", the composition of a "pseudo-Prisciliano".[3] In 1955 a paper of A. Casimassa on the Augustinian Rule—first published to be sure in 1921–1923—still presents without qualification this Priscillianist thesis.[4] Little wonder then that in 1967 Verheijen could express the opinion that the questions of place of origin and date still remained open.[5]

Nevertheless, the case presented above for identifying *CM* as a type of seventh-century Gallegan pactum has enjoyed increasing assent, and remains as strong as, indeed even stronger than, in 1948.[6] No formal defense of DeBruyne's chronology and Priscillianist attribution has been attempted nor has any refutation been made of the objections I raised against these, while further study of the vicinal, presbyteral and pactual cenobitism of Visigothic Galicia (Study I in this volume) has reinforced my own conviction that the piece can only be explained in the context of this region and

---

[1] Juan Manuel del Estatal, "Estado actual de la investigación sobre la historia de la Orden agustiniana," *Ciudad de Dios*, LXXXI (1966), 501–2; Luc Verheijen, *La Règle de Saint Augustin* (Paris, 1967), I, 7. Cf. A. C. Vega, "Notas histórico-críticas en torno a los orígenes de la Regla de San Agustín," *Bol. R. Acad. Hist.*, CLII (1963), 15, and note 4.

[2] Adalbert de Vogüé, *La Règle de Saint Benoît* (Paris, 1971–2; *Sources chrétiennes*, 181–186), I, 29, note 1, and elsewhere.

[3] Teófilo Ayuso Marazuela, *La Vetus Latina Hispana* (Madrid, 1953), I, 482 (no. 226).

[4] Antonio Casimassa, "Il più antico codice della regola monastica di Sant'Agostino," *Atti della Pontificia Accademia Romana di Archeologia*, ser. III, Rendiconti, I (1921–2, 1922–3), 95–105; reprinted in *Lateranum*, Annex XXI, no. 1–4 (Roma, 1955), where see 1, 107.

[5] *Op. cit.*, II, 9, with reproduction (7–9) of the text as edited by Hümpfner (note 7, below).

[6] See E. Dekkers, *Clavis patrum latinorum*, no. 1872 (*Sacris erudiri*, III, 1951, 319); M. C. Díaz y Díaz, *Index scriptorum latinorum medii aevi hispanorum* (Salamanca, 1958–9), I, 88 (no. 317); Claude W. Barlow, *Iberian Fathers* (Washington, 1969; *The Fathers of the Church*, 62–63), II, 215–6.

period, just as its incorporation into the *codices regularum* of the monastic communities of the Alta Reconquista demonstrates its wide use in thoroughly orthodox circles and tells heavily against the allegation of heretical Priscillianist composition. As far back as 1943 Arbesmann and Hümpfner, when rejecting DeBruyne's interpretation in a work of which in 1948 I was unaware, expressed themselves as confident "that it can be shown that the author is St Fructuosus and that its tendency is rather anti-Priscillianist."[7] On the chronological side this was a step in the right direction, although these authors, primarily concerned with the thought and writings of Jordanus of Saxony, offered no proof of their assertions or any real justification of the rubric prefixed to their improved edition of the text: *S. Fructuosi decretum observantiae regularis* alias *Regula Consensoria*.

In general, Spanish scholarship of recent decades has yet to reach a consensus. Fernández Alonso opts for a Fructuosan ambience as does Orlandis, although this latter specialist retains the misnomer *Regula Consensoria*; and T. González, citing only the brief reference to *CM* in my article "Pactos monásticos" (*Diccionario de historia eclesiástica de España*, ed. Q. Aldea, Madrid, 1973, III, 1858), classifies *CM* as a non-Priscillianist Rule, or rather *compromiso*, of uncertain date.[8] At Spoleto in 1956 Mundó noted the conflicting views;[9] Pérez de Urbel has on occasion spoken of "la profesión considerada como un pacto en la *Regula Consensoria*" and the "pacto de la *Regla Consensoria*;"[10] and Díaz y Díaz, whose preparation of a critical edition of the *Regula s. Isidori* has given him special interest in the *CM* as so strongly represented in the manuscript tradition of the Isidorian code, provides bibliography upon it without as yet expressing any final judgment as to date and origin. It can be expected, however, that in due time this able scholar's Isidorian investigations will shed fresh light upon various aspects of the *CM*'s use and diffusion.[11]

Meanwhile, the erudite student of Díaz y Díaz, Dr. Antonio Linage Conde, has had occasion to discuss *CM* at two points (pp. 263–66, 306–8) in the first tome of his massive *Los orígenes del monacato benedictino en la Península Ibérica* (León, 1973).[12] Here he expresses general, if somewhat qualified, agreement with my classification of the piece as a product of Gallegan pactual cenobitism; but he refuses to regard it as a genuine type of pactum, thus leaving in complete obscurity the reasons for its attachment to Hispanic manuscripts of the Rules of St Isidore and St Basil in precisely the same terminal position as that occupied by the pactum appended to the *Regula Monastica Communis* (*RCom.*). Furthermore, on the grounds that the ascription of *CM* to the decades before 711 is "el punto más flaco" of my argument, Linage Conde prefers to attribute the anti-monastic attacks, so fearfully envisaged in cc. vii–viii, to Muslim marauders, so that, in his own words, the work would have been composed in Galicia "inmediatemente después del 711, cuando aún no habían llegado a la zona

[7] Rudolphus Arbesmann and Winfridus Hümpfner, *Jordani de Saxonia Liber vitasfratrum* (New York, 1943), lxxvi–lxxviii, 484–488.

[8] J. Fernández Alonso, *La cura pastoral en la España romano-visigoda* (Roma, 1955), 491; José Orlandis, *La Iglesia en la España visigótica y medieval* (Pamplona, 1976), 233–4; *idem*, *Historia de España. La España visigótica* (Madrid, 1977), 248; Teodoro González in *Historia de la Iglesia en España*, ed. R. García-Villoslada, I (Madrid, 1979), 632–3.

[9] Anscari Mundó, "Il monachesimo nella penisola iberica fino al sec. VII," *Il monachesimo nell'alto medioevo e la formazione della civiltà occidentale* (Spoleto, 1957), 99.

[10] See his "Vida y caminos del Pacto de San Fructuoso," *Rev. port. de história*, VII (1963), 383; and "Carácter y supervivencia del Pacto de San Fructuoso," *Bracara Augusta*, XXII (1968), 227.

[11] Manuel Díaz y Díaz, "Aspectos de la tradición de la *Regula Isidori*," *Stud. monastica*, V (1963), 31 (note 16), 39; and "El códice monástico de Leodegundia (Escorial a. I. 13)," *Ciudad de Dios*, CLXXXI (1968), 578 (notes 30–32).

[12] See also his *El monacato en España e Hispanoamérica* (Salamanca, 1977), 29.

donde el monasterio estuviese enclavado los invasores islamicos." This is a solution I mentioned in 1948 only to dismiss it as no more persuasive than de Bruyne's Germanic conjecture, since in effect it reduces the genesis of *CM* to incomprehensibility by removing it from the crucial epoch of Gallegan cenobitic conflict and institutional experimentation between ca. 650 and 675, which alone can explain its peculiar features.

For at least two additional reasons Linage Conde's thesis does not in my judgment merit favorable consideration. The first of these is the undeniable fact, as affirmed above, that the *incursio repentina aut hostilitas* confronting the consensorial monks exhibits no overtones of foreign or anti-Christian assault but on the contrary harmonizes perfectly with the allusions of *RCom* 1, 14 and 17 and of the Pactum of *RCom*, which depict the monasteries of Galicia ca. 675–700 as existing in a social and juridical environment of close-knit blood relationships and inalienable familial property-holding. This is a milieu in which transfers of lands or other goods entail the potential destruction of religious communities at the hands of violently hostile kinsmen of disgruntled monks, either themselves attacking *cum gladiis et fustibus ac minis*, or alternatively employing the equally deadly juridical weapon of the public *iudices* and *saiones*. That is why, in that extraordinary supplementary c. 18, the heads of the *Sancta Communis Regula* absolutely forbid the federation's *coenobia* to accept any benefactions from converts. In short, *CM* uses *invasio* as a technical juridical, not a politico-military, term.

A second principal objection is that Linage Conde assumes there was only a single consensorial house ("el monasterio") which somehow survived inviolate despite the very early Muslim occupation of Galicia, presumably down to Alfonso I's transplantation of the region's monks in 740–750 to the safety of westernmost Asturias and Castella Vetula. This runs counter to the codicological proofs that *CM* had a more ancient and widespread history of use than so brief an interval as two or three decades in the highly disorganized first century of the Reconquest in Galicia. In three manuscripts of the pure or non-interpolated redaction of the *Regula s. Isidori* (Esc. a. I. 13, Brit. Mus. Addit. 30055, Paris B. N. 13090), *CM* is shown by the text itself or by the surviving *capitulationes* to have been terminally appended to the Hispalensian code in precisely the position of the pactum of *RCom.*[13] In Munich Staatsbibl. Clm 28 118 and Esc. S. III. 32 it is similarly attached to the Rule of St Basil, although here *CM* is not fused with this work as such, evidently because its form and content prevented its being mistaken for a final *interrogatio*. All these cases demonstrate that as a true pactum *CM* must originally have circulated for some time in quasi-monoregular houses of predominantly Isidorian or Basilian observance before, with the accompanying Rule, it became embedded in late 7th-century Gallegan *codices regularum*, the direct ancestors of those which by the commencement of the 9th century were being copied in the monastic *scriptoria* of Castile and the Carolingian Empire.

No definitive edition of *CM* has yet been published, although that of Arbesmann and Hümpfner marks an advance over the texts found in Holstenius-Brockie and *PL* 66: 993–996. and 32: 1447–1450. Professor Barlow bases his English rendering, the only one, upon collation of the variant manuscript readings.[14]

On questions relating to the biblical citations, there is now available Ayuso's guide to the versions and MSS of the Old Latin Scriptures circulating in ancient and

---

[13] "*Consensoria Monachorum*" (Study II), notes 31–2, and the *Introducción* By Julio Campos Ruiz to his edition of the *Regula s. Isidori* in *Santos Padres Españoles*, t. II, ed. J. Campos Ruiz and I. Roca Melia (Madrid, 1971), 84–6.

[14] *Jord. de Sax. Lib. vit.*, 484–488 (Appendix A); Barlow, *Iberian Fathers*, II, 217–220.

early medieval Spain.[15] Some further light is thrown upon the terms *doctor* and *doctrina*, with particular reference to the office and functions of the abbot in ancient western monasticism, in de Vogüé's edition of the *Règle du Maître*.[16] Finally, it may be suggested that closer attention to the MSS and circulation in Spain of Rufinus' compilation of the *Regula s. Basilii*, with which (as with that of St Isidore) *CM* is found associated in the Hispanic *codices regularum*, may well yield additional clues to the origins and popularity of this *opusculum*. It should be observed that the *Regula ss. Pauli et Stephani*, cited in this Study as a product of seventh-century Galicia, has been convincingly shown by Vilanova to have been written in Italy at the end of the sixth century.[17]

---

[15] See note 3; cf. also B. M. Metzger, *The Early Versions of the New Testament* (Oxford, 1977).

[16] A. de Vogüé, *La Règle du Maître* (Paris, 1964–5), I, 110–111; III, 136–7; cf. the discussion of "l'abbé docteur et le priscillianisme" in his *La communauté et l'abbé dans la Règle de saint Benoît* (Paris, 1961), 176–86. Neither work cites the passage in *CM* or the preceding Study.

[17] J. E. M. Vilanova, *Regula Pauli et Stephani: edició crítica i comentari* (Abadía de Montserrat, 1959; *Scripta et Documenta*, 11).

III

GALLEGAN PACTUAL MONASTICISM IN THE REPOPULATION OF CASTILE

Among the documentary sources for the monastic colonization which play so central a role in the repopulation of primitive Castile in the ninth and tenth centuries, there occur a number of monastic pacta. Argáiz, Yepes and, notably, Berganza edited certain of these texts, but only since 1907, when Herwegen published his excellent monograph on Gallegan monastic pactualism, has there been genuine understanding of their institutional origin and significance [1]. Herwegen, however, particularly in his treatment of the pacta of the Reconquista, employed a purely juridical approach, useful for illumining certain aspects of pactual evolution, but totally unrelated to the changing historical conditions in which these texts were used [2]. Since Herwegen's day the chief advance beyond his results has been the listing or publication of additional pacta unknown to him, principally by Barrau-Dihigo, Serrano, Pérez de Urbel and Sán-

[1] Ildefons Herwegen, *Das* Pactum *des heiligen Fruktuosus von Braga* (Stuttgart, 1907; *Kirchenrechtliche Abhandlungen*, ed. U. Stutz, Bd. 40); hereafter cited as Herwegen. [For aid in the preparation of this paper, the author wishes to acknowledge the assistance of the Institute for Research in the Social Sciences, University of Virginia.]

[2] Cf. Stutz's introductory remarks on the work's origin and aim, Herwegen, pp. viii-ix.

chez-Albornoz [1]. Yet to appreciate the great historical, no less than institutional, significance of the monastic pacta of the Reconquista, it is necessary only to classify them topographically. Then it immediately becomes evident that pactualism was unknown in Mozarabic Spania, the Spanish March states, Navarre above the Ebro, León and, virtually so, in central Asturias; while in Galicia, eastern Asturias, Liébana, and, above all, Castile, it was firmly established. This singular distribution pattern, too well documented to be merely accidental [2], demonstrates that in peninsular monasticism prior to the Cluniacs not only the recognized Visigothic tradition, but also a Gallegan pactual movement, must be reckoned with; and it provides a promising new clue to the institutional background and the course of the frontier colonization of the Reconquista. Numerous questions await investigation in this connection, but for early Castilian history two are of paramount importance: first, how did the pactual monasticism of seventh century Visigothic Galicia establish itself in distant Castile as the dominant monastic tradition of the first centuries of the Reconquista; and, secondly, what became of this Gallegan institutionalism as the county expanded southward toward the Duero and Carolingian Benedictinism entered the northern Meseta as a new monastic agency of Castilian repopulation?

The Gallegan origin of pactual monasticism is certain. By the middle seventh century, as Herwegen has shown, the monasteries of St Fructuosus of Braga (circ. 600-660) and doubt-

---

1 For lists of pacta, and treatments of pactualism after Herwegen, see L. Barrau-Dihigo, 'Chartes de l'église de Valpuesta du IXe au XIe siècle', *Revue Hispanique*, VII (1900), pp. 304-7; L. Serrano, *Cartulario de San Pedro de Arlanza* (Madrid, 1925), pp. 26-30; Z. García Villada, *Historia Eclesiástica de España* (Madrid, 1929-1936), II, 1, 291-8; III, 307-8; J. Pérez de Urbel, *Los monjes españoles en la Edad Media* (Madrid, 1933-4), I, 438-450; II, 372-5; idem, *Historia del Condado de Castilla* (Madrid, 1945), III, nos. 1, 3, 12, 26, 53, 115, 120, 310, 432, 459, 665, and Apéndice II, nos. iii, xxxix, and Apéndice III, no. viii; Cl. Sánchez-Albornoz, 'Serie de documentos inéditos del reino de Asturias', *Cuadernos de Historia de España*, I-II (1944), pp. 316-7.

2 In view of the expert examination of the archives by Sánchez-Albornoz and Pérez de Urbel, and my own search of the Madrid collections and the provincial and cathedral archives of northern Spain, it seems to me unlikely that future discoveries of pacta will be numerous enough to affect materially the generalizations here put forth.

less other houses, all located south of the Miño around Braga and farther to the northeast in Bierzo near Astorga, constituted a veritable monastic federation, the Sancta Communis Regula [1]. The abbots (or abbesses) of these Communities met in regular synods presided over by an *episcopus sub regula*, originally Fructuosus himself in his dual capacity of abbot-bishop of Dumio and metropolitan of Braga; and these assemblies enacted the ordinances incorporated into the *Regula monastica communis* [2]. Among these federated monasteries the normal monarchical abbatiate of cenobitic history was discarded in favor of a quasi-feudal, equalitarian monastic polity, resting upon the pactum or written covenant drawn up between abbot-*patronus* and monks-dependent. In the model pactum attached to the *RMC*, which is commonly but dubiously ascribed to Fructuosus himself and which becomes the archetype of so many pacta of the Reconquista, the rights and obligations of the two contracting parties are defined with precision: the monks surrender their persons to the abbot with vows of obedience and stability, but retain the right to protest against unconstitutional abuses of power and can even invoke against their abbot the intervention of other abbots, or of the *episcopus sub regula* and the local count *(comes defensor)*; the abbot, on the other hand, has full power to punish dissenters or those conspiring with kinsfolk to disrupt the community, and the right to expel recalcitrants and recover deserters *(fugitivi)* with government aid *(saiones)*, even from bishops, priests or laymen protecting them. Under this system, the bond between abbot and monks being personal, subscription of a new pactum with an abbot-elect was necessary to insure continuance of the monastic society. Use of the pactum, however, contrary to the assumption of Fita, Pérez de Urbel and others, did not impose observance of the *Regula monachorum* of Fructuosus [3], for Gallegan monasticism was

---

1 Herwegen, pp. 1-4, 24-60; Pérez de Urbel, *Monjes españoles*, I, 438-50.

2 L. Holstenius, *Codex Regularum Monasticarum* (3rd ed. by M. Brockie, Vienna, 1759), I, 208-219; Migne, *Patrologia Latina*, LXXXVII, 1109-1130. The chronology and nature of these enactments will be discussed in my study now in preparation of the *Regula monastica communis* (henceforth cited as *RMC)*.

3 F. Fita, 'El monasterio dúplice de Piasca y la regla de San Fructuoso

eclectic, each house developing its custom from a *codex regularum,* which might contain the Rules of Pachomius, Basil, Augustine, Isidore or Benedict as well as that of Fructuosus or the *RMC*. Types of pactum differing from the *RMC* archetype also circulated in Galicia outside the federation, such as the *Consensoria monachorum* and the *sacramentum* or *iuramenta* denounced in the first chapter of the *RMC* [1].

In the eighth century the closely knit federation of abbeys in the Sancta Communis Regula was destroyed, not (it would seem) by the Muslim invasion and occupation of Galicia, but by Alfonso I's depopulation of pactual monasticism's homeland below the Miño in the *territorium* of Braga [2]. Pactualism itself, however, as an effective instrument of cenobitic organization, did not disappear. In Galicia as well as in eastern Asturias, Liébana, the Rioja and Castile it persisted well into the eleventh century as the constitutional basis of numerous monastic foundations, providing them with a very different internal structure from that of the orthodox Visigothic houses of central Asturias, León and, indeed, all the rest of Christian and Muslim Spain. Yet for Galicia itself only four pacta of the Reconquista have been discovered: 1) the Sabaricus pactum of MS Escorialensis a I 13, from an unknown house, of either eighth or ninth century date [3]; 2) the unpublished Absalom pactum (826 or 876), from a monastery of Santa Eulalia, perhaps Santa Eulalia del Bubal, in the province of Orense [4]; 3) the Fulgaredus pactum (871) from Santa María

---

en el siglo x', *Bol. Acad. Hist.,* XXXIV (1899), 448-462; Pérez de Urbel, *Monjes españoles,* I, 449-450; II, 374-5.

1 C. J. Bishko, 'The date and nature of the Spanish *Consensoria Monachorum*', *American Journal of Philology,* LXIX (1948), pp. 377-395.

2 *Chron. Adefonsi III,* c. xiii (ed. Z. García Villada, *Crónica de Alfonso III* [Madrid, 1918], p. 69); L. Barrau-Dihigo, 'Recherches sur l'histoire politique du royaume asturien', *Rev. Hisp.,* LII (1921), p. 144. I hope to consider this and related problems in a forthcoming paper on the pactualism of Galicia between the eighth and eleventh centuries.

3 Herwegen, pp. 6-8. On the troublesome and controversial dating of this MS, see most recently, A. Millares Carlo, *Nuevos Estudios de Paleografía española* (Mexico City, 1941), pp. 106-7; Ángel Custodio Vega, 'Una adaptación de la «informatio regularis» de s. Agustín anterior al siglo IX para unas vírgenes españolas', *Miscellanea Giovanni Mercati* (Vatican City, 1946), II, 34-5.

4 *Tumbo de Celanova* (Madrid, Archivo Histórico Nacional, Códices, 986 B),

de Mezonzo, not far from Santiago[1]; and 4) the late Tudeildus pactum (1045) from the Portuguese abbey of São Salvador de Vacariça in the *suburbium* of Coimbra[2]. This scant list of what may be termed the western group of medieval Spanish pacta can be supplemented somewhat by a few references to pactualism in the charters; and unquestionably many pacta have been lost. Nevertheless, given the relative abundance of Gallegan monastic *pergaminos* surviving from the first centuries of the Reconquista, it is remarkable that more pacta have not come down to us from the ancient *reino*. It looks very much as if pactual monasticism never effectively reestablished itself in Galicia after the eighth century, partly because the Sancta Communis Regula had collapsed, partly because most monastic colonizers, in the repopulation of the western zone of the Peninsula, propagated the Visigothic tradition, but also because the chief center of pactual monasticism shifted to the eastern marchlands of the Asturo-Leonese state.

Certainly the contrast between Galicia and the East is sharp. Not four, but at least seventeen pacta, widely distributed over this area have been found: one from Asturias de Santillana, four from Liébana, one from the Rioja Alta and eleven from Castile. In addition, a fair number of references to lost pacta, and certain charters containing excerpts from the *RMC* pactum, attest considerable familiarity with pactual monasticism. The Castilian pacta, historically the most significant, fall into two clearly defined types, one more or less closely based upon the *RMC* model, the other markedly different in both language and juridical structure. To the *RMC* type four, probably five, Castilian pacta belong:

1. 855: the Rodanius pactum, from San Pedro de Tejada, north of the

---

fols. 151 v., col. 2-152 r., col. 2. This text will be edited in my study mentioned, *supra*, note 2, p. 516.

[1] A. López Ferreiro, *Historia de la Santa A. M. Iglesia de Compostela* (Santiago, 1898-1901), II, Apéndices, no. ix.

[2] *Portugaliae Monumenta Historica* (Lisbon, 1856-91), Diplomata, I, no. cccxlii, third part; also in Miguel Ribeiro de Vasconcellos, *Notícia Histórica do Mosteriro da Vacariça* (Lisbon, 1854).

Ebro in the Valdivielso valley (prov. Burgos, p. j. Lerma) [1]. This follows the *RMC* archetype fairly closely but omits the passages dealing with the *traditio* of the monks to the abbot, internal conspiracy, the role of *saiones* and bishops in the recovery of deserters and the appeal to the *episcopus sub regula* and *comes defensor* [2].

2. circ. 870: the Guisandus pactum, from San Juan de Orbañanos, near Valpuesta (prov. Burgos, p. j. Villarcayo, ayunt. Valle de Tobalina) [3]. Along with abridgement of certain *RMC* passages, this makes much the same omissions as the Rodanius pactum (although it does provide for direct access to the abbot in case of grievance) and is almost certainly connected with it through a common ancestor.

3. 924-5: the Nonna Bella pactum from San Miguel de Pedroso, south of Belorado (prov. Burgos) [4]. The pactual text proper has been lost; what remains is simply an abbatial *traditio* followed by the nuns' signatures, as in the codas of the Argilegus and Eufrasia pacta. Pérez de Urbel stoutly defends the 759 date found in the San Millán cartulary, but the cluster of Pedroso diplomas in the tenth and eleventh centuries corroborates Serrano's allocation of the text in the reign of Fruela II (924-5) [5].

4. 930: the Eufrasia pactum, from San Mamés de Ura, in the Mataviejas valley south of Burgos (prov. Burgos, p. j. Lerma) [6]. Here the excisions are

---

[1] Gregorio de Argáiz, *La Soledad Laureada por San Benito y sus Hijos* (Madrid, 1675), VI, 423-6 (with the impossible date 773, which is accepted by A. de Yépes, *Corónica General de la Orden de San Benito* [Irache, 1609-21], V, 331); Pérez de Urbel, *Historia del Condado de Castilla* [hereafter cited as *HCC*], III, 1058-60. Pérez de Urbel, *HCC*, I, 193, dates this text 'alrededor de 860'. Francisco de Berganza, who saw the lost original in the Oña archive, dates it 845 in his *Antigüedades de España* (Madrid, 1719-21), I, 241; this is also unacceptable, since Ordoño I's reign does not begin before 850, but permits restoration of 855 as the true reading.

[2] From the reference in this pactum to the Sancta Communis Regula, it should not be deduced that the Gallegan monastic federation reappeared in Castilian pactualism, but only that the Rodanius text descends from a period when the federal organization was still in existence.

[3] Barrau-Dihigo, 'Chartes de l'église de Valpuesta', no. viii; Argáiz, VI, 409-11. Cf. *HCC*, III, 1072-3; Z. García Villada, 'Valpuesta: una diócesis desaparecida', *Gesammelte Aufsätze zur Kulturgeschichte Spaniens = Spanische Forschungen der Görresgesellschaft*, erste Reihe, V (Münster i. W., 1935), 215-6. On the date, *HCC*, III, 1072-3.

[4] L. Serrano, *Cartulario de San Millán de la Cogolla* (Madrid, 1930), p. 1. See *HCC*, I, 94-5; III, 1035-6; L. Serrano, *El Obispado de Burgos y Castilla Primitiva* (Madrid, 1935), I, 76-7. The 778 or 858 document cited by L. Barrau-Dihigo, 'Recherches sur l'histoire politique du royaume asturien (718-910)', *Rev. Hisp.*, LII (1921), p. 340, and *HCC*, I, 231, n. 11, cannot be ascribed to Pedroso, which was a nunnery.

[5] Serrano, *San Millán*, nos. 35, 36, 37, 57, 58, 61.

[6] Herwegen, pp. 11-14; L. Serrano, *Cartulario de San Pedro de Arlanza* (Madrid, 1925), pp. 26-9.

much greater, the sections on conspiracy, punishment of recalcitrants and recovery of deserters all being omitted completely.

5. 1044: the Arcisclus or Arciselus pactum, from Santa María de Sotovellanos (prov. Burgos, p. j. Villadiego) [1]. This pactum, as yet unpublished, seems to follow rather closely (if I interpret Pérez de Urbel's précis aright) the Rodanius pactum of 855.

From these five chance survivors of doubtless scores of lost pacta, and from references in other *pergaminos*, the expansion of Gallegan pactualism in ninth and tenth century Castile can be reconstructed in more detail than might be supposed. The most striking fact is the way in which their geography and chronology attach these documents to successive stages of Castilian frontier repopulation [2]. The Guisandus pactum (ca 870) was drawn up at Orbañanos, where the monastery of San Juan is known to have been founded by the same Guisandus in 867 [3]. This put it well within the colonizing sphere of the monastic see of Valpuesta, so prominent in the ninth century resettlement of the whole Tobalina district above the Ebro [4]. The monasticism at Valpuesta and in its dependent areas was pactual in character, as can be seen from the Sonna and Munnina grant (865) to Santos Cosme y Damián de Val de Rama [5], Bishop Diego of Valpuesta's donation of 929 to his church [6], and the reference to the 'pactum regule'

---

1 Edited only in abridged form from Archivo de Silos, MS 29, fol. 1, by Pérez de Urbel, *HCC*, III, 1325; cf. Yepes, V, 333 v.-334; Berganza, I, 371. Publication of the complete text would be welcome.

2 On Castilian repopulation in this period, see in general R. Menéndez Pidal, *Documentos Lingüísticos de España. I. Reino de Castilla* (Madrid, 1919), pp. 1-12; ídem, *Orígenes del Español* (Madrid, 1929), I, 497-502; *HCC*, I, 107-140; 165-284; Cl. Sánchez-Albornoz, 'La repoblación del reino astur-leonés', *Humanidades*, XXV (Buenos Aires, 1936), 1.ª parte, pp. 37-55; ídem, 'Orígenes de Castilla. Cómo nace un pueblo', *Revista de la Universidad de Buenos Aires*, 3.ª época, I (1943), pp. 275-296; L. Serrano, *El Becerro Gótico de Cardeña* (Silos-Valladolid, (1910), pp. xv-xl; S. Ruiz, 'Burgos (Diocèse)', *Dictionnaire d'Histoire et de Géographie Ecclésiastique*, X (1938), cols. 1312-1319.

3 A. de Llorente, *Noticias históricas de las Tres Provincias Vascongadas* (Madrid, 1807), III, pp. 102-3; Serrano, *Cart. de San Millán*, no. 10; *HCC*, III, no. 35.

4 Barrau-Dihigo, 'Chartes de l'église de Valpuesta', 282-387; García Villada, 'Valpuesta: una diócesis desaparecida', p. 215; *HCC*, I, 117-124.

5 Barrau-Dihigo, no. v; *HCC*, III, no. 33.

6 Barrau-Dihigo, no. xiii; *HCC*, III, no. 109.

in the tenth century *traditio* of Gugina to the same bishop and Valpuesta [1]. This means that almost certainly from the erection of the Valpuestan see under Bishop Juan in 804 the monasticism of this important Castilian frontier diocese followed the Gallegan pactual tradition.

No less certainly does the San Pedro de Tejada pactum prove pactual monasticism accompanied the Castilian advance into the Valdivielso triangle of the Trueba, Losa and Ebro rivers [2]. In 855 Rodanius and his monks, indeed, must have been raising their abbey walls almost as early as Count Rodrigo of Castile (850-873) was constructing the nearby *castillo* of Tetelia as a safeguard for this dangerous frontier salient [3]. It was Rodrigo also who in 860 repopulated Amaya, from the vicinity of which we have the Sotovellanos pactum; but this text is too late to do more than attest that in 1044 Gallegan pactualism still flourished here, without throwing direct light upon its original introduction in the late ninth or early tenth century.

The next great Castilian colonization period, associated with Rodrigo's son, Count Diego Porcelos, who became the *poblador* of Burgos in 880, has left no pacta extant. But both the Nonna Bella and Eufrasia pacta, from districts lying east and south of Burgos, show pactualism continued to accompany new border expansion. The Nonna Bella pactum links the Gallegan tradition with Ordoño II of Leon's determined drive toward Nájera and the Rioja Alta, a drive followed by monastic settlement, as we know from his foundation in 923 of Santa Coloma on the Alesón, near Nájera [4]. The Eufrasia pactum (930) of San Mamés de Ura in turn demonstrates that pactualism also moved into the plains country south of Burgos, as far as the valleys of the Arlanza and the Ura (modern Mataviejas). This region was first opened to settlers at the end of the ninth century and, in the first quarter of the tenth

---

1 Barrau-Dihigo, no. ix.

2 *HCC*, I, 187-190.

3 Ibid., pp. 197-9. Note that San Salvador de Oña, which was located across the Ebro south of Tejada, and which eventually acquired San Pedro, was pactual from at least 922, as we learn from the 944 charter of restoration (*HCC*, III, no. 185).

4 Yepes, IV, 443 v. (esc. xx); Risco, *Esp. Sagr.*, xxxiii, 469-470.

century, was thickly planted with abbeys as eminent as Cardeña, Arlanza, and Silos [1]. Many, if not all, of these new houses must have been pactual. San Mamés stands, however, as the most southern outpost of pactualism of the *RMC* type in Castile, its further advance to the Duero and beyond doubtless being prevented by the advent of the Benedictine Rule.

While the Mataviejas line, or perhaps better, the Mataviejas-Arlanza line, thus represents the extreme limit reached by Gallegan pactual monasticism in Castile, the question of its original introduction into the county has still to be explored. First, however, it is imperative to examine two other, possibly earlier, eastern areas of pactual monasticism, the history of which is intimately linked with the Castilian problem. One of these is Liébana, the sierra-walled valley of the upper Deva, where a flourishing monasticism can be found as early as the second half of the eighth century. Here was San Martín, later Santo Toribio, de Liébana, then one of the foremost abbeys of the Peninsula, with an active scriptorium associated with the production of Beatus' magnificently illustrated *In Apocalipsin libri duodecim,* and the anti-Adoptionist tracts of Beatus and Etherius. Besides Santo Toribio there were numerous other houses in this region, which from a relatively early date yields important testimony to the pactual character of its cenobitism. Four Liébana pacta, dating between 790 and 941, have come down to us:

1. 790: the Alvaro pactum, from a monastery at or near Caldas, north of modern Potes (prov. Santander, p. j. Potes) [2]. This brief colorless text has no visible connection with the *RMC* archetype, and its relatively weak concept of the monastic polity recalls the communities based on the *sacramentum* or *iuramenta* attacked in *RMC,* c. i.

2. 818: the Argilegus pactum, from Santos Pedro y Pablo de Naroba, at or near modern Venta de Naroba, a few kms. south of Potes [3]. This follows

[1] Serrano, *Obispado de Burgos,* I, 161-6; A. Cotarelo Valledor, *Historia Crítica y Documentada de la Vida y Acciones de Alfonso III el Magno* (Madrid, 1933), pp. 411-6.

[2] E. Jusué, 'El libro cartulario del monasterio de Santo Toribio de Liébana', *Bol. Acad. Hist.,* XLV (1904), pp. 411-2; *HCC,* III, 1335-6.

[3] Sánchez-Albornoz, 'Serie de documentos inéditos del reino de Asturias', *Cuad. Hist. Esp.,* I-II, (1944), pp. 334-7; *HCC,* III, 1044-7. A photostat of this *pergamino* (A. H. N., Clero, San Julián de Samos, Leg. 794) in my possession

the *RMC* text fairly faithfully but omits the creed, combines the prescriptions on the punishment of rebels and conspirators, and, like the Guisandus pactum, sanctions direct approach to the abbot in cases of grievance.

3. 850-855?: the Osanius pactum, from San Pedro de Viñón, several kms. north of Potes [1]. A fairly simple pactum, chiefly devoted to the formal *traditio* of persons and property to the abbot, this draws upon the *RMC* text for only two passages, the vow of obedience ('quidquid nostrum', etc.) and the abbot's penal rights against rebels.

4. 941: the Ailo pactum, from Santa María de Piasca, southeast of Potes [2]. This belongs to the *RMC* type but deletes the sections on conspiracy and scourging; in contrast, the passage on the pursuit of *fugitivi*, which the Argilegus pactum omits, is retained.

Whether Santo Toribio itself was pactual cannot be securely determined in the absence of any pacta from this house, but since a 959 charter of the monk Flacinus to its abbot Opila employs phraseology borrowed from the *RMC* archetype [3], it may fairly be inferred that in the middle tenth century Santo Toribio was pactual, and that in view of its *ambiente* it may well have been so from its foundation in the eighth century. Certainly the four pacta just reviewed reflected an ancient and widely disseminated tradition, reaching back at least to the end of the eighth century and the first decades of the ninth. This is older evidence than we have found for Castile, and the descent of Castilian pactualism from that of Liébana becomes, therefore, a legitimate hypothesis.

At this point, a second pactual center on the margins of Castile demands consideration. From the abbey of Santillana del Mar, in Asturias de Santillana, there has been preserved the pactum of Indulfus (980) [4]. This is a late pactum, not

---

confirms the reading 'Naruoba' as against 'Nazaoba' (*HCC*, III, 1045). On Venta de Naroba, cf. *Mapa Militar Itinerario de España* (publ. by the Depósito de la Guerra), Hoja 14. Two modern copies of this diploma exist in the *Tumbo Nuevo* of Lugo (A. H. N., Códices, no. 363), fols. 336-8.

1 *HCC*, III, 1348-9. Pérez de Urbel reads 'ad baselica sancti Petri adiutum', but the illegible phrase after 'sancti Petri' in the Liébana *Cartulario*, fol. 25 v., col. 1, is clearly topographic; and a 942 charter of this same house (*Cartulario*, fols. 33 v.-34 r.) proves the reading should be 'sancti Petri ad uinionem', i. e., San Pedro de Viñón.

2 F. Fita, 'El monasterio dúplice de Piasca', *Bol. Acad. Hist.*, XXXIV (1899), pp. 449-450; *HCC*, III, 1372-3.

3 *HCC*, III, Apénd. II, no. lxi: 'contumax aut inobediens', etc.

4 E. Jusué, *Libro de Regla o Cartulario de la Antigua Abadía de Santillana del Mar* (Madrid, 1912), no. xxix.

only in its date but in its content. Its linguistic similarities to the *RMC* model are few; it retains only such elements as a creed, a *traditio,* a vow of obedience and recognition of abbatial rights of punishment and pursuit. It is a unilateral covenant, containing nothing to limit the abbot's authority or protect the rights of the monks. This document proves Santillana a pactual house in the second half of the tenth century, a conclusion sustained by the charter of circ. 965 from the *presbiter* Heredus and his *gasalianes* to the abbot Albarus, which, while not a pactum, contains an excerpt from the *RMC* archetype [1]. Undoubtedly, the Indulfus pactum descends from a more primitive prototype; but when this first reached eastern Asturias and how far beyond Santillana it once circulated, we have no means of determining. For central Asturias, one other house can perhaps be classified as pactual: San Vicente de Oviedo. For, although the 781 foundation charter of this monastery is interpolated and must be used with caution, yet it does have a pactum-like base authentic enough to go back to the eighth century [2]. It is a very simple type, unrelated to the *RMC* form, a mere foundation document with a simple *traditio* of their persons and property by the monks to the abbot, Fromistanus. Whatever the value of this text, it is unique in central Asturias, where monasticism almost invariably followed the Visigothic tradition. This contrasts with eastern Asturias where, limited as the documentation is, pactualism, as at Santillana, appears more firmly rooted. Nevertheless, with evidence so scant, one can hardly estimate the strength of pactualism in eastern Asturias or its contribution to that of Castile, influential as that contribution may have been.

The appearance of pactual monasticism as early as the end of the eighth century in Castile, Liébana and (probably at the same time) in eastern Asturias, and its absence (except for the lone San Vicente de Oviedo trace) in the intervening areas of central Asturias and León, point to the conclusion that the Gallegan tradition was introduced directly from the territory of Braga, where it survived as late as the mid-

1 *Ibid.,* no. lv.

2 L. Serrano, *Cartulario de San Vicente de Oviedo* (Madrid, 1929), no. 1.

eighth century. This would logically connect the shift from west to east with the repopulation policies of Alfonso I (739-757) who is known to have evacuated the Christian inhabitants of the trans-Miño area and to have transferred them elsewhere[1]. The Chronicle of Alfonso III specifically states that Alfonso I repopulated Liébana, Trasmiera (eastern Asturias beyond Santillana and across the river Miera) and 'Bardulies quae nunc appellatur Castella'[2]. Since Alfonso's depopulation between Duero and Miño occurred circ. 750 and the evidences of pactualism in Liébana and Castile first appear at the end of the eighth and beginning of the ninth centuries, it seems reasonable to conclude that soon after the middle of the eighth century the majority of Gallegan monks in the environs of Braga abandoned their old pactual houses and —probably along with numerous other Gallegos— were colonized in the eastern borderlands of the kingdom. From Bardulia, i. e., the lands along and beyond the Ebro, the fierce Muslim attacks under Alfonso I's immediate successors must soon have driven these hapless settlers[3]. Hence the pactualism that by 800 appears in the van of Castilian expansion must go back to unknown houses located in the northernmost nucleus of primitive Castile, and doubtless also to the pactual abbeys of eastern Asturias and Liébana.

Finally, it may be noted in passing that recognition of the existence of centers of Gallegan monasticism in the Asturo-Leonese East promises to throw new light upon the Spanish connections of Benedict of Aniane. It has always been a mystery how this Carolingian reformer of the early ninth century secured for his *Codex regularum* a mass of Gallegan material, including works only incompletely preserved, or not preserved at all in Spain, such as the *Regula sanctorum Pauli et Stephani,* Valerius' *De genere monachorum,* and the *RMC.* It can now be suggested that Benedict acquired these seventh century Gallegan writings from *codices regularum* and other MSS made available to him through eastern Asturo-Leonese houses of Gallegan origin.

---

1 A. Ballesteros y Beretta, *Historia de España,* (2nd. ed., Barcelona, 1943-4), II, 245-6; Barrau-Dihigo, 'Royaume asturien', pp. 143-4.

2 Ed. García Villada, p. 69.

3 *HCC,* I, 87-105.

What has been said so far of Castilian pactualism relates entirely, it should be understood, to pactualism of the *RMC* tradition, the direct Gallegan origin of which is indisputable. But in tenth century Castile there also circulated a second pactual formula, markedly different from the *RMC* covenant. Not contractual but unilateral, this pactum contains no elements of abbatial limitation; under it the monks, having formally affirmed their election of a named individual as abbot, hand themselves over to him without reservation, promising obedience and accepting his undefined powers of command. Herwegen, classifying this formula in his third category as furthest removed from the *RMC* model, noted these juridical features but left unexamined the problem of its development and distribution [1]. Five examples of it (six, if the unpublished Riojan pactum in the Conde de Mora Collection belongs to this group) [2] are known:

1. A model pactum, first identified as Spanish by Mabillon, who discovered it prefixed to the *Regula monachorum* of St Isidore of Seville in a 'codex vetustissimus' of Lérins [3]. The date, provenance and present whereabouts of this MS, if it still exists, are all unknown.

2. 921: the Petrus pactum, from Santos Pedro y Pablo 'in valle qui vocitatur Azadina', otherwise unknown but located in either the Rioja Alta or Castile [4].

---

[1] Herwegen, pp. 23-4, 35, 37-9.

[2] Discovered by Sánchez-Albornoz, 'Serie de documentos inéditos del reino de Asturias', *Cuad. Hist. Esp.*, I-II (1944), p. 317.

[3] J. Mabillon, *Annales Ordinis Sancti Benedicti* (Lucca, 1739), I, 332; Herwegen, p. 23.

[4] A. Tomás González, *Colección de Cédulas, Cartas-Patentes, Provisiones, Reales Órdenes y Otros Documentos Concernientes á las Provincias Vascongadas* (Madrid, 1829-33; vols. V-VI bear the title *Colección de Privilegios, Franquezas, Exenciones y Fueros Concedidos á Varios Pueblos y Corporaciones de la Corona de Castilla)*, VI, 7-9; *HCC*, III, no. 89 bis. González found this pactum in a *registro* at Simancas of *privilegios* from San Martín de Albelda, in the Rioja. For Pérez de Urbel, the citation of Ordoño II rather than a Navarrese ruler in the regnal formula proves the abbey Castilian. This is probably correct, although circ. 921 Ordoño II was making repeated efforts to annex the Rioja Alta and founding monasteries in that territory; cf. his 923 charter to Santa Coloma near Nájera (n. 4, p. 520, *supra)*. The fact that the *Becerro Gótico* documents never locate Cardeña 'in valle' but simply 'in locum qui dicitur Cardenia', 'in locum nominatum Caradigna', etc., militates against acceptance of Pérez de Urbel's conjecture that 'Azadina' (for reasons unknown to me Sánchez-Albornoz,

3. 931: the Stefanus pactum, from San Juan de Tabladillo, south of Burgos on the Mataviejas river, near Santibáñez del Val and Silos (prov. Burgos, p. j. Lerma) [1].

[4. 950: the unpublished pactum, probably of this type, in the Colección del Conde de Mora (Madrid, A. H. N.), no. 93; from 'San Martín' de Laturce, near Albelda in the Rioja] [2].

5. 959: the Urraca pactum, from San Julián de Villagonzalo Pedernales, a few kms. southwest of Burgos on the road to Arcos [3].

6. 975: the Azenarus pactum, from San Martin de Modúbar southeast of Burgos [4].

Four, possibly five, of the preceding pacta, all dating between 921-975, were drawn up in Castilian or Riojan monasteries. This provides the chief clue to the place and date of composition of this type of pactual formula. Three of the list emanate from well known abbeys, San Juan de Tabladillo, San Julián de Villagonzalo Pedernales and San Martín de Modúbar, located in the territory and diocese of Burgos. The Petrus pactum is either directly Castilian, as Pérez de Urbel's Cardeña hypothesis assumes, or indirectly so, since Riojan monasticism is a frontier offshoot, in this period, of the Castilian [5]. The Laturce text falls in the same category. Thus a Castilian or rather Burgalese provenance can be posited, and it will be convenient henceforth to cite this formula as the Burgos pactum to distinguish it from the *RMC* type.

On the chronological side, the Petrus pactum establishes 921 as the year before which the Burgos pactum must have been

---

'Serie de documentos', p. 317, reads 'Azadiba') is a corruption of 'Karadigna', i. e., Cardeña. Cf. also these *Estudios*, I, pp. 515-518.

1 M. Férotin, *Recueil des Chartes de l'Abbaye de Silos* (Paris, 1897), no. 2; Herwegen, pp. 19-20; Serrano, *Cart. de Arlanza*, pp. 29-30, and references there cited; *HCC*, III, no. 120. In his *Anti-Ferreras* (Madrid, 1724), p. 105, Diego Martínez de Cisneros lists three San Juan de Tabladillo pacta then in the San Pedro de Arlanza archive, but describes only two. One, of 931, is the Stefanus pactum; the other, dated 954 and now apparently lost, was probably the pactum of Stefanus' unknown successor and doubtless of similar type.

2 N. 2, p. 13, *supra*.

3 Berganza, I, 240-1; Herwegen, p. 22; Serrano, *Becerro Gótico de Cardeña*, no. cxv.

4 Yepes, I, 93; Berganza, II, 411-12; Herwegen, p. 21; Serrano, *op. cit.*, no. xlviii. Cf. Yepes, V, 66 v.-67 v.; Berganza, I, 339-40; *HCC*, III, no. 432.

5 C. J. Bishko, 'Salvus of Albelda and frontier monasticism in tenth-century Navarre', *Speculum*, XXIII (1948), pp. 559-590, especially pp. 583-589.

produced. A *terminus post quem* can be deduced from two other points. First, the non-appearance of this formula in Benedict of Aniane's *Codex regularum,* which, as already remarked, contains considerable monastic material from the eastern Asturo-Leonese pactual centers; this throws our text after 815. Secondly, the 931 Stefanus pactum from Tabladillo links it with an area not colonized before circ. 900; and if we assume that the Tabladillo text reached San Juan from the north and derives from lost ancestors of the Urraca (959) and Azenarus (975) pacta, then we must reckon in turn that the settlement dates for Amaya (860) and Burgos (880) establish the second half of the ninth century as the earliest date for that region. There is nothing in Mabillon's description of the lost Lérins codex as 'vetustissimus' to be of assistance here, but also nothing in contradiction to the foregoing data. In broad terms, then, the period 850-921 can be tentatively accepted as the time when this peculiarly Castilian type of pactum first circulated in the territory of Burgos.

These chronological and geographic limits could be defined more narrowly if it were possible to determine whether the text was written first in the older monasteries around Burgos itself, the group with which the Villagonzalo and Modúbar pacta associate it; or had been composed earlier to the south in the Arlanza-Mataviejas zone, as the early date of the Tabladillo pactum suggests. The assumption of older prototypes of the Urraca and Azenarus examples favors the first hypothesis, while the second finds support not only in the Tabladillo pactum's early date but in the probability that the earliest of all, the Petrus pactum, reached the Rioja from the south. For the Albelda documents indicate that Riojan monastic connections with Castile tended to run through Silos and the south, rather than directly across the Bureba from the northern Burgos area [1]. The Laturce text probably reached the Rioja through the same channel; and the fact that the Eufrasia pactum of San Mamés de Ura, which is of *RMC* type, survives only in the *privilegios* of Santa María la Real de Nájera [2], further attests that early Riojan connections with Casti-

[1] *Ibid.*, p. 589.

[2] Herwegen, p. 14, n. 1.

lian pactualism followed the southern route. In short, the earliest center of Burgos type pactualism may well have been the Arlanza-Mataviejas group of early tenth century frontier abbeys. This is a subject upon which some further light may be thrown by considering the circumstances under which the Burgos pactum evolved and the purpose for which it was designed.

The essential feature of the Burgos type of pactum, as Herwegen realized, is its abandonment of Gallegan contractualism for the orthodox monarchical abbatiate of Western monastic history. Such a radical Castilian shift from *RMC* pactual practice as this represents could have been motivated by recognition of advantages inherent in orthodox constitutionalism; or by adoption of Visigothic concepts from Asturo-Leonese houses to the west and north; or as a reaction to the spread of Benedictinism in Castile. There is every indication that the last motive was the decisive one. From the later decades of the ninth century, as the three earliest Castilian MSS of Smaragdus' *Expositio in regulam beati Benedicti* testify [1], the powerful reformed Benedictinism of Benedict of Aniane and the Carolingians was crossing the Pyrenees into the plains and valleys of Castile and the Rioja, as well as farther west all the way to Galicia [2]. Count Fernán González of Castile (931-970), Alfonso III of León (866-910) and Sancho Garcés I of Navarre (905-925) officially championed this foreign monastic invasion, with which the rise of such famous Spanish Benedictine centers as San Pedro de Cardeña, San Pedro de Arlanza, Santo Domingo de Silos and San Martín de Albelda, to name no others, is connected. Indeed, at the very time Gallegan pactualism was advancing south beyond Valpuesta and Tejada, Carolingian Benedictinism, leaping over the older northern foundations above the Ebro [3], was directing itself straight to the new frontier foundations below the river, and engaging pactualism in an intensive struggle for Castilian monastic supremacy.

It is from this clash between Gallegan pactualism and Carolingian Benedictinism on the Castilian frontier in the

1 Bishko, pp. 586, 588.

2 Pérez de Urbel, *Monjes españoles,* II, 384-9.

3 Bishko, p. 585.

early tenth century that the Burgos type of pactum must have emerged. San Juan de Tabladillo under its abbot Stefanus, was in fact a Benedictine abbey, apparently by 924 [1]. San Martín de Modúbar had been under the Monte Cassino observance at least three decades before, in 975, its monks subscribed to the Azenarus pactum [2]. There is no good reason for identifying the Burgos pactum with the Isidorian Rule simply because of their juxtaposition in Mabillon's Lérins MS [3]. Early medieval manuscripts of St Isidore's Rule alone are so extremely rare in Spain [4], that it seems very likely the Lérins MS was originally the initial section of a *codex regularum* which contained other rules as well as the Isidorian, and commenced with a pactual formula, just as the *codex regularum* of MS Escorialensis a I 13 opens with the Sabaricus pactum [5]. In just such *codices* or *libri regularum* many Spanish Benedictine abbeys found their text of the Rule of St Benedict [6]. It is not necessary to insist that only Benedictine monasteries used the Burgos pactum; the relatively numerous Villagonzalo Pedernales charters do not mention the Rule of Monte Cassino at all [7]. But the juridical content of the Burgos pactum approaches the Benedictine standard very closely, and its adoption in tenth century Castilian Benedictine houses is unquestionable. If we could determine whether Castilian Benedictinism first established itself on a large scale in the vicinity of Burgos, or in the Arlanza-Mataviejas zone, it would be possible to reach a conclusion as to whether the Burgos pactum originated near the town of Burgos or farther south. But this must wait upon closer critical study of Benedictine penetration into Spain.

While the appearance of the Burgos pactum can only be

---

1 Serrano, *Cart. de Arlanza,* no. iv.

2 Serrano, *Becerro Gótico de Cardeña,* no. xlvi.

3 Pérez de Urbel, *Monjes españoles,* II, 372-5.

4 C. H. Beeson, *Isidor-Studien* (Munich, 1913; *Quellen und Untersuchungen zur lateinischen Philologie des Mittelalters,* Bd. IV, Heft 2), pp. 58-9.

5 G. Antolín, 'Historia y descripción de un «Codex Regularum» del siglo IX', *Ciudad de Dios,* LXXV (1908), p. 305.

6 Pérez de Urbel, *Monjes españoles,* II, 376 ff.

7 Serrano, *Becerro Gótico de Cardeña,* nos. xcviii-cxxiii.

understood with reference to the rise of Castilian Benedictinism, it is no less vital to appreciate that the very invention of such an instrument, so alien to normal Benedictine practice, signifies that its purpose was to effect a compromise between the two rival monastic traditions — a compromise retaining traditional Castilian pactual elements in combination with Benedictine ascetic spirituality and ordinary regime. This Castilian effort at synthesis of peninsular and Carolingian Benedictine monastic institutions has already been discovered in other connections [1]. The recently identified *Libellus a regula sancti Benedicti subtractus,* written at San Martín de Albelda cir. 951/3-962 by the Benedictine abbot Salvus, reflects precisely the same effort at amalgamation in its mixture of pactual and Smaragdan-Benedictine materials. Albelda was itself, like Tabladillo and Modúbar, and probably also San Millán de la Cogolla, Silos, Arlanza, and others, both Benedictine and pactual. The unpublished Laturce pactum will doubtless provide another Riojan example of the same synthesis. A further by-product of the movement is the addition of two Spanish texts, *Item ex regula cuiusdam* and *Quid debent fratres uel sorores in monasterio serbare,* to Castilian Smaragdan MSS, from which they pass into Salvus' *Libellus* [2]. The Benedictinized pactual sections of the *Liber ordinum,* published by Férotin from the San Prudencio de Laturce MS, are also of prime significance in this connection, although the question whether they incorporate, as Herwegen thought [3], the juridical ideology of the *RMC* type pactum, or (as now seems possible) that of the Burgos type, remains unanswered. Thus the Burgos pactum fits perfectly into the framework of a Castilian-Carolingian monastic synthesis which persisted in Castile until the advent of the Cluniacs in 1033 under Sancho *el Mayor*.

Much still remains to be done before the role of Castilian monasticism in the first centuries of the Reconquista is fully understood. It will be enough for the present if we have

---

1 Bishko, 'Salvus of Albelda', pp. 583-9.

2 Pérez de Urbel, *Monjes,* II, 609-11; Bishko, pp. 581-2.

3 Pp. 39-50.

succeeded here in clarifying to some extent the significance of Gallegan pactualism in the whole process of Castilian repopulation. This is important not merely for medieval Spanish monastic history. If, as the pactual evidence would indicate, there occurred an extensive eighth century Gallegan colonization of the eastern districts of the Asturo-Leonese realm, the Gallegan element in the formation of Castile must henceforth be taken into serious consideration. It has often been noticed that, in comparison with those of Asturias and León, Castilian law, institutions, vocabulary and nomenclature are decidedly more Germanic [1]. Perhaps this puzzling phenomenon can now be at least partially explained by the settlement in early Castile of Gallegan colonists, both secular and ecclesistical, whose more Germanized juridical traditions, reaching back to the Suevic kingdom of Galicia, are attested by pactual monasticism itself.

University of Virginia.

[1] E. de Hinojosa, *El Elemento Germánico en el Derecho Español* (Madrid, 1915). For example, a Suevic origin may be suggested for the Germanic *gasalianes,* a term applied in primitive Castile to monks of a pactual community; cf. Pérez de Urbel, *HCC,* I, 175, n. 21, and Paulo Merêa in *Biblos,* XVI (1940), p. 55.

ADDITIONAL NOTE

In view of the extended discussion in Study I of this volume of the Galaico-Portuguese genesis and subsequent Castello-Riojan diffusion of Hispanic pactual monasticism, the present Note will address itself primarily to questions affecting certain of the pacta enumerated in the preceding catalogue. The completeness of this roundup of extant specimens has not been questioned by such leading authorities as Pérez de Urbel and Linage Conde.[1] Nevertheless, at several points revision is called for. No new pactual texts have been discovered since 1951 but some further traces of this distinctively peninsular cenobitism have been noted. In particular, one pactum, that associated with the abbot Sabaricus and long thought to be of Gallegan provenance, can now be ascribed to an eastern house; it therefore merits fresh consideration as an important adjunct to the Castilian group.

Antonio Floriano, in his *Colección diplomática*, rubrics as "pactos monásticos" seven documents of the Asturian epoch.[2] Of these, two are the Gallegan pacta of Absalon and Fulgaredus; another is the charter of San Vicente de Oviedo, allegedly of 781, which in addition to being heavily interpolated, as Floriano emphasizes, does not appear to me a true monastic pact at all; but the remaining three, those of Argilegus, Nonna Bella and Guisandus, are properly Castilian and were included in my catalogue above. Floriano however keeps in 900 the Guisandus pactum which I, following Argáiz and the evidence favoring an earlier date found also in Llorente (*Noticias hist. prov. vascongad.*, III, 102–3) and García Villada, fixed in "circ. 870" as against Barrau-Dihigo (900) and Pérez de Urbel (900?).[3] Floriano's reasoning in favor of the later chronology, as well as his incomplete coverage of the exegetical literature on the dating of this text, which indeed calls for an extended re-consideration impossible here, leave me of my original opinion. On the other hand, he omits altogether the pacts of Rodanius (855) and Osanius (850–855?) which I listed among the Castilian specimens. On the whole, Floriano's edition of the seven texts with its archival, bibliographical and toponymic exegesis is useful; but since he fails to draw upon either Herwegen's *Das Pactum des hl. Fruktuosus von Braga* or the section of Pérez de Urbel's *Monjes españoles* which summarizes the work of the German Benedictine,[4] this part of his

[1] J. Pérez de Urbel, "Vida y caminos del Pacto de San Fructuoso," *Rev. portuguesa de história*, VII (1963), 378; *idem*, "Carácter y supervivencia del Pacto de San Fructuoso," *Bracara Augusta*, XXII (1968), 233; A. Linage Conde, *Orígenes del monacato benedictino en la Península Ibérica* (León, 1973), I, 291–342.

[2] A. C. Floriano, *Diplomática española del periodo astur* (Oviedo, 1949–1951), I, nos. 7, 11, 14, 27, 62; II, nos. 102, 162. An eighth monastic pact, the Adaulfus fragment, is calendared, II, 396 (no. VIII), but not textually reproduced, from López Ferreiro (*Hist. Iglesia compost.*, II, Apéndices, 42–43, no. XXIII).

[3] *Supra*, p. 518, note 3.

[4] Pérez de Urbel, *Monjes*, I, 438–448; II, 372–375.

commentary is of severely limited value. To his credit, however, Floriano recognizes more adequately than either of the two monastic historians the interest of the abbatial component in what I have called in Study I, section 4, the binary pactum.

The Sabaricus pact found at the start of *Escorialensis* a.I.13 has now acquired much fresh import as a result of the illuminating study of this codex by Prof. Díaz y Díaz,[5] which demonstrates that this long hotly debated MS belongs not in the "eighth or ninth century" (p. 516, above), but in the tenth; and is furthermore to be assigned to the eastern, Castilian zone as against Galicia. The chronological problem had already been decided in favor of this later date by, *inter alios*, the authoritative Millares Carlo, for whom the famous colophon written *in monasterio Bobatele* by the nun-scribe Leodegundia, with its impossible coupling of era DCCCCL (912) and the reign of a King Alfonso, which various scholars corrected to 812 under Alfonso II, was at least in conformity with the manifestly tenth-century characteristics of the Visigothic hands used in the codex.[6] But on the basis of close paleographic analysis and a persuasive resolution of the colophonic chronological enigma Díaz y Díaz has now been able to fix the reign of Alfonso IV (925–931) as the authentic period not only of Leodegundia's portion of the MS (fols. 41–187) but—of more direct relevance to the present inquiry—also of the anterior section (now fols. 1–40).[7] This section contains the Sabaricus pact and also the Rules of St Benedict and St Fructuosus, extracts from the *Regula s. Isidori*, and various short prayers, all of which must have originally circulated as a separate "códice abacial", i.e., a *codex regularum*. At the commencement of these texts the abbot must have caused to be placed for safekeeping the juridical act of submission that still bears the subscriptions of the male and female members of his unknown community.[8] In the prominence given by *Regula s. Benedicti* in this primitive codex, and in the fact that the Isidorian materials clearly derive from the extra-Hispanic tradition of the code of the Andalusian metropolitan, Díaz y Díaz rightly finds that admixture of peninsular and trans-Pyrenean observances typical of 10th-century Castilian cenobitism.[9] Thus the monastic content confirms the chronology and geography posited by the paleographical data.

Codicological and other clues also induce Díaz y Díaz to ascribe the Leodegundia codex, and consequently the unknown monastery of Sabaricus, to a milieu of Leonese and Castilian cultural interchange; but if by this he intends to denote the Tierra de Campos, it may be objected that as yet we have no proof whatever of the presence of pactualism in the strongly Leonese cenobitism of this region where, as at Sahagún, Abellar, etc., only Visigothic, Mozarabic and Benedictine traditions are encountered

[5] M. Díaz y Díaz, "El códice monástico de Leodegundia (Escorial a. I. 13)," *Ciudad de Dios*, CLXXXI (1968), 567–587.

[6] A. Millares Carlo, "Manuscritos visigóticos," *Hispania Sacra*, XIV (1961), 352 (no. 17); also separately, Madrid-Barcelona, 1963.

[7] Díaz y Díaz, 572–577, 586–7.

[8] *Ibid.*, 575, 586. On the 93 subscriptions, with discussion of erasures and additions, the groupings of names added at the same time by particular scribes, and the evidence that, after some years of operating under the pact as an exclusively masculine community, Sabaricus' abbey accepted the admission of women and became a double house, see D. DeBruyne, "Les signataires du pacte de Sabaricus," *Rev. bénédictine*, XXVIII (1911), 80–86; Herwegen, "Die Unterschriften der Sabarikusurkunde," *ibid.*, XXIX (1912), 97–98. All these subscribants are unlikely to have affixed their signatures during the abbatiate of Sabaricus; probably the foundational pactum of the codex continued in use under his successors without change in the name of the abbot. Díaz y Díaz (582 and note 44) properly calls for onomastic study of these subscriptions in the context of the contemporary diplomas; this would throw light upon the chronology of use and doubtless narrow the geographical range as well.

[9] Pp. 576, 586.

in the 10th century. Even the great abbey of San Isidro de Dueñas (so close to and eventually incorporated into, the County of Castile) discloses no pactual symptoms in its relatively good documentation of the epoch, while its Benedictinism, and above all its dedication to and propagation of the cult of the Byzantine soldier-martyr Isidore of Chios, connects this house not with Galaico-Burgalese pactualism but with trans-Pyrenean France (Study VI). In short, the institutional signs point to an ambience well beyond Palencia to the south and west of Burgos for the Sabaricus pactum.

Certain other internal questions relating to this pactum also remain difficult to resolve. First there is the extraordinary business of the insertion of this text at the head of a *codex regularum*. All other Hispanic monastic pacts so far discovered that bear the name of a specific abbot or monastery exist in the form of single *pergaminos* or copies based upon these; none can be found in extant *codices regularum* or in the indices of contents of lost MSS of this type. To be sure, the formulaic pacta intended to serve as models do occur in close association with a Rule or Rules: the pactum of the *Regula communis* follows the final chapter of that work; of the four known occurrences of the *Consensoria monachorum*, two are appended to the *Regula s. Basilii*, and two appear as cap. 25 of the *Regula s. Isidori*.[10] In all these instances the position is terminal; but in the case of the lost MS of Lérins containing the model version of the Burgalese or Lérins formula, the pact apparently was intended to stand at the head of the index of capitular rubrics immediately preceding the *Regula s. Isidori*, although, since it followed in this codex the *Regula s. Benedicti* and the so-called *Capitulum de octo uitiis*, we cannot be sure that it ever actually formed the commencement of a separate MS of the Isidorian Rule.[11] In short, there is no exact parallel to the codicological position of the Sabaricus pact, or any firm basis for positing an ancient practice in which the implicitly ephemeral abbatial pacta were inserted in the permanent *codex regularum* of a house.

Nor is the mystery dispelled by the *ordines* of the Hispanic Rite where separation of pact and *liber regularum* seems plainly indicated, as we might expect. The rubric for the rite *in ordinatione abbatis* directs the abbot-elect to present to the bishop his *placitum tam pro se quam pro subditis de honestate uite regularis*, i.e., what we called above the binary pact; and after this ceremony and a prayer the bishop bestows the abbatial *baculum* and the *liber regularum*.[12] In the case of a newly consecrated abbess, no reference at all is made to the *placitum*; but once again we encounter episcopal presentation of *baculum* and *liber regule* (a significant shift to the singular).[13] Again, in connection with the reception of converts, it is ordered that the new monk's name be inscribed in the *pactionis libellus* or *testamenti libellus* which he himself, escorted by the priest and deacon celebrating the mass, places upon the altar.[14] This may be compared also with the practice followed, in the same century as the Sabaricus pact, at the Riojan nunnery of SS Nunilo and Alodia near Nájera: this proceeds without celebration of the sacrament: the *conuersa* receives the *carta pacti* from the hands of the abbess; places, or, if illiterate, has her name placed in this; and subsequently prostrates herself before the altar. While it may be unclear whether before this prostration she has deposited the pact upon the altar herself, or has merely returned it to the abbess, what is plain is the complete separation of pact from *liber regule*, especially plain since

[10] "*Consensoria Monachorum*" (Study II in this volume, 385–388).

[11] See M. Díaz y Díaz, "Aspectos de la tradición de la *Regula Isidori*," *Studia monastica*, V (1963), 27–57; and especially his "El manuscrito de Lérins de la *Regula Isidori*," *ibid.*, VII (1965), 365–382.

[12] *Liber ordinum*, ed. M. Férotin, *Ordo* XVIII (cols. 57–60).

[13] *Ibid.*, *Ordo* XXIII (cols. 67–68).

[14] *Ibid.*, *Ordo* XXVIIII (cols. 82–86).

we have the actual MS (*Aemilianensis* 62) of the *Libellus a regula sancti Benedicti subtractus* that served as the Rule of this convent.[15] Nowhere in any of these *ordines* does there appear the suggestion of a codex combining pact and *regulae*.

The Sabaricus pactum, as Herwegen noted, lacks the *invocatio* and *arenga* of the *Regula communis* archetype and commences abruptly in the middle of the *dispositio* with the words "et secundum editum apostolorum, etc." Now since the present arrangement of the initial *pliego* of a I.13 reveals that the folio now numbered 1 was almost certainly once preceded by two others,[16] and since this pact also adheres very closely to the order and content of the *Regula communis* model, with minor exceptions,[17] the chances are strong that the missing folia included a relatively extensive creed prefixed to the Gallegan archetype. But—a much more interesting possibility—did this credal passage itself follow a juridical act in which Sabaricus submitted himself to the constitutional authority of his congregation and made formal donation of his property to them or to the titular of the abbey? Space for such an abbatial pact would seem to have been available; but all we can safely believe is that a binary combination of abbatial and monacal pacts, of the sort occurring in other Castilian cases of this era,[18] cannot be entirely ruled out of consideration in any study of the Sabaricus text.

It should be noted that the Absalon pactum of 876 from Santa Eulalia de Búbal in Galicia, which in 1951 I termed unpublished (p. 516), had in fact been already twice edited, first by Sáez in 1947, again by |Floriano| in 1949 (Study I, note 95).

As for the distinctive Burgalese or Lérins pactual type, here again no new specimens have been discovered; but my classification of this formula as the product of a Carolingian-Hispanic synthesis of the ninth and tenth centuries in Castile and the Rioja has been directly challenged by Mundó, Pérez de Urbel and Díaz y Díaz, all of whom believe that this pact is of ancient and widespread Visigothic usage, and owes nothing to Galicia for its origin or later survival in Castile. Since I have tried at some length to refute this thesis in Study I, I shall not repeat here my reasons for maintaining the same position I adopted in 1951.

In two cases listed, however, brief comment is needed. Among the six pacts of Burgalese or Lérins type which are enumerated in this study, I included, although on a strictly tentative basis since I had not seen it, a supposedly Riojan example of 950 from San Martín (i.e., San Prudencio) de Laturce.[19] After some difficulty in tracking down this document, I have been able to determine that it is not a true pact at all, but simply a conventional *traditio* by which various monks surrender their persons to the authority of the abbot Dulquitus of San Martín de Albelda.[20] This item, bracketed above as no. 4 of the Burgalese type, and to be found in print in Ubieto Arteta's *Cartulario de*

[15] Cap. XXVI. Text in C. J. Bishko, "Salvus of Albelda and Frontier Monasticism in Tenth-Century Navarre," *Speculum*, XXIII (1948), 559–590, at 571–2), reprinted in my *Studies in Medieval Spanish Frontier History* (London, 1980), Study I; A. Linage Conde, *Una regla monástica riojana femenina del siglo X: el "Libellus a regula sancti Benedicti subtractus"* (Salamanca, 1973), 64–5.

[16] Díaz y Díaz, "Códice de Leodegundia," 573.

[17] The passages on conspiracy, pursuit of fugitives, excommunications, right of appeal; cf. Herwegen, *Pactum*, 11.

[18] "Pactual Tradition" (Study I, section 4).

[19] *Supra*, 526, no. [4].

[20] Profs. Cl. Sánchez Albornoz and H. B. Johnson, and Sra. Consuelo Gutiérrez del. Arroyo of the A. H. N., Madrid, have been of appreciated assistance in making it possible to identify this elusive diploma.

Albelda,[21] should therefore be eliminated entirely, thus reducing the known examples of this formula to five.

Finally, there is the Petrus pactum of 921 from a monastery of SS Pedro y Pablo *in ualle de Azadina*, which Pérez de Urbel on the basis of his own unjustified correction of this toponym to read *Caradigna* persists in identifying with San Pedro de Cardeña and using as the basis for claiming the foundation and continuing administration of Albelda on the part of the renowned Castilian abbey.[22] This arbitrary hypothesis, although it receives support from Ubieto Arteta's edition of the Albeldan diplomas, where once again without philological or documentary exegesis *Azadina* is revised to read *Karadina*,[23] finds no confirmation in the terminological usage of Cardeña's *pergaminos*, as I pointed out in 1951. The Petrus pactum is unquestionably of Riojan provenance, very possibly from a house that eventually passed into the hands of Albelda; but I have yet to see any good reason whatever for taking this community to be Albelda itself, or, on the grounds of an arbitrary alteration of the text, for linking Albelda and Cardeña.

---

[21] Ant. Ubieto Arteta, *Cart. de Albelda* (Valencia, 1960), 53–56 (no. 19).

[22] J. Pérez de Urbel, "La conquista de la Rioja y su colonización espiritual en el siglo X," in *Estudios dedicados a Menéndez Pidal*, I (Madrid), 495–534, at 516–17; the same dubious hypothesis reappears in his multi-volume works on the County of Castile.

[23] *Cart. de Albelda*, 9–10 (no. 1).

PORTUGUESE PACTUAL MONASTICISM IN THE ELEVENTH CENTURY: THE CASE OF SÃO SALVADOR DE VACARIÇA

Of recent years much interest has arisen in the question whether the pre-Benedictine Portuguese monasticism of the first four centuries of the Reconquista was continuous with the orthodox Mediterranean tradition of the Visigothic kingdom or, on the contrary, represents the survival in the western zone of the Peninsula of the heterodox, institutionally peculiar, «Fructuosan» or «pactual» form perfected between 650 and 711 in the Luso-Galaic northwest. The subject has secular connotations through linkage with, for example, the genesis of landlord-peasant-community associations of *incomuniação* and *benefactoria* type, or the formation of aristocratic domains clustered around familial *mosteiros privados*; and it illuminates certain lines of institutional-cultural diffusion in the complex convergence, between the Minho and Mondego, of indigenous «Mozarabic» elements and those penetrating the County of Portugal from Galicia or, via Trás-os-Montes and Beira Alta, from the Asturoleonese heartland.

In specifically historico-cenobitic terms, however, the key question is how to characterize the Portuguese monastic movement of the 8th-11th centuries within the remarkable (and hotly debatable) peninsular pattern of archaic but unmistakably orthodox tradition dominant in Asturias, Leon, eastern Spain from Pamplona to Barcelona, and al-Andalus, alongside varying forms of institutionalized pactualism found in comital Castile, the Rioja Alta and parts of the Atlantic West [1]. Distinctive of this second, in a non-theological sense «heterodox», tradition is its abandonment of the normal profession act,

(1) See in general Antonio Linage Conde, *Los orígenes del monacato benedictino en la Península Ibérica*, 3 t. (Léon, 1973), I, 289-342; C. J. Bishko, «Hispanic Monastic Pactualism: the Controversy Continues», *Classical Folia*, XXVII (1973), 173-185, and literature there cited; J. G. Freire and G. Rocca, «Patto», in *Dizionario degli istituti di perfezione*, VI, cols. 1292-1294 (in press).

addressed to God and the saints and entailing total personal submission to a virtually absolute monarchical abbot, and replacing it with the collective *pactum* (or *placitum*). This is a written covenant between an abbot and the whole corpus of his monks, who in making a *traditio* of their persons to his quasi-seigneurial authority (2), become members at the same time of the juridically privileged monastic congregation.

Because this uniquely Iberian cenobitic contractualism, which originally stipulated the rights and duties of both governor and community, including the latter's authorized rebellion against abbatial tyranny, first appears in late Visigothic Gallaecia, and is particularly well represented there by the model pactual formula appended to the so-called *Regula Communis*, it has traditionally but erroneously been ascribed to the metropolitan bishop of Braga St. Fructuosus († ca. 660--665). After 711 the pactum circulates in various forms and receives mention also in diplomatic and liturgical texts, while it displays with time an ever greater tendency to conform to the conventional unilateral cenobitic constitution. The collection and study of still extant specimens, first initiated in 1907 by Herwegen, has resulted in a considerable literature regarding their evolution and distribution, yet much of their history remains obscure and controversial (3).

So far as concerns the Galaico-Portuguese sector of the subject, with its special chronological and geographic problematics, this has been explored by, *inter alios*, Martins, Pérez de Urbel, Mattoso, Linage Conde and the present writer, but numerous questions remain acute. For Portugal, the argument necessarily gives particular prominence to the one known surviving specimen of a native monastic pactum, that drawn up at the relatively late date of 1045 between the abbot Tudeildus and the monks of the Beiran monastery of São

(2) Cf. José Orlandis, «"Traditio corporis et animae": laicos y monasterios en la Alta Edad Media española», *An. hist. derecho esp.*, XXIV (1954), 95-279; also in his *Estudios sobre instituciones monásticas medievales* (Pamplona, 1971), pp. 217-378.

(3) Ildefons Herwegen, *Das Pactum des hl. Fruktuosus von Braga: ein Beitrag zur Geschichte des suevisch-westgotischen Mönchtums und seines Rechtes* (Stuttgart, 1907; reprinted Amsterdam, 1965); Mário Martins, «O monacato de S. Frutuoso de Braga», *Biblos*, XXVI (1950), 315-342; J. Pérez de Urbel, «Vida y caminos del Pacto de San Fructuoso,» *Rev. Portuguesa de História*, VII (1963), 377-397; idem, «Carácter y supervivencia del Pacto de San Fructuoso», *Bracara Augusta*, XXII (1968), 226-242; J. Mattoso, «Sobrevivência do monaquismo em Portugal durante a Reconquista», *ibid.*, XXII (1968), 42-54: Linage Conde, *Orígenes*, I, 308-311, II, 741-746; C. J. Bishko, «Gallegan Pactual Monasticism in the Repopulation of Castile», in *Estudios dedicados a Menéndez Pidal*, II (Madrid, 1951), pp. 516-517.

Salvador de Vacariça. This is often taken to confirm beyond question the widespread existence of pactualism in Portuguese cenobitic circles through the 11th century. Nevertheless, for all the frequent mention of this instrument in the modern literature, its content and the precise circumstances of its promulgation have received little real analysis and stand in need of more serious scrutiny.

The Tudeildus pactum of 21 September 1045, originally published in 1854 from the *Livro Preto* of the Sé de Coimbra by Vasconcelos, and receiving a more critical redaction in the *Diplomata et Chartae* volume (1867) of the *Portugaliae Monumenta Historica*, can now also be consulted in the *editio princeps* of the *Livro Preto* recently issued by the University of Coimbra (4). Overlooked by Herwegen, it was first added to the corpus of Iberian pactual documentation, as then known, by P. Mário Martins, who in 1950 included it among other testimonia to the «evolução e sobrevivência do monacato de S. Frutuoso»; the following year I myself listed it as one of the only four discoverable Iberian monastic pacta comprising a «western» (i. e., Galaico-Portuguese) group within the class as a whole; and it has since been widely noticed (5).

In the pages of *Diplomata et Chartae* (henceforth *DC*) the act directed by the monastic community of São Salvador to their abbot Tudeildus stands last in a trio of inter-related texts which the editors have brought together from different parts of the *Livro Preto* and placed under the single number 342 (6). Each piece carries its own rubric (*pacti cartula, carta dimissionis, carta pacti uel placiti*), perhaps taken over from a lost cartulary of Vacariça, more likely imposed by the scribes of the Sé de Coimbra in assembling the *Livro Preto* from a mass of pergaminhos. Our act, the *carta pacti uel placiti*, since it precedes its two companions both in logic and indicated order

---

(4) Miguel Ribeiro de Vasconcel(l)os, *Noticia Historica do Mosteiro da Vacariça*... (Lisbon, 1854), pp. 26-27 (prova n.° 6) (also *Memorias da Academia Real das Sciencias de Lisboa*, classe sci: mor., n. s. 1, pt. 1, 1854); *PMH, DC*, I (Lisbon, 1867), pp. 211-212; *Livro Preto da Sé de Coimbra*, 3 t. (Coimbra, 1977-1979. Publicações do Arquivo da Universidade de Coimbra). Since the last named work has not been available to me, documents will be cited here as in *DC*.

(5) Martins, *Monacato*, pp. 405-411; Bishko, *Gallegan Pactualism*, p. 517; Mattoso, *Sobrevivência*, p. 45; Linage Conde, I, 310.

(6) In fact, the dossier of 1045 contains five texts, since the *Livro Preto* preserves a second version of the *cartula dimissionis*, of which *DC*, pp. 209-211, records the variant readings; *DC* 390, printed as of 1053 because it bears the date «XI kalendas octobris era LXXXXªIª superacta millesima» (a palpable scribal error for LXXXªIIIª), is a doublet of the *pacti cartula* to Floritus, with minor textual differences and slightly fuller list of attestations.

of composition (7), might well have been printed first of the triad. It is not possible here to reproduce it or attempt close exegesis, but the component elements can readily be summarized.

An opening sequence of credal and scriptural passages of ascetico--spiritual import precedes the formal declaration, addressed to God and the abbot Tudeildus by *nos omnes qui subter notati sumus*, of the monks' commitment to reside in the monastery obedient to his full authority. The entire remainder of the act defines this as embracing three specific powers: (i) flogging and denial of the sacrament to any monk guilty of actions *contra regulam et tuum preceptum*; (ii) pursuit and return of monks abandoning the community in order to dwell elsewhere, along with excommunication of any priest, monk, or laic sheltering such fugitive; and (iii) severe flogging of monks detected in secret conspiracy with their kinsmen or other persons. Lastly come the date, 21 September 1045, and the names of two confirmants: Petrus frater, Randulfus presbiter.

Several preliminary observations regarding the character of this unique Portuguese monastic pactum are in order. In language and content it looks very much like an abridged version of the celebrated formula attached almost four centuries previously to the *Regula Communis* of ca. 675, although we shall find reason below to qualify this conclusion to some degree. The various alterations and silences of the text show however that it departs in certain significant respects from the presumed prototype. It lacks an explicit personal *traditio*, and it also omits the original guarantees against abusive abbatial governance, and the right of appeal to the intervention of external ecclesiastical or civil authorities. The result is to emphasize the abbot's penal powers over refractory and subversive monks, suggesting current grave problems of indiscipline and instability within the monastery. Finally, the whole thrust is monolateral: profession is still collective but instead of the balanced counterplay between two privileged contracting parties we now have something much closer to the normal western cenobitic polity with its premise of relatively unlimited abbatial monarchialism.

How are we to account for the solitary emergence of the Tudeildus pactum in Beiran cenobitism so late as the mid-11th century? José Mattoso, whose admirable work on the monasteries of the diocese of Porto prior to the advent of Cluniac Benedictinism gave him a particular interest in this abbot as having become also the ruler of São Salvador de Leça above the Douro, answers this ques-

(7) Note references in the *pacti cartula* to «qui hunc nostrum pactum roborare uoluerint (p. 209:2) ... sicut in testamento et in pacto resonat» (p. 209:7-8); and in the *carta dimissionis* to «et quantuscumque in nostrum pactum roborauerint» (p. 210:1-2).

tion with assurance [8] For him the explanation lies in the tenacious retention throughout the ancient Lusitanian region of the legacy of 7th-century «Fructuosanism», attested in the diplomas of the 10th and 11th centuries by the presence of federations of abbeys, double communities of men and women, pluralistic use of *codices regularum* as against Benedictine monoregularism, extreme conservatism in ascetic practices and terminology, and of course pactualism. Although Vacariça was not founded before the close of the 10th century, Mattoso believes it would naturally have adhered to the Gallaecian traditionalism so strongly rooted among the monasteries of the Portuguese County, and indeed with such devotion that when ca. 1026 Tudeildus removed himself from this house to Leça he made his new seat a flourishing center of pactual and other «Fructuosan» usages long familiar to him in the Coimbran south.

This line of reasoning I find unconvincing. Mattoso's thesis of Portuguese cenobitic continuity with Visigothic Gallaecia down to the advent of the Cluniacs ca. 1085 depends excessively upon giving a «Fructuosan» explication of the admittedly archaistic but apparently conventional language of the diplomas. But, as Linage Conde argues and in my opinion soundly, the linguistic and institucional conservatism of these is more plausibly evaluated as stemming from the dominant orthodox monachism of the Visigothic period [9]. Again, on the historical *versus* the lexicographical side, no evidence is known to me that the monastic movement centering about St Fructuosus and his successors in the see of Braga ever crossed the Douro to invade the Romano-Visigothic province of Lusitania, or reached as far south as the environs of Coimbra. On the contrary, when the reformist King Wamba (672-680) tried to set up at Aquis (Chaves) in Lusitania a monastic see of the same type as Dume — Braga, i. e., involving the sort of *episcopus sub regula* associated with early pactualism, this manoeuvre was successfully blocked by the metropolitan church of Emerita with the full support of the fathers of the XIIth Council of Toledo (681) [10].

There are two alternatives to Mattoso's hypothesis. One is the possible establishment of pactual monasticism in Beira Litoral as a

(8) José Mattoso, *Le monachisme ibérique et Cluny: les monastères du diocèse de Porto de l'an mille à 1200* (Louvain, 1968), pp. 329-332; also his *Sobrevivência*, loc. cit.; and «O monaquismo ibérico e Cluny», *Do Tempo e da História*, II (1968), 79-95.

(9) Cf. the criticism by Linage Conde, II, 741-745, of Mattoso's methodology; and the latter's counter-thrust: «L'introduction de la Règle de S. Benoît dans la Péninsule ibérique», *Rev. d'hist. ecclés.*, LXX, n.os 3-4 (July-Dec. 1975), 731-742.

(10) *Concilios visigóticos e hispano-romanos*, ed. José Vives (Barcelona-Madrid, 1963), pp. 389-392 (canon 4).

consequence of the first Christian reconquest and colonization following Afonso III's extension of his kingdom's southwestern frontier to the Mondego in 878, and the consequent initial *repovoamento* of Coimbra and its countryside in the course of the 10th century (11). Under these circumstances pactual monks from Além-Minho, Entre Minho e Douro or elsewhere in the Asturoleonese state could have transplanted their distinctive form of monastic organization into the Baixo Mondego where Vacariça was to appear shortly before the year 1000, and where this and other pactual abbeys are known to have survived the Muslim re-occupation under al-Mansur and the earlier *muluk at-tawa'if*.

It is a serious objection to this solution and to that of Mattoso as well that although we have a fair number of Vacariçan pergaminhos, commencing in 1002 and running through various abbatiates before and after Tudeildus, none of these displays any recognizably pactual symptoms. This is not necessarily decisive: similar silence in what are essentially deeds of property transfer occurs in the documentation of several (but by no means not all) known pactual houses.

Nevertheless, the fact that no positive evidence links São Salvador with the pactual tradition either before or after 1045 forces consideration of a third possibility: that the Tudeildus covenant was a distinct innovation, quite unrepresentative of cenobitic practice in the diocese of Coimbra and introduced from outside for purposes yet to be determined. From this standpoint, what is required is a fresh look at certain facts in the history of the Beiran congregation and the career of the abbot Tudeildus, and the particular conditions under which these two parties entered into contractual agreement.

The tale turns on not one but two abbeys, Vacariça, and Leça. First, São Salvador (later São Vicente) de Vacariça (c. Mealhada), lying in the cerealiferous countryside below the historic Serra do Buçaco (*anglice* Bussaco), a house which was probably founded ca. 990 but enters into the light of record only in the earliest decades of the 11th century (12). When in 1018 Tudeildus became its third

(11) See the introductory section to vol. I of A. H. de Oliveira Marques, *História de Portugal* (Lisboa, 1972); L. Gonzaga de Azevedo, *História de Portugal*, 6 v. (Lisbon, 1935-1944; 2d ed., 5 v., Porto, 1954), II, chaps. 11-14; Pierre David, «Le sanctoral hispanique et les patrons d'églises entre le Minho et le Mondego du IXe au XIe siècle» in his *Études historiques sur la Galice et le Portugal du VIe au XIIe siècle* (Lisbon-Paris, 1947), pp. 185-256.

(12) On the medieval agrarian ambiente of Beira Litoral, cf. A. H. de Oliveira Marques, *Introdução à História de Agricultura em Portugal* (Lisboa, 1968), pp. 71-72. For the adventures of Tudeildus the biographical primary source is *DC* 311 (1040); equally indispen-

known abbot, the monks possessed but a modest temporal which included the small monastery of Rocas at Sever do Vouga halfway to the Douro (*DC* 191). This situation changed in 1021 when the widowed noblewoman Domna Unisco Mendes (or Menendiz) and her son Osoredo Trutesendes made the abbey a major benefaction above Portucale in the Terra da Maia (Amaia), This consisted of their familial *mosteiro privado* of São Salvador de Leça (*DC* 248) to which and its feminine counterpart of São Romão de Vermoim (c. Maia) these same two donors, as converts to the religious life, had already transferred in 1013 a long list of *villae, ereditates* and other possessions (*DC* 222). Unisco, daughter of the Portuensian noble Mendo Forjaz, and her late husband Trutesendo Osoredes († 995) ([13]) can both be closely associated with the Maian district of the county of Portugal and the lower valley of the river Leça where they accumulated the dispersed but in sum quite substantial holdings which, as attached to their abbey at Leça, now passed into the hands of Tudeildus and Vacariça.

The non-spiritual motivations of this inherently puzzling cession of a Minhotan abbey to relatively remote Vacariça remain obscure, as obscure indeed as the familial connections of Tudeildus and his one known relative, a nephew Randulfus the Presbyter (*DC* 344). Two things may be conjectured: some degree of blood relationship between the abbot and the line of Trutesindo Osoredes, and the possible trans-Douran provenance of Tudeildus himself. If these suspicions could be verified they would help explain the donation of 1021 and clarify why, when Tudeildus left Vacariça ca. 1026 and sought asylum from a Muslim invasion of the Baixo Mondego, he took shelter at São Salvador de Leça and remained there as its abbot during the last twenty years of his life. Of course, since this house had been a Vacariçan dependency for some half-dozen years at time of his flight northward, it was a natural refuge to choose. From 1025 down to 1045. Tudeildus completely disappears from the pergaminhos of Vacariça, two decades when he cannot be seen to have any active link with his old monastery, even though canonically he was still its head. Meanwhile, neither Muslim perils nor loss of

---

sable on his chronology and that of Vacariça are the meticulously compiled notices scattered through Mattoso's *Monachisme ibérique*, for which see the indices. Cf. also the valuable unsigned article «Vacariça» in *Grande Enciclopédia Portuguesa e Brasileira* (Lisboa--Rio de Janeiro, n. d.), XXXIII, 652-657.

([13]) See the authoritative prosopographic reconstruction of the local aristocracy by José Mattoso, «A nobreza rural portuense nos séculos XI e XII», *Anuario de estudios medievales*, VI (1969), 465--520, at pp. 471 (I A 2), 474-475 (II B).

their governor seems to have seriously affected the monks in the shadow of Buçaco. Under a new abbot, Floritus or Floridus, drawn from their own ranks and still in office as late as 1045, they continued as before under Muslim and eventually Christian control of the comarca ([14]).

What then of pactualism at our other São Salvador, that of Leça (c. Matosinhos), also founded in the late 10th century and, as a dependency of Vacariça after 1021, well represented in the *Livro Preto* as a consequence of both monasteries' having passed to the Sé de Coimbra in 1094? Concerning this quondam *mosteiro privado* of Trutesendo Osoredes, Unisco Mendes and their son Osoredo Trutesendes, Mattoso expresses the firm view that it was a pactual center from its very beginnings, indeed an exceptionally well attested instance of the persistence of the Visigothic past in Portuguese cenobitism; and he asserts that Tudeildus, abbot from 1026, brought with him from Vacariça a strong attachment to this same tradition and maintained his second command-post as a stronghold of «Fructuosanism» ([15]). We have already questioned the doctrine of unbroken continuity below the Douro with the Gallaecian past and denied the presence of the pactum at Vacariça before 1045. If we also note that down to that same year the diplomas of Leça reveal no recognizable pactual symptoms and that the notion of this monastery's being «un cas où la tradition wisigothique est attestée d'une façon exceptionelle», rests almost entirely upon the covenant of 1045, then the question cannot be avoided: is there really a better case to be made for pactualism at Leça than at Vacariça? I believe there is, but only if we achieve a more perceptive comprehension of the setting and objectives of the notable instrument of 1045.

What must be realized is that Tudeildus' apparent effort in 1045 suddenly to re-affirm a long quiescent abbatial power at Vacariça is far more explicable as stemming not from ambitious desire to resume active control of Vacariça after twenty years of absence, but from a deep concern for the future of São Salvador de Leça in the light of his own advanced age and approaching demise. This becomes very clear once we acknowledge that the pactum of 1045 cannot be separated from the two other Tudeildan texts of precisely the same

([14]) Floritus as monk of Vacariça: *DC* 248 (1021): «et de fratribus de illo abbate (teodegildo) Frater Floride»; as abbot: *DC* 290 (1036); *DC* 342 (1045): «praepositus».

([15]) Mattoso, *Monachisme ibérique*, pp. 114-116; see also the excellent assemblage of data regarding Leça, pp. 12-14 (documents and history), pp. 398-400 (patrimonies); and the toponymic index s. v. Cf. pp. 175-176 (with domanial map).

day, month and year, the *pacti cartula* and the *carta dimissionis*, which the editors of *DC* rightly place alongside it.

a. the *pacti cartula* (*DC* 342, p. 209). Tudeildus addresses himself in effect to two parties: one, Floritus (significantly given the reduced rank of *praepositus*) and his *fratres* of Vacariça; the other, Petrus and Randulfus the Presbyter, both (as we shall see) monks of Leça. With reference to São Salvador de Leça, its earlier patrimonies, and those additions made by Tudeildus himself — foundation of São Martinho de Anta, the *salinas* at Foz de Leça, one-half of the monastery of São Romão de Vermoim — the abbot swears not to alienate these during his lifetime; after his death they are to become possessions of the two previously named groups, which are also bound to abstain from their alienation.

b. the *carta dimissionis* (*DC* 342, pp. 209-211). Also of *post obitum* intent and now placed second in the triad of texts, this commences with an allusion to the two monasteries of São Salvador involved, meaning Vacariça, and Leça: «quorumue dispares et locis diuersis cimiteriis aule sunt nuncupate». Then Tudeildus, acting with the assent of the *fratres* of Vacariça, and in atonement for the sins of himself and his unnamed *parentes*, directs his act to the monk Petrus, the presbyters Electus, Tudeildus and Arias, to Lucidus and Randulfus the Presbyter, and to all subscribants to his pactum. Since the individuals named can all be identified as monks of Leça ([16]), while the anticipated subscribants to the pactum can only be monks of Vacariça, once again two abbeys are conjoined. As a first provision Tudeildus names Randulfus the Presbyter, i. e., his nephew, to serve after his death as *patronus*, meaning unmistakably of Leça, so long as he enjoys the approval of the abbot and *fratres* of Vacariça. Tudeildus goes on to place once again in the hands of both communities a slightly different list of his northern holdings: the monastery of Leça with all its possessions as granted by Unisco and her son Osoredo (*DC* 222: 1013), and his own subsequent acquisitions: São Martinho de Anta, the *vila* of Pousada, 1/2 + 1/10 of the *vila* of Custoias, the *salinas* of Foz de Leça. Finally, for reasons that escape us, it is ordered that monks coming to Leça from Lorvão be received into the congregation. An exceptionally long list of witnesses follows, headed by Gonçalo Raupariz «maiorinus regis domni fernandi qui pro iussione abba asignaui», so lengthy indeed as to suggest that this

---

([16]) See in *DC* the charters of Leça as follows: Petrus, 277, 298, 341; Randulfus presbyter, 273, 277, 283, 307, 325, 341, 395, 434-435; Electus, 295, 307, 313, 341; Tudeildus presbyter, 341; Arias, 274, 277; Lucidus, 277. All these must have been *seniores* of the community and in Tudeildus' intimate confidence.

piece originally closed the triad and carried the attestations validating all three acts.

c. the *carta pacti uel placiti* (*DC* 342, pp. 211-212). Sufficient has been said above on the content and nature of this text; what must now be noted is its relation to the two preceding pieces, since together these can be taken as the indispensable other half of the covenant between Tudeildus and the Vacariçan congregation. While it has always been recognized that pactual cenobitism implied reciprocal obligations and duties, the documentation confirming this on the abbatial side has been neglected since Herwegen because of concentration on the *pactum monachorum*. Such a document however an abbot could not subscribe. He required his own *pactum abbatis*, which seems to have taken the form of a normal donation act addressed to his monks at the same time they submitted to him; in bestowing property upon the community he thus by implication accepted the office and obligations of their ruler.

Of the limited number of such complete double pacta, the earliest discoverable is one of 818 uniting the monks of SS. Pedro y Pablo de Naroba, in the Liébana district of southeastern Asturias, with their abbot Argilegus ([17]). This embraces, within the bounds of a single pergaminho, the *pactum monachorum*, then what calls itself a *confirmatio uel compromissio* in which the abbot bestows properties upon the house, a second benefaction (this time by a kinsman of Argilegus), and only then the subscriptions of the religious of this double community. Another example is the Eufrasia pactum of 930 from the Castilian monastery of San Mamés de Ura (south of Burgos near Lerma), which puts together as of one date the pactum of the nuns, the corresponding donation act of the abbess, and a comparable gift by the famous Castilian count Fernán González ([18]).

In this context the Tudeildus triad of 1045 is of prime interest because it not only preserves our one known Portuguese *pactum monachorum* but is also one of the very few extant specimens from all medieval Iberia of a complete double monastic contract, containing the property transfers which constitute the *pactum abbatiale*. Since the instruments were drawn up, it must be emphasized, not at the beginning but towards the close of Tudeildus' long abbatial career, the monks' part of the covenant in no sense conforms to Herwegen's classification of such a text as *Professformel* and *Abtwahlinstrument*, for the triad represents no agreement at the commencement of an abbatiate, but a negotiated settlement to take full effect

([17]) Antonio C. Floriano, *Diplomática española del período astur*, 2 t. (Oviedo, 1949-1951), I, 146-150 (n.° 27).
([18]) Herwegen, pp. 11-14.

post obitum. By the *pactum monachorum* the Vacariçan community in effect acknowledged that Tudeildus was still its canonical governor, although clearly his term of office would have been envisaged as of only brief duration; and this acknowledgement was given in return for an acceptance of the juridical truth that in canon and secular law Leça was still subordinate to the suzerainty of the mother abbey despite the fact that it retained the right to its own *patronus* and the inalienability of its temporal. Vacariça thus regained *sub modo* long unexercised authority over her Minhotan dependency; Tudeildus secured for Leça, so long his principal base, guarantees of its relative independence and patrimonial security.

Whether all three members of the triad were originally inscribed in the same pergaminho, with the *pactum monachorum* at its head, there is no way to be sure; given their dispersion in the later *Livro Preto*, it is perhaps unlikely. In any event, since Tudeildus appears primarily as abbot of Leça and in behalf of this abbey, and since the names found within the bounds of these texts (aside from Floritus of Vacariça and those of the many unknowable confirmants and attestants declared present at the close of the *carta dimissionis*) are identifiable as belonging to Leçan monks, it would seem that the composition of the triad took place on the banks of the river Leça. It is improbable (although not impossible) that the old abbot travelled south to negotiate the agreement at distant Vacariça; the *pacti cartula* carries the name of the scribe, Ansemundus, well known from other Leçan documents of the period; and the territorial associations of the *maiorino* Gonçalo Rauparíz all lie above the Douro ([19]). All this woul explain the absence of the usual list of *adnotationes* of Vacariçan monks to the extant *pactum monachorum*, if what we have is a draft prepared at Leça, and not the actual instrument to which the names would have been attached.

After 1045 we hear nothing further of Tudeildus' ties with Vacariça; in 1046, presumably the year he died, the diplomas still designate him abbot of Leça (*DC* 344, 347). Floritus never re-appears after the *pacti cartula* of 21 September 1045, being replaced at Vacariça in December of that year by the abbot Alvitus (*DC* 348). At Leça, in the 1050's, after a gap in the documents, Randulfus the Presbyter turns up as abbot, no doubt as his uncle intended; although he is remembered more particularly for having attended Fernando I's major council at Coyanza in 1055, very likely as a *peritus* in canon law, and for bringing back to Portugal the so-called

(19) On Ansemundus, cf. *DC*, 296, 298-299, 307, 313; on Gonçalo Rauparíz, Mattoso, *Nobreza*, 511-512 (X C).

«Portuguese redaction» of the conciliar *decretos* ([20]). As for the old ties between the Minhotan dependency and the Beiran mother abbey, these seem to have continued unbroken throughout the 11th century but did not affect the de facto independence of São Salvador de Leça, precisely as Tudeildus had planned.

Can we then believe that the immediate prototype of the *pactum monachorum* of 1045 was a formula of similar content long in use at Leça and familiar to Tudeildus as the medium of his installation there as abbot ca. 1026? This now seems likely enough; but before declaring a positive conclusion on this point we are obligated to consider when and from what quarter pactual monacism could first have reached the Maian abbey. Several clues point towards a satisfactory resolution of these questions.

To be noted at the start is the striking, hitherto unnoticed correspondences between our Portuguese *pactum monachorum* and two earlier specimens of this genre from Castile. One of these was drawn up in 855 between an abbot Rodanius and the monks of San Pedro de Tejada, a house located south of Burgos in a zone of documented pactual-cenobitic colonization ([21]). The other, preserved in the noted Leodegundian codex *Escorialensis a. I. 13* of the first third of the 10th century, which was formerly attributed to a Gallegan scriptorum but is now shown by Díaz y Díaz to have been copied in Castile, unites an abbot Sabaricus with an unidentifiable congregation ([22]). Both instruments, like that of Tudeildus, sedulously follow the *Regula Communis* model pactum in various respects, yet they agree with one another in certain omissions from and modifications of this pattern, while at other times they differ from one another, e. g., in topical order and occasional phraseology. But what stands out with particular force is that all three texts preserve common elements which do not come from the Gallaecian formula at all. This can be readily established here by juxtaposing the section in all four pacta which deals with that ever-present danger of this period, confronting perhaps above all familial *mosteiros privados,* from monks conspiring with kinsmen against an abbey's integrity and patrimonial inviolability. The italics denote what is not found in the 7th-century text but occurs in the Castillian and Portuguese adaptations of the Reconquista.

([20]) Alfonso Gallo, «El Concilio de Coyanza», *An. hist. derecho esp.*, XX (1950), 275-633, at. pp. 303-320.

([21]) J. Pérez de Urbel, *Historia del Condado de Castilla,* 3 v. (Madrid, 1945), III, 1058-1060 (n.° 26).

([22]) M. C. Díaz y Díaz, «El códice monástico de Leodegundia (Escorial a. I. 13)», *Ciudad de Dios*, CLXXXI (1968), 567-587.

Pactum of the Regula Communis: Si quis sane ex nobis contra regulam occulte cum parentibus, germanis, filiis, cognatis, uel propinquis aut certe cum fratre secum habitante, consilium te absente supradicto patre nostro inierit, habeas potestatem in unumquemque qui hoc facinus temptauerit, ut per sex menses indutus tegmine raso aut cilicio, discinctus et discalceatus in solo pane et aqua in cella obscura exerceat quodlibet opus excommunicatus ([23]).

Pactum of Rodanius: Si quis sane ex nobis *quod ualde execratur regula uel omnes scripturam,* aut aliquis oculte consilium cum parentibus, germanis, filiis, cognatis uel *propinquis adprehenderit, sine consilio abbatis uel sancta communis regula,* habeas potestatem *in nos unoquaque, qui hoc tentauerit,* per sex menses indutum tegimen rasum, etc. ([24]).

Pactum of Sabaricus: Si quis sane ex nobis, *quod ualde execratur regula uel omnis scriptura,* aliquis occulte consilium cum parentibus, iermanis, filiis, cognatis uel propinquis *adprehenderit sine consilio abbati uel sancte communi regule,* habeas potestatem *in nos, in unumquemque, qui hoc temtaberit,* [ut] per sex menses indutum tecmen rasum, etc. ([25])

Pactum of Tudeilus: Siquis sane ex nobis *quod ualde exequatur regula* aliquis occulte consilium cum parentibus iermanis filiis cognatis uel propinquis uel cum quolibet extraneis *adprehenderit sine benedictione abbatis uel sancta commune regule* habeas potestatem *super nos unumquemque qui hoc temptauerit,* pro regulari disciplina corripere et accerrime flagellare ([26]).

Exegetical commentary on the foregoing passages, especially as regards the interesting alusion by the last three to the *sancta communis regula,* cannot detain us here; what is presently more noteworthy is the disclosure (i) that these Castilian and Portuguese pacta must have had a common ancestor in a somewhat different, slightly more extended, version of the *Regula Communis* archetype; (ii) that this was in circulation before the mid-9th century; and (iii) that descendants of this lost exemplar were being adopted at much the same time in both the Castilian East and the Portuguese or Galaico-Portuguese West. All this should warn us against attributing an exaggerated antiquity and ultra-tenacious conservatism to the cenobitism

([23]) «Reglas monásticas de la España visigoda», ed. Julio Campos Ruiz in *Santos Padres Españoles* (Madrid, 1971. Bibl. de Autores Cristianos), II, 210.

([24]) Pérez de Urbel, *Condado*, III, 1059.

([25]) Herwegen, pp. 6-7.

([26]) *DC*, p. 212.

of the Portuguese 9th-11th centuries which Mattoso ascribes to unbroken concatenation with the late Visigothic period. It should not be forgotten that a pactum of presumably this very same tenor surfaces in allegedly «progressive» Castile as late as 1044, at Santa Maria de Sotovellanos ([27]). After all, the formula available at Leça to Tudeildus in 1045 can have been instituted there at the earliest from ca. 990 when the house came into existence, i. e., only half a century previously. Admittedly, such a pactum must have already been in vogue at the time; but the impression is that the pactualism of Leça was part and parcel of the general monastic *repovoamento* of Entre Minho e Douro during the 9th-10th centuries and therefore in a broad sense innovative.

Fortunately, we have another unimpeachable witness to the spread of pactual monasticism in the diocese of Braga — the foundation charter of the major abbey of São Salvador de Guimarães ([28]). This double community which, according to Mattoso's authoritative judgment, had become the foremost abbey of the entire diocese by ca. 1000, was established in 959 by that eminent figure in the Portuguese high aristocracy, the countess Mumadona Dias, who richly endowed the new center with numerous *vilas*, lands and other goods. Since she dedicated all these patrimonies to the use of those who «in hunc locum sub manu abbatis et census regule fuerint Domino seruientes et in pactum roborati», the constitutional basis of the new community is placed beyond cavil, even if we cannot tell precisely what form its fundamental charter took. Furthermore, the strong affiliations of Mumadona's parents and kinsmen with the Gallegan nobility ([29]), and the inclusion of lands in Galicia among the properties conferred, give her donation a more than merely Minhotan significance. This is further supported by the appearance, in first place among the six confirmant bishops, of the celebrated San Rosendo of Mondoñedo, for many years abbot of the major Gallegan pactual house of San Salvador de Celanova ([30]), while the subscribants also include the current governor of that house: «Aloitus cellanouensis praepositus». Even if we are not justified in deducing that Celanova directly inspired the adoption of the pactum at Guimarães, the epi-

---

([27]) Unpublished, but cf. Pérez de Urbel, III, 1325 (n.° 665); Bishko, *Gallegan Pactualism*, p. 519.

([28]) *DC* 76 (p. 47, following note no. 136).

([29]) On Mumadona and her relatives cf. J. Mattoso, *As famílias condais portucalenses dos séculos X e XI* (Porto, 1970), pp. 46-49; Avelino de J. da Costa, «Mumadona Dias», in *Dicionário de História de Portugal*, ed. Joel Serrão, III (Lisbon, 1968), pp. 121-122.

([30]) *DC 76* (p. 48); cf. J. Mattoso, «S. Rosendo e as correntes monásticas da sua época», *Do Tempo e da História*, V (1972), 5-27.

sode serves to document what can be glimpsed from other sources as well — the bond of friendship and cultural-institutional exchange that united Minhotan cenobitism with the powerful revival of pactualism visible in many new monastic foundations of the 9th and 10th centuries in the peninsular northwest.

That such a movement existed in the Galicia and Portugal of the Alta Reconquista has yet to be perceived by monastic historians, but it is undeniable. In 1951, in the course of my study of the geographical distribution of the then known Iberian pacta, I expressed the view that since only four examples could be adduced for the entire Galaico-Portuguese zone, it would be valid to infer an extremely limited diffusion of this instrument in the region of its birth; and this judgment has been followed by, among others, Pérez de Urbel and Linage Conde ([31]). It is nevertheless erroneous, as I have now come to see, for although no new texts of pacta have come to light from this area in the last thirty years (so far as I am aware), it has grown increasingly manifest to me that the diplomas of the monastic houses of Galicia in the 9th and 10th centuries contain not a few references to pacta now lost or still awaiting rescue from the archives. These testimonies prove extensive use of the covenant in such major abbeys of Galicia as San Salvador de Celanova, San Salvador de Sobrado, San Julián de Samos, San Esteban de Ribas de Sil and, in Portugal, São Salvador de Guimarães and São Salvador de Leça ([32]). Thus the thesis wich I sponsored in 1951 is to be rejected — the pactual tradition was as firmly rooted in Galicia and northern Portugal above the Douro as it was in primitive Castile.

In the light (however flickering) of the antecedent pages, we may now assemble the principal results of this inquiry into 11th-century Portuguese pactual monachism and the particular case of São Salvador de Vacariça. It should be patent that, contrary to current belief, the Tudeildus *pactum monachorum* cannot be taken to establish this Beiran abbey as a late center of monastic traditionalism; on the contrary, its witness relates entirely to São Salvador de Leça in Minho, where it indicates that a formula of this type was in use from the 10th century. The deceptive connection with Vacariça is merely incidental to the authentic objective of this historically most interesting text, and its two companion pieces constituting the *pactum abbatiale*. The basic aim of the aged abbot Tudeildus was to insure the safe transfer to his nephew Randulfus of his own long-standing *padroado*

([31]) Bishko, *Gallegan Pactualism*, pp. 516-517; Pérez de Urbel, *Vida y caminos*, pp. 392-393; Linage Conde, *Orígenes*, I, 308-311.

([32]) The appropriate references are given in my study, «The Pactual Tradition in Hispanic Monasticism», awaiting publication in Spain.

over Leça and, *a fortiori,* safeguard for the future the virtual independence enjoyed by his cherished house for the last twenty years despite juridical subordination to Vacariça. The pactum of 1045, in consequence, lends no support to claims that pactual cenobitism prevailed everywhere below the Douro down to 1100; this problem, either because of our painfully limited and recalcitrant Beiran sources, or because in fact the heterodox contractualism never did cross that river, remains unresolved. It should however assist investigators to perceive that at Leça (as surely also at Guimarães) what we encounter in the pactum of 1045 is no anemic end-product of three centuries of ascetico-institutional stasis, but the expression of a vigorous tradition contributing positively to the new monastic foundations of the Luso-Gallegan West during the 9th-11th centuries.

13 January 1982.

Charlottesville, Virginia, USA.
University of Virginia.

Supplementary Note. The new Coimbra edition of the *Livro Preto* (cf. Note 4, *supra*), which I have been able to consult during final proofreading of this paper, presents the Tudeildan pactual dossier of 1045 in Vol. I, as nos. 150, 138 (*pacti cartula*), 148, 137 (*carta dimissionis*), 153 (*pactum monachorum*). For other principal acts, as cited above at pp. 138-140, *DC* 311, 191, 248, 222, 344, 290, 248, 290, 342 correspond, respectively, to *LP*, I, nos. 115 (also 140), 126, 142, 147; III, 520; I, 93, 142, 93, 150 (also 138). Textual variations appear minor.

V

SPANISH ABBOTS AND THE VISIGOTHIC COUNCILS OF TOLEDO

I

STUDENTS of medieval Spanish political and religious history have long recognized the peculiar importance in the development of the Visigothic monarchy of the great national assemblies held in the capital city of Toledo during the sixth and seventh centuries.[1] In origin purely ecclesiastical convocations at which the Spanish episcopate promulgated the famous series of Toletan canons, destined to exert so immense and abiding an influence upon the canonical literature of the medieval church,[2] the councils of Toledo early took on an increasingly noticeable secular character: the king and the high officers of state became regular members; the legislation, in the manner of the Byzantine *nomocanon*, included secular along with ecclesiastical enactments; and from *ca.* 650, as the doomed monarchy grew steadily more feeble, the supreme political authority of the realm passed into the eager hands of the Toletan assemblies. From these powerful bodies, by a process probably much more broken and indirect than the easy generalizations of constitutional historians acknowledge, seem to derive the *cortes* of the Reconquista kingdoms, the earliest true parliaments developed in Western Europe during the medieval period.[3]

1 The more important works dealing with the councils of Toledo are F. Dahn, *Die Könige der Germanen*, (Munich: Fleischmann, 1861–1909), VI, 501–504; E. Pérez Pujol, *Historia de las instituciones sociales de la España goda*, (Valencia : Vives Mora, 1896), III, 285–339; E. Magnin, *L'Eglise wisigothique au VIIe siècle*, (Paris : Picard, 1912), pp. 47–105; L. Duchesne, *L'Eglise au VIe siècle*, (Paris : Boccard, 1925), pp. 580–584; A. K. Ziegler, *Church and State in Visigothic Spain*, (Washington : Catholic University, 1930), pp. 32–43; Z. García Villada, *Historia Eclesiástica de España*, (Madrid : Fernando Fé, 1929–), II, 1, 107–130.

2 P. Séjourné, *Saint Isidore de Séville : son rôle dans l'histoire du droit canonique*, (Paris : Beauchesne, 1929), pp. 367–493; P. Fournier and G. LeBras, *Histoire des collections canoniques en Occident*, (Paris : Sirey, 1931–1932), *passim*.

3 M. Colmeiro, *Cortes de los antiguos reinos de León y de Castilla*, (Madrid : Rivadeneyra, 1883–1884), I, *introducción;* V. Piskorski, *Las cortes de Castilla*, trans. into Spanish by C. Sánchez Albornoz, (Barcelona, 1930); R. B. Merriman, "The Cortes of the Spanish Kingdoms in the Later Middle Ages," *Amer. Hist. Rev.*, XVI, (1910–1911), 476–495; *idem, The Rise of the Spanish Empire in the Old World and the New*, (New York : Macmillan, 1918–1934), I, 217–228; C. H. McIlwain, "Medieval Estates" in *Cambridge Medieval History*, (Cambridge: The University Press, 1911–1935), VII, 696; C. Sánchez Albornoz, *La curia regia portuguesa, siglos XII y XIII*, (Madrid : 1920).

In the seventh century the Toletan councils were attended not only by members of the secular hierarchy and the aristocracy, by bishops and nobles, but also by abbots; and among the numerous problems associated with the assemblies not the least obscure is that of abbatial participation. Upon the indubitable fact of the attendance of abbots monastic historians and canonists have constructed a general theory of abbatial attendance at medieval church councils which, reduced to simplest terms, asserts: (1) that in Spain, much earlier than elsewhere in Europe, abbots succeeded in compelling the episcopate to grant them the privilege of conciliar attendance hitherto monopolized by the bishops; (2) that the Spanish practice, advertised in extra-peninsular regions by the inclusion of the Toletan canons in all the great Carolingian and post-Carolingian collections, furnished the direct precedent for the admission of abbots to church convocations in France, in Italy, and in "toute la chrétienté."[4] Neither of these sweeping generalizations, however, rests on more than hasty inference, for the phenomenon of abbatial attendance has never been given the thorough investigation it emphatically needs. The subject is not an unimportant one, though its implications have scarcely been realized; it involves an examination from the ecclesiastical standpoint, and no less from the political and economic, of the rising juridical authority of the proto-feudal abbatiate in the pre-Carolingian West and the abbatial conquest of quasi-episcopal powers in the government of the church, questions themselves closely linked with the origins of monastic emancipation from episcopal control as defined by the Chalcedonian formula.[5]

4 *Cf.*, *inter alia*, Fr. Chamard, "Les abbés au moyen-âge," *Revue des Questions historiques*, XXXVIII, (1885), 71–108; Pérez Pujol, *op. cit.*, III, 186–87; Magnin, *op. cit.*, p. 59; Piskorski, *op.cit.*, pp. 30–31; T. P. McLaughlin, "Le très ancien droit monastique de l'Occident," *Archives de la France monastique*, XXXVIII, (Ligugé-Vienne : 1935), p. 145, and note 6.

5 Easily the best study along these lines is H. Barion, "Das fränkisch-deutsche Synodalrecht des Frühmittelalters," *Kanonistische Studien und Texte*, V–VI, (Bonn and Cologne: Röhrscheid, 1931), pp. 136–41. Barion is primarily interested in conditions of the eighth and ninth centuries, but he shows that in restricted numbers abbots attended Frankish councils of the earlier Merovingian period; he explains their presence in terms of (1) the growing religious and economic importance of the Frankish abbeys; (2) the influence of Irish monks upon the continental church. But as McLaughlin well remarks, *loc. cit.*, these abbots were almost invariably delegates of absentee bishops and not abbots present in their own right. Thorough examination of the Merovingian data might help to determine whether established Frankish custom was not more effective an element than imported Spanish practice in the marked rise in abbatial attendance at councils of the Carolingian period.

The object of the present paper, however, is not to treat this broad problem of abbatial attendance at church councils in medieval Europe, but rather to test the accuracy of the first of the two generalizations that make up the current doctrine: to examine the alleged Spanish precedent itself, and to determine whether the documents corroborate the ascription of conciliar rights to the peninsular abbatiate of the Visigothic period.

II

For the attendance of abbots at the Toletan councils our chief, practically our sole, source of information consists of the lengthy lists of subscriptions of bishops, clerics, abbots, and nobles, given in the MSS immediately at the close of the formal *acta* of each council.[6] From them can be ascertained the size and importance of the gathering, the relative proportions of churchmen and laymen present, the regions of the peninsula most heavily represented, and, more directly to our purpose, to what extent and upon what specific occasions Spanish abbots were admitted to the supreme deliberations of the Visigothic church. But in using them for these and other purposes historians and canonists alike have lost sight of one or two indispensable preliminary cautions, by ignoring which the entire testimony of the lists suffers serious misinterpretation.

6 For the purposes of this paper the conciliar lists, with variants, as published in J. P. Migne, *Patrologiae Cursus Completus, Series Latina*, (Paris : 1844–1864), LXXXIV, (cited henceforth as *P.L.* LXXXIV), have been carefully checked against the principal Spanish MSS of the *Hispana* collection, as follows: Madrid, Biblioteca Nacional, *MS. 1872; MS. 100 41;* El Escorial, *MS. d I 1 (Codex Aemilianensis); MS. d I 2 (Codex Vigilanus, Codex Albeldensis); MS. e I 12; MS. e I 13*. On these MSS, *cf.* G. Loewe-W. von Hartel, "Bibliotheca Patrum Latinorum Hispaniensis," *Sitzungsberichte der kaiserlichen Akademie der Wissenschaft zu Wien*, phil.-hist. Classe, CXI–CXIII, (1885–1886), as follows: CXII, (1886), 734; CXI, (1885), 457–58, 460–61; C. U. Clark, "Collectanea Hispanica," *Transactions of the Connecticut Academy of Arts and Sciences*, XXIV, (Paris : 1920), catalogue nos. 621, 519, 520–22; Z. García Villada, *Paleografía española*, (Madrid: [Revista de filología española], 1923), cat. nos. 123, 22–25; A. Millares Carlo, *Tratado de paleografía española*, 2nd ed. (Madrid: Hernando, 1932), cat. nos. 98, 116, 31–34; G. Antolín, *Catálogo de los códices latinos del Escorial*, (Madrid: 1910–1923), I, 320–404; II, 17–31. Examination of these MSS yielded only a few minor variations from the Migne text in *P.L.* LXXXIV; the lists may also be consulted, less confidently, in J. D. Mansi, *Sacrorum conciliorum nova et amplissima collectio*, (Florence-Venice: 1759–1798), IX–XII. For the Spanish canons, including the Toletan, the best edition is that of H. Bruns, *Canones apostolorum et conciliorum*, (Berlin: 1839), which, however, does not include the subscriptions.

In the first place, the distinction between national councils of the peninsular church and local synods of the *prouincia Carthaginensis*, convoked and presided over by the metropolitan bishop of Toledo, while familiar to all students, has been consistently ignored in practice.[7] For canonical purposes this equation of two very different sorts of council may be justified; the consecutive numbering of national and provincial assemblies as one series in the *Hispana* and the derivative collections proves that from an early date, even before the fall of the Visigothic monarchy, the canons of both types of council were regarded as of equal authority. For the historian, on the other hand, such procedure is utterly misleading, and the obscurities of abbatial attendance are only made the more impenetrable by the failure to discriminate between national and provincial evidence.

Secondly, not only must a sharp distinction be observed between two types of council, but no less between two types of abbot. Upon this the MSS themselves firmly insist in their classification of certain abbots as *uicarii episcoporum* and others as *abbates*. In the former instance the abbot's name and title are regularly coupled with the formula *agens uicem*, followed by the name and see of the bishop whose representative he is; in the latter, the abbot is placed under a special rubric, *abbates*, and is thus distinguished from the *uicarii* as a conciliar member in his own right. To disregard this distinction, as is commonly done, is to falsify the testimony of the MSS and to throw the whole question into utter confusion.

If now the conciliar lists are analyzed in the light of these two preliminary cautions, the information they contain as to abbatial attendance can be properly assessed. The abbots appearing as episcopal proctors or *uicarii* may be discussed first. From the Toletan as from other Spanish canons it is apparent that the Visigothic church experienced a certain difficulty in securing the attendance of bishops at ecclesiastical convocations. Signs of trouble in this quarter appear as early as the council of II Braga (571/3)[8] and continue all through the seventh century. The

7 For the classification of the councils as national or provincial, I accept the list drawn up by Magnin, *L'Eglise wisigothique*, pp. 48–50; for a somewhat different opinion, *cf.* Pérez Pujol, *Instituciones sociales*, III, 287–88, and the literature there cited; Ziegler, *Church and State*, pp. 35–36.

8 *Capitula Martini*, c. 19.

Lusitanian synod of Mérida in 666 denounced under threat of excommunication bishops absent from provincial assemblies; it permitted bishops, however, to send in their stead archpresbyters or presbyters, though not, be it noted, abbots.[9] In 675 another provincial synod, XI Toledo, repeated this warning to lax prelates and fixed one year as the term of excommunication to be imposed upon absentees lacking reasonable excuse.[10] The subject received national attention for the first time in 683 when the national council of XIII Toledo vigorously demanded the attendance of all bishops at assemblies of the church.[11] These efforts, as the repeated warnings and the conciliar lists both show, attained only partial success; they did, however, compel bishops to be more cautious about absenting themselves from important councils and led them to make wider use of the convenient and recognized system of procuration, so that the councils of the latter half of the seventh century included numbers of episcopal deputies, presbyters, deacons, abbots, all acting *uicem dominorum episcoporum.*

The extent to which abbots serving in this way as episcopal *uicarii* represented bishops at the Toletan councils can be determined with exactness from the conciliar subscriptions. The earliest episcopal proctors appear at III Toledo in 589, but the first example of an abbot's acting in this capacity comes from the middle of the following century when the abbot Crispinus confirms the canons of VII Toledo (646) "agens uicem domini mei Neufredi episcopi Olysiponensis ecclesiae haec statuta definiens subscripsi." At VIII Toledo (653) Osdulgus acts in similar fashion for Riccimirus, bishop of Dumio. At IX Toledo (655) there were no vicarial abbots present; at X Toledo (656) there were two; at XI Toledo (675) and XII Toledo (681), none. Thus, over a period of thirty-five years, embracing six councils, of which three were national councils of the Spanish church, only four cases of episcopal representation by abbots occur; at all of these assemblies by far the greater number of episcopal proctors were presbyters or deacons.

Suddenly, with XIII Toledo (683), comes a sharp increase in the number of abbot-proctors. Twelve of them attend this im-

9 Cc. 5, 7.
10 C. 15.
11 C. 8.

portant national council in the stead of their bishops.[12] The reasons for this abrupt rise in number are not altogether clear, but the fact that eight of the twelve abbots represent sees in the provinces of Narbonnensis and Tarraconensis strongly suggests some connection with the great revolt against the crown which after six months of hard fighting King Wamba had at last succeeded in crushing on the eve of the council itself.[13] No doubt conditions were still too unsettled to permit the bishops of the disaffected areas to leave their dioceses on the long journey to the capital, and recourse was had therefore to the abbatial proctors. The number of abbots drops again at XIV Toledo, a provincial council held in the following year, to six. At the same time an innovation in the use of *uicarii* appears; three of the bishops send not one but two delegates. In one pair both men were abbots; in the other two only one of the pair was an abbot. There is no further trace of this interesting experiment in limiting an abbot's procuratorial powers by a device familiar to Spartan and Roman constitutional history, and at XV Toledo (688), the last council at which abbatial proctors are known to have been present, the old practice is continued, two bishops sending single proctors to represent them.

From this survey it may be concluded that with the single exception of XIII Toledo (683), where unusual circumstances account for abbatial procuration on a comparatively large scale, the attendance of abbots at Toletan councils as episcopal proctors was confined within rather narrow limits. A comparison of the number of abbots present with that of the presbyters and deacons also acting *uicem episcopi* brings out very clearly how relatively few the abbot-proctors were and how definitely the bishops preferred to use members of the secular clergy. Over a period of a century, from 589 to 688, with 14 councils held at Toledo, the signatory lists furnish these statistics: 24 abbots as against 36 presbyters and 36 deacons, or a total of 72 clerics. But more important for us than the scant use of abbot-proctors is the fact that these abbots were

12 Note that in *P.L.* LXXXIV, col. 501, Ioannes *abbas* is designated proctor for Regineus Aucensis, but in col. 500 it appears that Stercorius is the bishop of Auca and present at the council. The error, to be found in the MSS listed, *supra*, n. 6, does not affect the present argument.

13 See the tract of Julian of Toledo, *Historia Wambae regis*, in *Mon. Ger. Hist., Scriptores rerum Merovingicarum*, V, 486–535; and *cf.* Dahn, *Könige der Germanen*, V, 207–212; 217–18; R. Altamira, *Cambridge Medieval History*, II, 179.

admitted to the councils not as abbots *sui juris* but, like the presbyters and deacons, solely as episcopal deputies; they cannot, therefore, be used to support a supposed abbatial privilege of conciliar membership.

III

We may consider next those abbots who, as noted above, attended the assemblies of Toledo not as *uicarii* but as *abbates*. That they were full members in the same sense as the bishops themselves there seems no good reason to doubt; a review of the evidence will demonstrate how regularly such abbots took part in the deliberations. Magnin incorrectly concluded that the beginnings of this type of abbatial attendance could be found in 589 at III Toledo,[14] where, as we learn from Ioannes Biclarensis, Eutropius, the abbot of the *monasterium Seruitanum*, then the leading monastic community of Spain, shared with the metropolitan bishop Leander of Seville the presidency of the great council.[15] Eutropius, however, did not subscribe to the canons, which is proof enough that the bishops did not recognize him as anything more than an honorary member; in no sense can his presence be taken to fix any tradition of abbatial attendance. As a matter of fact no *abbates* can be discovered at Toledo for sixty years after III Toledo. John and Germanus of Dumio, who attended III and IV Toledo respectively, were abbots, it is true, but they were also bishops;[16] and it is in their episcopal capacity that they enroll their names among those of the other Spanish bishops.

In short, no abbot *qua* abbot won the right of participation in a Toletan council until the middle of the seventh century. In 653 at the national council of VIII Toledo the admission of abbots to an episcopal assembly is for the first time formally effected. The list

14 *L'Eglise wisigothique*, p. 59.

15 Ioannes Biclarensis, *Chronica*, *sub anno* 584? : "Summa tamen synodalis negotii penes sanctum Leandrum Hispalensis ecclesiae episcopum et beatissimum Eutropium monasterii Seruitani abbatem fuit," (*Mon. Ger. Hist.*, *Auctores antiquissimi*, XI, 219); Isidore of Seville, *De uiribus illustribus*, cc. 42, 45.

16 The MSS read: "Iohannes Dumiensis monasterii episcopus," (not "ecclesiae" as in *P.L.* LXXXIV, col. 359); "Germanus ecclesiae monasterii Dumiensis episcopus." The Galician *monasterium Dumiense*, founded in the latter half of the 6th century by Martin of Braga, was a monastic bishopric long unique in the Spanish church; its character and far-reaching influence upon Spanish monastic history after 650 will be treated in the writer's forthcoming study of Spanish monasticism in the Visigothic period.

of subscriptions for this body contains thirteen names under the rubric *abbates*, placed immediately after the list of bishops and just before that of the *uicarii episcoporum*. After 653 *abbates* can be found at nearly all the Toletan councils, whether national or provincial. Six national councils fall in this period, but of two the subscriptions are lost.[17] At XII Toledo (681) there were four abbots present; at XIII (683), nine; at XV (688), eight; and at XVI (693), five. In addition, of four local synods of the *prouincia Carthaginensis* in the latter half of the seventh century, three included abbots: IX Toledo (655), eight; X (656), none; XI (675), eight; XIV (684), six.

It may be granted, then, that from 653 on Visigothic abbots possessed conciliar rights and were regular attendants of the Toletan assemblies; but one can hardly look at the figures just cited without being struck by the small number of abbots who participated in each case.[18] Can it be that the great majority of abbots over all Spain deliberately neglected to exercise a right that must have been acquired only after a long struggle? Or is it rather that the struggle was never won by more than a handful of monastic governors, favorably situated in communities of exceptional importance?

Fortunately, we are not without some materials for answering these crucial questions. If the names of the abbots appearing at two of the national assemblies which met only five years apart, XIII Toledo (683) and XV Toledo (688), are set down in parallel columns, it will be found that for the most part the abbots at the two councils were the same:

XIII Toledo (9 abbots)	XV Toledo (11 abbots)
Absalius	*Absfalius*
Faustinus	*Felix* ([19])
Gerontius	*Wisandus*

17 Those of XVII and XVIII Toledo. No abbots seem to have attended the important national council of III Saragossa in 691.

18 From this fact, indeed, Dom C. Butler, (*Cambridge Medieval History*, I, 533), mistakenly deduced the general unimportance of monasticism in Visigothic Spain.

19 At XIII Tol. Felix, though rubricked as *abbas*, is called *archipresbyter* in MS. *Aemilianensis* (*P.L.* LXXXIV, 500); at XIV and XV Tol. by all the MSS; so, too, Wisandus and Vincentius are *archidiaconus* and *primiclerus*, respectively, at XIII Tol. according to MS. *Aemil.;* and, according to all the MSS, at XIV Tol. There is no reason for doubting that all three were abbots, although clearly in orders and attached to monastic churches.

Castorius	*Vincentius*
Gabriel	*Gerontius*
Sisebertus	*Castorius*
Felix	*Gabriel*
Wisandus	*Sisebertus*
Vincentius	Eulalius
	Inuiolatus
	Adeodatus

Thus, only one of the abbots at XIII Toledo did not attend XV Toledo also, and only three of those at the later council had not attended the earlier. It seems, then, that at these two councils at least, the same monasteries were being represented. Now between the sessions of these two national councils occurred the provincial council of 684, XIV Toledo, to which, indeed, for special reasons, all the Spanish metropolitans sent *uicarii*, but which was fundamentally local and attended by no bishops except those attached to the metropolis of Toledo. There were six abbots at this council:

Asfalius
Felix
Gerontius
Gabriel
Castorius
Sisebertus

It will be perceived at once that all six of these abbots had already taken part in XIII Toledo the year before and were to sit in XV Toledo some four years later. It can be taken as proved, therefore, that the majority of the abbots at these two national councils came from the Toletan metropolitanate, and allowing for the slight difference in numbers and the possible change of abbots in one or two cases, the conclusion is certain that all of the abbots at the national councils came from dioceses subject to the capital, if not from the diocese of Toledo itself.

This is not the only suggestion of such a conclusion. Of the thirteen abbots subscribing to the canons of VIII Toledo in 653, seven, Eumerius, Fugitivus, Ioannes, Marcellinus, Siliculus, Ildephonsus, and Morarius, are found at IX Toledo in 656. The latter is a provincial, the former a national, council.

Only once, in the case of XI Toledo (675), is any information given as to the specific abbeys represented, and then no more than the titular saints of the houses are listed. The abbots and their monasteries are cited there as follows:

> Iulianus ecclesiae monasterii sancti Michaelis abbas
> Valderedus ecclesiae monasterii sanctae Leocadiae abbas
> Gratinidus ecclesiae monasterii sanctorum Cosmae et Damiani abbas
> Absalio ecclesiae monasterii sanctae Crucis abbas
> Florentius ecclesiae monasterii sanctae Eulaliae abbas

All of these monasteries, or, more properly, monastic churches, were situated either in or near the city of Toledo. The celebrated *monasterium Agaliense*, located *in suburbio Toletano*, was dedicated to Saints Cosmas and Damian.[20] The great basilica, also situated in the Toletan *suburbium*, in which at least three of the great councils met, bore the title of St. Leocadia.[21] As for the other two, there is no Visigothic evidence, but we know that there were ancient Mozarabic churches of Santa Cruz and San Miguel at Toledo in the twelfth century,[22] and this fact, taken together with the express statement of Eulogius in the ninth century that after the conquest the Moslems forbade the construction of new ecclesiastical edifices,[23] indicates that both of these Mozarabic foundations had their origins in the Visigothic period.

The Visigothic abbots, then, who attended Toletan councils would seem to have come from houses located in close proximity to the capital.[24] How is their presence to be explained? The documentation is much too scant to afford us any adequate understanding of the precise manner in which this handful of abbots won the privilege of conciliar membership; all we can do is to conjecture along what general lines developments must have moved. Two main factors, at least, need to be taken into consideration. First,

20 Cixilanus, *Vita s. Hildefonsi*, c. 1, (*P.L.* XCVI, 44): "In ecclesia sanctorum Cosmae et Damiani quae sita est in suburbio Toletano."
21 Concc. V, VI, and XVII Toledo; *cf. P.L.* LXXXIV, 389, 393, 551.
22 A. Martín Gamero, *Historia de la ciudad de Toledo*, (Toledo: 1862), pp. 383–401.
23 Eulogius, *Memorialis sanctorum*, III, 3, (*P. L.* CXV, 801–802).
24 For a similar conclusion as to the scope of abbatial attendance, *cf.* the brief remarks of J. Pérez de Urbel, *Los monjes espanoles en la edad media*, (Madrid: Maestre, 1933–1934), II, 56–57.

the membership in the councils, as the inclusion of laymen shows, was fluid rather than fixed; it was natural enough for the councils to admit to their sessions the heads of what were no doubt the greatest and most powerful abbeys of the peninsula, already exercising by reason of their wealth and the royal favor wide influence upon the affairs of church and state. Secondly, the practice of admission might develop very easily from an analogous custom of abbatial attendance at local councils; the Visigothic church, like the Merovingian,[25] was not unacquainted with the convocation of abbots to local assemblies, for throughout the seventh century Spanish bishops were required by the canons to summon frequent synods of the abbots and clergy of their dioceses.[26] We know from the equation of national and provincial canons in the *Hispana* MSS that the distinction between national councils and metropolitan synods of the Carthaginensis province, at both of which the bishop of Toledo was the ranking prelate, was soon blurred in practice. It seems possible that a similar tendency was at work obscuring the lines between metropolitan synods and local synods of the Toletan diocese, so that some, if not all, abbots called to attend diocesan synods secured, whether by custom or pressure, the right to appear at metropolitan synods, particularly in years when no special diocesan synod met at Toledo. Admittedly this hypothesis leaves much to be desired, but all things considered, it seems to explain as satisfactorily as any other the presence of abbots at the Visigothic assemblies.

IV

We are now in a position to summarize our conclusions. It has been shown, first, that in interpreting the phenomenon of abbatial attendance in Visigothic Spain, it is imperative to rule out of consideration the abbot-proctors who attended the councils only as episcopal delegates. Secondly, it has been proved that the few abbots who did participate *qua* abbots were not drawn from houses

25 McLaughlin, *op. cit.*, p. 145, and note 6.

26 *Conc. Oscense* (598), c. 1; XVI Toledo (693), c. 7. For the bearing on this whole subject of the extraordinary abbatial synods of the Galician metropolitanate, see Dom Ildefons Herwegen, "Das Pactum des heiligen Fruktuosus von Braga," *Kirchenrechtliche Abhandlungen*, ed. by U. Stutz, XL, (Stuttgart: 1907), 54–57; and the writer's general work referred to above (note 16).

scattered over the peninsula and that they cannot be used to posit a universal abbatial privilege; their presence is to be accounted for solely in terms of local conditions in the Toletan diocese and metropolitanate. The Carolingian assumption, therefore, that has dominated canonical thought and practice ever since, is thus seen to rest upon a misunderstanding of the MS evidence as to Spanish practice. Whether this fruitful error was the chief reason for the admission of Carolingian abbots to councils remains uncertain, though it may be guessed that the supposed Spanish precedent simply provided a further argument to an already advancing feudal abbatiate whose rights were strengthened, rather than suggested or determined, by the canons of Toledo. In any case the appeal to Spanish precedent, though sincere, was mistaken; the Spanish abbatiate of the Visigothic period never possessed the general privilege of conciliar attendance ascribed to it by the canonists and historians of a later age.

Corcoran School of History

ADDITIONAL NOTE

Since the original publication in 1941 of the preceding Study V, the new although not definitive edition by José Vives of the acts of the Visigothic councils has appeared.[1] This work, resting upon fresh examination of the MSS constitutes the most reliable guide in print to the subscriptions of abbots to the Toletan canons. Since, however, my own collation of these lists was made in Spain from the codices, no revision of the data supplied above seems to be required. As for the abbots themselves, whether acting as *vicarii* or *jure proprio*, they will now be found listed in the prosopographic monographs of García Moreno and Kampers.[2]

In recent decades there has been ever stronger recognition of the central role of the councils of Toledo in the political and social as well as the ecclesiastical formation of Visigothic Spain, and this has led to renewed interest in the composition of their membership. In the literature this has produced, the treatments by García Gallo, Moreno Casado and Abadal have little or nothing to say on the abbatial question.[3] Fernández Alonso, however, in his well known volume on the clerical structures of the Visigothic Church, has a section devoted to the membership of the councils; here, in discussing the enrollment of abbots in the Toletan assemblies, he follows the conclusions presented above.[4] So too Linage Conde, in his massive study of the context of Hispano-Benedictine beginnings, summarizes my views on the conciliar abbots.[5]

Three works from British presses have contributed notably to our understanding of the Visigothic epoch. P. D. King's book, and the collection of international papers edited by E. James, although they make abundant use of the conciliar *acta*, confine themselves to the rich materials they contain for social history.[6] On the other hand, the broad political survey by E. A. Thompson, which deals at some length with the composition of the ecclesiastical assemblies of the kingdom, accepts my general

---

[1] José Vives, ed., *Concilios visigóticos e hispano-romanos* (Barcelona-Madrid, 1963).

[2] L. A. García Moreno, *Prosopografía del reino visigodo de Toledo* (Salamanca, 1974); G. Kampers, *Personengeschichtliche Studien zu Westgotenreich in Spanien* (Münster, Westfalen, 1979), 40–62.

[3] A. García Gallo, *Manual de historia del derecho español*, 6th ed. rev. (Madrid, 1975), I, 545–6; J. Moreno Casado, "Los concilios nacionales visigodos: iniciación de una política concordataria," *Bol. de la Univ. de Granada*, XVIII (1946), 179–223; R. d'Abadal, "Els concilis de Toledo," *Homenaje a Johannes Vincke* (Madrid, 1962–1963), I, 21–45, reprinted in his *Dels visigots als catalans*, I (Barcelona, 1969), 69–93.

[4] Justo Fernández Alonso, *La cura pastoral en la España romanovisigoda* (Rome, 1955), 241–252.

[5] A. Linage Conde, *Los orígenes del monacato benedictino en la Península Ibérica* (León, 1973), I, 228–9.

[6] P. D. King, *Law and Society in the Visigothic Kingdom* (Cambridge, 1972); Edward James, ed., *Visigothic Spain: New Approaches* (Oxford, 1980).

conclusions but expresses a reservation regarding my hypothesis that the extraordinarily heavy attendance of abbot-proctors at XIII Toledo (683) would seem to be linked with King Wamba's suppression of the rebellion under Duke Paul in Narbonensis and Tarraconensis.[7] At the same time Prof. Thompson acknowledges his inability to offer any more convincing solution.

The distinguished Spanish authority who has done most to advance the study of the Toletan councils in recent years, Prof. José Orlandis, takes due note of my data regarding abbatial membership, but in his latest important studies published in Spain and Germany he clearly prefers a conceptual interpretation couched in terms of canonical jurisprudence.[8] Agreeing fully with the basic distinction to be made between abbots serving as episcopal *vicarii* and others subscribing the acts as full participants in an assembly, Orlandis considers that the small numbers of *abbates* in attendance from VIII Toledo (653) constitute an *ordo abbatum*. By this term he seems to mean that these subscribant abbots, although admittedly drawn from the monastery of Agalí and a few other leading houses close to Toledo, appear as representatives of a corporate estate, the abbatiate of the Church throughout the Peninsula. This I do not find a defensible thesis; nor does Orlandis adduce any juridical or historical evidence to support such a concept. Certainly it is not discoverable (as might be expected) in the versions of the *Ordo de celebrando concilio* of 675–681 or in any other seventh-century source.[9] Nothing in the admission of *abbates* exclusively from the environs of the capital indicates an intention to assure canonical representation of the monastic *ordo* existing in all the Visigothic ecclesiastical provinces. On the contrary, the simultaneous innovation in 653 of subscription to conciliar *acta* by both abbots and the palatine magnates of the *Aula Regia*—a coincidence Orlandis rightly emphasizes—points directly to a pragmatic decision on the part of the reformist king Recceswinth to strengthen his position by enlisting the collaboration of powerful monastic and lay figures close to the royal capital. It should also be emphasized once more that closer study is needed on the antecedents of abbatial presence in diocesan and provincial synods convoked in the Carthaginensis and other provinces (particularly Galicia) of the Visigothic Church.[10]

[7] E. A. Thompson, *The Goths in Spain* (Oxford, 1969), 275–96.

[8] See his *La Iglesia en la España visigótica y medieval* (Pamplona, 1976), 151–181 (at 176–7); "La problemática conciliar en el reino visigodo de Toledo," *Anuario de hist. del derecho español*, XLVIII (1978), 277–306, especially 289–294; "Los laicos en los concilios visigodos," *ibid.*, L (1980), 177–187; (with D. Ramos-Lissón) *Die Synoden auf der Iberischen Halbinsel bis zum Einbruch des Islam (711)* (Paderborn, 1981), 202, 234, 333–335.

[9] C. Munier, "*L'Ordo de celebrando concilio wisigothique*," *Rev. des sciences religieuses*, XXXVII (1963), 250–271; I. da R. Pereira, "Um 'ordo' visigótico para a reunião do concílio provincial," *Rev. portuguesa de história*, XIII (1971), 197–209.

[10] Cf. A. Mundó, "Les anciens synodes abbatiaux et les 'Regulae SS. Patrum'," *Studia Anselmiana*, XLIV (1959), 107–125.

VI

THE ABBEY OF DUEÑAS AND THE CULT OF ST ISIDORE OF CHIOS IN THE COUNTY OF CASTILE (10th-11th CENTURIES)

I

Not the least of the obscurities that surround the early history of the Hispano-Benedictine abbey of San Isidoro de Dueñas in the Tierra de Campos, founded by Alfonso III in all probability between 900 and 910,[1] is its unusual entitlature and the extent to which this throws light upon the foundational community and the house's place in the complex monastic evolution of 10th-century León and Castile. It has long been known that the Isidore of Dueñas is not the learned metropolitan of Visigothic Seville, but the homonymous soldier-saint of Alexandria who died on the Aegean island of Chios, a victim of the Decian (or more likely the Diocletianic) persecution.[2] But how this eastern martyr's devotion, altogether lacking in the traditional *sanctorale* of the Hispanic Rite before 711 and only rarely encountered in the hagiotoponymy of the peninsular churches or monasteries of the Alta Reconquista, came to be introduced into the monas-

1. The oldest extant privilegio is of King García I in 911 but another of Fernando I, probably of 1053 (rather than, as currently, 1043), cites the lost foundation act of Alfonso el Magno; cfr. A. de Yepes, *Corónica general de la Orden de San Benito,* IV, Irache, 1613, pp. 198v-199; abridged version, éd. J. Pérez de Urbel, Madrid, 1959-60, II, pp. 146-147; M. D. Yáñez Neira, *Historia del real monasterio de San Isidro de Dueñas,* Palencia, 1969, pp. 37-42.

2. For the life, cult and bibliography: *Acta sanctorum, Maii,* t. III, Antwerp, 1680, pp. 445-52, and *Supplementum,* pp. 72-3; A. P. Frutaz, "Isidoro di Chio," *Enciclopedia cattolica,* VII, Vatican City, 1951, cols. 252-3; G. Lucchesi, "Isidoro di Chio," *Bibliotheca sanctorum,* VI, Roma, 1966, cols. 960-68.

tic repoblación of the lands along the river Pisuerga remains a mystery.

The distinguished scholar, the *El Silense* of our time, to whom this collection of papers pays merited homage, has rightly rejected for Dueñas the Mozarabic origin that can be ascribed to other Alfonsine foundations at Abellar, Escalada and Sahagún; [3] but whether the first monks brought their eastern patron and Benedictine observance from more northern Asturo-Leonese centers, from Galicia, Catalonia, or directly from Carolingian Aquitaine, still requires to be explored. The subject is of distinct interest, not merely because of San Isidro's later destiny — its cession to Cluny in 1073 by Alfonso VI as the first authentic Burgundian dependency below the Pyrenees, and for long the administrative capital for all the Ibero-Cluniac priories west of Catalonia — but also because from the very beginning the abbey raises questions of prime historical significance. Outside the Marca Hispanica Dueñas ranks as a notable center of that Franco-Carolingian hagiographic and liturgical infiltration into Spain which was to culminate by the second half of the 11th century in the triumph of the Roman Rite. Because its two oldest diplomas, the reales privilegios of García I (911) and Ordoño II (915) [4] (as surely also the lost proto-pergamino of Alfonso el Magno) allude to observance of the *Regula s. Benedicti*, the abbey must be given serious consideration, as has not yet been done, in any study of the introduction and lines of diffusion of Carolingian Benedictinism into western Spain, for its possible ties with the pactual and mixed Hispano-Carolingian cenobitism of primitive Castile. Not least, there is the presently ignored fact that prior to Fernando I's translation to León in 1063 of the remains of St Isidore of Seville, it was not the Baetic bishop but the Chian martyr whose devotion enjoyed liturgical and patronal popularity in Christian Spain, although almost exclusively in the County of Castile and its monastico-cultural affiliate the Rioja — a peculiar geographic circumscription which must somehow be related to an eastward propagation from the cult center at Dueñas.

It is upon this last subject that the present pages will focus. The conclusions reached cannot claim to rest upon more than a partial realization of the search of the diplomatic documenta-

3. J. Pérez de Urbel, *Los monjes españoles en los tres primeros siglos de la Reconquista*, BRAH, 101 (1932), pp. 39-40; but the Mozarabic explanation offered by J. E. Díaz-Jiménez, *Inmigración mozárabe en el reino de León. El monasterio de Abellar o de los santos mártires Cosme y Damián*, BRAH, 20 (1892), p. 125, still finds favor in Antonio Linage Conde, *Los orígenes del monacato benedictino en la Península ibérica*, León, 1973, t. III, p. 164 (no. 502).

4. These texts, although published by Yepes, *Corónica*, t. IV, pp. 444v-445v (esc. xxiii-xiv), are not discussed by Linage Conde, *Orígenes*, t. II, chap. V.

tion proposed by B. de Gaiffier when the Bollandist authority noted the surprising infrequency of Isidorian patronal and toponymic references in the texts.[5] They should however serve to alert students of the great Sevillano to the presence of another Isidore, in this age of consecrations to the Savior, the Virgin or the martyrs, and force them to re-consider, for example, their automatic ascription — found even in Díaz y Díaz and Linage Conde — to the Andalusian polymath of an 11th-century Castilian monastery (itself a mistaken conflation by Serrano of two different houses) whose titulary is almost certainly the martyr.[6] It should be apparent further that in seeking to reconstruct the older, distinctively Castilian devotion to the Aegean soldier-saint we may well be on the track of one unnoticed motive behind the sudden Leonese enthusiasm in 1063 for the counter-promotion, with strong imperial Hispanic and therefore anti-Castilian overtones, of the previously little regarded cult of the peninsular metropolitan.

II

We commence on fairly firm terrain with the certainty that before 711 the commemoration of St Isidore of Chios, although conceivably known in Visigothic Septimania by reason of its spread in southern Gaul, was not among the many eastern martyr cults admitted to the formal liturgical and hagiological tradition of the Visigothic Church, and thus represents an innovation of the Alta Reconquista.[7] Outside the Peninsula, on the other hand, from at least the fifth and sixth centuries, the cult enjoyed wide esteem. In the East, the martyr's burial place and basilica on the Aegean island of his passion was a center of pilgrimage; at Constantinople the synaxaries and *typika* of the Great Church provide for an *acoluthia* on 14 May, with mention of the chapel for his relics built adjoining the church of Hagia Eirene by St Marcian in the 5th century;[8] inscriptions have been discovered

5. *Le culte de Saint Isidore de Séville. Esquisse d'un travail*, in M. Díaz y Díaz, ed., *Isidoriana*, León, 1961, pp. 271-83 (at p. 283); also, B. de Gaiffier, *Études critiques d'hagiographie et d'iconologie*, Brussels, 1967, pp. 115-129.

6. M. Díaz y Díaz, *Isidoro en la Edad Media, Isidoriana*, pp. 345-87, at p. 373, n. 117; Id., *Aspectos de la tradición de la Regula Isidori:* Studia monastica, 5 (1963), pp. 27-57, at pp. 53-4 and n. 90; Linage Conde, *Orígenes*, t. III, p. 205 (no. 669).

7. P. David, *Le sanctoral hispanique at les patrons d'églises entre le Minho et le Mondego du IXe au XIe siècle*, in his *Études historiques sur la Galice et le Portugal*, Lisbon and Paris, 1947, pp. 185-256, especially pp. 197, 211-3.

8. H. Delehaye, *Synaxarium Ecclesiae Constantinopolitanae*, Acta SS., Propylaeum Novembris, Brussels, 1902, cols. 683-4; Juan Mateos, ed., *Le Typicon*

in Byzantine North Africa; and at Rome the anniversary came to be included (as it still is) in the Roman martyrology under 15 May, with a church and monastery of Isidorian patronage located near the Porta Tiburtina.[9]

It is however from the Merovingian kingdom that the chief testimony comes, proving that the cult of the stratelate saint of Chios, like those of so many other Greek, Syrian and Egyptian martyrs infiltrating the Gallican Church at the commencement of the Middle Ages, was established at Arles, Clermont, Trier and Cologne, a geography that points to its northern transmission by bishops hailing originally from Aquitaine.[10] From late in this century comes also the literary notice which Gregory of Tours (cap. 101) places in the series of eastern saints that terminates his *Liber in gloria martyrum* (a work completed ca. 585); this omits the Alexandrine birth, military profession ,and circumstances of the passion, but enlarges upon the miraculous curative well in the Chian basilica.[11]

After Gregory there is a gap: to my knowledge, neither the Merovingian *vitae sanctorum* and *passiones,* nor the literary and historical texts, mention the Chian devotion,[12] and no inquiry has yet been undertaken to trace its persistance in the Gallican liturgical calendars of the 7th to the 9th centuries. It is therefore upon the major martyrologies of the period that we must depend for the immediate background to the emergence in Spain. Those of Bede (735), the anonymous of Lyon composed before 806 and represented by Paris B. N. Lat. 3879, and of Rabanus Maurus (ca. 850), make no provision whatever for commemoration of our St. Isidore.[13] In contrast, the expanded form of Lat. 3879 known as Recension *M,* which Quentin proved is the martyrolo-

---

de la Grande Église, Rome, 1962-3; Orientalia Christiana Analecta, vols. 165-6, I, pp. 292-3; II, 316-7; R. Janin, *La géographie ecclésiastique de l'Empire byzantin,* III: *les églises et les monastères,* Paris, 1953, 2d. ed., 1969, p. 271.

9. H. Delehaye, *Les origines du culte des martyrs,* 2d ed., Brussels, 1933, pp. 226-7, 239, 385-9, 401; *Acta SS.,* Propylaeum Decembris (1940), 189-190; *Codice topografico della città di Roma,* ed. R. Valentini and G. Zucchetti, Roma, 1940-42; Fonti per la storia d'Italia, 81, 88, t. II, p. 187, 301.

10. Eugen Ewig, *Die Verehrung orientalischer Heiliger im spätrömischen Gallien und im Merowingerreich, Festschrift P. E. Schramm,* Wiesbaden, 1964, t. I. pp. 385-400, at p. 393-4.

11. *M. G. H. SS. Rer. Meroving.,* I, ii, 2d ed. by B. Krusch and W. Levison, Hanover, 1969, p. 105. For the date of the *In glor. mart.,* René Aigrain, *L'hagiographie,* Paris, 1953, pp. 175, 182-3.

12. In the whole of t. VII of *M. G. H. SS. Rer. Meroving., Passiones vitaeque sanctorum,* ed. B. Krusch and W. Levison, Hanover, 1920, I have found only two references to St Isidore: p. 458, line 6, p. 462, line 6; both are from Clermont.

13. H. Quentin, *Les martyrologies historiques du moyen âge,* Paris, 1908, pp. 17-221, especially 47, 111-12 (Bede), 138 ff., 220-1 (Lat. 3879); *Martyrologium* of Rabanus: *PL,* 110, cols. 1121-87.

gy compiled by the deacon Florus in the first third of the 9th century, initiates a new stage in the history of the cult. For of the thirteen martyrs whom this learned Lyonese cleric resurrected from the *In gloria martyrum* of the bishop of Tours and to whom, by including them in his own decisively influential work, he gave renewed popularity in the Carolingian epoch, one is St Isidore of Chios. Florus severely abridges the text of cap. 101, retaining only brief mention of the Chian burial place and the basilica with its medicinal well. [14] In this form the Gregorian notice is reproduced *Idibus Maii* in the widely used martyrologies of Ado (850-859/860) and Usuard (ca. 875) — with variants that show independent adoption from their common model — and eventually finds its way into the modern Roman martyrology. [15]

It is not however to a crossing of the Pyrenees in the late 9th and 10th centuries that the original introduction of the Isidorian cult at Dueñas or elsewhere in Spain can be ascribed, for two unmistakable clues point to an entirely different medium of initial penetration. Florus, Ado and Usuard, like their ultimate source Gregory, have nothing on the Chian martyr's military profession, yet this knowledge was early familiar to the monks at Dueñas, as is proved by the real privilegio which in 924 King Fruela II addressed to their titular: "uobis dominis et sanctis martiribus quorum reliquie sunt condite in aula b. Isidori militis." [16]

Then there is the significant difference in the dating of the obit. Since the *In gloria martyrum* offers no such calendrical information, it must have been Florus himself who attached his précis of cap. 101 to 15 May, being followed in this by Ado and Usuard. The source from which he extracted this characteristically Roman date is unclear, since no Isidorian commemoration appears under the May Ides in the manuscripts of the *Martyrologium Hieronymianum* belonging to the major Epternacensis (*E*; saec. VIII in.) family. [17] Florus either did not know, or more likely deliberately rejected, the observance on 14 May (*II Id. Mai*) which is not only that of the ancient Byzantine tradition but is found, probably because this date had been kept by the churches of late imperial and Merovingian Gaul, in the other principal Frankish group of *Martyrologium Hieronymianum* codices headed

14. QUENTIN, pp. 314-18; on the Isidorian notice, p. 317.

15. *PL* 123, cols. 226-7 (Ado); 124 (Usuard).

16. Madrid, Acad. Hist., Col. Velázquez, t. IV, leg. 4, fol. 669r - 770r (no. 1382).

17. On the redactions of *MHE* and *MHB*, and the use of the former by Florus, see QUENTIN, pp. 324 ff.; AIGRAIN, pp. 32-50 (especially, 40-1).

by Bernensis 289 (*B*; saec. VIII ex.).[18] Yet it is this earlier feast by one day that is invariably encountered in the pre-12th-century Hispanic calendars, sacramentaries and passionaries, as well as in certain diplomas of Dueñas, where as late as the 17th century Yepes found the monks still celebrating their patron's anniversary according to the Greek fashion on 14 May.[19].

On these two grounds, the concept of Isidore as *martyr et miles* and the commemoration on 14 May, we can believe that the Hispanic cult followed originally a quite different line of transmission from that of the Florus-Ado-Usuard martyrologies or calendars based upon these. In view of the consecration of San Isidoro de Dueñas, this means it must have penetrated into western Spain by or before the end of the 9th century.

The next question is whether the Hispanic liturgical sources are in agreement with such a conclusion and whether, if so, they permit any more precise determination of the time, circumstances and area of diffusion. If we turn first to the Hispanic calendars dating after 711 but before the final adoption of the Roman Rite in the last third of the 11th century, most of which were collectively edited in 1949-50 by Vives and Fábrega,[20] we find that there are seven which stipulate a commemoration of the Chian St Isidore on *II. Ids. Mai* although in widely varying terms. These are the calendars contained in: the Codex Vigilanus or Albeldensis (*E*) of 976, and its reproduction in the Codex Aemilianensis (*E'*) of 1002; the *Antiphonarium* (or *Antiphonale*) of León (*L*), saec. X, but as interpolated in the first half of the 11th century;[21] the *Liber Ordinum* (*S3*) of 1052 from the Albeldan dependency of San Prudencio de Laturce; the two Silos manuscripts of the *Liber*

18. QUENTIN, p. 317. The two quite independent short forms of *MH* known to have circulated in Spain (Escorialensis I. III. 13, saec. X; fragment, fols. 2-3v of Acad. Hist. 18) mingle readings of both *E* and *B* redactions; the first omits St Isidore, the second commences only with 26 July. See B. de GAIFFIER, *Un abrégé hispanique du martyrologe hiéronymien:* Anal. Boll., 82 (1964), pp. 5-36, which corrects at various points the commentary of José JANINI, *Dos calendarios emilianenses del siglo* XI, *Hispania sacra*, 15 (1962), pp. 177-95.

19. YEPES, *Corónica*, IV, p. 198; ed. PÉREZ DE URBEL, II, p. 148.

20. José VIVES and Angel FÁBREGA, *Calendarios hispánicos anteriores al siglo* XII: *Hispania sacra*, 2 (1949), pp. 119-46, 339-80; 3 (1950), pp. 145-61. See also B. de GAIFFIER, *Un calendrier franco-hispanique de la fin du XIIe siècle:* Anal. Boll., 69 (1951), pp. 282-323, and especially p. 299, with important note 4 on Isidore.

21. On the still unresolved problem of dating the many additions in several hands made to the original 10th-century calendar, cfr. Serrano's minuscular *sci-sce* hypothesis (which would apply to St Isidore of Chios) in his Prólogo to *Antiphonarium mozarabicum de la catedral de León*, ed. Padres Benedictinos de Silos, Burgos, 1928; VIVES-FÁBREGA, *Calendarios*, pp. 344-7; J. PÉREZ DE URBEL, *Antifonario de León: el escritor y la época:* Archivos leoneses, 8 (1954), pp. 115-44, especially pp. 122-4, 143; José VIVES, *En torno a la datación del antifonario legionense:* Hispania Sacra, 8 (1955), pp. 117-24.

commicus of *ante* 1067 (*P1*) and 1072 (*P2*); and the 11th-century fragment now bound as fol. 6-11 of a Roman missal from San Millán de la Cogolla.[22] Three calendars complete for May lack an Isidorian entry: that of the Ripoll codex (*B*), 10th century; the so-called Primero of Silos (*S4*), very possibly from late in this same century; and that of the *Liber diurnus* (*C*) at Compostela, copied in 1055 for the *reyes* Fernando I and Sancha.[23]

From this tabulation it would appear that in the 10th century the cult of Isidore the Martyr, if known at all, was far from enjoying general acceptance in Catalonia or León, and in the latter kingdom was still ignored in court circles of the mid-11th century; that outside the Tierra de Campos it was chiefly observed in an area centering about the Castello-Riojan monasteries of Silos, San Millán de la Cogolla and Albelda; and that in this zone the notices come from the second half of the 11th century except for that of 976 (and its facsimile of 1002 at San Millán). The laconic Albeldan entry of 976 is the earliest of calendrical origin but it is to be observed that it follows by almost three-quarters of a century the foundation of Dueñas and displays no awareness of the martyr's insular passion or military status.

From what can be discovered in the sacramentaries and passionaries of the 10th and 11th centuries much the same chronological and geographic picture emerges. The precise terminology of the rubric used in the manuscripts of the Hispanic *Liber sacramentorum* is not reproduced by Férotin in his synthesized list but the four codices he adduces in this connection can be linked to 11th-century scriptoria in Castile and the Rioja.[24] In all probability the language used is that found in the text of the *Missale mixtum* as published in 1500 at the instruction of Cisneros by Fray Antonio Ortiz, an edition which despite certain readily distinguishable Romanist interpolations is known to have drawn largely upon trustworthy manuscripts of the 11th century from Silos and San Millán.[25] In this *Missale* the undated Isidorian

22. The actual entries for 14 May are as follows: *E*: Sci Ysidori; *E'*: Sci isidori; *L*: sci isidori cio insula; *S3*: sci isidori mr in Alexa(n)dria: *P1*: sci Ysidori mrtyris xpi; *P2*: sci ysidori mrtyris xpi; Cod. Aemil. 18: Uictoris et chorone mrum. Isidori mr. (JANINI, *Dos calendarios*, p. 187). The language of *L* may reflect a Carolingian martyrology, but like *S3* may have been influenced by the *Passio Isidori*.

23. VIVES-FÁBREGA, pp. 127, 352, 364.

24. *Le Liber mozarabicus sacramentorum et les manuscrits mozarabes*, ed. M. FÉROTIN, Paris, 1912, p. xlviii: Codd. *P, R, S, T*.

25. *PL* 135, cols. 655-1036. On the provenence and authenticity of the MSS used. Cfr. L. BROU, *Études sur le Missel et le Brévviaire 'Mozarabe' imprimés*: Hispania sacra, 11 (1958), pp. 349-398, especially p. 378; DAVID, *Études*, p. 195.

rubric reads: *Isidori militis: omnia dicuntur unius martyris.*[26] Since the appellative cannot have come from the calendrical tradition, which as evident above does not know it, or from the likewise silent Roman and Carolingian martyrologies, we plainly encounter here once more, as previously with the Dueñas privilegio of 924, the presence of a quite different source which is surely to be identified as the *Passio*.

Because the Latin version of the *Passio s. Isidori* has still not been published from the Hispanic *Passionarium* it remains unknown whether it represents a faithful translation of the Greek original (or the *Epitome* of this) or, alternatively, draws upon the account incorporated into the Byzantine *Vita s. Marciani*; but both these works of the 5th century record the martyr's military profession and the place and circumstances of his execution. Siegmund classifies the Latin redaction of the Isidorian *Passio* among the many such made from the Greek between the 7th and 9th centuries;[27] and we may add that while it was not used by Gregory of Tours or the Carolingian martyrologers, its circulation in Aquitaine by 900 (and perhaps not too long before this date) surely underlies, directly or indirectly, the foundation in Spain at the commencement of the 10th century of San Isidro de Dueñas, with its novel entitlature and its community's awareness of their patron's stratelatic character. Fábrega's valuable but incomplete study of the Hispanic *Passionarium,*[28] although it offers no help on the background of the new pieces added in the 11th century and does not attempt to correlate its findings with the chronology of monastic and parochial entitlatures, establishes very clearly one thing pertinent to our inquiry. Of the four extant codices, the two dating ca. 950-1000 — one, Brit. Mus. Add. 25600, copied at San Pedro de Cardeña ca. 950; the other, a Silos MS, Paris, B. N. nouv. acq. lat. 2180, of the second half of the century, from a Castilian house of San Pelayo 'in Baldem de Abellano' — make no place for St Isidore of Chios in their highly conservative Old Hispanic martyrology. In contrast the two others, both of the 11th century — Escorialensis b. I. 4, from Cardeña; Paris, B. N. nouv. acq. lat. 2179, from Silos — greatly

26. Col. 745; and cfr. in the synthetic *Calendarium* (col. 98): *Isidori militis IX lect.*

27. Albert SIEGMUND, *Die Überlieferung der griechischen christlichen Literatur in der lateinischen Kirche bis zum zwölften Jahrhundert,* Munich-Pasing, 1949, p. 237; cfr. pp. 201-2, 210-13, 226 ff.

28. Angel FÁBREGA GRAU, *Pasionario hispánico* (*siglos* VII-XI), t. I, Madrid-Barcelona, 1953; *Monumenta Hispaniae sacra,* ser. litúrg., VI; to be consulted with B. de GAIFFIER, *La lecture des actes des martyres dans la prière liturgique en Occident: à propos du Passionaire hispanique:* Anal. Boll., 72 (1954), pp. 134-66.

expand the older peninsular Passionario to take in numerous new pieces, and one of these, assigned in both collections to be read on 14 May, is the *Passio Isidori.*[29] This conforms with what we already know of the Castilian interest of the mid-11th century, but it does more: it demonstrates that even at such eminent abbeys as Cardeña and Silos it was not until after 1000, and very probably ca. 1050 or later, that St. Isidore of Chios, along with other eastern saints then popular in France, entered the passionary used in the monastic heartland of eastern Castile. And this despite the commemoration found in the Albeldan Calendar of 976, to say nothing of the dedication of Dueñas something like a century and a half before.

What are we to conclude from all this liturgical testimony? To be sure, the presence or absence of an Isidorian component in calendars, sacramentaries and passionaries cannot validly be evaluated without comparative study of its associations with the whole range of Franco-Roman martyr cults then swelling peninsular *sanctoralia,* and of their lines of codicological transmission. Nor can we overlook the fact that it is partly due to historical accident that so many of our surviving liturgical manuscript happen to come from Castile and the Rioja. Nevertheless it should be plain that by ca. 1050 veneration of the Aegean soldier-saint was well established among the monasteries of eastern Castile and the Rioja, and had probably by this time been carried also to at least one Leonese house by the interpolator of the *Antiphonale.* Nor is there any problem at this late date in recognizing in the references of *S3* to Alexandria and of *L* to Chios the influence of the *Passio* or the Carolingian martyrologies. Nevertheless, with the exception of the Albeldan Calendar of 976 (and the dependent Cod. Aemilianensis of 1002), none of the liturgical testimonies can be considered truly early, and some at least chart later repeated waves of Gallican and Roman hagiological penetration and need not be descended from the patently much more ancient first arrival of the Isidorian cult in Spain. In these terms the key centers for our inquiry become the Rioja (*ante* 976) and the Tierra de Campos (Dueñas, ca. 900-910); and the problem is one of determining the priority, affiliations, and (if any) inter-dependency of the two borderlands of the old County of Castile. Here the first need is to bring to bear the limited but valuable testimony provided by data of another category, the Isidorian entitlatures of Castilian monas-

---

29. FÁBREGA, pp. 225 ff., 233, 241, 273. The rubric in the Silos MS reads: "Passio sancti Isidori martyris Christi, qui passus est in Alexandria sub Decio imperatore, die II idus Maias"; de GAIFFIER, *Calendrier,* p. 299, note 4.

teries and churches erected prior to the Hispalensian revival of 1063, and the handful of Isidorian placenames still surviving in the landscape of Castile.

III

The list is not a long one but from it we can discern, first of all, the pattern of a spread of Chian patronage in certain districts of Castile between the rivers Arlanzón and Duero that must stem from the cult center at San Isidro de Dueñas. We commence with the more visible ecclesiastical cases:

A. *The Monastery of San Isidro de Clunia.* The sole known reference to this house occurs in an undated pergamino of the first half of the 11th century which was first published in 1912 by Serrano y Sanz under the rubric "Relación histórica de algunas divisas de Clunia que fueron de la Condesa Da. Ava y de otras que poseyó Ruy Gudestioz;" and in 1926 reproduced in a philologically more exact version by Menéndez Pidal, this time headed "Declaración de los derechos que los merinos de Coruña del Conde, a nombre del conde de Castilla, tenían en Espeja y otros pueblos vecinos." [30] This act, cast in what Serrano y Sanz styles "un latín sumamente bárbaro," is not always susceptible of ready comprehension, as the dissimilar rubrics intimate. It reaches back in its historical allusions to the days of the Castilian counts Fernán González (920-970) and Garci Fernández (970-995) and the latter's wife Countess Ava, but it was written at a time when King Sancho el Mayor of Navarre controlled Castile, i. e., between 1029 and 1035. The text displays two overriding concerns: (i) to trace the ownership of various land grants around Espeja and their subordination to the mandación of the Castilian comital merino based at Clunia; and (ii) to detail in this connection the terms of a partition affecting these lands, with particular reference to the properties held at the time of writing by one Rodrigo Godestioz or Gustioz. It is among the latter that a monastery of San Isidro de Clunia is enumerated:

> Illas hereditates de Fonteauria, de domno Seuero, et suas casas fecit eas Ruderico Godestioz palatjos, et tenet sancti Ysi-

30. M. Serrano y Sanz, *Noticias y documentos históricos del Condado de Ribagorza hasta la muerte de Sancho Garcés III*, Madrid, 1912, pp. 336-343; R. Menéndez Pidal, *Orígenes del español*, 3d ed., Madrid, 1950, pp. 35-38. Cfr. J. Pérez de Urbel, *Historia del Condado de Castilla*, Madrid, 1945, t. II, p. 937; A. Linage Conde, *Orígenes*, t. III, p. 147 (no. 438). Serrano y Sanz dates the text ca. 1023-30; Menéndez Pidal ca. 1030.

dori monasterio de Clunia cum suas sernas et suas uineas et suo mulino.

This house of San Isidro, with its modest abadengo, must have been located in the alfoz of Clunia (mod. Coruña del Conde, prov. Burgos, part. Aranda de Duero), perhaps close to the town in the direction of the cited Hontoria (i. e., Hontoria de Valdearados, to the southwest). Since Clunia, although first re-peopled by Count Gonzalo Fernández in 912, had to be abandoned after the battle of Valdejunquera (920), remained for decades a frontier outpost of contention, and as late as 1007-1010 shows up among the fortified places surrendered by the Moors,[31] the community of San Isidro is not likely to have anticipated by much the year 1000. While we have no way of telling whether its erection as a familial abbey was the work of Rodrigo Gustioz, his father or some other kinsman, we can therefore tentatively assign its beginnings to the first third of the 11th century, i. e., to the time of Count Sancho García (995-1017).

Rodrigo Gustioz himself, the proprietor of San Isidro de Clunia, is also known as a subscribant to diplomas of Covarrubias (1024) and Cardeña (1032),[32] and from our Clunian pergamino he can be identified as a rico hombre or infanzón of considerable landed wealth. He was undoubtedly a prominent member of one of the most celebrated Castilian noble families of the epoch, that descended from Gonzalo Gustioz and linked to the immortal legend of the Siete Infantes de Lara of the 10th century. This family, closely connected with Lara and Salas de los Infantes to the north of Clunia, has been much studied in its political and literary aspects by Menéndez Pidal, Pérez de Urbel and others,[33] but still awaits study of its prime role in the Castilian repoblación below Burgos of the fertile mesopotamia between the rivers Arlanza and Duero, where its members can be found acquiring numerous aldeas, sernas, casas, molinos and other properties as far west as the Pisuerga and even beyond. D. Rodrigo's own holdings, according to the text of 1030-35, embraced in addition to the numerous pieces near Clunia and Espeja, lands to the

---

31. Pérez de Urbel, *HCC,* t. I, pp. 277-82, 301-2; t. II, pp. 593, 811-2; R. Menéndez Pidal, *Documentos lingüísticos de España,* t. I, Madrid, 1919, pp. 5-6; Id., *Orígenes del español,* p. 476.

32. *Cart. del Infantado de Covarrubias,* ed. L. Serrano, Silos-Valladolid, 1907, nos. 13 (p. 40), 15 (p. 45); *Becerro gótico de Cardeña,* ed. L. Serrano, Silos-Valladolid, 1910, n. 71 (p. 85).

33. On the Gustioz linaje and its territorial connections, see R. Menéndez Pidal, *La leyenda de los Infantes de Lara,* 2d ed., Madrid, 1934, pp. 175-99, 451-9; J. Pérez de Urbel, *El Condado de Castilla,* Madrid, 1969-70, t. II, p. 425 ff.

northwest in the area of Lerma and still others scattered to the southwest of Clunia beyond Roa as far as Peñafiel on the south side of the Duero.[34] If, as the reference in our Clunian act to a partition implies, all these estates constitute his share of a señorío which had come to be divided between himself and Da. Tarasia — perhaps his sister but at any rate a kinswoman, whose own aldeas of Valdezate, Pinillos de Esgueva, Villafruela and others lie in this same country towards the Leonese border — then we have before us here the outlines of a domain that in the preceding generation reached well beyond Clunia into the valley of the Esgueva and on to Roa and Peñafiel.[35]

Although the pergamino does not distinguish which Isidore was the monastery's titular, everything about the rare dedication points to the martyr as against the metropolitan. Since this branch of the Gustioz linaje has no ties within the Rioja, it is evident that we must look to the west. The far-flung distribution of its holdings would have brought this family at various points close to, and doubtless into, Cerrato and the immediately adjoining portion of the Tierra de Campos on the west or Castilian side of the Pisuerga, i. e., into the comarcas which before the expansionist era of Count Sancho García marked the extension of the County of Castile to the eastern fringes of the Leonese kingdom. This would have brought the Gustioz within easy distance of San Isidro de Dueñas at the confluence of the Pisuerga and the Carrión. Furthermore, we know — and the proof of this will be given below — that during the 10th and 11th centuries this abbey was acquiring patrimonies and at least three monasteries across the river in that part of the Campos under Castilian rule. It can safely be assumed that where the monks of Dueñas extended their abadengo they introduced the veneration of their patron, so that the contacts made possible through the possessions of the Gustioz in this same area offer a plausible explanation of how the cult of St Isidore of Chios could have been carried, whether by Rodrigo himself or by one of his family, to their monasterio propio in the alfoz of Clunia.

---

34. See the careful geographical exegesis of MENÉNDEZ PIDAL, *Orígenes del español*, pp. 37-8.

35. Cfr. also, as possibly another component of this partition, the familial *porciones* bestowed conjointly by Momadona, daughter of Godesteo Díaz and Domna Taresia, and her brother Munnio Gostioz, upon San Pedro de Arlanza in a donation charter of 1054, where holdings are mentioned at Peñaranda de Duero, Paúles del Agua, Terradillos de Esgueva and other points west of Clunia and between Lerma and the Duero, as well as in Cerrato at Antigüedad (prov. Palencia, part. Baltanás) and Sequilla in the vega of Riofranco: *Cartulario de San Pedro de Arlanza*, ed. L. SERRANO, Madrid, 1925, no. 55 (pp. 114-6); cfr. p. 106, n. 12.

B. *The Monastery of San Isidro de Hontoria de Riofranco.* This second Castilian house of Isidorian entitlature is attested by two brief but trustworthy notices. The real privilegio of 1 July 1043 (not, as invariably now stated, 1048) [36] in which Fernando I and Da. Sancha transferred to San Pedro de Arlanza their *abadía propia* of Santa María de Retortillo, lists as belonging to this community located near Palenzuela (prov. Palencia, part. Baltanás), a monastery dedicated to St Isidore: "et in Fonte Oria monasterium sancti Ysidori cum suas terras et suas uineas et suos molendinos et suos pratos." Since Serrano identifies this Hontoria, one of several of the name in Castile, as that of Valdearados just west of Clunia, it has been natural to assume that it is the same community as that of Clunia. [37] This conflation is certainly erroneous. We have no basis for assuming that between 1030-35 and 1043 Rodrigo Gustioz lost or transferred his familial monastery to the real abadía of Santa María de Retortillo which the first king of Castile was to turn over to Arlanza. Given the proximity of Retortillo itself to the Río Franco, an affluent of the Arlanza near its juncture just below Palenzuela with the Arlanzón, it is the nearby Hontoria de Riofranco that is both inherently more likely and indicated by the diploma itself. For the text does not associate *Fonte Oria* with an earlier mention of Clunia and the church there of San Esteban but places it after *Villa Froila,* possibly a hamlet on the Río Arauzo as Serrano conjectures, but more convincingly taken to be the important Villafruela southeast of Palenzuela. Finally, this reasoning finds full corroboration in Alfonso VI's Fuero of 1074 to Palenzuela, which mentions a district of *Sanctus Isidorus* adjoining the municipal alfoz on its eastern, i. e., Río Franco, side. [38]

San Isidro de Hontoria de Riofranco cannot have been of any great size or importance, to judge by its subordination to Retortillo; but we can at least infer that its foundation preceded the

---

36. *Cart. Arlanza,* n. 51 (pp. 103-7) carries the date 1 July 1048, as found in Alfonso X's confirmation of 1255; but for Serrano's own correction of this, with brief discussion of the abbey of Retortillo, see his *El obispado de Burgos y Castilla primitiva,* Burgos, 1935-6, t. I, pp. 237-8.

37. *Cart. Arlanza,* p. 105, n. 10; Díaz y Díaz, *loc. cit.*, in note 6 above. Yepes, *Corónica* (ed. Pérez de Urbel, t. I, p. 127, col. 2) confuses this cenobium with that of Santa Eugenia at Tabladillo, which follows it in the pergamino's tabulation, an error which persists in Flórez, *ES* XXVII, 110. Linage Conde correctly distinguishes the two San Isidros of Clunia and Hontoria: *Orígenes,* t. III, p. 147 (no. 438); p. 205 (no. 669).

38. "... de campo de Lagunas [Laguna] fasta Autier de Ferro; et deinde usque ad Sanctum Ysidorum circam Villamroderici [Villodrigo on the Arlanzón] comodo semita discurrit en acca": *Colección diplomática de San Salvador de El Moral,* ed. L. Serrano, Madrid-Valladolid, 1906, p. 20; also T. Muñoz y Romero, *Colección de fueros municipales,* Madrid, 1847, 275 ff.

death of Sancho García, since Alfonso VI's Palenzuelan code presents itself as basically a confirmation of the previous fuero given the town by "el conde de los buenos fueros." This means that the municipal confines shortly before 1017 would have touched, as they did in 1074, the land known as that of San Isidro, and that the house of Hontoria already existed. It might throw some light upon its origins if we could ascertain something of how and when Santa María acquired not only San Isidro but seven other monasteries: San Millán and Santa María de Belbimbre (above Palenzuela), Santa Juliana de Burgos, San Fausto de Cerezo del Río Tirón, San Juan Bautista de Huerta del Rey, Santa Eugenia de Tabladillo, and Santos Facundo y Martín de Valdecañas. If we can consider the transfer of Santa María de Retortillo to Arlanza in 1043 to be part of Fernando I's plan to build up the latter house as the major monastic center of the lower Arlanza valley, as indicated by his series of closely spaced donations to San Pedro between 1039 and 1048, then behind this we may discern an earlier similar program initiated by one of his comital predecessors with Retortillo as its keystone. This would explain why Santa María — an abbey of which we never hear before this date and but rarely thereafter [39] — appears in 1043 with the surprisingly large, meticulously inventoried temporal of subject houses and other patrimonies that stretches over the whole zone of Castilian repoblación from Burgos south to the Ura Valley and thence westward to Antigüedad and Sequilla in Cerrato and on past Palenzuela to the banks of the river Arlanzón. [40] In such case, the author of the anterior scheme can only have been Sancho García, whose strong interest in promoting the rapid settlement of his county's western districts is illustrated in the liberal fuero to Palenzuela; and San Isidro de Hontoria would have been one of the eight smaller monasteries in comital hands Sancho used to promote the rise of Retortillo.

If this hypothesis throws no light upon Hontoria's origins and entitlature, it at least suggests the house was already in existence not only before 1043 but before 1017. What is in any case beyond dispute is that here on the banks of the Río Franco, and close to the line of the Pisuerga, we stand once again within the shadow of the cult center at Dueñas, only some 40 kms. away. Lastly, we encounter, as with San Isidro de Clunia but in this case quite firmly, a connection with the great count of Castile; and perhaps another with the house of Gustioz, for the visible clustering of many of Retortillo's patrimonies around Espeja, Clunia and Arau-

39. *Cart. Arlanza,* p. 258 (no. 143, 1217).
40. Cfr. *Cart. Arlanza,* nos. 32, 34-6, 41, 46-7, 53.

zo de Salce, as disclosed by the Fernandine act of 1043, may well point to the common interest of the count of Castile and his infanzón Rodrigo in the propagation of the Chian devotion.

C. *The Parroquia of San Isidro de Muñó.* On 14 May 1013, the anniversary of the martyr of Chios as celebrated in Spain, the Condes Sancho García and Urraca of Castile addressed to San Isidro de Dueñas a donation act which bestowed upon the Campestrian abbey their church of San Isidro at Muñó or Castillo de Muñó. The full text no longer survives but we have two short extracts from it, based on the lost Becerro. The first of these, preserved in the Colección Velázquez of the Academia de la Historia (with a copy in B. N. 720) makes hash of the dispositive clause by confusing the church with Dueñas itself: "Nos autem famuli uestri Sancius Dei gratia comes cum coniuge Vrracha comitissa ... hacen donacion y oblacion de la misma yglessia del monº de Sant Isidro dando sus terminos y limites hasta san Chyriacum y otros mojones."[41] Fortunately, this can be clarified by an entry in the *Indice de Dueñas* which records: "Vna donacion de Sancho, Conde en Castilla, y la Condesa D. Urracha ... dona(n) al Glorioso S. Ysidro y a S. Martin, cuius Basilica Fundata est in suburbio atque Regimine Legionense, y a su abb(ad) la Iglesia de S. Ysidro que esta cerca del Castillo que se llama Munio en loco predicto super Benbibre."[42] Between them these two notices suffice to fix the site of the parroquia bestowed upon Dueñas as near the castle of Muñó (mod. Villavieja de Muñó), i. e., on the south side of the lower Arlanza, just upstream from Belbimbre and midway between Palenzuela and Burgos. A charter of 929 delimiting the bounds of the monastery of San Millán de Belbimbre (which as we have seen had by 1043 become a dependency of Santa María de Retortillo) mentions as adjoining the abadengo on its northern side an *Otero de sancti Quirici,*[43] which must be the mojón of *San Chyriacum* preserved in connection with the church of San Isidro by the scribe of Colección Velázquez. But since in this act of 929 there is no reference to the parroquia, it may not yet have been in existence.

The implications of the Sanchan grant of 1013, the only one so far as we know that this great Castilian count conferred upon the monks of Dueñas, are of considerable interest. Once more we find ourselves at a site of Isidorian ecclesiastical patronage in close proximity to the Campos and the valley of the Pisuerga, this time in a context disclosing Sancho García's personal as-

41. Col. Velázquez, t. IV, leg. 4, no. 1433; Madrid, B. N. MS 720, no. 54.
42. AHN, Códices, *Indice de Dueñas,* fol. [11], s. v.
43. *Cart. Arlanza,* p. 22 (no. 6).

sociation with Dueñas as benefactor and with an Isidorian iglesia propia as proprietor. That the parroquia itself existed prior to 1013 is patent, so that we may conjecturally place its construction between that date and the *post quem* of 929 suggested above. A second inference is that the comital generosity of 1013 is inseparable from Sancho's recent seizure of the Tierra de Campos from León and a desire to win the influential adherence of San Isidro de Dueñas. The rising lords of Castile had long sought to wrest this fertile comarca from their Leonese rivals, but it was Sancho García who in 1010 or thereabouts, during the minority of Alfonso V, successfully overran the Campos and was still holding the area down to his death in 1017, at which point the Leonese monarch was able to expel the Castilians.[44]. Thus it is in the years between ca. 1010 and 1017 that all three of the Isidorian foundations we have inspected might naturally fall, the consecration of the monasteries at Clunia and Hontoria, the cession to Dueñas of the Muñó parroquia marking a definite attraction at this time on the part of the ruler of Castile and at least one of his magnates, Rodrigo Gustioz, to the cult of the Chian saint.

D. *The Isidorian placenames in Castile.* In addition to the sites at Clunia, Hontoria and Muñó, a preliminary search of Castilian toponymy has turned up a small number of other Isidorian placenames within the bounds of the old County of Castile.[45] These could assist in charting the cult's lines of diffusion if only they could be pinned down chronologically so as to avoid the possibility that they may stem from the Hispalensian, not the Chian, Isidore. The San Isidro which lies just below Salas de los Infantes, and another south of Clunia near Rocigas de Perales, are both sufficiently close to Clunia to be classified, if not as outlying patrimonies of the monastery of San Isidro, then at least as locales of churches consecrated in the martyr's name. Just to the north of Aranda de Duero is San Isidro de las Vi-

---

44. Note that when, after Alfonso V's own passing in 1028 and the murder at León the following year of Count Sancho's son the Infante García, Sancho el Mayor occupied Castile and the Tierra de Campos, the Navarrese monarch similarly rewarded San Isidro de Dueñas by the donations in 1030/1 of the church of San Pedro de Avellano, and on 14 May 1033 (the anniversary of the Chian martyr) the church of San Miguel de Baltanás. Both parroquias are in the Campos on the Castilian side of the Pisuerga. Cfr. J. PÉREZ DE URBEL, *Sancho el Mayor de Navarra,* Madrid, 1950, p. 426; C. J. BISHKO, *Fernando I y los orígenes de la alianza castellano-Leonesa con Cluny:* Cuadernos de historia de España, 47-48 (1968), pp. 65-6.

45. I have examined the Mapa Militar Itinerario de España, chiefly sheets 24 and 25 but further search needs to be made in the topographical dictionaries of Miñano, Madoz and Bleiberg.

ñas; and in the partido of Castrogeriz west of the Arlanzón there is a Villasidro. These two are slightly less probable; but it is noteworthy that all four of these sites lie within easy distance of Clunia, Hontoria or Muñó. Finally, two 13th century pergaminos from San Salvador de Oña speak of "la esglesia de sant Esedro de Uillasant," which Alamo identifies as Villasante, some 6 kms. from Espinosa de los Monteros in the partido of Villarcayo, where there still exists a church of San Isidro; [46] but this is far enough from our other locations to make the precise patronage more uncertain.

IV

If we now undertake to relate the foregoing liturgical, diplomatic and toponymic testimonies to the problems of the Hispanic propagation of the cult of St Isidore of Chios and the early history of the abbey of Dueñas, the following conclusions may be formulated:

(i) The extreme rarity of Isidorian data in general, and the strongly marked concentration of those discoverable in the zone Tierra de Campos-Castile-La Rioja, are confirmed by examination of the Asturian charters (to 910) edited by Floriano, Linage Conde's alphabetical "Monasticon Hispanum" (to 1109), [47] the printed cartularies, and my own notes on selected holdings in the Madrid archives. In Asturias there was a church of San Isidro near the venerable monastery of Santo Toribio de Liébana but so far this is untraceable before the 14th century; [48] Yepes ran across an otherwise unknown urban monastery of San Isidro at Astorga, apparently in documentation of the 11th and 12th centuries;[49] there is the already noted 11th-century interpolation of the *Antiphonale* of León; and in Catalonia the church at Martorell on the Llobregat below Barcelona is said to have possessed (but from what date is unclear) relics of the Chian martyr. [50]

---

46. *Colección diplomática de San Salvador de Oña,* ed. Juan del ALAMO, Madrid, 1950, t. II, nos. 516-17, both of 1249 (pp. 630-2).

47. Antonio C. FLORIANO, *Diplomática española del período astur,* Oviedo, 1949-51; A. LINAGE CONDE, *Orígenes,* III.

48. *Cartulario de Santo Toribio de Liébana,* ed. L. SÁNCHEZ BELDA, Madrid, 1948, pp. 283-4 (no. 237: 1316); p. 309 (no. 261). In the Indice de lugares, San Isidro appears as "iglesia lebaniega que no hemos identificado" (p. 499, col. 2).

49. *Corónica,* ed. PÉREZ DE URBEL, t. II, p. 209, col. 1; cfr. FLÓREZ, *ES,* XVI, 68.

50. *Acta SS, Maii, III* (1680), 448, col. 2, citing Antonio V. DOMÉNECH, *Flos sanctorum o historia general de los santos y varones en santidad del Principado de Cataluña,* Barcelona, 1602, and Juan TAMAYO DE SALAZAR, *Martyro-*

These constitute at present the only other known sites of Chian relevance.

(ii) The calendars, sacramentaries and passionaries from the areas dominated by Cardeña, Silos and Albelda prove regular commemoration of our St Isidore on 14 May but primarily in the second half of the 11th century, presumably due to successive waves of what de Gaiffier aptly calls "cette invasion pacifique d'hagiographie française,"[51] not to a simple preservation of the Albeldan Calendar notice of 976. The latter date is sufficiently early to merit attention; but I believe that like the later cases from the Rioja and eastern Castile it represents a direct Franco-Hispanic line of martyrological transmission quite distinct from that found at Dueñas and in western Castile, one indeed — to judge by the pergaminos of Albelda, San Millán de la Cogolla, Valvanera, Silos and other houses of the region — which struck no real roots and cannot be found incorporated in a single monastic or parochial entitlature.

(iii) In western Castile, from Clunia to Campos, we encounter an authentic Isidorian cult, finding expression in ecclesiastical patronages and some placenames, that can be associated with San Isidro de Dueñas as its chief center. The entitlatures at Clunia and Hontoria, and the donation of Muñó in 1013, point to an era of intensified Castilian interest under Sancho García which apparently coincided with that count's conquest of the Campos ca. 1010; but the way for this must have been prepared by the much older expansion of the Dueñas abadengo across the Pisuerga into Cerrato and its vicinity. As early as 924 by deliberate purchase San Isidro acquired from King Fruela II the monastery of Santa María de Remolino *ultra flumen Pisorice*; in 971 by gift of Count Fernán Ansúrez of Monzón, then seeking to create a buffer county between León and Castile, it became proprietor of the lands, church and monastery of Santa Coloma at Tariego, just above Dueñas but again on the opposite side of the Pisuerga; in 974 it received near Cevico de la Torre, to the southeast of Tariego, the monastery of Tobilla;[52] and, as we have mentioned (Note 44), Sancho García and Sancho el Mayor bestowed the churches of San Isidro de Muñó, San Pedro de Avellano and San Miguel de Baltanás. These outposts manifestly gave the monks well before Sancho García's time a strong natural interest in cultivating friendly relations with Fernán González and his succes-

logium Hispanum, Lyon, 1651-9; LUCCHESI, *Isidoro di Chio*, col. 967, erroneously reads "Martonello."

51. *Calendrier franco-hispanique,* p. 284.
52. Col. Velázquez, t. IV, nos. 1382, 1414, 1434.

sors; it is significant that after 936 no further reales privilegios of Leonese kings appeared in the Becerro. How much the growing Castilian orientation of the abbey, which both Sancho García and Sancho el Mayor patently fostered by their benefactions in this territory which from the second third of the 11th century was to be part of the restored diocese of Palencia,[53] displeased the Leonese we can only surmise; but it is not unreasonable to conjecture that their displeasure found vent in 1063 so that the celebrated translation of St Isidore the Bishop from Abbadid Seville to León may stem from something more than simply a failure to locate the previously requested bones of St Justa. At any event, the vogue henceforth of St Isidore of León, the symbol of the Leonese program of Hispanic imperialism which Fernando I so enthusiastically espoused after the battle of Atapuerca (1054), coincides with the nonappearance of new Chian patronage, although of course in the martyrology of the Castilian Church and above all at Dueñas, even after the house's transfer in 1073 to Cluny, the old Isidorian devotion continued to be honored.

(iv) We return, finally, to the recalcitrant problem that underlies the eventual trans-Pisuergan penetration of Dueñas and the propagation of its non-Hispanic patron's cult in westernmost Castile: the provenance of the foundational community itself, which at the very beginning of the 10th century represents much the oldest proof we have of an introduction of the Chian devotion below the Pyrenees and which ranks also among the early significant instances of Carolingian Benedictine influence in ultra-Catalan Spain. Of the possible hypotheses, we can confidently rule out as contra-indicated by the data reviewed above, Mozarabic, Gallegan, Catalan and Leonese solutions. A Riojan line of transmission, despite possessing some appeal by reason of the commemoration in the Albeldan Calendar of 976, finds no support in face of the lack of visible exchanges between the monasticisms of the Tierra de Campos and the Rioja, or of any intermediate links of Isidorian diffusion between these two widely separated comarcas. The church at Muñó and the scattered Isidorian toponyms of Castile might seem to point to a diagonal passage in the late 9th century across the County from around Valpuesta or Burgos, following the pattern of the repoblación of the lower Arlanzón and Arlanza valleys; but the ignorance of or indif-

53. See also the section devoted to the Merindad de Cerrato, with references to cis-Pisuergan possessions of San Isidro de Dueñas, in *Becerro. Libro famoso de las behetrías de Castilla*, ed. F. Hernández, Santander, 1866, pp. 1-15; and cfr. Cl. Sánchez Albornoz, *Estudios sobre las instituciones medievales españolas*, México, 1965, pp. 159-62, with map.

ference to the Chian devotion found in the pre-11th-century charters of Valpuesta and in the Becerro gótico and codices of Burgalese Cardeña, tells heavily against this. There is also the fact, perhaps due only to documentary losses but certainly thought-provoking, that the Dueñas pergaminos disclose no verbal or institutional traces of that pactual cenobitism characteristic in its Gallegan and Burgalese forms of the houses of this part of Castile and of the Rioja, and inseparably connected in the late 9th and 10th centuries with the reception there of the Benedictine Rule.[54]

There remains a line of descent by the founding monks, with their Isidorian relics and patronage, straight down the valley of the Pisuerga from communities in Asturias de Santillana and Liébana which during the 9th century were in contact with the new cenobitic revival affecting Carolingian Gascony and Aquitaine. This hypothesis would imply a center or centers in the eastern zone of his kingdom upon which Alfonso III drew for the establishment of his new abbey in the distant Campos; and in my judgment it has the best claim to at least tentative acceptance. Even so, much is still, and perhaps always will be, uncertain. Meanwhile, what we need is investigation into south French interest in St Isidore of Chios during the 8th and 9th centuries, and into that other equally primordial feature of Dueñas, its Benedictine observance, which requires to be related to the now little known story of Asturian reaction to the advent of the Cassinensian code and its Frankish exegetical counterpiece, the *Expositio* of Smaragdus. But these are obviously questions beyond the scope of this paper.

---

54. See the initial essay, "The Pactual Tradition in Hispanic Monasticism," in my forthcoming *Estudios de historia monástica hispánica*.

Addendum to Note 28: Observe that the *incipit* of the *Passio* emphasizes *militia, militabat, militauit* (*Cat. cod. hagiog. lat... B. N. Paris.*, t. III, Brussels, 1893, p. 481).

VII

THE LITURGICAL CONTEXT OF FERNANDO I'S LAST DAYS

ACCORDING TO THE SO-CALLED "HISTORIA SILENSE"

In one of the many illuminating annotations that adorn the pages of his classic edition of the *Liber Ordinum,* Dom Marius Férotin associates with the *Ordo penitentie* of the Hispanic Rite that passage of the so-called *Historia Silense* which describes the dramatic scene in the basilica of San Isidro de León when the aged, mortally stricken Fernando I of León and Castile puts off his royal robe and crown and assumes the *cilicium* and ashes of the penitential state [1]. This is but one of several episodes in the great king emperor's last days at the end of december 1065, which, as so vividly described in the pages of the unknown chronicler, display a strongly liturgical and ceremonial character [2]. When, in addition, we note the citation of texts from the Office celebrated *more Toletano,* and the close correlation of the final events in Fernando's life with the ecclesiastical calendar of the Nativity octave, it becomes evident that this terminal section of the *Historia* constitutes a document of distinct interest for the history of the Hispanic Rite just a decade and a half before the liturgical crisis of 1080 and Leonese-Castilian adoption under Alfonso VI of the Roman tradition [3].

[1] M. Férotin, *Le Liber Ordinum en usage dans l'église wisigothique et mozarabe d'Espagne du cinquième au onzième siècle,* in Monumenta Ecclesiae Liturgica, t. 5 (Paris, 1904), col. 88, n. 1.

[2] The passages of the *Historia* to be discussed here can be found in *Historia Silense,* ed. Francisco Santos Coco (Madrid, 1921), pp. 89-91; *Historia Silense,* ed. Dom J. Pérez de Urbel and Atilano González Ruiz-Zorrilla (Madrid, 1959), pp. 207-209. I shall cite the Santos Coco text but with due attention to the readings of the recent Pérez de Urbel and Ruiz-Zorrilla edition.

[3] Pierre David, *Études historiques sur la Galice et le Portugal du VIe au XIIe siècle* (Lisbon-Paris, 1947), pp. 391-430; Richard B. Donovan, *The Liturgical Drama in Medieval Spain* (Toronto, 1958), pp. 20-29.

Familiar and often reproduced as are these passages from the *Historia,* they do not seem ever to have been examined as a whole from the liturgical standpoint. This is clearly desirable. It is now agreed that the *Historia* is a work of the first half of the twelfth century composed most probably under Alfonso VII (1126-1157), in the city of León, very likely at San Isidro itself [4]; the chance of its monk-author's having been an eye-witness of the events of december 1065 is therefore minimum. The question then arises of his source of information, whether an oral tradition or a written account, for Fernando I's last days, and of the degree of reliability of the liturgical data presented. The discovery that the text contains certain ambiguities and marks of calendrical confusion makes it all the more necessary to subject this concluding portion of the *Historia* to closer analysis.

The account commences with Fernando's abandonment of his successful campaign in the region of Valencia against the Muslims and, with the shadow of death upon him, his return to León, which he reaches on 24 december. This means he missed by two days the commemoration there of the Translation of St Isidore, the feast instituted in 1063 after the envoys of the *serenissimus rex* had transported the sainted metropolitan 's body from Seville to the banks of the Bernesga and amid solemn pomp placed it in the newly reconstructed imperial basilica of St John the Baptist, better known henceforth as San Isidro de León [5]. Between the monarch's arrival in the capital and his death the *Historia* allows for the passage of four days, which may be identified as follows:

a) Saturday 24 december, the vigil of the Nativity: «VIII kalendas ianuarii die sabbato» [6]. Fernando, arriving in León, repairs to San Isidro and kneels in prayer before the *memoria* of the saint.

[4] Pérez de Urbel, p. 87, places the *Historia* in the second decade of the twelfth century, under Urraca; but cf. the more cogent argumentation for a date in the reign of Alfonso VII in CLAUDIO SÁNCHEZ ALBORNOZ, *Sobre el autor de la llamada Historia Silense,* in «Cuadernos de Historia de España» 23-24 (1955) 307-316; idem, *De nuevo sobre la Crónica de Alfonso III y sobre la llamada Historia Silense,* ibid. 37-38 (1963) 292-317, especially pp. 313-314. On San Isidro de León as the place of composition, see MANUEL GÓMEZ MORENO, *Introducción a la Historia Silense* (Madrid, 1921), pp. XXI-XXII; Antonio VIÑAYO GONZÁLEZ, *Cuestiones histórico-críticas en torno a la traslación del cuerpo de San Isidoro,* in *Isidoriana,* ed. M. DÍAZ Y DÍAZ (León, 1961), pp. 285-297, especially pp. 292-293.

[5] VIÑAYO GONZÁLEZ, op. cit.; JULIO PÉREZ LLAMAZARES, *Historia de la Real Colegiata de San Isidoro de León* (León, 1927), pp. 26-35.

[6] Reading 'VIII' with Pérez de Urbel and Ruiz-Zorrilla, p. 207, as against

b) Night of Saturday 24 december | Sunday 2 december: «in ipsa celebri natiuitatis Dominice nocte». As the *clerici* festively chant the Matins of the Nativity, the king joins them in the singing *more Toletano* of the final *sonus:* «Aduenit nobis» ; and the *succentores* respond with: «Erudimini omnes qui iudicatis terram». Of these extracts from the Hispanic breviary, the first, which I myself have not yet located, Gómez Moreno wrongly styles the final psalm of the Matins [7]; the «Erudimini omnes», as Pérez de Urbel points out, occurs in the Nativity Matins according to the *Antiphonarium mozarabicum* of the Cathedral of León, although Lorenzana's edition of the *Breviarium Gothicum* places this *sonus* in the Lauds of the Nativity [8].

c) Sunday 25 december, Feast of the Nativity: «illucescente natiuitatis Filii Dei clara uniuerso orbi die». With his limbs failing him, Fernando requests the singing of the Mass, and after receiving the Sacrament, is carried off to bed.

d) Monday 26 december: «in crastinum uero luce aduenïente». On this day Fernando participates in four distinct acts of liturgical character:

1. Having called together bishops, abbots and *religiosi uiri,* he is carried in their midst into the basilica, dressed in the royal vestments and wearing the crown, probably looking very much as in his still extant portraits preserved in the Libro de las Estampas of the Cathedral of León or the Tumbo A of Santiago [9]. This initial mention by the chronicler of the monarch's appearing in the *regalis chlamys* and with the *gemmata corona* or *aureum diadema* on his head establishes this as a formal *coronamentum* or crown-wearing, such as characterizes monarchical practice in eleventh century France, Germany and England, although the customary accompanying acclamations of the *laudes regiae* do not seem to have been introduced into the Leonese-Castilian state before the time of Alfonso VII [10]. It will be recalled

Santos Coco, whose 'VIIII' is clearly impossible since in 1065 it was the eighth day before the Kalends of January which fell on Saturday.

7 *Introd.*, p. CXXXV. On the Hispanic Office, consult M. FÉROTIN, *Le Liber Mozarabicus Sacramentorum et les manuscrits mozarabes,* in Mon. Eccl. Liturg., t. 6 (Paris, 1912), pp. LIV-LXXI; F. CABROL, *Mozarabe (la liturgie),* in DACL, t. 12 (1953), cols. 443-446.

8 PÉREZ DE URBEL, p. 207, n. 264. *Brev. Goth.* in PL 86, 122 C.

9 See the reproductions in A. BALLESTEROS Y BERETTA, *Historia de España,* vol. II (^{2} 1944), pp. 298-301.

10 Cf. ERNST KANTOROWICZ, *Laudes Regiae: A Study in Liturgical Acclamations and Mediaeval Ruler Worship* (Berkeley-Los Angeles), 1958, pp. 92-101; PERCY E. SCHRAMM, *A History of the English Coronation* (Oxford, 1937), pp. 31-32, 56; idem, *Herrschaftszeichen und Staatssymbolik,* in Schriften der Mon. Germ. Hist., t. 13, vol. III (1956), pp. 727-730, 817 (= *Las insignias de la realeza en la Edad*

that Christmastide was one of the regularly appointed seasons for such display of the *Herrschaftszeichen.*

2. Before the altar of St John the Baptist and the bodies of SS Isidore and Vincent, Fernando surrenders his kingdom, and commits his soul, to God. The moving prayer which accompanies this renunciation, and which is quoted at length in the *Historia,* is of unmistakably liturgical origin, being a somewhat abbreviated adaptation of the Davidic canticle «Benedictus Dominus Deus Israhel patris nostri» in I Chronicles 29. In the Hispanic Office this canticle has no known connection with 26 december (St. Stephen's Day), and is used (so far as I have been able to determine) only at Lauds on the Saturday after the second Sunday in Lent and again in the course of the third feria after Ascension Day [11]. Familiar as he was with the Hispanic breviary [12], Fernando may have called to mind this highly appropriate prayer from having heard it sung; or knew it from its inclusion in both the famous codices copied in his time for the imperial library and to which Dom Férotin devoted a justly celebrated study: the *Liber Diurnus* of 1055, now at the University of Compostela, and the *Liber Canticorum* of the Biblioteca de Palacio in Madrid [13]. Since in the Roman Rite the canticle is assigned to the Lauds of the second feria throughout the year, and since in 1065 St. Stephen's feast fell on Monday, we may conceivably have here a conflation of the two liturgical traditions, although it is essential to note that the *Historia* has the *Benedictus Dominus Deus* recited by the king alone and not by the clergy. Certainly it cannot altogether be ruled out that this highly appropriate prayer may have been suggested by a churchman accustomed to the Roman use, in which case a likely candidate would be Bishop Bernard Ramón of Palencia, a Catalan, perhaps a Cluniac, and a close counsellor of Fernando and his son Alfonso VI [14].

3. Fernando divests himself of the chlamys, removes the crown,

Media española, trans. L. Vázquez de Parga (Madrid, 1960), pp. 25-35); Cl. Sánchez Albornoz, *Un ceremonial inédito de coronación de los reyes de Castilla,* in «Logos» 3 (Buenos Aires, 1943) 75-97.

11 *Brev. Goth.,* in PL 86, 373 D; W. S. Porter, *Cantica Mozarabici officii,* in «Ephemerides liturgicae» 49 (1935) p. 140, col. 2 (n.° 64). Cabrol, *Cantiques,* in DACL., t. 2 (1925), cols. 1991-92, wrongly assigns this canticle to the Saturday following the first Sunday in Lent.

12 Santos Coco, p. 87. 21-24.

13 *Deux manuscrits wisigothiques de la bibliothèque de Ferdinand I.er, roi de Castille et de Léon,* in «Bibl. de l'École des Chartes» 62 (1901) 374-387.

14 Pedro Fernández del Pulgar, *Teatro clerical, apostólico y secular de las Iglesias Catedrales de España* (Madrid, 1679), vol. II, pp. 85-119.

and weeping prostrates himself on the church floor, imploring forgiveness of his sins. This ceremony constitutes the formal abdication of the imperial office, a *decoronatio*.

4. The bishops administer the rite of penance, placing the *cilicium* upon the monarch and asperging him with ashes. If, as can be supposed, this ceremony followed the procedure prescribed for mortally sick penitents in the *Ordo penitentie* of the *Liber Ordinum* (Ordo xxx), Fernando would first have been given the tonsure; then, draped in the *cilicium* with the ashes placed upon him in the form of a cross, after recitation of the set *orationes, benedictiones* and Psalm 50, he would be given communion [15].

e) Monday 26 december, and Tuesday 27 december «in tali permanenti penitentia duobus diebus». Fernando survives for two days in this state of penitence.

f) Tuesday 27 december, Feast of St. John the Evangelist: «sequenti autem die que est feria tertia, hora diei sexta, in qua sancti Iohannis Euangeliste festum celebratur». Fernando dies at noon.

Let us note that this liturgical, ceremonial obitus of the Leonese ruler shows a striking similarity to the last days of St. Isidore of Seville in april 636, as these are described in the short *Relatio de transitu beatissimi Isidori episcopi* of the cleric Redemptus [16]. In this presumably contemporary account [17], manuscripts of which were unquestionably available to Fernando I, and almost certainly familiar to him in view of his interest in the saint, the metropolitan's death is carefully detailed. Four days before he dies, the ailing Isidore, accompanied by two bishops and a throng of clergy, monks and faithful, has himself transported from his *cellula* to the cathedral church of St. Vincent, where he makes a public confession and becomes a simple

[15] Ed. FÉROTIN, cols. 87-92. On the doctrine and administration of penance according to the Hispanic Rite, see SEVERINO GONZÁLEZ RIVAS, *La penitencia en la primitiva Iglesia española* (Salamanca, 1950); J. M. CARDA, *Doctrina y práctica penitencial en la liturgia visigótica,* in «Rev. esp. de Teología» 6 (1946) 223-247.

[16] PL 81, 30-32. Cf. ÁNGEL C. VEGA, *Cuestiones críticas de las biografías isidorianas,* in *Isidoriana* (1961), pp. 75-98, especially 95-96; B. DE GAIFFIER, *Le culte de Saint Isidore de Séville. Esquisse d'un travail,* ibid., p. 271. Observe also the account in *Hist. Sil.* (SANTOS COCO, p. 53; PÉREZ DE URBEL, p. 168) of Ramiro II's death (951), after penitential *confessio* and renunciation of office before bishops and abbots; cf. PÉREZ DE URBEL, *Sampiro, su crónica y la monarquía leonesa en el siglo X*, (Madrid, 1952), p. 403.

[17] See J. MADOZ, *S. Isidoro de Sevilla* (León, 1960), pp. 3-21, as cited by J. N. HILLGARTH, *The Position of Isidorian Studies: A Critical Review of the Literature since 1935,* in «Isidoriana», pp. 49-50.

penitent. Then, in the choir, before the altar, the bishops impose upon him the *cilicium* and ashes (which implies a previous laying aside of canonical vestments). In a long prayer, drawn from several scriptural passages, he implores God's pardon for his sins and is given the Sacrament by the prelates. Finally, after forgiveness from clergy and people, distributing his last charities, and beseeching divine favor for his flock, he returns to his cell, where death comes to him on the fourth day of this *confessio et paenitentia.*

To be sure, at various points the two cases differ, partly because the liturgical context of an archbishop dying in his cathedral in april would not coincide with that of a king dying during the Nativity octave; and in certain respects the resemblances of the two accounts result from the use of the same formula of public penance. Yet the parallel remains quite close and impressive, especially given the uniqueness of Fernando's ceremonial death-scene and his fervent devotion to the great Baetic archbishop, whose body just two year before, in the climactic religious event of the reign, the king-emperor had had translated to León. In my opinion, therefore, it is very probable that when in the Isidorian basilica Fernando renounced his supreme authority and undertook to spend his last remaining hours in the *cilicium* and ashes of a penitent, he was deliberately emulating the noble example of his venerated patron, the metropolitan of Seville.

As the so-called *Silense* presents the sequence of events at the end of Fernando s life, their correlation with the ecclesiastical calendar of the Nativity week seems, at first glance, straightforward and has been universally accepted; but on closer consideration a serious chronological difficulty presents itself. If the king's penance began on Monday, and the period of *duobus diebus* comprises Monday and Tuesday, 26 and 27 december, then *sequenti die* ought to designate Wednesday 28 december. But such an identification is expressly contradicted by the text's assertion that Fernando's death occurred on the third feria, the Feast of St. John, i, e., Tuesday, 27 december. The suspicion that there is something wrong with this equation becomes a certainty when we note that at the abbey of Cluny the Fernandine obit was solemnly observed not on 27, but on 29, december.

On this point we possess two convincing testimonies, both hitherto unappreciated. The first is the notice regarding the commemoration at Cluny of Fernando's death as recorded in the magnificent custumal of

Bernard of Cluny, commonly cited as the *Ordo Cluniacensis* but probably more accurately styled *Consuetudines coenobii Cluniacensis* [18]. Compiled at the abbey itself by a learned monk thoroughly acquainted with the congregation's daily regime under Abbot Hugh the Great in the second half of the eleventh century, this work can be dated between 1078 and 1083, i. e., ca. 1080 [19]. Among Bernard's several interesting references to the intercessional prayers offered at Cluny for the king-emperors of León *(reges Hispaniarum),* one informs us that in Fernando's name a daily alms portion of food was served the poor; another that on his anniversary all the monks enjoyed a full refection of fish and honeyed, spiced wine [20]. But most pertinent is a passage in Part II, cap. 32, which describes how at night during the entire Nativity octave the Cluniacs omitted recitation of the Office (i. e., of the Dead) with one single exception:

> Sciendum tamen quia in octauis Dominicae natiuitatis usque post octauum diem, nullum sit in nocte Officium, excepto uno solo, in crastino festivitatis Innocentium quod D. Hugo abbas fieri instituit pro Fredelano Hispaniarum rege, qui multa bona loco Cluniacensi contulit, pro quo etiam sicuti pro abbatibus nostris sit; praecepit ut singuli sacerdotes qui ad hoc idonei uidentur, missas ipsa die pro eo cantent [21].

Since above the Pyrenees Holy Innocents fell on 28 december, and the following day was yet to be assigned in the Roman calendar, as it now is, to the martyred Archbishop of Canterbury, the feria of the 29th would naturally be designated the *crastinum* or morrow of the immediately preceding feast [22]. In 1065 Holy Innocents would have been a Wednesday; hence for Cluny Fernando I must have died on the fifth feria of Christmas week, i. e., Thursday 29 december, and not — as the *Historia* alleges — on the third feria, Tuesday 27 december. Certainly, in ca. 1080 Bernard found the former date being solemnized in an extraordinary fashion reserved otherwise only for deceased abbots of Cluny herself. Now, on so essential a liturgical particular as the date of the Fernandine obit, the abbey can hardly have

[18] Edited by MARQUARD HERRGOTT, *Vetus disciplina monastica,* (Paris, 1726), pp. 134-364.

[19] See my *Liturgical Intercession at Cluny for the King-Emperors of Leon,* in «Studia monastica» 3 (1961) 53-76, especially pp. 60-65.

[20] HERRGOTT, *Ordo,* I, 13; I, 51 (pp. 158, 246).

[21] *Ordo,* pp. 355-356.

[22] In the peculiarly Spanish tradition, this feast as the *Allisio infantum* was celebrated on 8 January: CABROL in DACL, t. 12, col. 418.

been mistaken: Abbot Hugh's friendship with the Spanish monarch who had granted 1000 gold *metcales* a year for clothing his congregation, and who ranked among the very greatest of the *socii* and *magni benefactores* (for the celebration of whose anniversaries Bernard provides such abundant detail), and the regular communication with the Leonese court provided by the collection of the annual census [23], insure that the Burgundian abbey would have been at exceptional pains to possess accurate information as to the exact day of the emperor's demise.

Furthermore, additional evidence, if this is needed, confirming 29 december as the day in question, can be had from an independent, equally unimpeachable source of peninsular origin: the imperial diploma of 1073 by which Alfonso VI gave Cluny the ancient dynastic monastery of San Isidro de Dueñas, located south of Palencia and the very first of the abbey's permanent acquisitions in the Leonese-Castilian state. As published among the charters of Cluny in Bruel's collection, this document bears the date «IIII kalendas junii, millesimo CXI» or 29 may 1073, under which it now circulates [24]. This text, however, reproduced not from the lost original, but from the early twelfth-century portion of the Cluniac Cartulary B (Bibliothèque de la Ville de Cluny, ms. 3), has had its date mishandled (cf. the loss of *era* before the misspelled *millesimo*) and has been split by the copyist at the *imprecatio* into two separate acts (Nos. CVII and CVIII) [25]. An incomplete but superior transcript of the copy of the Alfonsine *privilegio* which was contained in the lost *Becerro* of San Isidro de Dueñas survives in Madrid in the Colección Velázquez of the Academia de la Historia [26]. This establishes that at several points in the text as in the list of subscriptions the Burgundian version commits errors of omission and orthography. Most significantly, however, the Spanish transcript dates the diploma not by reference to the *kalendas junii,* but on «III kals januarias era. M.CXI», or 29 december 1073. This

[23] BISHKO, *Liturgical Intercession,* pp. 61-62.

[24] A. BERNARD and A. BRUEL, eds., *Recueil des chartes de l'abbaye de Cluny* (Paris, 1876-1903), t. 4, n.° 3.452 (pp. 560-562).

[25] Ibid., p. 560, n. 1; on the Hugonic section of Cartulary B, cf. t. 1, pp. XXII-XXIII.

[26] Col. VELÁZQUEZ, t. IV, leg. 4, n.° 1.388. I expect to include a more satisfactory text of this diploma in my forthcoming edition of the unpublished charters of San Isidro de Dueñas. The Madrid text, for example, gives as *comes Munio Gonçaluez* the garbled *comes Grunnio Gunsalbus* of *Chartes de Cluny,* t. 4, p. 562, and supplies the missing name of the scribe Ariulfus.

complete and almost certainly original chronological formula allows us to perceive for the first time that the cession of Dueñas, so decisive a turning point in Hispanic-Cluniac history, was timed to coincide with the anniversary of Fernando I's death. This in turn gives new emphasis to the clauses by which Alfonso, acting imperially as *rex Hispaniarum et Legionensis,* devotes his grant «pro remedio animę meę et pro anima patris mei et matris meę et omnium parentum meorum», and defines it as including all possessions of the house «sicut fuit donatum et confirmatum ... in tempore patris mei uel parentum meorum». To be noted also, as something more than conventional piety, is Alfonso's justification of Dueñas' transfer to Cluny in words drawn from the very Davidic canticle «Benedictus Dominus Deus Israhel patris nostri», which must have been indelibly associated in memory with the Fernandine renunciation in San Isidro de León eight years before: «Tua sunt enim omnia, Domine, et que de manu tua accepimus, in tuo sancto timore detulimus tibi» [27]. Thus the evidence of the Dueñas charter of 1073, earlier by some half-dozen years than the Bernardine notice of ca. 1080, confirms 29 december as the true date of the obit and shows that at the Leonese court no less than in Burgundy the anniversary was observed two days later than reported by the so-called *Historia Silense.*

This correction of the date of Fernando's demise bears also upon the *Historia*'s final assertions that the monarch died «era millesima c^{a}III^{a}» and that he was buried in San Isidro «anno regni sui XXVII, mensibus VI, diebus XII» [28]. The latter calculation, frequently offered as the length of the reign and which Pérez de Urbel regards as «el cómputo exacto desde que (Fernando) había sido coronado en León el 22 de junio de 1037» [29], can hardly be accepted without scrutiny. For if the 27 years of the reign run from 22 june 1037 to 22 june 1065, and the six months carry us to 22 december of that year, the twelve days beyond the 22nd would terminate in era 1104 on 2 january 1066. Since the text actually declares that burial, not death, occurred at the end of the 12 days, this would mean that if Fernando died on 27 december, as the *Historia* says, he was not interred until a week later; or, if he died on 29 december, as we have argued, five days later. The

27 *Chartes de Cluny,* t. 4, p. 561: I Chronicles 29: 14.
28 SANTOS COCO, p. 91; PÉREZ DE URBEL, p. 209.
29 P. 209, n. 266.

latter is perhaps more credible. But if it was the writer's intention to mean that the king was buried on the day he died, as has been generally inferred, a scribe may have wrongly written *XII diebus* for an original *VII diebus;* for 7 days after 22 december would bring us to the date accepted by Cluny and Alfonso VI. At any rate, the present reading of the text cannot be regarded as a precise measure of the reign's duration.

In view of the convincing testimony from two authoritative quarters, Cluniac and Leonese, that Fernando I died on 29, not 27, december, how are we to account for the *Historia*'s universally accepted error? The answer is not far to seek, and will doubtless have already occurred to the reader: we confront here a confusion caused by the conflation of the Hispanic and Roman ecclesiastical calendars in the years following adoption of the latter Rite in the Leonese Empire in 1080. For while in the Roman *sanctorale* St. John's Day is the 27th, in the Hispanic tradition the feast which the manuscript calendars list under some form of *Adsumtio S. Iohannis apstli et euangeliste* falls on the 29th [30]. The *Historia*'s unknown composer, we may therefore confidently assume, possessed the information that the monarch died on the apostolic *festum,* but despite his explicit awareness that in 1065 the older liturgy was still in use at San Isidro, so that the Matins of the Nativity were sung *more Toletano,* he must have overlooked the fact that the ecclesiastical year would also then be ordered according to the same tradition. In consequence, he was driven to compress within a period of four days, from the 24th to the 27th, a series of events that we can now realize must have extended over six, to the 29th; and his difficulty in effecting this can be seen in the obviously forced and ambiguous language of this part of his narrative. For if, as the *Historia* makes plain, Fernando became a penitent on Monday 26 december, and remained in that condition for two days *(duobus diebus),* then the fellowing day *(sequeti die)* ought either to be the fourth feria, Wednesday, the 28th (assuming the count begins on Monday), or else the fifth feria, Thursday, the 29th (with Tuesday and Wednesday as the *duobus diebus*). Between these alternatives we need not hesitate, since both the Bernardine *Consuetudines* and the Alfonsine diploma of 1073 for San Isidro de Dueñas agree, as we have seen, on 29 december.

[30] DAVID, *Études,* pp. 201, 205.

In this light, and in the context of the Hispanic liturgical calendar, the true sequence of Fernando I's last days in San Isidoro de León can be reconstructed as follows [31]:

a) Saturday 24 december, the vigil of the Nativity. Fernando appears in the basilica.

b) Night of Saturday 24 december | Sunday 25 december. He participates in the celebration of the Nativity Matins.

c) Sunday 25 december, Feast of the Nativity. He attends the Mass.

d) Monday 26 december, St. Stephen's Day. He renounces the imperial office and enters into the penitential state.

e) Tuesday 27 december, Feast of St. Eugenia. The first full day as a penitent.

f) Wednesday 28 december, Feast of St. James the Brother of the Lord. The second of the *duobus diebus* as a penitent.

g) Thursday 29 december, Feast of the Assumption of St. John the Evangelist. Fernando dies at noon.

Now the discovery of an error of two days in the length of Fernando's life in not in itself of earth-shaking moment, although we humbly submit it to the attention of any bodies planning to celebrate in 1965 the nine-hundredth anniversary of this great Spanish ruler's passing. What is, however, genuinely significant is the fact that the *Historia's* error, and the specifically liturgical genesis of this error, make it possible to discern for the first time the nature of the original source lying back of the conclusion of the king-emperor's biography and to relate this to the history of liturgical change in eleventh-and twelfth-century Spain. We shall therefore conclude this inquiry by drawing certain deductions that now appear justified.

1) As the extracts from the Nativity Matins of the Hispanic Breviary, and also (if somewhat less certainly) the canticle «Benedictus Dominus Deus Israhel patris nostri», attest, the original description of Fernando I's last days must be contemporary and can be ascribed to an ecclesiastic — surely one of the *episcopi et abbates et religiosi uiri* in attendance upon the dying monarch — who was thoroughly

[31] For the Hispanic calendar in the Nativity octave, see the detailed analysis of the manuscripts in José Vives and Ángel Fábrega, *Calendarios hispánicos anteriores al siglo XII*, in «Hispania sacra» 2 (1949) 119-146, 339-380; 3 (1950) 145-161. This definitive study replaces both Férotin, *Liber Ordinum*, pp. xxx-xxxv; cols. 449-497; and M. Álamo, *Les calendriers mozarabes d'après Dom Férotin: Additions et corrections*, in «Rev. d'Hist. ecclés. 39 (1943) 100-131.

familiar with the prayers and *ordines* of the Hispanic Rite and an eyewitness of the ceremonial scenes in San Isidro. This could not have been, as often asserted, the author of the *Historia* itself in its present form.

2) The description, as it reached the author of the *Historia,* was unquestionably in written form. The already noted signs of editorial revision and chronological compression, manifested in the addition of the gloss «quem tunc temporis more Toletano canebant» to identify for a later generation the then unfamiliar passages from the Hispanic matutinal *sonus* of the Nativity, and in the insertion after «sequenti autem die» of a second gloss «que est feria tertia» so as to make the two penitential days terminate on the Roman feast of St. John, establish beyond dispute a written original. One does not insert phrases of this type into an account based on memory or oral tradition. Furthermore, that the chronicler's editorial method when taking over an earlier document into this Fernandine portion of his work is of precisely this order, can be seen from what is known of his account of the bringing of St. Isidore's body to León in 1063. In this case, the original source still survives independently in the form of a *Translatio,* and collation of this with the shorter redaction in the *Historia* has made it clear that various minor changes of phraseology or addition of brief glosses have been introduced [32]. This piece posed no such chronological problem as the Johannine correlation (and indeed nowhere else in the *Historia* does a similar confusion of calendars seem to have arisen); but its editorial modifications offer an instructive parallel to the two glosses we have encountered in the story of Fernando's death.

3) Unlike the *Translatio,* which seems to have been inspired by liturgical needs [33], the account of Fernando's death cannot be found existing apart from the *Historia;* and nothing in its opening words («Ingressus est enim ciuitatem», etc.) or general vocabulary and style indicate an origin different from that of the Fernandine biography as a whole (the Isidorian translation acts excepted). This implies that the account was an integral part of a general history of the reign composed by an unknown Leonese ecclesiastic, which was incorporated into the present so-called *Historia Silense;* but contrary to Cirot's

[32] Gómez Moreno, *Intród.,* pp. xv-xvii; Pérez de Urbel, pp. 45-49; Viñayo González, *Cuestiones histórico-críticas,* pp. 289-293.
[33] Viñayo González, p. 294. The MSS preserve the text in the form of nine lessons for the Matins of 22 december, the anniversary of the Translation.

argument that on liturgical grounds the composition of such a Life of Fernando must be dated subsequent to the introduction of the Roman Rite, «en 1077, ou l'année suivante», just the opposite conclusion has now emerged: the liturgical evidence requires that this portion of the *Historia* already existed in written form before the change of rite [34].

4) Given the high probability that the *Historia* was compiled at San Isidro de León itself or, alternatively, at Santa María la Regla or other center in León, it is likely that its erroneous dating of Fernando's death was due to the actual liturgical practice of the monastery or church to which the chronicler was attached. Between 1066 and 1080 the anniversary would have been celebrated both in Burgundy and in Spain on the same day, 29 december. When in 1080, or by degrees thereafter, the Roman *sanctorale* established itself in the Leonese-Castilian state, there may well have occurred a number of cases where anniversaries, designated in the necrologies by reference to the ecclesiastical calendar, were wrongly shifted to a new date, particularly when, as with St. John's Day, the dates according to the old and new observances stood quite close together. It would be useful to know just where the Fernandine obit appears in the extant necrology of San Isidoro de León [35], and to check on this point any surviving necrologies of Hispano-Cluniac priories. For we may suppose that when, after 1080, a divergence developed, the communities of Cluniac affiliation would have continued, like the mother abbey, to celebrate the 29th, while Leonese centers — or at least the one with which the *Historia* is to be linked — abandoned this date for the 27th. Certainly, we have here one more reason of several that might be presented for rejecting the hypothesis that the *Historia* emanates from a Cluniac *ambiente* [36]. If it did, its author would surely have been well aware of the correct chronology and authentic liturgical context of the last days of Fernando I.

University of Virginia.
(Charlottesville, Va., U. S. A.).

[34] GEORGES CIROT, *La Chronique Léonaise et la Chronique dite de Silos*, in «Bull. hispanique» 16 (1914) 15-34, especially pp. 28-30.

[35] JULIO PÉREZ LLAMAZARES, *Catálogo de los códices y documentos de la Real Colegiata de San Isidro de León* (León, 1923), pp. 24-25: Codex n.° 4, 73 fols. in 'letra minúscula francesa'; the Necrologium is contained in fols. 1-6. Cf. VIÑAYO GONZÁLEZ, p. 286, n. 7.

[36] CIROT, pp. 24-28. PÉREZ DE URBEL, p. 71.

VIII

LITURGICAL INTERCESSION AT CLUNY FOR THE KING-EMPERORS OF LEON

AMONG the neglected factors in the still very imperfectly understood relations between Cluny and Christian Spain during the eleventh and twelfth centuries is the great Benedictine community's immense repute as a center of intercessory prayer [1]. In an insufficiently appreciated study W. Jorden has claimed that from the time of her foundation Cluny's intercessions for the living, and above all her devotion to the commemoration of the dead, attracted so many pious — and generous — benefactors that at any given moment the abbey's success and significance *(Hauptblüte, Hauptbedeutung)* could be measured by the number of her anniversary observances [2]. Somewhat exaggerated as it is, this thesis possesses much merit and urgently requires to be carried beyond the mid-tenth century, where Jorden left it, and to be further investigated along with its inseparable corollary, Cluny's admission to her prized confraternity or *societas* of those numerous princes, nobles, church-

1. There is no satisfactory comprehensive treatment of Hispano-Cluniac history; for the general problems, and more recent bibliography, consult Pierre DAVID, *Études historiques sur la Galice et le Portugal du VIe au XIe siècle* (Lisbon and Paris, 1947; Collection portugaise publiée sous le patronage de l'Institut Français au Portugal, vol. 7), pp. 341-439; J. PÉREZ DE URBEL, *Los monjes españoles en la Edad Media* (2nd ed., Madrid, 1954), 2, chap. 6; M. DEFOURNEAUX, *Les français en Espagne aux XIe et XIIe siècles* (Paris 1949), pp. 17-49; G. de VALOUS, *Cluny* in *D.H.G.E.*, t. 13, 1956, cols. 144-149, 171-172.

[To the Research Committee of the University of Virginia I am indebted for financial aid in the preparation of this paper.]

2. Willibald JORDEN, *Das cluniazensische Totengedächtniswesen* (Münster in Westf., 1930; Münsterische Beiträge zur Theologie, Hft. 15), esp. pp. 112-113. See also G. SCHREIBER, *Kluny und die Eigenkirche. Zur Würdigung der Traditionsnotizen des hochmittelalterlichen Frankreich* in *Archiv für Unkundenforschung*, t. 17, 1941-2, pp. 370-405.

men and other donors who came to enjoy remembrance both in life and death through the abbey's intercessory prayers and the regular commemoration of their obit [3].

Of the medieval rulers who became *socii* and *benefactores* of the Burgundian congregation, none appear more important, or more influential for the abbey's own material development, than the Leonese king-emperors Fernando, or Ferdinand, I (1038-1065) and his son Alfonso VI (1066-1109). Much has been written in recent decades concerning the imperial traditions of the medieval kingdom of Leon; and we now know that both Fernando and Alfonso were strong champions of the Leonese doctrine of the *regnum Hispaniae* or *regnum Hispaniarum,* which envisaged an Iberia freed from all Muslim domination and united under the hegemony of the kings of Leon as *imperatores* transcending in authority all merely regional kings or counts from Barcelona to Galicia [4]. It has however not yet been appreciated how closely Cluny became associated with Leonese imperialism. Too much attention has been paid to the introduction of Cluniac Benedictinism into Navarre, Aragon and Castile by the celebrated Navarrese monarch Sancho *el Mayor* ca. 1025 [5], too little to the fact that within three decades after his death Cluny's really significant connections with the Iberian Peninsula shifted westward to center almost exclusively in the imperial state of Leon, with far-reaching implications for the character and (no less) the limits of Cluniac activity below the Pyrennes.

Cluny's bond with Leon, and with its rulers Fernando I and Alfonso VI, can readily be shown to have been far more intercessory than reformist [6]. Furthermore, this has left important but neglected liturgical

3. Rich materials for the study of Cluniac *societas* in its intercessory no less than reformist implications exist in the charters, narrative sources, custumals, and other texts. That this confraternity was not only with laymen but also numerous churches and monasteries is proved by the *rotulus* entitled *Hae sunt societates ecclesiarum et monasteriorum ecclesiae siue abbatiae Cluniacensi conjunctarum* in *Bullarium sacri ordinis Cluniacensis* (ed. P. SIMON, Lyons 1680), pp. 225 (erroneously, 215) to 230 (erroneously, 220). This appears to contradict C. H. TALBOT, *Odo of Saint-Remy, a Friend of Peter the Venerable* in G. CONSTABLE and J. KRITZECK, ed., *Petrus Venerabilis, 1156-1956* (*Studia Anselmiana,* fasc. 40), 1956, p. 22, who regards such ties as rare.

4. Hermann HÜFFER, *Die leonesischen Hegemoniebestrebungen und Kaisertitel* in Bd. 3 of *Gesammelte Aufsätze zur Kulturgeschichte Spaniens* (ed. H. FINKE, Münster in Westf., 1931), pp. 337-384; R. MENÉNDEZ PIDAL, *El imperio hispánico y los cinco reinos* (Madrid, 1950); J. A. MARAVALL, *El concepto de España en la Edad Media* (Madrid, 1954); Cl. SÁNCHEZ ALBORNOZ, *España, un enigma histórico* (Buenos Aires, 1956), 2, pp. 373-386.

5. Good accounts in E. SACKUR, *Die Cluniacenser in ihrer kirchlichen und allgemeingeschichtlichen Wirksamkeit bis zur Mitte des elften Jahrhunderts* (Halle a. S., 1892-94), 2, pp. 101-113 (now somewhat dated); J. PÉREZ DE URBEL, *Sancho el Mayor de Navarra* (Madrid, 1950), pp. 297-321; idem, *Monjes españoles,* loc. cit.

6. In forthcoming papers I propose to examine at length the ecclesiastico- political factors determining Cluny's Leonese alignment and the major consequences for the geographical distribution of its peninsular holdings.

traces in the Cluniac custumals and other documents, both Burgundian and Hispanic; and these this paper proposes to examine with a twofold aim: (i) to reconstruct as fully as possible the actual stages by which Cluny, as from ca. 1060 on her Leonese alignment tightened, came to bestow upon the imperial sovereigns of the Bernesga intercessory privileges surpassing even those granted her cherished benefactors in the ruling dynasties of the Holy Roman Empire; and (ii) to apply the results thus achieved to the more accurate dating and interpretation of the monastic and diplomatic texts that constitute our chief sources of liturgical information.

1. *The Evidence of Bernard of Cluny's* Consuetudines

The offering of intercessory prayers at Cluny for Spanish monarchs commences in the abbatiate of Odilo (†1048). From the latter's two well-known epistles, one directed to King Garcia III of Navarre, the other to the ex-abbot Paterno of the Aragonese house of San Juan de la Peña, with its cordial references to King Ramiro I of Aragon, it seems certain that as a *socius* of Cluny King Sancho el Mayor, the fervent promoter of Cluniac reformism in his domains, must have shared in the monks' general prayers for their benefactors, although in fact we cannot document the commemoration of his obit as we can the anniversaries of his chief monastic collaborators, Bishop Sancho of Pamplona and Abbots Paterno and Garcia, by means of the Necrologium of Villers [7]. It is evident also from these letters that on specific occasions of great moment — for King Garcia, a time of victory; for King Ramiro, a time of acute distress — special prayers were recited at Cluny, either privately by the abbot or formally by the monks. Thus for a time, in behalf of the harassed Ramiro, the psalm *Domine, quid multiplicati sunt* was said after Matins (i. e., modern Lauds) and the psalm *Levavi oculos meos* at the other hours [8].

But such prayers — the possible Sanchan commemoration apart — were strictly occasional, not permanent additions to the abbey's liturgical customs. To find the earliest testimony to continuous, regular intercession for, and commemoration of, peninsular rulers we must turn to the Hispanic passages in the *Consuetudines cenobii Cluniacensis* of Bernard of Cluny, the earliest of the three great Cluniac custumals of the second half of the eleventh century. This work contains, as the older custumals

7. Text of Necrologium in SACKUR, I, pp. 383-386. Sancho's name is also lacking among the royal and imperial *amici* of Cluny in the so-called *Consuetudines Farfenses* in Br. ALBERS, ed., *Consuetudines monasticae* (Stuttgart-Vienna, 1900), I, p. 205.

8. Odilo, *Epp.* 2-3 in *P. L.* 142, 941-943; PÉREZ DE URBEL, *Sancho el Mayor*, pp. 453-454.

of the abbey do not, a detailed description of the procedures followed at Cluny in the intercessory remembrance of all *socii* and *benefactores;* and it will be useful to summarize this material before considering in detail the data relating solely to the Leonese king-emperors [9].

Bernard's *Consuetudines* treat (i) the general prayers said for the abbey's lay donors in their lifetime and after death; and (ii) those commemorating a specific individual obit. The chapter entitled *De societate nostra danda extraneis* informs us that in life the benefactors were remembered in all prayers, alms and good works, and particularly in each hour of the daily Office through the responsory *Deus, in adiutorium meum intende* and the collect *Praetende, Domine;* and also in the intention of both the Morrow and the High Mass [10]. As for deceased benefactors, in their general behalf the collect *Omnipotens sempiterne Deus, in cuius humana conditio* was recited as the first collect of any Mass or Office to which it was not already assigned, as well as in the Matins of the Dead from Septuagesima to November Ist, after days of twelve lessons, and at Vespers and Matins on the feasts in Lent and on the Rogation Days [11]. In addition, three times a year — at the commencement of Lent, on the feast of SS Peter and Paul (a day of great solemnity at Cluny) and after All Saints — the Office and Morrow Mass were said for dead benefactors and followed by seven days of Masses and Offices for them. Finally, immediately after the death of an individual donor, it was the practice to serve a portion of food (*prebenda*) to the poor for thirty days, just as for a monk of Cluny who died away from the abbey, although the singing of private Masses, as done for such a brother, was expressly denied benefactors [12].

In the matter of obit commemorations Bernard elsewhere carefully distinguishes the *magnum anniuersarium,* reserved to the abbots of Cluny and kings, from the *anniuersarium mediocre,* of which there were three classes, differing from the *magnum* and each other in the liturgical content of Office and Mass, and in the number of bells rung, candlesticks placed before the altar, and poor fed by the sacristan [13]. Assignment to each

9. Citation of Bernard of Cluny's *Consuetudines* is by part, chapter, and page, to the edition of Marquard HERRGOTT, *Vetus disciplina monastica* (Paris, 1726), pp. 134-364, which badly needs replacing by a modern annotated text. The commonly used title found in Herrgott of *Ordo Cluniacensis* does not occur in the chief MS (Paris, B. N. 13875) which has *Consuetudines cenobii Cluniacensis;* cf. Rose GRAHAM, *English Ecclesiastical Studies* (London, 1929), pp. 5-7, 25-29; A. WILMART, *Cluny (MSS liturgiques de)* in *D.A.C.L.*, t. 3, pt. 2 (1948), col. 2084.

10. Bernard, *Consuet.*, 1, 26 (200).

11. Ibid. The full title of the collect, not given by Bernard, is supplied by the slightly later *Consuetudines* of Udalric, 1, 7 in *P. L.* 149, 652B.

12. Ibid.; cf. also 1, 13 (158).

13. 1, 74, sect. 27 (272); sect. 63 (278). See also E. MARTÈNE, *De antiquis ecclesiae ritibus* (2nd ed., Antwerp, 1736-38), t. 4, pp. 470-477; G. de VALOUS, *Le monachisme clunisien des origines au XVe siècle* (Ligugé, 1935), 1, pp. 326-372.

class was made by the abbot. The *magnum anniuersarium* was limited to emperors, empresses and kings *qui magnum quid contulerunt ecclesiae*, a list which in Bernard's time seems to have included only five persons: the German emperors Henry II and Henry III; the empresses Adelaide and Agnes; and King Fernando "of the Spains" [14]. On these great occasions (i) all bells, including the two great ones, were pealed for a considerable time at the Vespers, Office and Mass of the Dead; (ii) the Tract was sung in the Mass in copes, and the responsory in tunics; (iii) antiphons and psalms were added to the Vespers; (iv) the entire Office, and the responsory, were intoned; (v) five candlesticks were set before the altar; (vi) twelve poor were fed with a hearty meal of bread, wine and meat; and (vii) a full refection was served the monks [15].

In addition to such general intercessory provisions for benefactors as such, and for the solemn commemoration of the *magna anniuersaria*, Bernard also records in five widely scattered passages the existence of special liturgical or eleemosynary practices devoted to King Fernando I, his consort (Doña Sancha) and "the kings of the Spains". These are as follows:

(1) of the three daily alms portions of food (*prebendae*) served the poor by the almoner from the high table in the refectory, two of which were dedicated to Abbot Odilo and Emperor Henry II, the third commemorated Fernando, his wife and the *reges Hispaniarum* [16];

(2) in the High Mass on ferial days between the octave of Easter and Michaelmas the fifth collect was said *pro regibus Hispaniarum aliisque principibus* [17];

(3) in the Morrow Mass *pro defunctis* the collect *Omnipotens sempiterne Deus, in cuius humana conditio* was said for an unnamed

14. 1, 51 (246); not, as commonly, Henry I (e.g., Graham, p. 38) but Henry II *primus Henricus imperator*. On Cluny's relations with the Emperors Henry II and Henry III, see Sackur, 2, pp. 155-290; Valous, *D.H.G.E.*, t. 13, cols. 44-49.

15. For the full refection *(plena refectio)* of fish and spiced honeyed wine *(pigmentum)* see 1, 51 (246). Cf. D. Knowles, *The Reforming Decrees of Peter the Venerable* in *Petrus Venerabilis*, p. 7.

16. 1, 13 (158): "Praeterea tres fratrum praebendae dantur quotidie ad eleemosynam quae et in refectorio super mensam principalem apponuntur; scilicet pro beatissimo patre d. Odilone, pro Henrico primo imperatore, pro Fredelano et eius uxore et regibus Hispaniarum."

17. 1, 41 (232): "Et ab octauis Paschae usque ad festum s. Michaelis. *A domo tua, quaesumus, Domine*. Quarum quinta et pro regibus Hispaniarum aliisque principibus..."

monk of Cluny, the *reges Hispaniarum,* and Abbot Hugh's father (Count Dalmace de Semur) [18];

(4) of the five anniversaries on which the sacristan served a full refection of fish and spiced honeyed wine, four were obits of the German emperors Henry II and III and the empresses Adelaide and Agnes; but the fifth commemorated the death of King Fernando of Spain (*rex Hispaniae*); and on such occasions, if *ornamenta* given by these rulers were among the treasures of the house, these were to be displayed in their memory upon the altar [19];

(5) to the practice of celebrating no Office at night throughout the entire octave of the Nativity, there was a unique exception: by Abbot Hugh's express command, the Office was celebrated on the morrow of the feast of the Holy Innocents for King Fernando, the abbey's generous benefactor, and in the same fashion as for Cluny's own abbots; and that day all qualified priests sang their private Masses for his repose [20].

To appreciate the full meaning of these five intercessory customs, it is necessary to recognize, first of all, that they relate solely to the king-emperors of Leon and not to medieval Spanish *reges* in general. In this period the abbey no longer had close ties with Aragon, whose king,

18. I, 42 (233): "Quod si nullum praecessit officium per omne iam dicti temporis spatium, post duodecim lectiones, *Deus, qui inter apostolicos* prima dicitur, et similiter illae duae adimuntur, et caeterae in ordine supradicto sequuntur. Haec missa, *Deus, qui inter,* proprie deputata est sanctis patribus nostris pontificibus Romanis: *Omnipotens sempiterne Deus, in cuius,* cuidam fratri nostro et regibus Hispaniarum et patri domni abbatis..." For Cluny's celebration of the anniversary of Count Dalmace de Semur, father of Abbot Hugh I, cf. A. BERNARD and A. BRUEL, eds.,*Recueil des chartes de l'abbaye de Cluny* (Paris, 1876-1903), 4, nos. 2940, 3346; 5, no. 3742 (esp. p. 94).

19. I, 51 (246): "Ad eumdem apocrisiarium pertinet in quibusdam anniuersariis plenam refectionem fratribus exhibere de piscibus uidelicet atque pigmento; in anniuersario scilicet primi Henrici imperatoris et alterius Henrici, domni quoque Fredelani regis Hispaniae, et domnae Adelaidis augustae, domnae quoque Agnetis imperatricis, in quorum quoque memoriis, si qua in thesauris ecclesiae de ipsorum donariis habentur ornamenta, pro illorum memoria commendanda superponuntur."

20. 2, 32 (355-356): "Sciendum tamen quia in octauis Dominicae Natiuitatis usque post octauum diem, nullum sit in nocte officium, excepto uno solo in crastino festiuitatis Innocentium, quod d. Hugo abbas fieri instituit pro Fredelano Hispaniarum rege qui multa bona loco Cluniacensi contulit, pro quo etiam sicuti pro abbatibus nostris sit; praecepit ut singuli sacerdotes qui ad hoc idonei uidentur missas ipsa die pro eo cantent." On the basis of the *Historia Silense,* ed. Fr. SANTOS COCO (Madrid, 1921), pp. 89-91, and in complete neglect of this passage of Bernard, the death of Fernando I has universally been placed on December 27th; I expect to demonstrate shortly that the author of the *Silense* was confused, and that the true obit was the 29th, as observed at Cluny.

from 1068, was a vassal of the pope, or with Navarre, as in Sancho el Mayor's era, but only with the *reges* of the united states of Leon and Castile. It is to them that Bernard's passages unquestionably apply. Cluniac and papal documents alike avoid calling any ruler below the Pyrenees *imperator,* the term which in Burgundy and Italy, as elsewhere outside the Peninsula, normally designated the Holy Roman emperor. So too the Spanish chanceries, even that of Leon, frequently employ in their official diplomas the term *rex,* with or without qualifying attributes, for the Leonese-Castilian sovereign. But the majestic phrases *rex Hispaniae, rex Hispaniarum,* circulating in Spain alongside their equivalent *imperator Hispaniae, imperator Hispaniarum,* unmistakably meant only one of the various Iberian rulers, the Leonese king-emperor of the *regnum Hispaniae* or *Hispaniarum*[21]. There are moreover two clear signs that Cluny, conscious of its imperial connotations, accepted this peninsular usage: the restriction of *rex Hispaniae, rex Hispaniarum,* to the Leonese monarch in Cluniac texts such as the Spanish correspondence of Abbot Hugh, the *Vitae* of this abbot, and the *Liber de miraculis* of Abbot Peter the Venerable; and in the consistent bracketing by the Cluniac custumals and the *Statuta s. Hugonis abbatis* of the Leonese sovereigns and their consorts with the *imperatores* and *imperatrices* of the Holy Roman Empire[22].

Secondly, it is to be noted that on Bernard's showing the abbey paid substantially greater intercessory honor to the Leonese king-emperors than to the imperial Germans[23]. Fernando's obit, like theirs, was not only an imperial *magnum anniuersarium* but was marked by the only Matins recited in the whole Nativity octave, elevated to the supreme level of the anniversaries of Cluny's own abbots, and assigned that singing of private Masses which was prohibited to other benefactors. In comparison, the *plenum officium* and feeding of twelve poor on July 13th, and the seven-day alms serving of food and drink (*justitia*) for the Emperor Henry II ("nostrae societatis et fraternitatis karissimi") represent a distinctly less solemn commemoration[24]. Furthermore, while special collects had long been recited on the obits of imperial and royal benefactors, there appears neither in the earlier custumals nor in Bernard any parallel — other than the nondescript *pro ...aliisque principibus* that the latter attaches to ferial High Masses between the Easter octave and Michaelmas — to the offering of frequent, regular prayers for specific national rulers such as are here prescribed for the *reges Hispaniarum,* living and dead.

21. R. Menéndez Pidal, *Imperio hispánico,* pp. 86-89, 99-113; idem, *La España del Cid* (4th. ed., Madrid, 1947), 2, pp. 725-731.

22. Cf. Bernard, *Consuet.* 1, 51 (246), quoted *supra,* n. 19; references to the other sources listed will be found below.

23. See the details of imperial commemorations in the *Consuetudines Farfenses,* ed. Albers, pp. 201-202; of those of abbots, pp. 201-202, 204.

24. Ibid., p. 204.

Lastly, of the three Leonese parties for whom intercession is being made — Fernando I, his wife Doña Sancha, and the *reges Hispaniarum* — each possesses great interest. The attention given Fernando himself is no great problem: whatever other *multa bona* he may have given Cluny — and the phrase recalls Bernard's mention of the *magnum anniuersarium* for rulers *qui magnum quid contulerunt ecclesiae* — by far the richest was the famous census of an annual thousand gold *metcales* or dinars for clothing the monks of Cluny, an extremely large sum as such by extra-peninsular monetary standards in the eleventh century, and made enormously more so by the promise of its annual repetition. Abbot Hugh's gratitude for this substantial charity would alone explain his institution of the exceptional obit observances. But what of the Queen-Empress Sancha and the *reges?* Are we to suppose their intercession was begun at the same time as Fernando's, perhaps by previous arrangement with abbot Hugh? or are we dealing in the Leonese passages with customs combining several stages of post-Fernandine liturgical evolution? The answer depends in large part on the date we assign the *Consuetudines cenobii Cluniacensis.*

2. *Bernard of Cluny and the Alfonsine Diploma of 1077*

While there has not been any agreement on the date of the Bernardine *Consuetudines,* other than that they belong in the second half of the eleventh century, the prevailing belief is that they were completed by the years 1067 or 1068 [25]. If true, this would compel us to place all the five Hispanic references within the period of not over three years following Fernando I's death on 27/29 December 1065. But this date for the custumal cannot be accepted. It rests upon two assumptions now several centuries old: Duchesne's view of 1614 that Bernard's work preceded the *Consuetudines* of Udalric or Ulric (ca. 1085), which is sound enough although still in need of careful demonstration [26]; and the assertion by the Maurist author of the two-page account published in 1746 in Tome VII (pp. 595-597) of the *Histoire littéraire de la France* that "Bernard l'avoit fait dès 1067, ou l'année suivante", a claim for which no proof is offered and which reflects superficial examination of the text. For the very fact that in the list of imperial anniversaries Cluny celebrated in his time Bernard includes that of the Empress Agnes, the widow of the Franconian emperor Henry III, who did not die until December 14, 1077, indicates

25. Graham, p. 29; Valous, *Monachisme Clunisien,* 1, 20 suggests 1063-1087; but in *D.H.G.E.*, t. 13, col. 135, says ca. 1063.
26. M. Marrier, *Bibliotheca Cluniacensis* (Paris, 1614), Notae, p. 23, as cited by Graham, p. 26, n. 3.

that the *Consuetudines* appeared at least a decade later than now commonly supposed [27]. And that the Agnes obit is no later interpolation finds confirmation in three, possibly four, of the Hispanic passages, which also point to 1077 as the *terminus post quem*.

The principal clue to dating Bernard's Leonese texts is their revelation of Cluniac intercessory customs affecting not only Fernando I but his wife and the *reges Hispaniarum*. Several possibilities suggest themselves. First, prayers and the daily *prebenda* might conceivably have been organized immediately after news of Fernando's death reached Cluny, presumably in 1066. Indubitably this is what happened as regards the anniversary commemoration which Abbot Hugh ordered; but it does not explain the *prebenda,* unless we imagine that this was originally for Fernando alone, and, even less, the intercession for Doña Sancha and the *reges*. It was on 7 November 1067 that the queen-empress died, two years after her husband [28]; again it is difficult to believe that at that time she was included in a hypothetically existent Fernandine *prebenda,* because Cluny did not automatically include their consorts, male or female, in the high liturgical honors rendered her imperial benefactors, as the German cases prove; and there are no grounds for assuming any special Cluniac gratitude to Sancha, a point confirmed by the lack of an obit observance comparable to her husband's. Furthermore, this leaves the *reges* still unaccounted for. There remains, then, the strong probability that the appearance of Doña Sancha and the *reges Hispaniarum* in Bernard's custumal reflects liturgical and eleemosynary practices established at Cluny after 1067, in the reign of Fernando I's son and successor on the imperial Leonese throne, the fervently Cluniaphile Alfonso VI.

In the entire history of Hispano-Cluniac relations Alfonso VI (1066-1109) stands as the peninsular sovereign with whom the great Burgundian abbey developed the closest bonds of friendship and *societas,* and from whom she received more splendid gifts than from any other medieval European monarch. Filial loyalty to Fernando's pro-Cluniac orientation only partially explains this Alfonsine policy. More important is the fact that at various points in the reign, e. g., the early struggle against Sancho II of Castile, the conflict with Gregory VII over abolition of the Hispanic Rite, the crises over the imperial sucession, Alfonso depended heavily upon Cluny's counsel and powerful support [29]. Particularly significant for the present inquiry is the abbey's intervention in the fratricidal wars among Fernando's three sons after the old emperor's partitioning of his realms and his death in 1065 [30]. For when, after the battle of

27. Bernard, *Consuet.*, I, 51 (246); F. L. BAUMANN, ed., *Necrologia Germaniae,* I (*M.G.H.* Berlin, 1888), t. I, pp. 128, 659.
28. MENÉNDEZ PIDAL, *España del Cid,* I, p. 165.
29. DAVID, *Études,* pp. 399-430; idem, *Le pacte successoral entre Raymond de Galice et Henri de Portugal* in *Bulletin hispanique,* t. 50, 1948, pp. 275-290.
30. Cf. MENÉNDEZ PIDAL, *España del Cid,* I, pp. 165-192.

Golpejera in January 1072, Sancho II deposed Alfonso, assumed for himself — after annexing Leon — the imperial title, and imprisoned his defeated brother in the *castillo* of Burgos, it was Abbot Hugh and his monks who came to Alfonso's rescue with their prayers and influence. These prayers, as earlier with Kings Garcia and Ramiro, were purely occasional, being designed to save the life and liberty of the enchained ruler; but it is to be noted that they were offered in behalf of that son of Fernando who was the legitimate king-emperor of Leon, and that they were successful. The reluctant Sancho was coerced into allowing his brother to go into safe exile at Moorish Toledo; and a few months later, in October 1072, after Sancho's assassination before the walls of Zamora, Alfonso triumphantly returned from the banks of the Tagus to rule over all his father's old dominions [31].

In the years that followed the restoration of 1072 there are four major occasions on which the king-emperor publicly exhibited his profound thankfulness to his Burgundian liberators and his earnest desire for Cluniac intercessory remembrance. These are: (i) his transfer to Cluny between 1073 and 1081 of various Leonese and Castilian monasteries; (ii) the concession in 1077 of a census double that of his father's, the additional thousand dinars to be used for feeding the monks; (iii) the contribution, from ca. 1088 on, of vast sums for the construction of Abbot Hugh's new abbey church; and (iv) the re-grant in 1090 of the doubled census. Given the natural sequence of extraordinary gift and liturgical recognition, any one of these generosities might lie back of the post-Fernandine elements in Bernard of Cluny; but in fact the last two can safely be ruled out, as too late in time for the *Consuetudines* and also as linked with still other liturgical intercessions, to be discussed below.

Moreover, the first possibility mentioned, that Alfonso's monastic cessions motivated the intercessory practices for Doña Sancha and the *reges Hispaniarum,* can likewise be dismissed. Inspection of the *pro remedio* clauses of the donation charters, in which Alfonso designates the spiritual beneficiaries of his gifts, yields no counterpart to the liturgical trio of Fernando, Sancha and the *reges,* or to the last two alone. To cite the major cessions: that in 1073 of San Isidro de Dueñas, was made "pro remedio anime mee et pro anima patris mei et matris mee et omnium parentum meorum" [32]; that of San Juan de Hérmedes de Cerrato (May 22, 1077), "pro remedium anime mee" [33]; that of Santa María de

31. Ibid.; but n. 4, p. 175 wrongly rejects the account of Cluniac aid as anachronistic. L. G. de VALDEAVELLANO, *Historia de España,* t. 1, pt. 2 (2nd ed., Madrid, 1955), pp. 317-320, curiously ignores Cluny's important role in the crisis of 1072. On Cluny's prayers for the fettered emperor, see *P. L.* 159, 866B, 912C; *Bibl. Clun.*, 443, 452; A. L'HUILLIER, *Vie de Saint Hugues* (Paris, 1880), p. 584; G. CIROT, *Une Chronique Léonaise inédite* in *Bulletin hispanique,* t. 11, 1909, p. 273.

32. *Chartes de Cluny,* t. 4, no. 3452.

33. Ibid., no. 3508.

Nájera (1079), "propter remedium anime mee uel parentum meorum"[34]; that of Santa Coloma de Burgos (1081), "pro remedium anime mee uel parentum meorum"[35]. In each case where these *pergaminos* mention *parentes,* the context — for example, *omnium* in the Dueñas text — shows that the *parentes* in question are not merely Fernando and Sancha, but Alfonso's *parientes,* i. e., in the Romance sense of the word still current in Spanish, all his kinsmen or relatives; and in no case can these be taken as the counterpart of Bernard's *reges Hispaniarum* who are, as we have said, the Leonese king-emperors.

If, on the other hand, we turn to a more munificent benefaction than any or all of the monastic cessions, to Alfonso's doubling of the Fernandine census to Cluny, we discover at once an exact parallel with the three subjects of intercession recorded in Bernard's *Consuetudines.* Two imperial documents, sent to Cluny at the time the doubled subsidy was given, and long preserved there, are extant. Alfonso's personal letter announcing the gift to Abbot Hugh displays no manifestly liturgical symptoms[36]. But the actual donation charter of July 10, 1077 is more illuminating, for it carefully lists the spiritual beneficiaries of the imperial generosity: "pro remedio anime mee et pro anima patris mei regis Fridenandi et pro anima matris mee Sanctie regine et pro animabus parentum meorum qui post me uenturi sunt ut habeant uitam et requiem sine fine"[37]. This list is remarkably interesting in several respects. It commences with Fernando I, thus ignoring that initial royal Iberian benefactor of Cluny in the Navarro-Basque dynasty, Sancho el Mayor. It disregards no less the old line of Leonese emperors ending at the battle of Tamarón (1037), when Fernando I overthrew his brother-in-law, Vermudo III. It includes Doña Sancha, Alfonso's mother, but omits (perhaps somewhat ungraciously) his then still living first wife, Agnes of Aquitaine[38]. Not unexpectedly, spiritual benefits are sought for the king-emperor himself. But the most striking thing of all is the concern here manifested for the repose of Alfonso VI's own future successors as king-emperors, for there can be little question that the phrase *parentes post me uenturi,* which occurs in none of the monastic charters alluding to his *parentes* in general, means not all descendants, but precisely those who are to come after him on the imperial throne. The same language recurs a little later in the diploma of 1077, where Alfonso binds his successors to faithful discharge of the doubled census: "Et si quis ex meo genere qui post me uenturus sit... hunc uotum mei testamenti infringere uoluerit et qualiscumque fuerit qui hoc regimen post me gubernauerit

34. Ibid., no. 3540.
35. Ibid., no. 3582.
36. Ibid., no. 3441 (wrongly dated); *P. L.,* t. 159, cols. 938-939.
37. Ibid., no. 3509, esp. pp. 627-628.
38. David, *Études,* p. 387, following Sandoval, places her death on June 6, 1078.

et si hunc censum ita duplicatum persoluere non quesierit, etc.". Here then is the hope of intercession for Fernando, Sancha and the *reges*.

If this reasoning is sound, as we believe it to be, then it seems possible to reconstruct the chronology of liturgical and eleemosynary innovation that underlies the five Leonese texts in Bernard of Cluny. In 1066, as we have said, the anniversary commemoration of Fernando I must have been begun by abbatial order. Perhaps in 1068, after Doña Sancha's death, observation of her anniversary commenced but without the exceptional solemnity of her imperial husband's. Then in 1077, perhaps in the late summer or early autumn, the diploma of July 10, 1077 reached Cluny; and in its light Abbot Hugh instituted probably three new intercessory measures. At this time, doubtless, the third daily *prebenda* was established, supplementing the older ones for Abbot Odilo and Emperor Henry II; as a commemoration of the dead, this gave immediate intercession to Fernando and Sancha; after their deaths, it would include Alfonso VI and his successors, the *reges Hispaniarum*. Secondly, the fifth collect in all ferial Masses between the octave of Easter and Michaelmas was now prescribed to be said *pro regibus Hispaniarum;* since this was a prayer for the living, it would be said for Alfonso VI and, in the future, for each of his reigning successors in his lifetime. Thirdly, the collect *Omnipotens sempiterne Deus, in cuius humana conditio,* which was being used for benefactors in general in all Masses and Offices of the Dead when not among the regularly assigned collects, and which had previously been recited in all Morrow Masses for the special benefit of the anonymous Cluniac monk and Dalmace de Semur, was to be offered in such Masses for the *reges Hispaniarum,* i. e., Fernando I immediately, Alfonso VI and his successors after death.

The extraordinary nature of these intercessory customs of 1077 should be marked. The new Leonese *prebenda* placed Fernando, Sancha and the *reges Hispaniarum* alongside Cluny's most revered abbot of the past and her hitherto greatest imperial benefactor. Specific commemoration of the *reges* in Morrow Masses of the Dead represented an intercessory frequency never accorded the German emperors and empresses. The introduction of regular prayers for the reigning Leonese king-emperor in ferial Masses of the long summer season gave Alfonso VI a privilege that Cluny had never yet bestowed on any ruler. And the implicit promise of continuing prayer for the Leonese king-emperors yet to come, which corresponds exactly to the hereditary character of the doubled census, means that in Burgundy as in Spain the bonds of *societas* and intercession were envisaged as henceforth perpetual.

The bearing of all this also upon the dating of the *Consuetudines cenobii Cluniacensis* should now be patent. Its mention of the anniversary of the Empress Agnes has already been cited as pointing to post-1077. Now it can be seen that this was no interpolation. The Hispanic materials show that Bernard is describing intercessory customs that were not in existence prior to Alfonso VI's promulgation of the diploma of July 10, 1077 which led the abbot of Cluny to create the new liturgical and prebendary elements which the *Consuetudines* combine with those going back to 1066. Bernard's work cannot have been completed before 1078; if we are to allow for its use, possibly as early as 1083, by Udalric, we may tentatively place it between 1078 and 1082 or, in short, ca. 1080.

3. *The* Dies Liberationis *of Alfonso VI*

In still another quarter we encounter further neglected evidence of intercessory observance for Alfonso VI. Among the extant medieval biographies of Abbot Hugh I four make mention of an anniversary feast at Cluny celebrating Alfonso's release from imprisonment in 1072 through the intervention of Cluny and her patron St. Peter [39]. The *Vita s. Hugonis* of Gilo, written — according to Schieffer — in 1120 and at most points the best informed of the abbot's Lives, describes Alfonso VI as rewarding the abbey by doubling the Fernandine census and leaving to Cluny the observance of the day of his liberation: "diemque liberationis celebrem nostris relinqueret" [40]. This same passage re-appears in the later *Epitome* based on Gilo's work, the so-called Anonymous I [41]. Another early and well-informed *Vita,* that of Hildebert of Lavardin, which probably appeared very shortly after Gilo's in 1121 or so, declares that in gratitude for Cluny's aid in securing his release Alfonso doubled his father's census while also "diem utriusque exitus et de carcere scilicet et de corpore celebrem habere desiderans" [42]. So too the so-called *Alia miraculorum quorundam s. Hugonis abbatis relatio* (Anonymous II) preserves the tradition that following his escape the king thanked his intercessors by doubling the annual tribute and "diem suae ereptionis festiuum apud nos reddidit" [43].

From these texts it is clear that (a) Cluny observed the anniversary of Alfonso's liberation from prison which she associated with her intervention in his behalf and the subsequent concession of the doubled census; (b) observance of the day was instituted, and coupled with the future com-

39. On the chronology of the *Vitae* of Abbot Hugh, I have followed T. Schieffer, *Notice sur les vies de Saint Hugues, abbé de Cluny* in *Le Moyen Age*, t. 46, 1936, pp. 81-103, but my collation of the Alfonsine passages has both strengthened doubts of his prematurely precise datings and suggested the desirability of meticulous analysis of the component materials and complex interrelationships of the Hugonic biographies.

40. Text in A. L'Huillier, *Vie de Saint Hugues*, pp. 574-618; the words quoted are on p. 584.

41. *P. L.* 159, 912C.

42. *P. L.* 159, 867A.

43. *Bibl. Clun.*, cols. 452-453.

memoration of the royal obit, at the king's own request. These points can be clarified somewhat further. First, it must have been with the doubling of 1077, not its later renewal in 1090, that the *dies liberationis* was inaugurated. Hildebert, to be sure, links his account with Abbot Hugh's visit to Spain, which took place probably in early 1090, and after which — as we shall see — Alfonso issued a *real privilegio* dated Easter 1090, again pledging himself and his successors to payment of the doubled subsidy. But the other *Vitae* avoid this obvious confusion of original grant and re-grant, and rightly connect the *dies* with the concession of 1077, which was made when the event was still fresh in men's minds and the imperial sense of gratitude strong. There is, however, no reason to doubt another piece of information Hildebert alone reports, that the king-emperor asked for observance of both his *dies exitus de carcere* and *dies exitus de corpore*. The obit request is at least implicit in the charter of 1077; but the *dies liberationis* must have been requested either in a lost letter to Abbot Hugh or orally through a Cluniac intermediary, very probably the notorious Robert, Alfonso's chief counsellor on ecclesiastical affairs at this time. The creation of such an anniversary, a curious kind of anticipation of the *magnum anniuersarium* awaiting the obit of this greatest of the abbey's donors, seems to have no parallel in Cluniac history. It is all the more regrettable, therefore, that the liturgical details of its celebration remain completely unknown. At least we know it was *festiuum*.

When was this day of liberation? The custumals and later *statuta* do not mention it at all. Since the doubling charter of 1077 was issued on July 10th, it is possible that this was the anniversary of the king's escape. Certainly this fits in with the events of 1072 when they are reconstructed as follows: the king-emperor's capture in January; some months of imprisonment while the Infanta Urraca, the Leonese nobles, and the abbot of Cluny labored to effect his release, which may well have occurred in early July; and then the sojourn at Toledo, until Sancho's death in October [44]. It appears furthermore from the Cluniac biographers quoted above that the observance of Alfonso's liberation continued even after his death. Hildebert's language seems to imply that both it and the obit were commemorated on one and the same day. In this case it might be conjectured that since Alfonso actually died on June 30th or July lst 1109, and may have been liberated from prison on July 10th, as suggested above, the proximity of these two dates may have led to an amalgamation of obit and *dies liberationis* in the Cluniac calendar. But this is admittedly sheer surmise.

44. In my opinion, MENÉNDEZ PIDAL, *España del Cid*, I, pp. 175-176 and VALDEAVELLANO, I, pt. 2, pp. 317-318, fail to allow sufficient time for the length of Alfonso's stay in prison and to the period during which his supporters in Spain and Cluny labored for his release; I hope to discuss this at an early date.

4. *The Hispanic References in Udalric's* Consuetudines

A very few years after the completion, ca. 1080, of Bernard's *Consuetudines,* Udalric compiled the second of the great Cluniac or Cluniac-inspired custumals of the last quarter of the eleventh century [45]. This work, which like Bernard's still awaits careful study of its composition, is generally thought to have appeared by 1085, and perhaps as early as 1083, although Hauviller places Book III as late as 1087 [46]. It draws freely upon Bernard, with many changes in order and content, and with new material reflecting either the passage of the years or different sources of information. Between Bernard's and Udalric's notices of the Leonese intercessions there are certain differences. Udalric, writing for the German priories, is less detailed on customs peculiar to the mother abbey, omitting entirely Bernard's sections on anniversary commemorations. He is also less informative on matters Hispanic: he has only three such passages as against Bernard's five; he leaves out all mention of Fernando I's obit; and as for major anniversaries, he adduces only the example of Emperor Henry II, without any reference to the display of *ornamenta* [47]. He cites however in somewhat the same words as his predecessor the daily *prebenda* commemorating Fernando, Sancha and the *reges* [48].

As we have seen, Bernard limits the Hispanic collect in ferial High Masses to the period between the Easter octave and Michaelmas, and has it offered *pro regibus Hispaniarum aliisque principibus.* But Udalric describes it as said throughout the year *pro regibus Hispaniarum per uices* [49]. For Bernard this is the fifth collect, for Udalric the seventh. While Bernard loosely includes among the collects of Morrow Masses of the Dead the *Omnipotens sempiterne Deus* and has it said *pro cuidam fratri et regibus Hispaniarum et patri domni abbatis,* Udalric provides a carefully drawn up *ordo collectarum* for these Masses, in which he assigns sixth place to the *Omnipotens sempiterne Deus* as recited solely *pro regibus Hispaniarum;* and seventh place to an unidentified collect

45. Text in *P. L.* 149, 635-778; cf. GRAHAM, pp. 25-28, and on the MSS, WILMART, *D.A.C.L.*, 3, pt. 2, col. 2089.
46. GRAHAM, loc. cit.
47. The three passages are: 1, 6 (*P. L.* 149, 651D); 1, 7 (652B); 3, 24 (767A). For Henry II, 3, 12 (756D).
48. 3, 24 (767A): "praeterea trium fratrum praebendae dantur ad eleemosynam, scilicet pro beatissimo patre dom. Odilone, pro Henrico primo imperatore, pro Fredelando et eius uxore et regibus Hispaniarum".
49. 1, 6 (651D): "Quarta [collecta] est pro regibus aliisque principibus; quinta pro episcopis et abbatibus nostris; sexta pro familiaribus nostris; septima pro regibus Hispaniarum per uices, et aliae collectae."

recited *pro regina Hispaniarum et pro sororibus et aliis feminis familiaribus*[50].

Now certain of these variations between the two custumals can doubtless be accounted for satisfactorily as due either to Udalric's incompleteness — which led his original patron, Abbot William of Hirsau, to produce his own *Consuetudines Hirsaugienses*[51] — or his deliberate neglect of topics irrelevant to the needs of the monasteries his work addresses. This may explain the mention of Henry II's anniversary, which would interest German readers, as Fernando's would not; doubtless it also lies back of the entire silence regarding the Fernandine obit, which Bernard had emphasized and which was surely still being observed at Cluny, and the dropping of the *quidam frater* and Dalmace de Semur from the Morrow Masses *pro defunctis*. On the other hand, Udalric throws light on how the prayers for the *reges Hispaniarum* in the ferial Masses were expected to continue: *per uices,* i. e., for each succeeding monarch in his turn[52]. But his divergences from Bernard in extending the Hispanic collect in ferial High Masses to the whole year; his different order of the Hispanic collects in these and in the Morrow Masses of the Dead; and the insertion among the collects for the dead of one *pro regina Hispaniarum et pro sororibus et aliis feminis familiaribus;* must be attributed to a post-Bernardine revision of the Leonese provisions. When and why were these changes made?

If, as concluded above, the *Consuetudines cenobii Cluniacensis* date after 1077 and Udalric's *Consuetudines* appeared ca. 1083-85, we have a period of only a decade in which to place the new arrangements. One possible clue presents itself in the collect *pro regina Hispaniarum,* etc. Udalric's language here abridges several sentences in the parallel chapter of Bernard which assert "*Quas dicet* [deputata est] sororibus nostris et aliis feminis familiaribus nostris... similiter quoque officium facimus pro regina uel pro alia femina familiari nostra. Quod si anniuersarius sit pro regina uel comitissa, praemissa *Quaesumus, Domine* sequitur *Praesta, Domine*"[53]. Bernard's alternatives here of *regina uel... alia*

50. I, 7 (652B): "...quarta [collecta] pro familiaribus nostris; quinta pro fratribus; sexta pro regibus Hispaniarum, *Omnipotens sempiterne Deus in cuius humana conditio;* septima pro regina Hispaniarum et pro sororibus et aliis feminis familiaribus..."

51. *P. L.* 150, 929C-D.

52. On the meaning of *per uices,* cf. also Madrid, Archivo Histórico Nacional, MS 258: Archivo de Sta. Maria de Naxera. Privilegios y cartas reales, t. I, fols. 166r-166v; this *real privilegio* of Alfonso VII of January 30, 1149 (era 1180 is incorrect) records the gift of a tenth of the *portazgo* of Logroño "...deo et ecclesie sancti Petri de Cluniaco et domno Petro ejusdem ecclesie abbati ecclesie quoque sancte marie de Naiara qui deo ibi seruiunt et in perpetuum seruient. singulis annis uestiendis. ut in suis orationibus cotidie mei et parentum meorum *singulariter* faciant mentionem..."

53. Bernard, *Consuet.*, I, 42 (233).

femina, regina uel comitissa effectively destroy any assumption that he or his copyists might have inadvertently suppressed *Hispaniarum* after *regina*. Thus the Udalric text represents a genuine change in the meaning of *regina* from a general to a specific application; and it is noteworthy that the use of the singular connotes a single individual, not as with the *reges Hispaniarum*, a succession.

Who was this deceased queen-empress of the Spains now newly assigned commemoration in Cluny's Masses of the Dead? Certainly not Constance of Burgundy, Alfonso VI's consort in these years, for she did not die until 1093 and was then granted much more solemn commemoration along with her husband, as the *Statuta Hugonis* attest [54]. She could be Alfonso's first wife, Agnes of Aquitaine, whose death on June 6, 1078 might have come too late for mention by Bernard [55]. Yet the king-emperor's failure in the diploma of 1077 to mention Agnes among the persons for whose repose he gave the doubled census, and his early re-marriage within less than a year, this time to Constance, make it unlikely that he would have pressed Cluny for so exceptional a memorial to his first consort, and under the title now borne by her successor. Nor did Cluny have reason herself to initiate extraordinary commemoration of a queen of no known special devotion to the abbey who was followed on the throne by Abbot Hugh's own niece. This leaves us with Alfonso VI's mother, the empress of Fernando I, Doña Sancha of Leon; and in my opinion there can be little doubt that she is the *regina Hispaniarum* of the Udalrician collect.

The precise point, however, between 1077 and ca. 1085 at which this commemoration commenced, it seems impossible to determine. If it resulted from Sancha's inclusion in the diploma of 1077, we should expect it to have been reported by Bernard. No undue interest in his mother can be found in Alfonso's donation charters of Santa María de Nájera (1079) or Santa Coloma de Burgos (1081), where, as we have seen, the *parentes* cited are in fact the *parientes* [56]. It might be contended that Bernard was mistaken and should have included the Sanchan collect; but against this is the fact of Udalric's two other significant innovations in the Hispanic intercessory customs, and one of these — the extension to the entire year of the Hispanic collect in ferial Masses — constitutes also, like the addition of the *regina*, an enlargement of the liturgical honors paid the Leonese imperial house. Nor can we dispose of any or all of his variations from Bernard in terms of Udalric's alleged carelessness; indeed, his *ordines collectarum* for ferial High Masses and Masses of the Dead are more carefully organized than Bernard's. Thus the only conclusion justifiable at the moment is tentative: presumably,

54. See *infra*, sect. 6.
55. David, *Études*, p. 387.
56. See nn. 34-35, *supra*.

within a few years of his original intercessory measures of 1077, and in continuing appreciation of the *multa dona* from across the Pyrenees, the abbot of Cluny supplemented in several respects the liturgical honors already paid Alfonso VI and his mother. Whether this coincided in time with the foundation of the *dies liberationis* observance, we have, however, no means of determining.

5. *The Imperial Diploma of Easter 1090*

The next stage in the history of the Leonese intercessions is contemporary with two further instances of Alfonso VI's devotion to the Burgundian abbey in or about the years 1088-1090: his huge contributions to the construction of Cluny's new church, and his re-grant of the doubled census. The circumstances surrounding both these actions are by no means wholly understood, but are certainly connected with the Almoravid invasion of Spain in 1087 and the Leonese king-emperor's bloody defeat at Sagrajas (Zallaka). The rise of the powerful expansionist empire of the North African sultan Yusuf ibn Tashfin brought with it the abrupt collapse of the system of tributary *parias* under which enormous quantities of dinars had poured into the imperial Leonese fisc. That this immediately affected the Cluniac census is shown by the fact that Abbot Hugh, probably ca. 1088, sent to Spain his abbatial chamberlain Seguin to reproach the Leonese monarch for his non-payment of the annual subsidy upon which the abbey's economic welfare now so largely depended [57]. What may have saved the situation both for Alfonso and Cluny was the unexpected windfall of 30,000 dinars which the Zirite ruler Abdallah of Granada paid the king-emperor in the vain hope of preserving his kingdom from Almoravid annexation and himself from deposition [58]. At any rate, Seguin returned to Cluny with 10,000 *talenta,* i. e., dinars, for the new abbey church, and with a letter in which Alfonso passionately avowed his boundless affection for Cluny, implored Hugh and his monks to offer prayers for him, and urged the abbot to come to Spain so that he might profit by his counsels [59]. The result of this moving epistle was Hugh's one journey to Spain, the first but not the last time an abbot of Cluny pased the Pyrenees [60]. The two men met at Burgos, presumably in early

57. See Alfonso's letter to Hugh in *Chartes de Cluny,* 4, no. 3562, with wrong date.

58. Menéndez Pidal, *España del Cid,* 1, pp. 392-396; the date 1090 here assigned seems to me somewhat dubious.

59. See n. 57.

60. See my articles *The Spanish Journey of Abbot Ponce of Cluny* in *Studi in onore di Giorgio La Piana, Ricerche di storia religiosa,* t. 1, Rome, 1957, pp. 311-319; and *Peter the Venerable's Journey to Spain* in *Petrus Venerabilis,* pp. 163-175.

1090; and from Alfonso's *real privilegio,* which was issued at Easter in the Castilian capital, after Hugh had left for Burgundy laden with still more Muslim gold for the building of Cluny III, it is evident that the future of the census had been the principal subject of discussion in their conference [61]. In this diploma Alfonso binds himself to faithful discharge of the census, once more pledging himself and his successors to its perpetual payment, but this time securing formal ratification of his promise by an assembly of Leonese-Castilian notables, including Queen Constance, Archbishop Bernard of Toledo, and the bishops and magnates of his realm. In return, as the same *pergaminò* informs us, Abbot Hugh promised the king-emperor to impose by decree *(preceptum)* upon all his successors at Cluny the perpetual *commemoratio uel obsequium* of certain members of the dynasty: Alfonso's parents (Fernando and Sancha); his brothers (Sancho II of Castile, García of Galicia); himself and his queen (Constance); and his children.

The roll of spiritual beneficiaries in this imperial proclamation offers thought-provoking comparison with that of the first census donation charter of 1077. Here we have in the persons for whom Alfonso aimed to secure Cluny's lasting commemoration a new tendency to include members of the Navarro-Basque line outside Doña Sancha and the *reges* of the strict imperial succession. Alfonso and his parents are common to both lists; but in 1090, aside from the fact that the heir presumptive, the Infanta Doña Urraca, would be included among the *liberi,* there is no reference to the successors *post me uenturi.* Patently they were thought of as provided for in the collects of 1077. On the other hand, Queen Constance appears as the second Leonese queen-empress for whom after death Cluny was to pray. She, we know, as Abbot Hugh's niece, was the zealous champion of Cluny's interests in Spain and a close collaborator with the monk Robert in the liturgical crisis of 1080; and her alleged responsibility for the cession of Santa María de Nájera in 1079 later gave rise to a controversy which Rome itself had to decide [62]. As for the royal children, in 1090 these would include at least three living daughters, the future queen-empress Urraca, and her illegitimate sisters, Elvira and Teresa [63]. Finally, there are the two brothers, and here we witness a touching final act in the civil wars of twenty years before. By this act Alfonso laid to rest the bitter memories of his defeat and imprisonment at Sancho II's hands, the suspicions of his complicity in his brother's assassination at Zamora, and the famous oath at Santa Gadea in the presence

61. *Chartes de Cluny,* 4, no. 3638; P. L. 159, 973-974.

62. DAVID, *Études,* pp. 388-423; P. KEHR, *Papsturkunden in Spanien.* II. *Navarra und Aragon,* 2. *Urkunden und Regesten,* pp. 51-52, in*Abhandlungen der Gesellschaft der Wissenschaften zu Göttingen,* philolog.-hist. Kl., N. F., t. 22, 1 (Berlin, 1928).

63. L. VÁZQUEZ de PARGA, *Alfonso VI* in *Diccionario de Historia de España* (Madrid, 1952), 1, p. 110, col. 1 lists the more important of the children.

of the Cid. Cluny on her part was engaging to pray for her old enemy, whom the abbey's tradition — as the Gilo *Vita Hugonis* demonstrates — continued to depict a *tyrannus* [64]. García, the youngest of the brothers, and so very briefly the king of Galicia, had lived out his sorry life in chains as Alfonso's prisoner for over a score of years until his death on March 22, 1090 [65], exactly a month before the promulgation of the Easter *privilegio* and very probably while Abbot Hugh was still in Burgos. Alfonso had directed earlier grants to Cluny to the repose of his *parientes* in general, but this appears the unique instance, on the morrow of Garcias's death, of his specific concern for Cluny's intercession in behalf of his two ill-fated brothers.

6. *The* Statuta s. Hugonis abbatis

It must have been not long after his return from the Burgos meeting of 1090 that the abbot of Cluny promulgated the short liturgical ordinance which has been published under the title of *Statuta sancti Hugonis abbatis Cluniacensis pro Alphonso rege Hispaniarum tanquam insigni benefactore* [66]. This text cannot be regarded as the fulfillment of the intercessory promises Hugh is said to have made Alfonso VI in their discussions on Castilian soil. The *Statuta* address themselves to all the monks of Cluny, present and future, and impose upon them faithful execution of their prescriptions; they salute Alfonso *Hispaniarum rex* as a *fidelis amicus* who has given, and continues to give, to the abbey and to her priories, *tanta et talia bona* as no other king or prince of former or present times has done; and they describe him as one who both in life and death merits special participation in the abbey's spiritual benefits.

Therefore, in his behalf, during his lifetime, the *Statuta* order that (i) the psalm *Exaudiat te Dominus* is to be sung without intermission at Terce; (ii) the collect *Quaesumus, omnipotens Deus* is similarly to be said at each daily High Mass; (iii) a maundy of thirty poor is to be provided on Maundy Thursday; (iv) on Easter the chamberlain is to feed at least 100 poor; (v) every day at the high table a *prebenda* of food such as the king himself would eat if dining with the monks is to be served one of the poor, and this is to continue after Alfonso's death; and (vi) in the new abbey church built through the king-emperor's gifts one of the principal altars is to be reserved, Masses said at which are to be for his salvation. After death, it is prescribed that in addition to the daily *prebenda,* and the Offices, Masses and alms for him, he is to be commemorated by

64. L'Huillier, *Vie de Saint Hugues,* p. 584; also, *Epitome, P. L.* 159, 912C.
65. Menéndez Pidal, *España del Cid,* 1, 203-204.
66. *P. L.* 159, 945-946; incorrectly listed ca. 1070 by *Chartes de Cluny,* 4, no. 3442.

(i) the daily singing of Mass especially for his soul during an entire year at the aforesaid altar; and (ii) by the celebration of his *anniuersarium* as for the Emperor Henry II — namely, all bells to be pealed at the Vespers, Office and Mass; the Tract to be sung in copes; the Mass to be celebrated at his own altar; twelve poor to be fed; a portion of food and drink *(justitia)* to be served the poor for seven days in addition to the daily *prebenda* at the high table; and the monks to be served a full refection by the sacristan.

The *Statuta* conclude by declaring that Alfonso's *regina* and *coniunx deuotissima* is to share in all these provisions, and is further granted her own maundy of twelve poor on Maundy Thursday and the observance of her anniversary in the same manner as for the Empress Agnes [67].

The principal questions this document raises are those of its date, relationship to the Burgos conference, and place in the history of Cluniac intercession for the imperial Leonese dynasty. Since it distinguishes Constance's association in her husband's vitalicial intercessions, and her own maundy, from the commemoration of her obit, it follows that the queen-empress was alive at the time. This fixes the *terminus ante quem* at 1093, the year in which — according to David, between 3 April and 25 October — Constance died [68]; and removes any temptation to infer from the use of the perfect infinitive in the passage on Alfonso's altar ("in ecclesia beatorum apostolorum Petri et Pauli noua quam ipse de propriis facultatibus construxisse uidetur") that this points to an advanced stage of construction, e. g., that signalized by Pope Urban II's dedication of the chevet in 1095 [69]. As for the *post quem*, this is obviously later than 1088, when Alfonso was contributing to the building, and almost certainly after the 1090 meeting. Thus the date of composition would seem to fall in the period 1090-1093.

For several convincing reasons the *Statuta* cannot be identified as the *preceptum* embodying Abbot Hugh's liturgical regulations of which Al-

67. *P. L.* loc. cit., 946C.
68. David, *Études*, p. 389.
69. Kenneth J. Conant, *Carolingian and Romanesque Architecture, 800 to 1200* (Harmondsworth, Middlesex , 1959; The Pelican History of Art, vol. 13), p. 116. In the abbatial *preceptum* of 1155-56 (*Chartes de Cluny,* 5, no. 4183) establishing certain liturgical intercessions for Henry II of England after his death, Peter the Venerable speaks of the king's grandfather, Henry I, as "Donis autem multiplicibus et magnis omnes jam dictos (latinos reges) exsuperans, etiam majorem ecclesiam a rege Hispanorum Aldefonso inchoatam miro et singulari opere inter universas pene tocius orbis ecclesias consummavit". But this is not to be taken seriously: Henry I's census of 1130 or 1131 (*Chartes de Cluny,* nos. 4015-4016), giving the abbey an annual census of 100 marks of silver, cannot compare with the 2000 gold dinars of Alfonso VI; and, as for the building of the church, Henry I's doubtless substantial contributions are placed in more accurate proportion by the unknown Cluniac who wrote on the back of this charter (4183) the words: "De rege Henrico primo Anglie, basilice nove nostre precipuo constructore post regem Hispanie."

fonso VI speaks in his Easter diploma, for the contrast in content and purpose of the two documents bars this conclusion. The 1090 *real privilegio* is wholly dedicated to the subject of the census and twice mentions the persons to whose spiritual repose the subsidy is directed: in addition to the king and queen, the former's parents and brothers, and the royal children. The *Statuta,* however, envisage only Alfonso and Constance; although surely subsuming the doubled census among the *tanta et talia bona,* they do not allude to it, but to the construction of the abbey church. Abbot Hugh's instructions, therefore, for the dynastic conmmemorations, if ever actually written down, have perished.

The true purpose of the *Statuta* is plain: they are the supreme expression of the gratitude of the abbot and monks of Cluny to their imperial Leonese *socius* whose lavish benefactions have no counterpart in Cluniac annals. It may be only chance that we possess no similar written ordinance for the commemorations of the German emperors and empresses, but the fact is Hugh's *Statuta* have only one known precedent, the *Statutum* by which Abbot Odilo commanded the *commemoratio omnium fidelium defunctorum* [70]. It is to be noted further that the *Statuta* establish for Alfonso intercessory action over and above that already in existence since 1077; and while Hugh assigns him an anniversary similar to that of Henry II, it should be remembered that his daily commemoration in the Masses of the Dead and in the intention of Masses sung at his altar in the abbey church, assured him of more frequent intercessory prayer than ever offered for this greatest of the German benefactors. And finally, we may conclude that the primary inspiration of the *Statuta* was gratitude for the subsidizing of the new church within the walls of which Cluny was to offer the most elaborate and solemn of her intercessions for any medieval ruler.

7. *The Post-Alfonsine Evidence*

With the death of Alfonso VI, on June 30 or July 1, 1109, we can assume that liturgical intercession for the monarch took the form prescribed in the *Statuta Hugonis,* with the year of Masses and Offices of the Dead and thenceforth solemn commemoration of the imperial anniversary. If we are right in thinking that, according to Hildebert of Lavardin, the latter was combined with the previous observance of the *dies liberationis,* this must have been ordered not by Abbot Hugh, who died two months before the monarch, but by the next abbot, Ponce de Melgueil. Peter the Venerable, writing soon after 1142 his *Liber de miraculis,* attests the lively gratitude Cluny still felt towards her greatest benefactor with evidence brought home from Spain of the efficacy of Cluny's prayers for

70. *P. L.* 142, 1037-1038.

him. This is a story circulating in the Rioja of which Peter knew before crossing the Pyrenees, but now heard in person near Estella from the lips of Pedro Engelbertiz himself. This old soldier of Alfonso's, now a monk of Nájera, had had a vision a few years previously in which he was visited by several spirits of the dead; and one of these informed him that King Alfonso after his death had been suffering torments among the other sinners until he was rescued (once again!) by the intercessions of the monks of Cluny: "aliquandiu tormentis acribus inter reos excruciatus, postmodum a Cluniacensibus monachis inde sublatus est" [71].

No doubt the monks of Burgundy long continued their daily prayers for the souls of Alfonso VI and the *reges Hispaniarum* in the great choir of SS Peter and Paul; but well before the mid-twelfth century the age of Cluniac-Leonese friendship can be looked upon as drawing to its close. The dearth of new custumals or other pertinent evidence may exaggerate this impression, and it is possible that thorough search of the surviving Cluniac liturgical manuscripts of the mother house and her dependencies, especially the Iberian ones, might be rewarding. But the collapse of the imperial tradition in later twelfth-century Spain, the virtual termination of the annual census, and the diversion of royal Leonese and Castilian interest from a declining Cluny to Cîteaux and other new monastic movements, usher in a different age. Alfonso VI's daughter Urraca (1109-1126) possessed her father's faith in the Burgundian abbey but her troubled reign, with its internal disorders, long wars against her husband, King Alfonso *el Batallador* of Aragon, and acute financial distress, drastically reduced the generosities to Cluny, even though Urraca did cede certain monasteries, churches and lands for the *remedium anime* of herself, her parents and her first husband, Count Raymond of Burgundy [72]. Doña Urraca's son, Alfonso VII (1126-1157), displayed no special affection at all for Cluny and in 1142 negotiated with Abbot Peter the Venerable the reduction of his grandfather's doubled census to a mere 200 maravedis a year [73]. Yet in 1149, when giving the priory of Santa María de Nájera a tenth of the portazgo of the town of Logroño, Alfonso VII showed himself not entirely unmindful of the ancient family bond with Cluny. For he dedicated this gift to the clothing of the Riojan monks in the expectation that they in turn "in suis orationibus cotidie mei et parentum meorum singulariter faciant mentionem" [74]. Nevertheless, as this very donation illustrates, royal gifts now tended to be relatively minor and offered to

71. *Bibl. Clun.*, 1293-1296; *P. L.* 189, 903-908.

72. Anselm G. Biggs, *Diego Gelmírez, First Archbishop of Compostela*, pp. 65-139 in *The Catholic University of America, Studies in Mediaeval History*, New Series, vol. 12 (Washington, 1949). For Urraca's Cluniac charters, see, e. g., A. de Yepes, *Corónica general de la Orden de San Benito* (Irache, 1609-1621), t. 6, Apénd., pp. 462r-v, escr. xviii; F. Fita, *Primer siglo de Santa María de Nájera* in *Boletín de la R. Academia de la Historia*, t. 26, 1895, pp. 264-266.

73. Bishko, *Peter the Venerable's Journey to Spain*, pp. 169-170.

74. Cf. n. 52.

Cluny's peninsular dependencies rather than to the mother house. Alfonso VII's successors to his divided kingdom, Fernando II of Leon (1157-1188) and Alfonso VIII of Castile (1158-1214), and for the rest of the Middle Ages the kings of the reunited Leon-Castile, continued to make petty grants of land or privileges to Nájera, San Zoil de Carrión and other Cluniac houses in their domains; but all these ranked far below the munificent benefactions that evoked the great intercessory concessions of the epoch of Abbot Hugh I. Perhaps it was with some sense of this fading of the old dynastic tie between Cluny and the King-Emperors of Leon that Alfonso VIII, granting in 1165 the *heredad* of Villagiga to the Cluniac priory of San Isidro de Dueñas, looked back across the years to a policy neither he nor his successors would emulate: "hoc facio pro remedio animarum omnium parentum meorum qui especiali deuotione Cluniacensem ecclesiam dilexerunt" [75].

The full meaning of Cluniac intercessory ties with the Leonese king-emperors of the eleventh and twelfth centuries must of course be determined within the larger framework of medieval Hispano-Cluniac relations as a whole. We may, however, conclude with the hope that as pursued in these pages the subject has revealed its utility for at least four lines of historical investigation:

(i) the plotting of the actual course of the close personal, confraternal, liturgical and financial steps by which Cluny came to ally herself below the Pyrenees principally with imperial Leon, and above all with Alfonso VI, in the era of her most significant penetration into the Peninsula;

(ii) clarification of the predominantly intercessory rather then reformist character if this relationship, despite the cessions of Leonese-Castilian houses and the continuing leaven, since Sancho el Mayor's time, of the customs and ideals of Cluniac Benedictinism;

(iii) demonstration of the prominence of the imperial Leonese dynasty in Cluny's daily liturgical life and the swiftness with which the great donations found intercessory response, itself an index of the high degree of liturgical and customary fluidity existing under Abbot Hugh [76];

(iv) the provision of useful clues to the chronology and purpose of the pertinent passages in the custumals and other Cluniac and Hispanic texts.

University of Virginia — August, 1960

75. Antonio Suárez de Alarcón, *Relaciones genealógicas de la casa de los marqueses de Trocifal* (Madrid, 1656), Apénd., p. 10, escr. xvii.

76. For other instances of Hugh I's liturgical or customary innovations, see Bernard, *Consuet.*, 1, 23 (188-189); 1, 24 (195, 198); 2, 9 (297); 2, 24 (332); 2, 25 (334); 2, 30 (347); 2, 31 (351).

ADDITIONAL NOTE

On the emphatically imperial character of Cluny's bond with Alfonso VI and the Leonese-Castilian ruling dynasty, there must now be consulted the important work (with full recent bibliography) of Peter Segl, which ably re-examines Hispano-Cluniac relations in the 11th and 12th centuries.[1] The same imperial context can be further confirmed from the notable late 11th-century codex, now preserved at Parma, of St Ildephonse of Toledo's *De virginitate beatae Mariae*, which Abbot Hugh I presented to the Hispanic-king-emperor.[2] This sumptuous illuminated manuscript, done at Cluny in gold letters on purple vellum, is reminiscent of the famous imperial presentation codices produced by the Echternach School in 10th- and 11th-century Germany; and could have been sent to Spain in grateful acknowledgement shortly after the census doubling of 1077 or, alternatively, in the wake of Hugh's visit to Burgos in 1090, at the time of his promulgation of the special pro-Alfonsine liturgical *Statuta* of 1090–1093 (above, 72–4). Segl notes (204–207) that, contrary to p. 59 above, Peter the Venerable, St Bernard of Clairvaux and others do occasionally designate the *rex Hispaniae* as *imperator*. It may be added that the Burgundians also coupled the monarchical benefactors of Spain and England (73, above, note 69): see Peter's Letter 89 to Bishop Albaro of Liège: "post reges Hyspanos et Anglos", and the special intercessional ordinance for the year 1200 decreed by Abbot Hugh V: "pro . . . regibus Anglorum et Hispaniarum".[3]

The Hispano-Cluniac coalition in the papal crisis of 1080 has been usefully treated at some length by H. E. J. Cowdrey, although I am not in entire agreement with his contentions.[4] By some scholars Alfonso VI's donation in 1089–1090 of 10,000 *talenta* (gold dinars) continues to be seen as an extravagant new benefaction made by an overly pious ruler for the express purpose of funding the construction of Cluny III. But as I have insisted elsewhere, this (by trans-Pyrenean standards) enormous sum was in fact the overdue settlement of five years' arrears in the discharge of the doubled Hispanic census of 1077;[5] it was the abbot who *motu proprio* decided to dedicate it to his ambitious building program.

---

[1] Peter Segl, *Königtum und Klosterreform in Spanien* (Kallmünz, 1974), 193–217.

[2] M. Schapiro, *The Parma Ildefonsus: A Romanesque Illuminated Manuscript from Cluny and Related Works* (n. p. 1964); but this study errs on the historical context of the gift. Cf. also C. R. Dodwell, "The Gospel-Book of Goslar," *Times Literary Supplement*, 19 Nov. 1976, 1463–4.

[3] *The Letters of Peter the Venerable*, ed. Giles Constable (Cambridge, Mass., 1967), I, 229 (Ep. 89); II, 157–9; *PL* CLXXXIX, 279A (Ep. III, 2); *Statuts, chapîtres généraux et visites de l'Ordre de Cluny*, ed. G. Charvin (Paris, 1965–), I, 52.

[4] H. E. J. Cowdrey, *The Cluniacs and the Gregorian Reform* (Oxford, 1970), 214–47.

[5] See my "Fernando I and the Origins of the Leonese-Castilian Alliance with Cluny" in *Studies in Medieval Spanish Frontier History* (London, 1980), 46–50; Spanish version in *Cuadernos de historia de España*, XLVII–XLVIII (1968), 122–7.

Something more needs to be said regarding the remembrance by the Cluniacs of Fernando I's consort, the queen-empress Sancha, so patently a major influence upon her Leonicizing husband and her son Alfonso VI in their intimate alliance with the Burgundian abbey. Sancha must have been highly regarded by the monks as *socia* along with Fernando, and perhaps also as *benefactrix* in her own right. Nevertheless, while commemoration of her obit on VII. Id. Nov. (7 November; she died in 1067 not, as erroneously above, in 1077)is attested by the Necrology of Villars-les-Moines[6]—and Wollasch has shown this obituary to be in fact that of the foremost Cluniac nunnery of Marcigny-sur-Loire and therefore closely based upon Cluny's own lost Necrology[7]—it remains true that at the time of her death in 1067 the queen-empress does not seem to have been allotted anything more than the customary annual commemoration of her anniversary. Only in later years, and thanks to the eleemosynary and intercessional negotiations of her son Alfonso VI, can Doña Sancha be found enjoying also the exceptional privileges of inclusion alongside her husband in the Fernandine *praebenda* and the assignment of a special, if anonymous, collect.

On several topics raised in the foregoing Study, some further brief observations may be made. The subject of intercessional commemoration linking the Cluniacs with lay rulers, nobles and other benefactors is being fruitfully pursued by Prof. Joachim Wollasch and his students. A recent byproduct is the quantitatively based monograph by Dietrich Poeck, which ably analyzes the donors, motives and benefactorial concessions connected with the numerous lay burials made at Cluny in the 10th and 11th centuries.[8] On the major 11th-century Cluniac custumals or consuetudinaries of Bernard and Udalric, the badly needed and long awaited modern critical editions promised in the *Corpus Consuetudinum Monasticarum* directed by Dom Kassius Hallinger have yet to appear. Since neither Philippeau nor Hallinger in their valuable studies (published before my paper of 1961) on the codices and chronological problematics of these works exploited the Hispanic intercessional passages assembled above,[9] the utility of my data in helping to narrow the respective dates of composition has yet to be assessed within the manuscript tradition as a whole. The statement (58, above) regarding non-celebration at Cluny of the nocturnal office during the Nativity octave should probably be restricted to mean only that *pro defunctis*.

The view of the preceding Study that in the later 11th and early 12th centuries Cluny offered no such liturgical supplications for any other Iberian sovereigns as she did for the king-emperors of Leon, demands a certain degree of modification regarding the Navarro-Aragonese monarchs Pedro I (1094–1104) and Alfonso I *el Batallador* (1104–1134). Fifty years ago Ramackers published from the Collection Baluze in the Bibliothèque Nationale a text which Baluze himself had taken from fol. 74^{v} of Cluny's

---

[6] *Necrologium des Cluniacenser-Priorates Münchenwiler* (*Villars-les-Moines*), ed. Gustav Schnürer (Freiburg, Schweiz, 1909. Collectanea Friburgensia, N. F., X). Under VII. ID. Nov. appear the words *Sanctia Regina* (p. 83); the Longpont necrology reads *Sanctia regina Hyspanorum* (*ibid.*).

[7] Joachim Wollasch, "Qu'a signifié Cluny pour l'abbaye de Moissac?" in *Moissac et l'Occident au XIe siècle* (Toulouse, 1964), 13–24 (also, *Annales du Midi*, LXXV, 1963, 345–52); *idem*, "Ein cluniacensisches Totenbuch aus der Zeit Abt Hugos von Cluny," *Frühmittelalterliche Studien*, I (1967), 406–43.

[8] D. Poeck, "Laienbegräbnisse in Cluny," *Frühmittelalterliche Studien*, XV (1981), 68–179.

[9] H. R. Philippeau, "Pour l'histoire de la coutume de Cluny," *Rev. Mabillon*, XLIV (1954); 141–51; K. Hallinger, "Klunys Bräuche zur Zeit Hugos des Grossens (1049–1109)," *Zeitschrift der Savigny-Stiftung für Rechtsgeschichte, Kanonist. Abteil.*, XLV (1959), 99–140. On the unexplored Iberian circulation of Bernard's custumal, and a hypothesis of its passage via Sahagún to São Vicente de Pombeiro and other Portuguese houses, see J. Mattoso, *Le monachisme ibérique et Cluny* (Louvain, 1968), 125, 204, 216, 223, 272–4, 375–7.

lost Obituary. This is a *statutum* or *praeceptum* of Abbot Hugh I which describes the admission to the abbey's *societas* of the French-born bishop Peter I of Pamplona (1083–1115), also known as Pierre d'Andouque, Pedro de Roda or Pedro de Anduque.[10] In addition to detailing various intercessional privileges accorded this celebrated prelate for his repeated generosities to the abbey, this piece also contains two highly interesting references to King Pedro I of Aragon-Navarre. In one passage, where the charities of Bishop Peter to the Burgundian congregation are warmly acknowledged, the text goes on to declare that not only did he journey all the way to Cluny "cum suis praeclaris muneribus" but that "secumque etiam munera domni Petri regis detulit."[11] A second such passage, after relating the Pamplonese bishop's admission to confraternity and the list of intercessional honors granted him in life, at the time of his death, and in commemoration of his anniversary, makes the following stipulation: "Hoc etiam disponimus, ut in omni uita sua oratio illa, quam pro salute domni Petri regis cotidie in missa dicendam stabiliuimus, pro ipso similiter dicatur, ut quae pro rege singulariter pronuntiaretur, nunc pluraliter pro ambobus proferatur."[12]

These two extracts from the Cluniac Obituary provide firm evidence that at some point in his ten-year reign King Pedro I of Aragon-Navarre, abandoning the coolness towards Cluny characteristic of both the Navarrese and Aragonese royal houses from ca. 1040 on, became a generous benefactor of the abbey and the recipient of exceptional liturgical intercession, through the inclusion, at Abbot Hugo's express order, of a special *oratio* on his behalf in the daily Mass. We can safely assume a substantial act of royal charity preceded this concession: one that took the form not of a census, as with Fernando I and Alfonso VI, or Pedro's own current annual stipend to Rome,[13] but a donation of money or treasure, made at one specific time. When this occurred, under what circumstances, and with what relevance for Cluny's previous imperial link with the *reges Hispaniarum* of Leon and Castile, are all questions calling for brief consideration.

The chronology can be fixed with fair assurance. Since the Petrine *oratio*, once instituted, was still being observed at the time when Bishop Peter brought a second royal charity—as well as his own *munera*, so *praeclara* as to induce the abbot to couple his name with that of his sovereign in the daily supplication—it follows that we can distinguish two separate occasions of royal Aragonese-Navarrese benevolence. These in turn are most logically correlated with the two climactic points in Pedro I's reign when major victories over the infidel and acquisition of abundant spoils would prompt placing Cluny among the monasteries and churches with which the monarch piously shared his good fortune. The first of these would have been the reconquest of Huesca in 1096, and since this city with its rich booty did not capitulate until 27 November,[14] the royal *munera* are not likely to have reached Burgundy until the following spring or summer. Thus the year 1097 is most probably to be taken as the time when Hugo

[10] Johannes Ramackers, "Analekten zur Geschichte des Reformpapsttums und der Cluniacenser," *Quellen und Forschungen aus italienischen Archiven und Bibliotheken*, XXIII (1931–32), 48–9 (no. XVIII); cf. 30–2. See also H. E. J. Cowdrey, "Unions and Confraternity with Cluny," *Journ. Econ. Hist.*, XVI (1965), 161, to which I owe this reference. On Peter, see J. Goñi Gaztambide, "Los obispos de Pamplona del siglo XII," *Anthologica Annua*, XIII (1965), 147–95.

[11] Ramackers, 48.

[12] *Ibid.*, 49.

[13] P. Kehr, "El papado y los reinos de Navarra y Aragón hasta mediados del siglo XII," in *Estudios de Edad Media de la Corona de Aragón*, II (1946), 130–3; Ant. Ubieto Arteta, *Colección diplomática de Pedro I de Aragón y Navarra* (Zaragoza, 1951), 159–60.

[14] Ant. Ubieto Arteta, *Historia de Aragón*. [I] *La formación territorial* (Zaragoza, 1981), 122–8.

introduced a new daily collect in the Mass for the ruler of Pamplona and Jaca. Similarly, Pedro's I's second bestowal of *munera*, after what is clearly an interval of several years, can be linked to his capture of Barbastro in 1100. Once again, the date of the city's surrender falls in the autumn, on 18 October,[15] so that Bishop Peter's crossing of the Pyrenees and appearance at Cluny with his monarch's new benefaction are most naturally placed in the summer of 1101.

If we can thus perceive that from 1097 on, during Alfonso VI's later years, a reciprocal bond of benefaction and liturgical recognition for the first time united Cluny with the king-emperor's principal opponent in Christian Spain, the resolutely anti-imperial monarch of the Aragonese-Navarrese federation, are we to interpret this as the extension of the bitter political enmities of the Peninsula into the very choir of the Burgundian abbey-church?[16]

Three things seem reasonably plain. First, the two royal Petrine donations, of presumably 1097 and 1101, must reflect in part at least the persuasive influence upon Pedro I of the bishop of his Navarrese capital. The latter's ties with the Cluniacs, although secondary to those with his old *alma mater* Sainte-Foi de Conques, possibly go back to soon after his installation in 1084, under Sancho Ramírez, as head of the Church of Pamplona.[17] He was present with the king at the fall of both Huesca and Barbastro, when spoils were being distributed to religious centers on both sides of the Pyrenees;[18] and, in the case of Sainte-Foi de Conques at least, we have direct testimony to his ability to induce both Sancho Ramírez and Pedro I, as well as their nobles, to bestow alms upon foreign monks.[19] Secondly, the collect *pro salute domni Petri regis* stands as a vitalicial, purely personal supplication, with no provision for dynastic continuation. Thirdly, although impressively honorific, the Petrine *oratio* fails to place the Aragonese-Navarrese sovereign on anything like the exalted plane of the imperial Hispanic intercessional privileges, as these are recorded in the custumals of Bernard and Udalric and in the Hugonic *Statuta*; and the fact that Bishop Peter's *praeclara munera* could equate him with his king in the *oratio* confirms the distinctly secondary level of liturgical solemnity allowed the king of Jaca and Pamplona.

Other implications are less readily determinable, and merit further inquiry. A highly probable factor in bringing about the novel friendship of Cluny with Pedro I may have been the increasingly strained relations between Abbot Hugh and Alfonso VI in the latter's last two decades, although the Aragonese-Navarrese benefactions of 1097 and 1101 both precede by some years the apparent disruption of Alfonsine-Cluniac amity. This estrangement intensifies, probably, in 1103, when the king-emperor first begins publicly to acknowledge his half-Moorish son, the Infante Sancho, as his heir designate, and culminates in 1105, when Cluny's mediation of the

---

15 *Ibid.*, 129–30.

16 On Aragonese-Navarrese relations with Castile under Sancho Ramírez and Pedro I, see Ant. Ubieto Arteta, "Homenaje de Aragón a Castilla por el condado de Navarra," *EEMCA*, III (1947–48), 7–28; *idem*, *Col. dipl. de Pedro I*, 129–31.

17 Cf. Abbot Hugh's words "in episcopatu suo nobis . . . magna et multa exhibuisset karitatis seruitia" (Ramackers, 48).

18 Ubieto Arteta, *Col. dipl. de Pedro I*, 96–7 and Docs. nos. 24, 25 (Huesca), 96 (Barbastro).

19 See the prose prologue to the versified biography of Peter preserved in t. 143 of the Collection Doat, Bibl. Nat., Paris: "Procurauit etiam multa bona conferri dicto Conchensi monesterio . . . a felicis memoriae Sancio et Petro Sancii filio ipsius regibus pampilonae et aragonum" (fol. 177^{v}).The same prologue cites Bishop Peter's establishment of a permanent confraternal *sociale foedus* between the *fratres Conchenses* and the cathedral chapter of Pamplona (fols. 177–177^{v}); this must have antedated his personal entry into *societas* with Cluny.

successoral pact between the Burgundian counts Raimundo of Galicia and Henrique of Portugal demonstrates her defiance of Alfonso and determined adhesion to the original plan, the co-succession of Raimundo and Doña Urraca.[20] Yet, even before 1103–1105 or Pedro's first donation of 1097, we can suspect a marked cooling of Abbot Hugh's affection for the Leonese-Castilian emperor caused by an undocumentable but strongly indicated suspension of the Hispanic census by reason of Alfonso's loss of his Taifa tributaries and the financial demands of the Almoravid war.

Thus it becomes possible to conjecture that in Aragon-Navarre in 1097, following the lucrative conquest of Huesca, it was not only royal piety but also conscious foreign policy that motivated the sending of Muslim booty from the fallen city to Cluny in a calculated effort to exploit the abbey's strained ties with Leon and attract Hugo's influential support towards Jaca-Pamplona. And are we similarly justified in deducing that the Cluniac abbot, desperate for funds to maintain his costly building program, to say nothing of the burden of feeding and clothing his large congregation, cordially welcomed this Iberian charity from an unexpected source, the long hostile Aragonese-Navarrese royal house, and, even at the risk of displeasing the Leonese-Castilian *rex-imperator*, gratefully elevated King Pedro I to the limited ranks of those exalted persons who, along with the *reges Hispaniarum*, received daily mention in the formal supplications of his famed center of liturgical intercession? There is reason to think that to both of these questions affirmative answers are in order; but pending further archival investigation and much closer study of Hispano-Cluniac affairs in Alfonso VI's two terminal decades, the case must obviously be left *sub judice*.

On the other hand, Pedro's successor in 1104, Alfonso I, may for some few years between 1109 and 1113 have received full imperial intercessional privileges as the consort of the queen-empress Urraca, if not in consequence of the latter's accession to the Leonese-Castilian throne in July 1109, then during and after the years of bitter hostility between the two spouses when *el Batallador* claimed and used the Hispanic imperial title in his own right. Alfonso reputedly made gifts to Cluny and may have briefly enjoyed the abbey's recognition; obscurity surrounds this never seriously investigated question;[21] but any friendship between the Burgundian monks and this formidable reconquistador who regarded himself as the legitimate ruler of both Navarre-Aragon and Leon-Castile must have terminated by 1113. This was the year—as I have contended ("The Spanish Journey of Abbot Ponce," Study X in this volume)—of the intervention in the Spanish dynastic crisis of the Cluniac head, Ponce de Melgueil, and the abbey's henceforth open alignment with the anti-Aragonese cause of Doña Urraca and her young son Alfonso Raimúndez, the future Alfonso VII.

One possible by-product of these royal Aragonese contacts with the abbey under Pedro I and Alfonso I has never been given the attention it surely merits. This is the gift to the Cluniacs, made first in 1133, and again in 1141 and 1145, by the Aragonese

[20] P. David, "Le pacte succesoral entre Raymond de Galice et Henri de Portugal," *Bull. hisp.*, L (1948), 275–90, at 285–8. On the date 1105, and the historical circumstances of the intervention of the Cluniac chamberlain Dalmace Geret in the imperial succession crisis, see my "Count Henrique of Portugal" (Study IX in this volume).

[21] Some suggestive data on Alfonso I's imperial status down to 1126 (Urraca's death) or 1127 (Peace of Támara) can be found in J. M. Ramos y Loscertales, "La sucesión del rey Alfonso VI," *An. hist. derecho esp.*, XIII (1936–41), 36–99 (at 62 ff.); J. M. Lacarra, *Alfonso el Batallador* (Zaragoza, 1978), 62 and note 14; Bernard F. Reilly, *The Kingdom of León-Castilla under Queen Urraca, 1109–1126* (Princeton, 1982), 106–7, 121, 170–1, 180, 194; but none of these works considers the bearing on the Leonese-Cluniac alliance.

magnate Fortún Garcés Cajal of what became the one Burgundian priory in Navarre, San Adrián de Vadoluengo near Sangüesa; see "Peter the Venerable's Traverse" (Study XIII in this volume), from around note 44 of text. Cajal, long governor of Nájera and other Alfonsine *tenencias* in the Rioja, is the one Aragonese baron known to have endowed Cluny; his generosities may well be connected with those of the two kings, with whom he claimed a blood relationship.

IX

Count Henrique of Portugal, Cluny, and the antecedents of the Pacto Sucessório

Despite more than a century of intense scrutiny, the genesis, date and circumstances of the so-called Pacto Sucesório mediated by the Cluniac chamberlain Dalmácio Geret between the two Ibero--Burgundian counts Henrique of Portugal and Raimundo of Galicia remain subject to considerable contention. The last detailed exegetical studies, by Pierre David (1948) and Rui de Azevedo (1947 [1953], 1962), notably advance our control over this problematic text, with its subsequently influential guarantees of Portuguese territorial enlargement and its manifest relevance for the prolonged crisis in the Hispanic Empire over the succession to Afonso VI; but they diverge sharply regarding its chronology (1105-1107 as against 1095-1107) and motivation (1). Much clearly remains to be learned; and prominent here among other promising lines of inquiry is the as yet only perfunctorily examined role of Abbot Hugo of Cluny, a role the contracting parties themselves proclaim is central when in transmitting their covenant to him they describe it as negotiated in conformity with his command (2). It is in this

(1) Pierre David: *Le pacte successoral entre Raymond de Galice et Henri de Portugal, in Bulletin hispanique,* L. 1948, pp. 275-290; Rui de Azevedo: *Data crítica do convénio entre os condes Raimundo da Galiza e Henrique de Portugal,* in *Revista portuguesa de história,* III, 1947, pp. 539-552 (actually published in 1953, with coda criticizing David); idem, Nota ao Doc. 2, in his edition of *Documentos Medievais Portugueses, Documentos Régios* [henceforth cited as *DR*], vol. I, t. II (Lisboa, 1962), pp. 547-553. Azevedo's two treatments review the previous interpretations, with bibliography, some of which will be cited below.

(2) Text in *DR,* n.º 2 from Luc d'Achery: *Spicilegium,* 2.ª ed. (Paris, 1723), III, p. 418; also in Migne; PL, CLIX, cols. 944-946; David, *op. cit.,* pp. 275-276.

connection that the present paper, in warmly associating itself with the homage of the learned world to Professor Paulo Merêa, would call attention to an unknown Henrician diploma that not only throws fresh light upon the Portuguese count's relations with the Burgundian abbey but provides also a possible means of determining more accurately the date and immediate antecedents of the celebrated Pacto.

I

The document in question is a privilégio of Henrique of Portugal that finds no place among the count's collected charters in the first *Régios* volume of the *Documentos Medievais Portugueses*. In form an act of donation, prepared like most of Henrique's known diplomas outside his own official *scriptorium* (3), and bearing the date *Era M. C. XLIII. et noto die qui fuit III Kalendas Februarias,* or 30 January 1105, its explicit purpose is to confer certain tithes and churches which belonged to Henrique and his wife D. Teresa in the Galician comarca of Sanabria upon Cluny and, more specifically, upon S. Isidro de Dueñas. This is the Benedictine royal monastery, founded in the tenth century, which Afonso VI gave to the Cluniacs in December 1073 as their first Leonese-Castilian (and indeed proto-Iberian) dependency, and which served as chief center of their trans-Pyrenean possessions until, under Urraca, it was superseded by the more strategically located priory of S. Zoil (or Zoilo) de Carrión de los Condes, henceforth the administrative capital of the Province of Hispania (4).

The original of the Henrician privilégio has long since vanished, but the greater part of the text is preserved in the form of copies contained in two 18th-century diplomatic collections in Madrid, the Colección Velázquez of the Academia de la Historia, which includes two copies in different hands, and the Codex 720 of the

(3) Azevedo, *DR,* t. I, pp. XXVI-XXVII.

(4) Cf. C. J. Bishko: *The Cluniac Priories of Galicia and Portugal: Their Acquisition and Administration,* in *Studia monastica,* VII, 1965, pp. 338--339; but the organization of the Cluniac Province of Hispania and shift of administrative center from Dueñas to Carrión still await close study.

Biblioteca Nacional (5). All three of these versions, like those of the other Isidorian charters with which they appear, go back to a manuscript terminating with a colophon which begins with the words *Todos estos Privilegios y donaciones se sacaron del libro que dicen del Vecerro del dicho monasterio de sant Issidro de duenas*. This contained copies of a number of the monastery's documents, chiefly but not exclusively of royal origin, extracted from its 13th-century cartulary or *Becerro* in April 1594 by order of the Licenciado Gil Ramírez de Arellano, a member of the Consejo Real under Felipe II and oidor of the Real Chancillería de Valladolid (6). This now lost manuscript, obviously prepared for legal purposes in connection with defence of S. Isidro's patrimonies and rights, did not transcribe from the *Becerro* the absolutely complete text of each act, but often omitted or abbreviated conventional penal and similar passages and even, as in Count Henrique's case, certain secondary dispositive or topographic details. But the invocatory and other initial protocol, the principal dispositive prescriptions, the chronological clauses, and the full list of subscriptions, are nearly always given as the compiler of the *Privilegios y Donaciones* found them in the *Becerro*; and since both the *Becerro* and the Ramírez de Arellano transcript presumably perished along with almost all of the rich archives of Dueñas in the destructive campaigns of the Napoleonic wars in northern Castile during 1808 and after, the 18th-century copies of the *Privilegios y Donaciones* are fundamental to reconstruction of this great Cluniac priory's history and temporal.

In addition there survives also at Madrid in the Archivo Histórico Nacional an invaluable *Índice* of the entire documentation of the Isidorian archive as this existed, still inviolate, in the years 1683-1693 (7). Prepared by the house's archivero Dom Bernardo Gutiérrez following his reorganization of the vast collection of materials, this calendars with brief but adequate summary not

(5) Acad. Hist., Col. Velázquez, t. IV, leg. 4, fols. 668r-817v, and 23 unnumbered folios appended, containing docs. 1444-1477; B. N., MS 720, 234r-314r.

(6) The relationship of this transcript to its surviving 18th-century copies, as well as to the lost *Becerro* itself, will be treated in the Introduction to the edition I am preparing of the diplomatic collection of S. Isidro de Dueñas.

(7) A. H. N., Códices, Dueñas, no. 41.

only the medieval pergaminhos, many of which were by this date sewn together in long rolls *(rollos de pieles);* but also itemizes, folio by folio, each act included in the *Becerro* of the 13th-century, similarly noting the content. Thus it records acts of which no separate exemplar existed; and at times provides data not carried over into the abridged text of the *Privilegios y Donaciones*. Such is the case with the Henrician donation, which the *Índice* informs us was originally on fols. 54-55 of the *Becerro*. From this entry we learn that the grant included tithes omitted from the version of the *Privilegios y Donaciones*.

The following text is essentially that of Academia de la Historia, Madrid, Colección de Velázquez, tomo IV, leg. 4, fols. 804r-805r, no. 1422 (also no. 43), which has been collated with the second copy found among the unnumbered fols. in a different hand at the end of this same legajo, where it has been given the number 1446; and also with the copy in Biblioteca Nacional, Madrid, MS. 720, fols. 300r-301r, no. 43. Appended is Gutiérrez' summary from the *Becerro* as recorded in his *Índice*, fol. 13 (8).

Donación del Conde Don Enrrique Conde de Portugal

In nomine sancte et indiuidue Trinitatis Patris et Filij et Spiritu(s) Sancti. Ego Henrricus nutu Dei Portugalensis et Colum-briensis prouintie comes regisque gener cum consensu uxoris mee infantis domne Tharasie facio hanc testamenti seriem Sancto Petro de Cluniaco et eius monasterio prenominato de Sancto Issidoro de Donnas. Ubi offero omnem decimam partem mei panis et uini seu animalium et peccorum que mihi omnibus annis nata fuerint in terra de Sanabria uel in omnibus meis palatijs que de Sanabria in hac parte modo habeo uel deinceps acquisiero, de omnibus tribuo decimam partem fruct(u) um. Et in Villa Quesxita do ibi duas ecclesias Sancti Romani et Sancte Columbe. Et in Pausata de Rey concedo alias duas ecclesias Sancte Marię et Sancti Petri, *etc.*

(8) Variant readings from no. 1422 in the other two copies, all of which are either minor orthographic changes or manifest scribal errors or omissions, will be indicated in my above mentioned edition of the Isidorian charters. In using the *Índice* in microfilm, I have had to resort to conjecture in several (bracketed) places, none of which affects the meaning of the text.

Hoc autem facio anime me(e) et ut Sanctum Petrum paradissi clauigerum cuius famulos subleuare studeo in terris pium et propitium merear habere in celis, *etc.* Siquis tamen quod fieri non credo contra hoc nostrum factum ad disrrumpendum uenerit, *etc.*, sit excommunicatus et ab omni Christianorum consortio separatus, *etc.*

Facta autem hac carta firmitatis Era M. C. XLIII. et noto die qui fuit III Kalendas Februarias. Ego Enrricus Dei gratia comes et gene(r) regis quod feci comfirmo. Tharasia regis filia et predicti comitis uxor quod dominus meus (MSS: Deus) feci (t) comfirmo.

Martinus Flaynez comes conf. Raymundus Palentine sedis episcopus conf. Petrus Legionensis sedis episcopus conf. Pelagius Astoricensis episcopus conf. Didagus Sancti Facundi abbas conf. Didacus Sancti Claudi(i) abbas conf. Didacus sancti Petri de Montes ab(b)as conf. Petrus prior Sancti Zoyli de Carrion conf. Bernardus prior de Sancti Saluatoris de Nogal conf. Munio prior Sancti Saluatoris de Villaceyd conf.

Munius prepositus regis in terra de Carrion conf. Michael Alfonso prepositus terre legionense *(sic)* conf. Erus Gutierrez Campestris et Astoricensi(s) terre prepositus conf. Gomez Martinez filius comitis et potestas conf. Didacus Martinez filius comitis conf.

Petrus Pelaez maiordomus comitis conf.

2.ª col. Alfonsus Petriz conf. Petrus Goncaluez conf. Ferlez conf. Pelagius Petri conf. Didagus Pelagij conf. Egas Pelaez conf. Egas Munioz conf. Ermigio Munioz conf. Menendo Nunez conf. Alfonsus Tellez conf. Martinus Munoz conf. Gomez Menendez conf. Petrus Menendez conf.

2.ª col. Alfonsus Petriz conf. Petrus Goncaluez conf. Fernandus Goncaluez conf. Aluaro Velazquez conf. Menendo Venegas conf. Gomez Venegas conf. Egas Venegaz conf. Menendo Pelaez conf. Ramiro Arias conf. Pelagius Gomez conf. Gutier Pelaez conf. Garcia Menendez conf.

Pelagius Erigit cognomento Botam regalis palatij notarius conf.

Diezmos de Sanabria y de otras quatro Iglesias [*Índice*, fol. 13]

Fol. 54. Vna Donacion del Conde D. Henrrique conde de la Prouincia Portugalense y Coimbrense y Yerno del Rey por estar casado con su hija la Infanta D. Teresa. Fecha en Era 1143 en Honor de S. Pedro de Cluni y del Glorioso S. Ysidro cuy(o) Monasterio [es clunia]cense. Dona la decima parte de todos los frutos y Ganados que le nacieren en tierra de Sanabria, y todo el partido que de Sanabria le pertenece. Mas dona dos Iglesias suyas (?) En Villa quexita la vna de S. Roman la otra de S.ta Coloma con todo s(u) Diezmo. [Mas dona en] Posada de Rey otras dos Iglesias dedicadas a N. Señora y al Glorioso S. Pedro con todo su Diezmo y con todo el Diezmo de Valletronco, y quiere que todo esto lo posean los Monjes de [S. Y.].

In the foregoing document we have what appears at first glance to be, except possibly for the unusually large number of confirmations, a conventional monastic donation. The dispositive stipulations can be readily summarized. On 30 January 1105 Henrique count of Portugal and Coimbra and son-in-law of King Afonso VI, with the approval of his wife the Infanta Teresa, for the benefit of his soul and in the hope of future reward from S. Pedro whose earthly servants he thus succors, makes to Cluny and her dependency of S. Isidro de Dueñas a triple benefaction. This consists of (i) a tenth of the grain, wine and livestock annually produced on all paços he then posesses or shall in future acquire in the Terra de Sanabria; (ii) four igrejas propias there belonging to him, together with their dízimos, namely, S. Romão and Santa Comba in «Villa Quesxita» and Santa Maria and S. Pedro in «Pausata de Rey»; (iii) the dízimos of «Valletronco».

To dispose first of certain preliminary questions, there is no reason to suspect the accuracy of the date as transmitted by all four sources from the *Becerro* of S. Isidro, which raises no discoverable difficulties for the itineraries of either Condes or confirmants. The locations of the vilas and churches named cannot all be satisfactorily identified in the present state of toponymic investigation of the region of Sanabria, lying to the north of Bragança, beyond the traditional frontier of Trás-os-Montes in what is now the northwestern panhandle of the Spanish province of Zamora. Presumably they lay not far west of the comarcal capital of Puebla de Sanabria where the inhabited places of San Román and Santa Columba survive, although it has not proved possible to trace the terms «Villa Quesxita», «Pausata de Rey» or «Valletronco» in the medieval texts or modern maps and geographical works pertaining to this area (9). There is however no doubt that the Portuguese

(9) Cf. E. Flórez; *España Sagrada,* XVI (Madrid, 1795), with map between pages 68 and 69; Sebastián de Miñano: *Diccionário geográfico-estadístico de España y Portugal* (Madrid, 1826-1828), VII, pp. 434-435; Mapa Militar Itinerario de España, Hoja 23 (1918); *Enciclopedia universal ilustrada europeo-americana* (Barcelona, 1907 ff.), LIII, p. 1117; Fritz Krüger: *Die Gegenstandskultur Sanabrias und seiner Nachbargebiete* (Hamburg, 1925), especially p. 322 (Orts-und Landschaftsnamen) and folding map at end. It might be contended that the reading *Sanabria,* although found in all the 18th-century copies as well as in the *Índice,* results from a misreading in the *Becerro* for some Portuguese locale, in which case two possibilities suggest themselves: (i) *Senabria,* in Beira Litoral not far from Sobrado, to the east of the junction of the Paiva with the Douro (see Paulo Merêa and Amorim Girão: *Territórios portugueses no século XI, in Rev. Port. de Hist.,* II, 1943, pp. 255-263, especially p. 260 and Map I); or (ii) *Sena* (mod. Seia), in Beira Alta, distrito da Guarda, then a concelho of some importance to judge from its repeated mention in the documents of Henrique and his successors (cf. DR, pp. 14, 1. 21; 35, 1. 2; 63, 1. 5; 77, n.º 62; 154, 1. 9; 176-179, n.º 152; 202, 1. 6). Henrique undoubtedly possessed paços, igrejas and other reguengos in both comarcas; their situation below the Douro might explain why in his diploma to S. Isidro as in only one other of his known documents, the count entitles himself *Portugalensis et Columbriensis prouintie comes.* But the dual formula frequently occurs with Henrician subscriptions in the documentation; see, e. g., Paulo Merêa: *De «Portucale» (civitas) ao Portugal de D. Henrique* (Porto, 1944; separata from *Biblos,* XIX), pp. 36-37, citing cases from 1096, 1098 and 1103; Luciano Serrano: *El obispado de Burgos y Castilla primitiva* (Madrid, 1935-1936), III, pp. 103 (1099), 112 (1100); A. González Palencia: *Los mozárabes de Toledo en los siglos XII y XIII* (Madrid, 1926-1930), vol. preliminar, p. 119 (1101). Nor does either site help on the vilas or «Valletronco»; certainly nothing can be based upon the existence at Seia of freguesias of Santa Comba and S. Romão (*Grande enciclopédia portuguesa e brasileira, Lisboa-Rio de Janeiro,* 1950 ff., XXVIII, pp. 124-134). A third alternative, the possible misreading of an original *Saldania* as *Sanabria,* might be linked to the location of «Valletronco». On 21 March 1101 Count Henrique exchanged with the abbey of Sahagún an herdade belonging to him *in Villa Mirelli* for what is described as *in territorio de Tronco monasterium Sancti Petri cum sua uilla ab integro* (*DR,* n.º 7). Azevedo, loc. cit., p. 11, places this herdade at modern Villameriel in the comarca of Saldaña, prov. Palencia; but he does not identify the monastery, which indeed finds no notice among the possessions of Sahagún mentioned in Antonio de Yepes: *Corónica general de la Orden de San Benito,* (Irache, 1609-1621), III, fols. 167r-203v (abridged edition by J. Pérez de Urbel: *Biblioteca de autores españoles, Madrid,* 1960, I, pp. 256-310); Romualdo Escalona: *Historia del Real Monasterio de Sahagún* (Madrid, 1782);

comital house possessed properties in this Luso-Leonese borderland: between 1129 and 1135 Henrique's son Afonso was to give here to the Sanabrian abbey of S. Martinho de Castanheira (San Martín de Castañeda) the vila of Mahide between Puebla and Alcañices (10); and in 1169 he similarly transferred to the cathedral church of Zamora his domains at Manzanal in the Terra de Aliste (11). In view of Sanabria's inclusion during this epoch in the diocese of Astorga, it is to be remembered that the metropolitans of Braga long claimed provincial jurisdiction over this diocese and that the whole zone of Western Leon was also the object of Portuguese expansionist claims under Henrique, Teresa and Afonso Henriques (12).

or the numerous charters calendared by V. Vignau: *Índice de los documentos del monasterio de Sahagún de la Orden de San Benito* (Madrid, 1874). To the southwest of Valladolid and Simancas, in territory apparently then regarded as lying within the County of Saldaña, there exist a Villamarcial (in the valley of the Pisuerga) and a Vega del Val de Tronco (on the Hornija, another tributary of the Douro); and the interest of S. Isidro de Dueñas in this zone of the Leonese estremadura is certain from the priory's close collaboration with the Leonese magnate and Cluniophil Pedro Ansurez, count of Carrión and Saldaña, in the foundation there of the abbey (later cathedral) of Santo Antonino at Valladolid. This solution likewise throws no light upon the two vilas of Henrique's pergaminho; and on the whole there seems to be no good reason to question that his donation to Dueñas lay in Sanabria, a conclusion which the motives of his action, to be considered below, confirm. It should be added that the inclusion of *Senabria et ripeira et valdaria et baronzeli* among the territorial concessions promised D. Teresa by the Queen-Empress D. Urraca in their pact of *circa* 1120 (?) further evinces Portuguese interest in the Sanabrian comarca. Cf. Alexandre Herculano: *História de Portugal,* 8 th ed. (Lisboa, s/d.), II, pp. 102-103, 255-259 (Nota X); Luiz Gonzaga de Azevedo: *História de Portugal* (Lisboa, 1935-1942), III, pp. 233-236 (Nota XIII); J. M.ª Lacarra: *Dos documentos interesantes para la história de Portugal,* in *RPH,* III, 1947, pp. 291-305.

(10) *DR,* n.º 103; cf. t. II, pp. 616-618.

(11) *DR,* n.º 298.

(12) On the ecclesiastical side, see P.e Avelino de Jesus da Costa: *O Bispo D. Pedro e a organização da diocese de Braga* (Coimbra, 1959), I, pp. 106-114 (northern and northeastern limits of the Bracaran diocese); and the references cited in note 57, *infra.* Observe the significant absence of Portuguese ecclesiastics from the Henrician diploma of 30 January, even though two weeks previously on 16 January 1105 (A. López Ferreiro: *Historia de la S. A. M. Iglesia de Santiago de Compostela,* Santiago, 1898-1909, III, Apénd. 19), Archbishop Geraldo of Braga had attended the same junta of notables which met with Count Raimundo in Galicia and from which

It seems plain however that the Henrician diploma of 1105 was drawn up neither in Sanabria nor in the County of Portugal but somewhere farther to the east in the kingdom of Leon. Along with the complete absence of Portuguese episcopal subscriptions, the decisive testimony on this point is the corroborations of the Leonese bishops, abbots, priors and royal officials. The precedence given the name of Bishop Raimundo of Palencia among the ecclesiastics, and the fact that of the six monastic confirmants four — the abbot of Sahagún and the priors of S. Zoil de Carrión, S. Salvador de Nogal and S. Salvador de Villaceite (or Villacet) — also belong to this same diocese, make it almost certain that the whole company attesting the comital donation to S. Isidro was gathered in the then Leonese Terra de Campos along the Palencian sector of the Santiago pilgrimage road. The cathedral city of Palencia itself can safely be dismissed as situated too far south of the great highway, and the same is even more true of the priory at Dueñas. Since not only the abbot of Sahagún, but also the priors of two of his dependent houses, were present, that great Benedictione abbey is a strong possiblity; on the other hand, the Cluniac priory of S. Zoil de Carrión, also on the *camín francés* a few kilometres farther east, is perhaps even more likely as the most suitable place for making a grant to Cluny.

On the other hand, the size of the corroborative assembly and the validation of the diploma by the Leonese-Castilian palatine notary Paio Eriges *cognomento Botan* suggest the need to relate the document somehow to the imperial court of Alfonso VI, which in 1105 can be found moving eastward along the pilgrimage road to Burgos; and this is a problem to which we shall presently return. Before doing so however it is necessary to consider in some detail the extraordinary composition of the body of ecclesiastics and laymen who appear in Count Henrique's Sanabrian benefaction to S. Isidro.

Bishops Pelágio of Astorga and Pedro of Leon proceeded to join Henrique's assembly in the Terra de Campos. Portuguese political interest in eastward expansion into Leon, much less satisfactorily studied than the ecclesiastical, can be followed in Herculano II, Livro I; Gonzaga de Azevedo, III, chaps. 15-23, 25-26.

II

Prosopographic analysis of the forty-three persons other than the Condes of Portugal who subscribe the donation of 30 January 1105 reveals that they fall into two distinct categories, one Leonese, the other Portuguese. Of the twenty-six Portuguese or Portuguese-linked confirmants commencing with «Petrus Pelaez», virtually all can be identified as leading members of the Minhotan aristocracy who in the years before and after 1105 served Count Henrique as administrative officers or mesnadeiros, and whose names repeatedly occur in the Portuguese diplomas of this era. At the head of the list stand the two ranking officials of the comital household: the *maiordomus comitis* Pedro Pais (Pedro Pelaez), the well-known mordomo-mor who can be found in the count's documents between 1101 and 1112 (13); and the alferes Soeiro Nunes (Suero Nuniz) who can similarly be traced between at least 1097 and 1108 (14). There follow familiar names of magnates from the comarcas around Braga. The five Pais other than Pedro (Nuno, Diogo, Egas, Mendo, Gutierre) are doubtless close kinsmen of the mordomo-mor; at least two, Mendo (Menendo Pelaez) and Nuno (Nunes Pelaez) — the latter once Henrique's alferes — are his brothers and appear with him in the act of 21 August 1105 relating to the cession of the monastery of Tibães to the see of Braga (15). Of the three Moniz confirmants, Egas (Egas Munioz) must be the

(13) *DR*, n.ºs 13, 15, 20, 25, 27; *Documentos Medievais Portugueses, Documentos Particulares*, III, ed. Rui de Azevedo (Lisboa, 1940), n.ºs 197, 299; *Liber Fidei sanctae Bracarensis ecclesiae* ed. P.^{e} Avelino de Jesus da Costa, I (Braga, 1965), n.ºs 230, 232. Here and in the following notes only the references suficient to establish the identity of the Henrician mesnadeiros will be cited; for a number of these figures the sources afford further data on their familial and regional conections and careers under Henrique, Teresa and Afonso Henriques.

(14) *DR*, n.ºs 5, 8; *DParticulares*, n.º 299; *L. Fidei*, n.º 232; Escalona, *Hist. de Sahagún*, n.º cxxxix (p. 506, col. 1).

(15) *DParticulares*, n.º 197. Cf. further, for *Mendo: DR*, n.ºs 15-17, 19; *DP*, n.ºs 112-197; *L. Fidei*, n.ºs 172, 230; for *Nuno: DR*, n.ºs 4 (*armiger comis)*, 5, 15, *DP*, n.ºs 197, 280, 334; *L. Fidei*, n.ºs 169, 171, 230; for *Egas: DR*, n.º 17; *DP*, n.º 100; *L. Fidei*, n.ºs 167, 231; for *Gutierre: DR*, n.º 15; *L. Fidei*, n.ºs 158, 161, 162, 170, 230.

celebrated later aio of Afonso Henriques, *o honrado e bem-venturado Dom Egas Moniz de Ribadouro,* to whom *circa* 1100 the charters assign the lordships of S. Martinho and Arouca (16). Ermígio Moniz (Ermigio Munioz), who subscribes other Henrician diplomas, is the brother of this legendary figure (17). As for Martim Moniz (Martin Munioz), he may well be the adventurous senhor of Montemor who succeeded, by 1092, his father-in-law Count Sisnando as Count of Coimbra, was shortly thereafther deprived of this post in favor of Afonso VI's son-in-law, Count Raimundo, and became an open opponent of both the Burgundian prince and the king-emperor. This led him to take service with the Cid in the Levante and he is mentioned in the Poema as *Martin Munoz que mando a Mont Mayor* (18). Apparently this high-born Portuguese aristocrat had returned to his native land after the Cid's death in 1099 or following Valencia's fall to the Almoravids in 1102, and thrown in his lot with Count Henrique, alongside whom he can later be found fighting, under the banner of King Afonso I of Aragon, in the civil wars that swept the Hispanic Empire after 1109 (19).

Other powerful clans are likewise represented by prominent members: the Viegas (Venegas) by three (20); the Mendes (Menendez) by three; (21); the Gonçalves (Goncalvez) by two (22). Mendo Nunes (Menendo Nunez), possibly a kinsman of the alferes,

(16) *DR,* n.os 11, 13, 17, 21, 24, 26, 30, 32, 39, 45; *DP,* n.os 125, 213, 230, 295, 319, 411. Cf. Alexandre Herculano: *História de Portugal*, 8 th ed., (Lisboa, s/d), II, pp. 23-24; GEPB, XVII, pp. 624-629; A. de Almeida Fernandes: *Dom Egas Moniz de Ribadouro «o honrado e o bem-aventurado»* (Lisboa, 1946); A. H. de Oliveira Marques: *Moniz, Egas,* in *Diccionário de história de Portugal,* ed. Joel Serrão (Lisboa, 1963 ff.), III, pp. 98-99 (with bibliography).

(17) *DR,* n.os 39, 62, 64; GEPB, XVII, pp. 629-630.

(18) Damião Peres: *Como nasceu Portugal* (Barcelos, 1938), pp. 45-46; Ramón Menéndez Pidal: *Cantar de Mio Cid* (Madrid, 1944-1946), II, 749-751; idem: *La España del Cid,* 4th ed. (Madrid, 1947), II, pp. 553-554, 607. The line quoted is 738 of the poem.

(19) Menéndez Pidal: *España del Cid,* II, p. 554.

(20) See for *Mendo: DR,* n.os 16, 17, 20, 21, 25, 26, 45; *DP;* n.o 125; for *Gomes: DR,* n.os 17-39; and for the Viegas in general, GEPB, XXXV, pp. 205-210.

(21) For *Gomes: DR,* n.os 55, 67; for *Pedro: DR,* n.o 36.

(22) For *Pedro: DR,* n.os 34, 39, 43.

may well have a similar background ([23]), while Paio Pires (Pelayo Petri), who attests numerous charters *circa* 1105, is recognizable as an outstanding Minhotan magnate. He and Afonso Pires (presumably the Alfonsus Petriz of our catalogue) are mentioned by the *Vita s. Geraldi* as *duos regionum magnates;* according to this same work, Paio left to join the Moors after being accused of incest by the saintly archiepiscopal reformer of Braga ([24]). By 1105 he must have returned from this self-imposed exile.

Not all the names in this section of the list necessarily conform to this same pattern. Alvaro Velazquez, Ramiro Arias and Pelagius Gomez are still to be identified. As for the important figures of Telo Teles (Tel Tellez) and Afonso Teles (Alfonso Tellez), these two brothers were comparative newcomers to Portuguese soil, who had once been among the chief Leonese proceres of the Terra de Campos and Palencia but had joined forces with Henrique and D. Teresa ([25]). As late as 1103 Afonso was still serving as *maiordomus* of Afonso VI, although it is evident from Portuguese pergaminhos of 1108 and 1112, as well as from our text of 30 January, that soon after 1103 he — and presumably Telo as well — abandoned the imperial household and aligned himself politically with Henrique ([26]).

Now it is true that not a few of these nobles regularly accompany Henrique and Teresa down to the former's death in 1112, as their documents demonstrate. So, in 1097, we find with the condes Nuno Pais (then still Henrique's alferes) and Soeiro Nunes ([27]); in 1101, Soeiro Nunes and Pedro Pais ([28]); in 1106, in February (with Teresa

([23]) *DR*, n.os 16, 48, 56.

([24]) *DP*, n.os 112, 125, 179, 189, 244, 258, 259, 305, 351; *L. Fidei*, n.os 147, 150, 165, 219, 226, 231; *Portugalliae Monumenta Historica, Scriptores*, I (Lisboa, 1856), p. 55.

([25]) *DR*, n.os 10, 13, 28, 29, 36; Vignau: *Índice de Sahagún*, n.os 1444, 1538, 1544, 1575.

([26]) 26 July 1102: *major domus in domo regis Adefonso Telliz* (Vignau, n.º 1444); 10 February 1103: *Adefonsus Telici maiordomus regis* (A. López Ferreiro: *Historia de la S. A. M. Iglesia de Santiago de Compostela*, Santiago, 1898-1909, III, Apénd. XVII); 23 March 1103: *Adefonsus Telliz maiordomus regii palatii* (*Colección diplomática de San Salvador de Oña*, ed. Juan del Álamo, Madrid, 1950, I, n.º 116).

([27]) *DR*, n.os 4, 5.

([28]) *DR*, n.º 8.

alone), Egas Moniz, and in August, with both condes, Telo Teles, Afonso Teles and Egas Moniz (29); in 1108, Pedro Pais, Telo Teles and Egas Moniz (30); in 1109, Martim Moniz and Mendo Viegas (31); in 1110, Mendo Viegas, Gomes Viegas, Egas Moniz, Egas Pais, Mendo Pais and Pedro Pais (32); and in 1111, when they are all explicitly styled members of the *scola comitis,* Pedro Gonçalves, Mendo Viegas, Mendo Pais and Pedro Pais (33). But in no single extant Henrician document other than the Sanabrian donation to Dueñas do we encounter more than five of such subscriptions; in none does there ever appear so impressively complete a muster of the Portuguese count's chief partidários. Clearly, we are dealing with an unusual occasion that must be reckoned with in assessing the historical setting of the act of 30 January 1105.

The fifteen Leonese subscriptions are no less indicative of a gathering of special significance. Of the nine churchmen present, the three bishops — Raimundo of Palencia, Pedro of Leon, Pelágio or Paio of Astorga — all govern sees in Leon (34). On the monastic side, Abbot Diego of Sahagún is well known as having ruled that great Leonese abbey from 1087 to 1110 (35); the second Diego must be affiliated with the important but sparsely documented house of S. Claudio de Leon in the imperial capital (36); and the third abbot of this name, from the venerable monastery of S. Pedro de Montes in the Bierzo to the north of Astorga, turns up also in a royal charter of Afonso VI promulgated at Astorga on 31 March 1105 (37). Each abbot hails from the diocese of one

(29) *DR,* n.os 9, 10, 11.

(30) *DR,* n.o 13.

(31) *DR,* n.o 16.

(32) *DR,* n.os 17, 19, 20.

(33) *DR,* n.o 25.

(34) Raimundo Pal.: 1085-circa 1109 (Pedro Fernández del Pulgar: *Teatro clerical, apostólico, y secular de las iglesias catedrales de España... Parte primera... historia secular y eclesiástica de la Ciudad de Palencia* (Madrid, 1679), II, pp. 120-163; Pedro Leg.: 1087-1112 (ES, XXXV, p. 133); Pelágio Astor.: 1097-1121 (*ES,* XVI, pp. 194-197).

(35) Cf. Vignau: *Índice de Sahagún,* n.os 1202-1535.

(36) On this house, see Yepes: *Corónica,* ed. Pérez de Urbel, I, pp. 35-43 (without abbatial list); ES, XXXIV, pp. 357-360.

(37) See Prudencio de Sandoval: *Historia de los reyes de Castilla y de Leon don Fernando,* etc. [*Cinco Reyes*] (Madrid, 1792), I, p. 307,

of the three bishops, so that we have representing Palencia, Bishop Raimundo and Abbot Diego of Sahagún; Leon, Bishop Pedro and Abbot Diego of S. Claudio; Astorga, Bishop Pelágio and Abbot Diego of S. Pedro de Montes.

The three priors however do not conform to this distribution. Something has gone wrong with the name of the first of the trio, for between 1101 and 1107 a Prior Bernardo ruled this major Cluniac dependency at Carrión de los Condes ([38]); nor can this error be explained as simple transposition of the next name on the list, since it is certain that at this time S. Salvador's prior was in fact named Bernardo ([39]). In any event, the prior was a Cluniac of the Palencian diocese; and the other two priors, Bernardo of Nogal and Munio of Villacet, although not Cluniacs, have the same provenance. Both these latter monasteries must, at the time of Count Henrique's charter, have been possessions of Sahagún. S. Salvador de Nogal (or Nogar), situated a little north of Carrión, had been given to the great abbey by Afonso VI in 1093, and remained in Sahagún's hands until Afonso VII briefly alienated it to certain nobles of his court before returning it in 1127 to the

presumably from the lost *Becerro* of the Church of Astorga. From the same source Sandoval, p. 313, also gives the subscriptions of another escritura of Afonso VI of 1106, no day or month, where the abbot of San Pedro is given as Pedro, apparently by dittography.

([38]) See the exchange made on 3 June 1101 with Count Pedro Ansurez his wife Eilo and the abbot Salto by *ego Berardus obediens et frater Cluniacensis Ecclesiae necnon et prior monasterii sancti Zoili* (Manuel Mañueco Villalobos and José Zurita Nieto: *Documentos de la Iglesia colegial de Santa María la Mayor (hoy Metropolitana) de Valladolid. Siglos XI y XII*, Valladolid, 1917, n.° 11); also, in the grant of 23 May 1107 to the see of Braga by the Countess D. Urraca, daughter of Count Pedro Ansurez, the confirmation: *Bernaldus Sancti Zoili prior conf.* (*L. Fid.*, n.° 143). Yepes, drawing up the catalogue of priors on the basis of S. Zoil's then inviolate archive, supplies no name between Hugo in 1095 and Verila in 1110 (*Corónica*, VI, 88^{v}; ed. Pérez de Urbel, III, p. 71). M. Álamo: *Carrión (San Zoil de Carrión de los Condes), in Dict. d'hist. et de géog. ecclés.*, XI (Paris, 1949), col. 1137, assigns Verila to the decade 1100-1110; but it is possible that Bernardo and Verila are the same person, since a copy at Madrid of the Valladolid pergaminho of 1101 reads *Ego Berildus obediens*, etc. (Acad. Hist., Col. Velázquez, t. VI, fols. 410^{v}-411, n.° 2263).

([39]) See Vignau, n.ºs 1313 (30 June 1095); 1469 (27 June 1104); (1482 (15 May 1105); 1510 (29 March 1107); 1533 (6 June 1110).

mother house ([40]). S. Salvador de Villacet, although its status *circa* 1105 is less readily determinable, also appears to have then belonged to the Leonese abbey. We know that when, in 1103, Hordonius Sarraciniz acquired one-third of S. Salvador from his wife, Fronildi Ovequiz, the pair immediately transferred this portion of the house to Sahagún ([41]). Presumably Fronildi did likewise with the other two-thirds, although her donation act is missing; at any rate, by 1113 she was excommunicated by the Council of Palencia for having taken back Villacet into her own hands, and in 1115 she had formally returned most of it to Sahagún's possession ([42]). Furthermore, as late as 1104 Villacet was still ruled by an abbot, Pedro, not a prior ([43]), so that Munio's confirmation of the charter of 30 January — apparently the unique occasion on which he can be discovered in the available documentation — suggests that he was either acting in his abbot's stead, or that Pedro by 1105 had been replaced by a prior. In any case, our three priors all hail from the same diocese of Palencia, one of them a Cluniac, the other two delegates of Sahagún's daughter-houses.

As for the lay subscriptions here, the six names that immediately follow those of the ecclesiastics belong to persons high in the aristocracy and official bureaucracy of the Leonese monarchy. Martin Flainez, once the alferes of Afonso VI and, other than Henrique himself, the only count present, is familiar from ca. 1090 for his associations with the districts of Valladolid, Simancas, Aguilar and Cea, and appears in numerous royal documents ([44]).

([40]) Cf. Escalona, *Hist. de Sahagún,* Apéndice III, n.os 126, 154; Vignau, n.os 71-74, 83. See also Francisco Simón y Nieto: *El monasterio de San Salvador de Nogal,* in *Bol. R. Acad. Hist.*, XXXV, 1889, pp. 187-210, where it is erroneously supposed that at the time of the cession of 1093 Sahagún belonged to Cluny.

([41]) Vignau, n.os 1452-1454; Escalona, n.° 136.

([42]) Escalona, n.° 145; Vignau n.° 1544. The portion of S. Salvador's patrimonies Fronildi confesses to having given to Telo Teles was surrendered to Sahagún by Afonso Teles in 1130 (Vignau, n.° 1575).

([43]) Vignau, n.os 1467 (26 May 1104) and 1473 (26 August 1104). The next entry in Vignau for Villacet is of 1115 (n.° 1544), and the subsequent n.os 1545, 1552, 1575, 98, 1594, 1598) are silent both on title and name of the community's head.

([44]) See the disquisition on this Leonese magnate in Mañueco and Zurita: *Documentos de Valladolid,* pp. 19-20, note 1 to doc. n.° 4. For his

He was also, as a benefactor in 1089 of S. Zoil de Carrión, a good friend to Cluny. Of his two sons who confirm the Isidorian act, Gomez Martinez, the elder and holder of the title *potestas,* also subscribes along with his father a pergaminho of Count Pedro Ansurez to Sahagún in 1101; of Diego Martinez nothing more can be learned [45]. The other three figures in this group, the *prepositi terrarum,* Munio, i. e., Munio Diaz of Carrión and Saldaña, Miguel Alfonso of Leon and Cea, and Ero Gutierrez of Astorga and Campos, are royal meirinhos in charge of administrative areas at this time [46]. These meirinhados of Carrión-Saldaña, Leon-Cea and Astorga-Campos correspond geographically to the bishoprics of Palencia, Leon and Astorga, so that from each of these districts surrounding the imperial capital in the heartland of the Leonese state, a bishop, an abbot and a royal meirinho corroborate Henrique's gift to Dueñas.

To sum up, the impression is of an unusual assembly of notables, partly Leonese, even more Portuguese, brought together by the Count of Portugal at the end of January in the Terra de Campos.

III

While the unmistakably dual composition of Count Henrique's confirmatory assembly might possibly be explained as a fortuitous (or even deliberately selected) fraction of the imperial court, and such an hypothesis might seem to gain support from the role

subscriptions, Escalona, n.ºs 109, 115, 120, 122, 125-127, 134, 135, 137-140; Vignau, n.ºs 1180, 1469; Serrano: *Obispado de Burgos,* III, n.ºs 15, 23, 29, 31, 35, 47, 53; *López Ferreiro: Hist. de Santiago,* III, Apénd.; n.º 14; Mañueco and Zurita, n.ºs 4, 6, 7, 15.

(45) Mañueco and Zurita, n.ºs 3, 11; Escalona, n.º 134.

(46) *Munio Diaz:* Escalona, n.ºs 125-127, 133-136, 138; Vignau, n.ºs 1469, 1510; Mañueco and Zurita, n.º 11. *Miguel Afonso:* Escalona, n.ºs 40, 130, 131, 133, 136-138, 140; Vignau, n.ºs 1398, 1485; Sandoval: *Cinco Reyes,* I, pp. 312-313; *Cartulario del monasterio de Eslonza,* ed. V. Vignau (Madrid, 1885), n.ºs 50-52. *Ero Gutierrez:* Escalona, n.º 127, 135, 137. The foregoing citations confirm the affiliation of Munio Diaz with Carrión (and Saldaña), of Miguel Afonso with Leon (and Cea), and of Ero Gutierrez with Astorga; but only our pergaminho of 30 January records that the last also came to administer the meirinhado of the Terra de Campos.

of the palatine notary Paio Eriges in the drawing up of the diploma, the weight of the evidence is against this solution. No known testimony places Afonso VI or his curia in the Terra de Campos as early as January 1105; on the contrary, in late March, the king-emperor was still far to the west at Astorga in the course of his slow progress across Leon and Castile towards the Campos and eventually to Burgos (47). From the imperial documents falling between 31 March and 12 December, furthermore, it is demonstrable that relatively few of the persons present with Henrique and Teresa in January shared the subsequent itinerary of the court during the remainder of the year. Of the Leonese,, only the three bishops, the Abbot Diego of S. Pedro de Montes, Count Martin Flainez,and the latter's son, the *potestas* Gomez Martinez, act as confirmants (48). In contrast with certain household officers or retainers of Count Raimundo of Galicia (49), no Portuguese, not even the mordomo-mor Pedro Pais or the alferes Soeiro Nunes, witnesses these diplomas, even if we suppose that some of Henrique's mesnadeiros must have attended him and Teresa in Burgos. As for the notary Paio Eriges, whose name also appears in a Henrician diploma of 1097, although only in its subsequently appended confirmation

(47) Sandoval: *Cinco Reyes,* I, pp. 309-310.

(48) Docs. régios of 31 March 1105, Astorga: Bishop Pelágio of Astorga, Abbot Diego of S. Pedro de Montes, Count Martin (F)laynez (Sandoval, ibid.); 14 May 1105, Burgos: Bishops Pedro of Leon, Pelágio of Astorga, Raimundo of Palencia, Count Martin Flainiz, «Gomez martinci filius comitis» (Cl. Sánchez-Albornoz: *La primitiva organización monetaria de León y Castilla,* in *Anuario de historia del derecho español,* V, 1928, pp. 342-344; reprinted in his *Estudios sobre las instituciones medievales españolas,* México, 1965, pp. 479-481); 22 September 1105, Burgos: Bishop Pedro of Leon (Serrano: *Obispado de Burgos,* II, n.º 62); 12 December 1105, Burgos: Bishops Pedro of Leon, Raimundo of Palencia (*Cart. de Oña,* n.º 21). Since Pelágio and Pedro also subscribe Count Raimundo's charter of 16 December 1105, issued in Galicia in confirmation of the forais of the city of Compostela (López Ferreiro, III, Apénd. 19),, there is a chronological difficulty here yet to be resolved.

(49) Cf. the appearance of Count Pedro Froilaz and the *iudices* Pelágio Godesteiz and Pedro Danieliz on 14 May 1105 at Burgos (Sánchez-Albornoz, loca citata); and in Raimundo's company in Galicia on 16 December (López Ferreiro, loc. cit.). But if López Ferreiro, III, Apénd. 18, is right in reading the date of D. Pedro Froilaz donation to S. Tomé de Nemeno as 6 May 1105, this count then may still have been in Galicia.

of Afonso VI ([50]), he may well have been available while awaiting at Sahagún or Carrión the king-emperor's arrival as he moved toward the Castilian capital. Finally, neither Henrique nor Teresa seems to have joined the court until some time shortly before 14 May, when Afonso had reached Castrogeriz just east of the Campos in Castile ([51]). It looks, then, as if in late 1104, or at the very beginning of 1105, the Count of Portugal, his wife and an exceptionally large escort of Portuguese magnates travelled to the Terra de Campos well in advance of the king-emperor; and at Sahagún or Carrión met in conference with Leonese churchmen, meirinhos and nobles, after which most, if not all, of the Portuguese other than the condes returned to Minho ([52]), while half of the Leonese contingent dispersed to their customary stations.

But if this makes it highly unlikely that our charter is a product of the imperial court, at any rate the roll of its subscriptions must be evaluated in the light of the imperial succession problem which at that moment dominated all Leonese-Castilian-Portuguese political activity. By January 1105, some two years after Afonso manifested his intention to abandon his previous commitment to Count Raimundo and in effect designated the Infante Sancho as his heir, the governing classes of the Hispanic Empire, ecclesiastical and secular, must have been in a state of acute polarization between the two candidates for the throne; and the king-emperor's advanced age — he was in January 1105 just three and a half years away from his final agony at Toledo — brought ever closer the moment of national distuption and civil war. Under such

([50]) Donation to Soeiro Mendes, 23 November 1097 (*DR*, n.º 4), cf. Rui de Azevedo, *ibid.*, t. II, pp. 554-556, on the posterior confirmation and also on Paio Eriges *cognomento Botan* as a well-known notary of Afonso VI. Paio's name should be added to the list of royal scribes in Agustín Millares Carlo, *La cancillería real en León y Castilla hasta fines del reino de Fernando III*, in AHDE, III, 1926, pp. 227-306, especially pp. 248-249. Note also that in the four Afonsine documents of 1105 cited above, those of 31 March, 14 May and 22 September contain no notarial colophon; but that of 12 december terminates with the validation of *Pelagius Erigiz cognomento Boitum regalis notarius qui scripsi confirmo.*

([51]) Cf. their confirmation of the documento régio of this date in Sánchez-Albornoz, loca citada.

([52]) Note the reappearance in Portugal by 21 August 1105 of the mordomo-mor Pedro Pais and of Nuno and Mendo Pais (*DP*, n.º 197).

circumstances it is difficult, if not impossible, to believe that Count Henrique's bipartite assembly of 30 January could have been convoked solely or even chiefly for the purpose of securing corroboration of a conventional monastic donation. Behind the eleemosynary intent a more fundamental, distinctly political purpose can be discerned, the winning over of key figures in the Leonese Church and bureaucracy to some measure of agreement or cooperation with him — in short, an attempt to create a Luso-Leonese coalition in the face of the Raimundist-Sanchist factionalism.

It by no means follows that such a scheme was intended to defend Raimundo's rights to the Hispanic throne against Sancho; on the contrary, given what we know of Count Henrique's political goals, the reverse is almost certainly the case, especially when it is observed that the Pacto Sucesório vividly reflects a state of acute antagonism between the imperial sons-in law. Most writers, to be sure, have assumed that this agreement attests a close collaboration of the two Burgundians in mutual defiance of Afonso's succession formula: such, for example, is the view, explicit or implied, of Saraiva, Herculano, David and Rui de Azevedo (53). But others,

(53) This does not mean that these and other authorities agree on the motives of the collaboration. Cardinal Saraiva (D. Francisco de S. Luiz) in 1837 envisaged a secret family compact uniting the counts and their wives in defense of personal interests and Christendom against the half-Moorish Sancho (*Memorias historicas e chronologicas do Conde D. Henrique,* in *Memorias da Academia Real das Sciencias de Lisboa,* XII, Parte II, 1837, especially pp. 69-76; reprinted in *Obras Completas do Cardeal Saraiva,* II, Lisboa, 1873 pp. 167-174), a view also held by David: *Pacte successoral,* pp 277-279. Herculano: *Hist. de Port.,* II, pp. 28-32, in full anti-clerical cry, finds Abbot Hugo, after failure to dissuade Afonso VI from naming the undesirable Sancho as his heir, organizing a conspiracy with Raimundo and Henrique to block this eventuality; similar emphasis upon Cluniac initiative in bringing the counts together can also be found in Luiz Vieira de Castro: *A formação de Portugal* (Funchal, 1938); D. Peres: *Origens da nacionalidade, in Congresso do mundo português, Publicações* (Lisboa, 1940), II, pp. 23-26. But for Rui de Azevedo, in RPH, III, 1947, pp. 551-552, and in DR, t. II p. 553 as, more recently for Henrique Barrilaro Ruas: *Henrique, Conde D.,* in *Dicionário de história de Portugal,* ed. Joel Serrão, II (Lisboa, 1965), p. 418, col. 1, and M. T. Campos Rodrigues: *Raimundo, Conde D.,* ibid., III (1968), pp. 531, col. 2 — 532, col. 1, the Cluniac factor is much less decisive than the counts' fear of Sancho and hope of attracting the Leonese-Castilian nobles to the defense of the Raimundist succession. None of these interpretations explores adequately Raimundo's reaction to Henrique's aims in Leon.

notably López Ferreiro and Gonzaga de Azevedo, have much more convincingly seen behind the Pacto an underlying conflict between its principals (54); and it is hard indeed, in view of the major political, territorial and financial concessions made to the Count of Portugal, to reach any other conclusion than this: that these were extracted from Raimundo — even if in return for a pledge of political and military support — only because the Galician prince faced the fatal consequences of Henrique's opportunistic opposition and stood in desperate fear of being denied the indispensable Portuguese assistance against Sancho.

Aside from the Pacto, Count Henrique's role in the dynastic crisis prior to Raimundo's death at the end of 1107 has hitherto been more readily conjectured than documented. Whether with Herculano we fix in 1103, or with Ruas in 1101, the prince's presumed departure for the Holy Land, Gonzaga de Azevedo has proved from four Henrician confirmations to pergaminhos of Sahagún, that he was present in the Peninsula during 1104 (55). This agrees perfectly with the implication of the Sanabrian donation of late January 1105, that decisions and plans for the Luso-Leonese meeting in the Terra de Campos must have been made in the preceding year. In any case, we can be confident that Henrique's policy in the face of Afonso VI's proposed dynastic revolution would

(54) López Ferreiro: *Hist. Iglesia de Santiago,* III, pp. 174-175; Gonzaga de Azevedo: *Hist. de Port.,* III, pp. 171-176. Both writers, however, erroneously link the Pacto to Afonso's original plan of 1093/1094 for Raimundo's succession.

(55) Herculano: *Hist. de Port.,* II, pp. 25-26; Ruas, pp. 417, col. 1 — 418, col. 2. Herculano, p. 26, n. 1, tries to dismiss the Sahagún confirmation of February 1104 (Vignau, n.º 1460), the only one he knew, on the unconvincing grounds that either the Henrician subscription was arbitrarily inserted or the donation as a whole was a forgery. But Gonzaga de Azevedo, III, pp. 55-56, cites from A. H. N., Madrid, three other Sahagún charters for March, May and September of this year that contain the Portuguese count's subscription and similarly attest his presence in Leon. These four documents, in which according to Gonzaga de Azevedo Raimundo's name also appears, point to a prolonged sojourn of both counts in the strategic Terra de Campos during much of 1104; along with the other data adduced by Dom José Mattoso: *Le monachisme ibérique et Cluny* (Louvain, 1968), p. 88 and note 121, they can be used to prove Henrique's contacts with Sahagún. It should be remembered that at this time Sahagún was not in Cluny's possession or governed by an abbot of Cluniac origin.

be determined not, as so often facilely reiterated, by sentiments of affection towards Raimundo on grounds of their supposed kinship and common Burgundian origin (neither of which factors need be taken seriously), but by the dazzling opportunity that the imminent struggle for the Empire presented in furtherance of two objectives he vigorously pursued down to his death in 1112: maximum emancipation of Portugal from centralizing imperial rule; expansion of Portuguese territory not merely to the south against the infidel, but eastward into the Leonese kingdom and its newly annexed estremaduras. For the second of these objectives we can adduce his assumption, in 1111, at a time when Raimundo and Afonso were both dead and Urraca was hard pressed by civil strife, of the title *comes in Alçamora et Asturica et in Portugal* (56); and his encouragement of the Church of Braga's metropolitical claims over the diocese of Astorga against Toledo and Compostela (57).

It is on this question of Henrician-Raimundist schism during the climatic years of the succession crisis that the Isidorian diploma is particularly suggestive. Leon obviously was the big prize, if war with Sancho's partisans shattered the unity of the Hispanic Empire, partly because of its significance for the imperial office, hardly less because its annexation promised enormous increase of power and prestige to the ruler of either Portugal or Galicia. In the years before 1105 Raimundo's presence in the Leonese territories was already strong by reason of his employment by Afonso VI as administrator of Zamora and as repovoador of Salamanca, where in 1102 the count installed as bishop the Cluniac Jerónimo, a refugee from the Cid's fallen Valencia (58). But the Galician prince was also well established in the heartland of the older Leon through his

(56) Vignau, n.º 1544; cf. note 12, supra.

(57) For the historical background, see P.e Avelino de Jesus da Costa: *O bispo D. Pedro e a organização da diocese de Braga* (Coimbra, 1959), I, pp. 242-253; and for the Henrician epoch, Demetrio Mansilla, *Formación de la Provincia Bracarense después de la invasión arabe*, in *Hispania sacra*, XIV, pp. 5-25; David, *Études historiques sur la Galice et le Portugal* (Lisboa--Paris, 1974), pp. 456 ff.: Juan Francisco Rivera Recio: *El arzobispo de Toledo don Bernardo de Cluny, 1086-1124* (Roma, 1962), pp. 57-58, 84; Manoel Ramos, in *História de Portugal*, ed. Damião Peres, I (Barcelos, 1928), pp. 489-493.

(58) Julio González: *Repoblación de la «Extremadura» leonesa*, in *Hispania, III*, 1943, pp. 204-206.

possessions of lands and political authority to the south of Sahagún at Grajal, where he tended to reside in his last years and where in November-December 1107 he died (59). In Grajal also in 1106 he can be found, for example, giving to the church of Santa Maria Magdalena at Sahagún the vila of «Vulxote» (60); here also he exercised governmental power over the district through his own personal meirinho Martin Ceidiz (61). As legitimate heir, consort of the king-emperor's oldest daughter, D. Urraca, and ruler of Galicia, Raimundo must have seemed to many Leonese far preferable to the more visibly Castilian-oriented Infante Sancho; and when we encounter him on 16 January 1105, at the time when Enrique was busy in the Campos, he and Urraca are in Galicia presiding over a mixed company of clerics and nobles that included four interesting non-Galicians: the metropolitans Bernardo of Toledo and Geraldo of Braga; and also the two Leonese bishops Pelágio of Astorga and Pedro of Leon who a fortnight later are to subscribe Henrique's donation to S. Isidro (62). Evidently Raimundo was busy constructing his political fences in the northwest at the very time Henrique in the Campos was also seeking to enlist supporters.

The Count of Portugal's position in Leon was of course far weaker. Other than the patrimonies in Sanabria that are the subject of his benefaction to Dueñas, Henrique is known to have possessed within the kingdom only Villameriel near Saldaña, a property he exchanged with Sahagún in 1101 for the monastery of S. Pedro de Tronco, also, perhaps, in the same area (63); nor do we find him participating in the repovoação of the Leonese Estremadura. In seeking to secure allies beyond the Portuguese frontier, he was therefore at a distinct disadvantage as compared with Raimundo; but Henrique

(59) Raimundo can be connected with Grajal as *tenens* or *presidens* from at least February 1102 (cf. Vignau, n.os 1439, 1440, 1450); on his final illness there, the visit of Bishop Gelmirez of Compostela, and death between 17 November and 13 December 1107, cf. López Ferreiro, III, pp. 295-297; Anselm G. Biggs: *Diego Gelmirez, First Archbishop of Compostela* (Washington, 1949), pp. 61-62.

(60) Escalona: *Hist. de Sahagún,* n.º 139; Vignau, n.º 1502.

(61) Vignau, n.º 1450 (13 February 1103).

(62) Sandoval: *Cinco Reyes* I, p. 309.

(63) *DR,* n.º 7; cf. note 9, supra.

must have expected to attract to his banner not Leonese magnates who, like the powerful Count Pedro Ansurez, loyally accepted their monarch's choice of heir, but rather those churchmen and nobles in the kingdom who opposed Afonso and the Infante Sancho but were not yet formally committed to a Raimundist alternative.

In this context the conference of 30 January, with its Portuguese and Leonese but no Galician, attendants is most naturally seen as a major step in Count Henrique's plan to secure control of all or part of Leon. Such an interpretation, furthermore, of the Campestrian assembly, which if valid would provide important new testimony to the background of comital hostility preceding the Pacto Sucesório, becomes even more persuasive when we consider the Cluniac aspects of the Sanabrian benefaction and relate these to Abbot Hugo's intervention in Spain, the immediate prelude to the negotiation of the comital covenant.

IV

The Cluniac factor in the genesis of the Pacto Sucesório and indeed the entire Leonese-Castilian succession crisis under Afonso VI and D. Urraca, although usually touched upon by the authorities, has been little investigated in depth, even otherwise so brilliant a diagnosis as that of Ramos y Loscertales dismissing it much too briefly ([64]). Yet nothing could be more certain than that the abbatial command leading Afonso VI's sons-in-law to arrange their pact of mutual assistance was no isolated or arbitrary act, but one of a series of Hugo of Cluny's interventions in Iberian political affairs made on the firm basis of the confraternal and censive *coniunctio* or alliance existing between the Burgundian abbey and the *regnum Hispaniarum* since its foundation, most probably in 1063, by Fernando I and renewal by Afonso VI in 1077 and 1090 ([65]). Long

([64]) José María Ramos y Loscertales: *La sucesión del rey Alfonso VI*, in *AHDE*, XIII, 1936-1941, pp. 36-99.

([65]) See my forthcoming study of Fernando I and the origins of the Leonese-Castilian alliance with Cluny, to be published in *Cuadernos de historia de España.*

before 1105 the enrollment of Afonso as *socius-benefactor* of Cluny, the abbey's heavy dependence upon the annual Hispanic *census duplicatus* of 2000 gold dinars *(metcales)* for its financial liquidity and costly building program, and the institution throughout the Burgundian monastic federation of daily intercessional prayers for Afonso VI and future *reges Hispaniarum* that equalled or surpassed in solemnity those conceded members of the German imperial house ([66]), had established Hugo's position as the *patronus* (Afonso's own term) ([67]) and protector of the Navarro-Basque dynasty; and the quasi-feudal implications of such status were reinforced by consanguineal ties: Constança of Burgundy, Afonso's second wife and mother of D. Urraca, Count Raimundo's consort and future queen-empress, was the abbot's niece, Count Henrique of Portugal the grandson of his sister Hélie de Semur ([68]).

In the light of such intimate involvement on Cluny's part in the dynastic politics of the Leonese-Castilian monarchy, it is surely significant that Henrique's grant to S. Isidro de Dueñas on 30 January 1105, made in the midst of the crisis over the Afonsine succession, marks two noteworthy innovations in the Portuguese count's previous relations with the abbey. These are, first, the gift of annual revenues and churches outside Portugal itself, in Leonese Sanabria; and, secondly, their conferment upon Cluny herself and her Leonese dependency of Dueñas, a reversal of the previous Portuguese policy of approaching the mother abbey indirectly and along non-Leonese lines through the agency of the Nivernais priory of La-Charité-sur-Loire. On both these grounds our diploma can be viewed as intended to create for Count Henrique a new, specifically Leonese and therefore potentially imperial, line of affiliation with Hugo, one which in the eyes of Raimundo of Galicia must have represented a direct challenge to his own hopes of the abbot's undivided support in his struggle for the succession.

(66) C. J. Bishko: *Liturgical Intercession at Cluny for the King-Emperors of Leon*, in *Studia monastica,* III, 1961, pp. 55-60.

(67) *Recueil des chartes de l'abbaye de Cluny,* ed. A. Bernard and A. Bruel (Paris, 1876-1903), IV, n.° 3562.

(68) On Constança, see David: *Études,* pp. 388-390; on Henrique, as grand-nephew (not, as often, nephew) of Hugo, cf. Jean Richard: *Sur les alliances familiales des ducs de Bourgogne aux XIIe et XIIIe siècles,* in *Annales de Bourgogne,* XIII, 1958, pp. 37-46; Ruas, op. cit., p. 416, col. 1.

To appreciate this more fully, it is important to advance beyond the usual assumption that, since Henrique and Raimundo came of high Burgundian Cluniophil families, and had originally been recruited by Hugo to aid Afonso VI against the Almoravids, the two counts maintained in the Peninsula identical ties with Cluny. This is simply not true. Raimundo before coming to Spain had participated along with his father Count Guillaume Tête-Hardie in the donation of Salins to Cluny (*circa* 1086) (69); but once on Iberian soil, whether as Count of Galicia-Portugal, Count of Galicia alone, or as Afonso VI's leading repovoador of Salamanca, Ávila and Segovia, he does not seem at any time to have given the Burgundian congregation a single monastery, piece of land or regular revenue. Conceivably, there may have been occasional gifts of money or spoils of which no record survives; and Raimundo had a direct hand in the designation of the Cluniacs Dalmace d'Auvergne and Jerónimo as bishops respectively of Compostela and Salamanca (70). But no Cluniac counterpart can be found for his many donations of vilas and lands to Galician monasteries and even to Sahagún, or for the annual subsidy of 1000 *solidi* he bestowed upon the non-Cluniac Burgundian house of Saint-Bénigne-de-Dijon (71). Such lack of discernible benefactorial zeal towards Cluny can hardly denote estrangement between Abbot Hugo and the Galician count; more likely it can be attributed to Afonso VI's insistence upon excluding both his sons-in law from imitation of or infringement upon his own personal confraternal and censive alliance with the Burgundian monks. It is to be observed also that in the same way Raimundo's wife, D. Urraca, although a generous benefactor of the Cluniacs after becoming queen-empress, herself abstained from making them any donations of lands, churches or monasteries until over a year after her husband's death; and when on 22 February 1109 she ceded them the well-endowed Galician house of S. Vicente de Pombeiro, this was done, as the Infanta explicitly informs us, at her father's own suggestion, undoubtedly because at the time Afonso VI

(69) *Chartes de Cluny,* IV, n.° 3615.

(70) See Bernard F. Reilly: *Santiago and Saint Denis: The French Presence in Eleventh-Century Spain,* in *The Catholic Historical Review,* LIV, 1968, pp. 467-483, especially pp. 472-473, 477-478; and cf. note 58, supra.

(71) *Chartes et documents de Saint-Bénigne de Dijon,* ed. Georges Chevrier and Maurice Chaume, II (Dijon, 1943), n.° 420.

was seeking to secure Hugo's approval of Urraca's succession (72). At any rate, down to his death at the end of 1107, Raimundo does not seem to have enjoyed the status of Cluniac *socius* or *benefactor,* so that something more than merely rhetorical style may well lie behind the distinction made in the protocol of the Pacto Sucessório between *Raimundus filius* and *Henricus familiaris.* We can however be certain from the Pacto that after Afonso's plan of 1103 to displace Raimundo by Sancho as his heir, the Count of Galicia's legitimate rights to the throne continued to be recognized at Cluny, however painful a situation this created between king--emperor and abbot.

A quite different pattern characterizes the Count of Portugal's Cluniac relations (73). Even before his arrival in the Peninsula Henrique can be found among the *laudatores et testes* confirming a donation to the abbey by his brother Duke Eudes of Burgundy (74); and once he was across the Pyrenees this association intensifies. Entrusted in 1095-1097 by Afonso with lordship over Portugal, Henrique immediately associates himself with the reform program previously initiated in the diocese of Braga in 1071 by Bishop Pedro I and installs there as metropolitan the Cluniac Geraldo, a one-time monk of Agen who had become a canon of the cathedral church of Toledo under the Cluniac archbishop Bernardo (75). By 1099 another French Cluniac from Toledo, Maurício Burdino, has been made bishop of Coimbra, from which see by 1109 he was to be translated to that of Braga (76). Then in March 1100 Henrique and Teresa bestow upon the Cluniac nunnery of La Charité-sur--Loire the Church and Termo of S. Pedro de Rates near Braga,

(72) *Text: Chartes de Cluny,* IV, n.º 3533; on the date, David, *Études,* p. 454, n. 4; on the context, C. J. Bishko *The Cluniac Priories of Galicia and Portugal: Their Acquisition and Administration,* in *Studia monastica,* VII, 1965, pp. 316-319.

(73) On this subject in general, see P.e Avelino de Jesus da Costa: *A Ordem de Cluny em Portugal,* in *Cenáculo,* IV, 1948 (also, separately, Braga, 1948), pp. 9-15; Miguel de Oliveira: *História eclesiástica de Portugal,* 3ª ed. (Lisboa, 1958), pp. 110-111, 141-142; José Mattoso: *Cluny em Portugal, Ordem de,* in DHP, I, (1963), pp. 595, col. 2 — 596, col. 1.

(74) *Chartes de Cluny,* IV, n.º 3516 (before 1078).

(75) Gonzaga de Azevedo, III, pp. 46-52; Mattoso: *Monachisme ibérique,* pp. 103-105.

(76) David: *L'énigme de Maurice Bourdin,* in *Études,* pp. 441-501.

for conversion into a monastic center, and the dízimas on bread, wine and flax from all their estates (reguengos) in the extensive region between the rivers Douro and Mondego (77). This donation establishes at Rates the first and largest of what were to be eventually three Cluniac houses on Portuguese soil; creates in effect an annual census of presumably substantial amount in the form of the dízimas of Entre Douro e Mondego; and gives the Portuguese condes the status of Cluniac *benefactores* and probably also *socii,* at least at La Charité. This charter, incidentally, looks like the model for that addressed to S. Isidro: both combine tithes on frutos e gados with transfer of ecclesiastical properties.

The assignment of these charities not to the mother abbey but its Nivernais affiliate cannot be disposed of by positing a personal or familial interest in La Charité on the part of either Henrique, Teresa or their episcopal counsellors Geraldo and Maurício, for no such sentiments can be detected in any of the four. The bishop of Coimbra in 1102 gave the Cluniacs within his diocese the church of Santa Justa for conversion into a priory; but this looks like nothing more than conformity with his count's action two years before (78). The true explanation lies elsewhere, in part in Afonso VI's apparent desire to monopolize for himself alone the imperial family's association with Abbot Hugo; in even greater part in Henrique's preference for a line of connection that would safeguard Portuguese autonomy aims by keeping Rates out of the hands of the strongly imperialist community of S. Isidro de Dueñas and simultaneously maintain the separate identity of the dízimas of Entre Douro e Mondego alongside Afonso's far more munificent *census duplicatus.*

The reversal of this policy in January 1105 and the bestowal of the Sanabrian tithes and churches upon Cluny herself and S. Isidro thus falls convincingly into the very different political circumstances created in 1103 by Afonso VI's switch to the Infante Sancho. The king-emperor's opposition to his son-in-law's direct approach to the Cluniacs, or Portuguese fears of imperial domination of S. Pedro de Rates and Santa Justa de Coimbra if subordinated to Dueñas, no longer mattered. What was crucial was to secure for

(77) *DR,* n.º 6; cf. Bishko: *Priories,* pp. 311-315.
(78) *DP,* III, n.º 523; Bishko, op. cit., pp. 315-316.

Count Henrique as much support as possible within Leonese monasticism, the hierarchy and the nobility, and for this the friendship of S. Isidro would be helpful. Even more important, Hugo's favorable attitude toward his kinsman's penetration of Leon and the Terra de Campos could best be sought through the Isidorian priory and in direct benefactorial ties wth the abbot. In short, the Sanabrian concession constitutes a calculated move to strengthen Henrique's chances in the Leonese kingdom on the eve of the anticipated struggle for power.

One thing is plain, that even more than to Afonso and the Sanchistas, such possible diversion of Cluniac sympathies towards the Count of Portugal presented a sharp challenge to Raimundo, threatening not only to weaken his indispensable support in Burgundy and Leon but confronting him with the need to make major concessions to Henrique as the price of cooperation. Indeed the combination of the new Portuguese approach to Cluny through Leon and the attempted organization of a Luso-Leonese union of anti-Sanchist notables must have aroused the Count of Galicia like an alarm-bell in the night. We can therefore suppose that in the late winter or early spring of 1105, following the assembly of the Terra de Campos at the end of January, he addressed an urgent message to the Cluniac abbot as the protector and blood relative of the imperial Navarro-Basque-Burgundian line, warning him of the dire consequences, inherent in Henrique's opportunistic scheme, to both the legitimist sucession and the maintenance of the Leonese-Cluniac *coniunctio* and the *census duplicatus*. There is no need to ascribe to the abbot in this conjuncture Machiavellian motives of extending his abbey's domination below the Pyrenees, or to picture him as acting in terms of a holy war to avert secession of Spain from Christian Europe under the leadership of an allegedly Mozarabic Sancho. Hugo must already have reacted against Sancho's succession; it was unnecessary for the count to stress how fatal to the abbey's huge interests would be a triumph of the Sanchista party.

The prologue to the Pacto Sucessório makes it perfectly clear that some such appeal reached the abbot and led him to issue the blunt command to both counts — to Henrique, surely, much more than to Raimundo — to meet with his envoy Dalmácio Geret and to arrive at terms for their mutual collaboration on the death of

Afonso VI. The hypothesis that Raimundo's call for help came in early 1105 and was followed later in that same year after the abbatial chamberlain had arrived in the Leonese-Castilian kingdom by the conclusion of the Pacto, gains confirmation from the diplomatic evidence that allows us to trace the movements of the two counts during the crucial years 1105-1107.

V

The dating of the Pacto Sucessório imposes certain prerequisites which Count Henrique's Sanabrian diploma now makes it possible to define more sharply than ever before. For Rui de Azevedo the comital treaty might belong anywhere between 1095 and Raimundo's death; for David, who fails to confute his own evidence that it could fall any time after 1103, the limits are 1105-1107 (79). In our opinion, it is impossible to go back of 1103, when Afonso VI's intention of changing the succession from Raimundo to Sancho becomes a matter of public record in the acts of his chancery, and the stage is set for a contest over the imperial throne. It is, however, not the succession as such that immediately underlies the Pacto, but Raimundo's being confronted with a Portuguese challenge to his anticipated possession of Leon (and, more remotely, Castile).

The Pacto plainly provides not for a succession, Raimundo's being accepted throughout, but for a territorial partitioning of the Hispanic Empire, assuring to Henrique on vassalic terms possession of either Toledo or Raimundo's own Galicia in addition to his Portuguese holdings. Either of these promised territories represents the heavy price the Count of Galicia agreed to pay in return for Henrician support against the Sanchistas in Leon and Castile. The prime danger of course for Raimundo lay in possible loss of Leon, the imperial kingdom, without which he could not hope to establish himself as *rex Hispaniarum*. Henrique's expan-

(79) Rui de Azevedo, *RPH*, III, 1947, pp. 552; idem, *DR*, II, p. 553; David: *Pacte Succesoral*, p. 290. Both scholars review and in part refute the various chronological hypotheses advanced since the days of Saraiva and Herculano.

sionist interest in Leon may well have preceded 1105 by some years; but the Sanabrian diploma enables us to determine that it was at the start of that year that he took two major steps overtly challenging Raimundo's position there: alliance with leading figures in the episcopate, the monasteries and the royal bureaucracy; and the opening of the new direct line to Cluny through Dueñas. If valid, this reasoning means that in January 1105 the Pacto Sucessório, with its major premise of the political and military collaboration of the two counts, did not yet exist, which *a fortiori* rules out the years 1103 and 1104 (80).

On the other hand, the final biennium of Raimundo's life, 1106--1107, also appears improbable. One would expect the Luso--Leonese assembly and Henrician benefaction to S. Isidro of 30 January 1105, as major threats to Raimundo's hopes in Leon, to be followed fairly quickly by strong countermeasures on his part; and since in this conjuncture Henrique had no reason to invoke Cluniac intervention, it must have been, as Gonzaga de Azevedo cogently argues (81), Raimundo who, as the legitimate heir supported by Cluny even against Afonso VI, appealed for Hugo's help in checking the dangerous Portuguese attack upon his whole position. The Pacto demonstrates that in consequence of the abbot's response to some such appeal, there was held, unquestionably on Iberian soil, a joint conference of the two counts with his deputy Dalmácio Geret. When could such a meeting of the trio have taken place?

The Cluniac *camerarius,* still in this period an itinerant envoy of the abbot, and not yet as he would become under D. Urraca a provincial governor permanently stationed at Carrión, would normally come to the Peninsula once a year during the summer in order to collect at the imperial court the 2000 goldpieces of the census and also perhaps to make a visitation of the Leonese--Castilian priories (82). The odds are against such a meeting of the

(80) This refutes the assumption by Ruas, DHP, II, p. 418, col. 1, of a supposed meeting at Sahagún in 1104 for the negotiation of the Pacto.

(81) III, pp. 175-176.

(82) Cf. Bishko: *Priories,* pp. 338-339, as against David's view, op. cit., p. 281, that even this early the chamberlain was stationed in Spain «d'une façon à peu près permanente». It need not, however, be supposed that in 1105, when deprived of most if not all of his parial revenues, and facing

trio at court in 1106, since throughout much of this year Raimundo, already seriously ill, seems to have remained at Zamora or Grajal, while Henrique cannot be shown to have gone outside the boundaries of his county ([83]). For the same reasons 1107, at the end of which the Count of Galicia dies, is even less likely; adverse also to such a solution is the known presence of Dalmácio Geret in Burgundy, at Berzé-la-ville, *circa* 13 August 1107 ([84]). To be noted also during both 1106 and 1107 is Raimundo's sudden assumption of the imperial title. In a diploma of 1 May 1106 he abruptly styles himself *comes Raimundus habens principatum apud Hispanie,* while D. Urraca employs the honorific phrase *regalibus orta natalibus ego Urracha,* as if both condes were deliberately flaunting their sovereign rights to the succession ([85]). Again, in a pergaminho of March or April 1107, Raimundo acts as *ego comes Raimundus totius Galecie imperator seu toletani principis gener,* another novel proclamation of his approximation to the imperial office ([86]). Both these protocolic entitlatures, breathing defiance of Afonso VI's plans to bar him from being the next *rex Hispaniarum,* may well be explained as due to the fact that just before the spring of 1106, i. e., in the course of 1105, Raimundo's position had been greatly strengthened through the conclusion of the Pacto, which assured him the powerful support of Henrique and the Portuguese, while renewing Abbot Hugo's complete adhesion to his cause in flat opposition to the king-emperor.

In another quarter, what we can learn of the itineraries during 1105 of Raimundo, Henrique and the imperial court — for Dalmácio Geret

the gravest danger from the Almoravids, Afonso VI was in fact able to discharge the annual stipend; on the contrary, the census was then probably in a state of suspension, which would not necessarily deter Hugo from sending his chamberlain to Spain at the appointed time for its collection or prevent him from nursing hopes that on Raimundo's accession the precious dinars would once again flow across the Pyrenees.

([83]) López Ferreiro, III, pp. 293-294.

([84]) Cf. *Chartes de Cluny,* V, n.os 3862, 3867; Rui de Azevedo, DR, II, p. 550; David: *Pacte,* pp. 283-284 (but n. 1 on p. 284 reads incorrectly «3667»).

([85]) Escalona, n.º 139; Vignau, n.º 1502. Note also that elsewhere in this document the Condes refer to *regalem morem* and *reges nostri antecessores,* while Gelmirez' eschatocol describes the text as *testamentum regale.*

([86]) López Ferreiro, III, Apénd., n.º 22.

of course we have no record, other than the Pacto itself, for his presence in Spain until well after Afonso VI's death — makes it extremely probable that this is the one year of the triennium in which the three parties actually could come together, and that their meeting took place in Burgos. The pertinent chronology here commences on 16 January when, as we know from Sandoval's summary of Raimundo's grant to S. Juan de Poyo, the count along with D. Urraca and their daughter D. Sancha, was still in Gallicia ([87]). By 31 March, however, he must have joined Afonso VI's court at Astorga, for the real privilégio the king-emperor granted that day to the canons of the cathedral church of this city contains the confirmations, significantly in this order, of the Infante Sancho and Raimundo ([88]). Beyond Astorga we cannot chart in detail the stages of the court's eastward progress, but some time around the beginning of May it must have crossed the Pisuerga into Castile and reached Castrogeriz. A halt here is attested by the *Historia Compostellana,* which describes how, after Pope Paschal II had appointed Bishop Garcia of Burgos to judge the quarrel between the sees of Santiago and Mondoñedo over the archpresbyterates of Besoucos, Trasancos and Seaya, Bishop Gonzalo of the latter see and the procurators of Gelmirez of Compostela found that Garcia could not because of illness make the scheduled trip to Astorga to hear the case. They were therefore compelled to seek out the Castilian prelate in his own diocese, and found him with King Afonso and the court at Castrogeriz ([89]). This must have been in late April or early May, since by 14 May the court had gone on to Burgos, as would appear from Afonso VI's celebrated concession to the bishop of Santiago of the right to operate a mint. Although this royal document actually bears the date 14 May 1108, Sánchez-Albornoz has shown that it must have been drawn up three years previously at Burgos, so that it fixes for us on 14 May 1105 the presence of Raimundo and Urraca in the Castilian capital ([90]).

([87]) Sandoval: *Cinco Reyes,* I, p. 309.

([88]) *Ibid.,* pp. 309-310.

([89]) *Hist. Compost.,* Lib. I, c. 34 (PL, CLXX, col. 929 D); cf. Biggs: *Diego Gelmirez,* p. 51.

([90]) Sánchez-Albornoz: *Primitiva organización monetária,* pp. 324-329 (*Instituciones medievales españolas,* pp. 461-466). López Ferreiro, III, Apénd., n.° 23, whose text Sánchez-Albornoz reproduces, assigns this document

But the charter of 14 May also contains the subscriptions of the Condes Henrique and Teresa of Portugal. Henrique's movements between the Luso-Leonese assembly of late January and his appearance here in Burgos on 14 May are unknown. Unlike Raimundo he was not present in Astorga on 31 March, and he and Teresa may therefore have tarried in the Terra de Campos until the court arrived on its way to Burgos. At any rate, from 14 May on, both Henrique and Raimundo were residing for some months with the court in the Castilian city. As late as 22 September a charter granted by Afonso to one Pedro Ibannez bears the confirmations of both the Burgundian princes and their consorts (91). But by 12 December an imperial confirmation of various rights to Abbot João and the Castilian monastery of S. Salvador de Oña mentions of the quartet only Count Henrique (92), so that sometime between the end of September and early December Raimundo and Urraca must have left for Galicia (93), perhaps in connection with the birth of their son Afonso Raimundes, the later Afonso VII; and Teresa may have returned to Portugal.

We have, therefore, a firm basis for placing Henrique and Raimundo in Burgos between 14 May and 22 September 1105; what remains conjectural, in the absence of direct documentary proof, is whether in fact during that time Dalmácio Geret arrived on the chamberlain's regular visit to the king-emperor and brought with him the abbot's instructions for both counts to meet with his envoy and terminate their dangerous quarrel. Still, better than any hypothesis yet proposed or that seems extractable from the evidence, the assumption of a meeting in Burgos during the summer of 1105 at which the terms of the Pacto were hammered out to be carried back to Hugo when Dalmácio recrossed the Pyrenees, satisfies the requirements of the historical conjuncture, above all as this can now be reconstructed in the light of Count Henrique's Sanabrian

to 1107 but everything points to 1105 at Burgos. The subscriptions merit much further study.

(91) Serrano: *Obispado de Burgos,* III, n.° 62.

(92) *Col. Dipl. de Oña,* I, n.° 121.

(93) On 16 December 1105 Raimundo and Urraca confirm the forais of Santiago at a large gathering of notables, chiefly Galician but including the archbishops Bernardo of Toledo and Geraldo of Braga and the bishops Pedro of Leon and Pelágio of Astorga.

donation. On this basis therefore, tentatively but with some fair measure of confidence, we can posit for the genesis of the Pacto the following order of events:

(i) in late 1104, the decision by Henrique to intervene in the succession crisis of the Hispanic Empire for the purpose of annexing all or part of the kingdom of Leon;

(ii) at the end of January 1105, the attempted creation on Leonese soil of a Luso-Leonese coalition embracing Henrique's chief nobles and various leading members of the Leonese Church, monasteries and royal bureaucracy;

(iii) simultaneously, through concession of tithes and churches in Leonese Sanabria, an Henrician effort to forge new Portuguese benefactorial and financial bonds with Cluny, operative through S. Isidro de Dueñas and threatening to infringe upon the Burgundian abbey's hitherto total commitment to Raimundo;

(iv) in the late winter or spring of 1105, the successful appeal by the Count of Galicia to Abbot Hugo as the ally and protector of the Navarro-Basque dynasty, seeking his help in thwarting a Portuguese political and monastic policy undermining the legitimist cause in the looming conflict with the Sanchistas;

(v) between 14 May and 22 September 1105, the arrival of the two counts at Burgos and the conference with the Chamberlain Dalmácio Geret, at which Henrique agrees to surrender his Leonese schemes in return for compensation in Toledo or Galicia, and where the conditions of his collaboration with Raimundo are incorporated into the epistle addressed to the Cluniac abbot that we know, by no means accurately, as the Pacto sucessório.

University of Virginia
Charlottesville, Virginia, U. S. A.

ADDITIONAL NOTE

Since 1970 the timing and circumstances of the Pacto Sucessório have been commented upon by three authorities in the field.

Prof. T. de Sousa Soares (1974), rejecting David's case for 1105–1107, Azevedo's for 1095–1102, and my own for the summer of 1105, defends the year 1103.[1] It was then that Alfonso VI's public acknowledgement of Sancho as his heir would have alarmed not only the two politically motivated Burgundian counts but also Cluny and the Leonese-Castilian and Portuguese Churches, fearful of a dangerous anti-European reaction in favor of Mozarabic, if not actually pro-Islamic, isolationism. Hence, in 1103, Archbishop Bernard of Toledo's sudden willingness to accept restoration of the Bracaran metropolitanate under Gerald of Braga, the journey of both Gerald and Count Henrique to Rome in order to obtain Paschal II's sanction, and the new cooperation of Raimundo and Henrique to prevent Sancho's succession, all fix this as the indicated year.

None of these basically ecclesiastical arguments is impressive. The Pacto is totally free from overtones of metropolitical or other ecclesiastical concern; the thesis (pressed by David) of the Sanchistas as anti-European and potentially pro-Islamic, is completely unrealistic when the actual Castilian particularist leanings of this nebulous faction are considered; and Sousa Soares' reasoning does nothing to meet my contention that Abbot Hugh pragmatically intervened in order to safeguard Raimundo's imperial hopes against the schemes of the powerful and ambitious Henrique. Sousa Soares also asserts that in contracting a designedly secret treaty the count of Portugal could not have taken along so large a company of Portuguese barons as the charter of 30 January 1105 discloses; but this misses my whole point: that the barons went only as far as the Tierra de Campos, assisted in the formation of a Luso-Leonese coalition, and then returned home well before Henrique himself went on to the imperial court at Burgos and the negotiations with Raimundo and Dalmace Geret.

Dr. Peter Feige's discussion (1978) is content simply to cite Azevedo and me (although not Sousa Soares), while placing the Pacto broadly in the years just before Raimundo's death in 1107.[2]

As for Prof. Bernard Reilly's virtually page-length footnote in his notable biography of Urraca (1982), this proposes an (in my opinion) incredibly early

[1] T. de Sousa Soares, "O governo de Portugal pelo Conde Henrique de Borgonha: sus relacões com as monarquias leonesa-castelhana e aragonesa," *Rev. port. hist.*, XIV (1974), 365–97, at 380–5, especially 380, note 43.

[2] Peter Feige, "Die Anfänge des portugiesischen Königtums und seiner Landeskirche," *Gesammelte Aufsätze zur Kulturgeschichte Spaniens*, XXIX (Münster Westfalen, 1978), 85–436, at 130–2.

assignment to 1093–1097, in the years before Henrique had even been named count of Portugal.[3] This radical view (which ignores the treatments of both Sousa Soares and Feige) faults my "interesting attempt [as] less than convincing" on the following grounds. First, I do not sufficiently appreciate that the mixture of Portuguese and Leonese subscribants to the diploma of January 1105, and its drafting by an imperial notary, prove it was drawn up at the court. This possibility is of course the very one I raised and dismissed for reasons that still seem to me sufficient and unrefuted by anyone. Next, in a quarter where his unrivalled expertise in the diplomatics of the period merits all respect, Reilly re-dates to 1 May 1096 the charter I adduced as evidence of the reconciliation of Raimundo and Henrique in 1106; and to 1107 the charter I used under the date 14 May 1105 to narrow the time-span for the meeting of the two counts with Dalmace Geret.

Even if he is right on both heads, neither of these texts is in any sense central to my explication of the Pacto. For my part, here as elsewhere in his book Reilly (like Sousa Soares and Feige) seems to me to pay far too little attention to the Cluniac side of the story, the abbey's unique role in Leonese-Castilian dynastic and imperial crises under the alliance that dated from Fernando I's last years. As I have sought to emphasize in connection with the Pacto and the various controversial climaxes of Alfonso VI's *grosse Politik*, abbatial intervention below the Pyrenees has to be diagnosed within this framework. The reinforcement of liturgical commemorative honors assigned to Alfonso and Queen Constance after 1090, the subsequent precarious status of the *census Hispanicus* in the face of Murābit (Almoravid) shut-off of the *parias*, Hugh's significant turn for financial aid after 1096 to King Pedro I of Aragon (see the Additional Note to "Liturgical Intercession at Cluny," Study VIII in this volume) are factors affecting the abbot's anti-Alfonsine sponsorship of the Pacto and pointing to a date after 1100. All this patently awaits further study; meanwhile it is difficult to take seriously Reilly's contention that because the Pacto does not mention Portugal (which after all was not up for grabs), its formulation must precede Henrique's acquisition of the country by 1097.

Finally, of the two recent general histories of Portugal, that of Oliveira Marques favors "1106?" for the Pacto; while that of Serrão follows Sousa Soares on 1103.[4]

---

[3] B. F. Reilly, *The Kingdom of León-Castilla under Queen Urraca, 1109–1126* (Princeton, 1982), 26 and note 55, 38 and note 78.

[4] A. H. de Oliveira Marques, *História de Portugal* (Lisbon, 1972), I, chap. 1; English version, *History of Portugal* (New York, 1972), I, 38; J. Serrão, *História de Portugal*, I (Póvoa de Varzim?, 1977), 77.

X

The Spanish Journey of Abbot Ponce of Cluny

Contrary to common assumption the abbots of Cluny in the eleventh and twelfth centuries rarely crossed the Pyrenees to visit the Iberian Peninsula. Throughout this period of Cluniac greatness in medieval Spain only three abbots, Hugh the Great, Ponce de Melgueil and Peter the Venerable, made the arduous journey from Burgundy, and they each but once in a long abbatiate. Furthermore, these visits, although commonly attributed to the abbot's duty of inspecting Cluny's peninsular priories and his desire to make the pilgrimage to Compostella, unquestionably had a predominantly economic objective in two of the three cases. Abbot Hugh traveled to Burgos in 1090 for the express purpose of securing from King Alfonso VI of Leon and Castile the solemn imperial confirmation of that monarch's earlier lucrative grant to Cluny of an annual census of 2000 gold *mithkals;* and Peter the Venerable's celebrated traverse of 1142, as his negotiations with Alfonso VII at Salamanca prove, was likewise inspired by a crisis in the collection of the same prized Cluniac revenue[1]. But if the principal motive of Hugh's and Peter's Spanish journeys is plain, the same cannot yet be said of that of Ponce de Melgueil, which, as regards its circumstances and accomplishments, still remains in the darkness that veils so much of this abbot's turbulent career. Only with the aid of unknown or hitherto improperly used evidence from the Spanish sources does it seem possible to restore this least known of the three abbatial crossings of the Pyrenees to its proper place in the history of Spanish-Cluniac relations.

The sole authority now cited for Abbot Ponce's peninsular trip is a brief passage in the *Chartularium Sithiense* of the French abbey of St. Bertin (Saint-Omer) stating that Ponce « post paucos annos ordinationis sue, peragratis superioribus monasteriis Hispanie, Burgundie, Francie, Abbatis Villam tandem devenit »[2]. Since Ponce was elected abbot of Cluny in 1109, and since he presumably reached Abbeville in the winter of 1111, it seems to follow that his Spanish

1. The peninsular visits of Abbots Hugh and Peter will be treated in my forthcoming paper on the history of Cluny's Spanish census.

2. *Pars secunda,* II, 81, in M. Guérard, *Cartulaire de l'abbaye de Saint-Bertin* (Paris, 1840; *Collection de documents inédits sur l'histoire de France, Collection des cartulaires de France,* III), p. 280

journey occurred in 1110 or 1111, and was directed towards visitation of Cluny's major trans-Pyrenean subject-houses.[3] But this testimony of the St Bertin chronicle, although the basis of current statements about Ponce's visit to Spain, requires to be re-examined in the light of the Spanish documents.

First of all, in view of the fact that Hugh's and Peter's Spanish trips were directly inspired by crises in the payment of the Alfonsine census, it is of prime significance that total suspension of this important revenue by the Leonese-Castilian crown must have confronted Ponce de Melgueil from the very start of his abbatiate. The reasons for this are clear. In 1109, the year of Ponce's election, Alfonso VI had died and been succeeded on the throne by his daughter Queen Urraca, who almost immediately married her second cousin, King Alfonso I *el Batallador* of Aragon. This marriage, which might conceivably have foreshadowed by some four centuries the unification of the Spains under the Reyes Católicos, actually resulted in a series of violent quarrels and short-lived reconciliations between the two rulers, accompanied by prolonged and bitterly destructive warfare in Castile, Leon and Galicia [4]. Queen Urraca thus found herself involved in a costly and, for long, a losing struggle with the powerful Aragonese king and his supporters, a struggle in which she was constantly hampered by lack of funds for military and political purposes, as the sources show. Under such circumstances, although the evidence is indirect, it can be safely concluded that from 1111, on, if not as early as 1110 itself, the hard-pressed queen had been driven to halt the customary annual delivery of the 2000 gold *mithkals* into the hands of the Cluniac abbatial chamberlain then serving in Spain, Dalmace Geret. [5]

So far as can be determined, from at least 1111 on, Urraca never again discharged the Cluniac census in gold. But, as has yet to be recognized, in mid-January 1114 for the first time the queen commenced making to Cluny almost annual donations of monasteries, churches and royal estates. This is proved by a group of hitherto unknown charters of this queen in the Madrid Academia de la Historia documents on the Cluniac priory of San Isidro de Dueñas in Leon[6]. So regular are these Urracan cessions in their virtually annual se-

3. Guérard, pp. lvi-lvii, dates the trip 1111; J.-H. Pignot, *Histoire de l'ordre de Cluny* (3 vols. Autun - Paris, 1862-1868), III, 87-8, places it in the period 1110-1111.

4 A. Herculano, *Historia de Portugal* (8th ed. Paris-Lisbon, no date), II, 34 ff.; A. López Ferreiro, *Historia de la santa A. M. iglesia de Santiago de Compostela* (Santiago, 1898-1909), III, 317 ff.; A. Ballesteros y Beretta, *Historia de España* (2nd ed. Barcelona, 1943-44), II, 335-349; A. G. Biggs, *Diego Gelmírez, First archbishop of Compostela* (Washington 1949; Catholic Univ. of America, *Studies in mediaeval history*, N. S., XII), pp. 65 ff.

5. P. David, « Le pacte successoral entre Raymond de Galice et Henri de Portugal », *Bulletin Hispanique*, L (1948), 282-285.

6. Colección de Velázquez, IV, carpeta 4.

quence, and so contradictory to the consistent policy of Alfonso VI who with his grant to Abbot Hugh of the doubled census completely reversed his earlier practice of monastic cessions to Cluny, and from 1081 made no further such grants for the remaining three decades of his reign that they can only be understood as demonstrating a conversion of the census from payment in gold, which the queen did not possess, to payment in kind from her *realengo* holdings of lands, churches and monasteries.

Now, so important a transformation in what Cluny regarded as her major source of external income in this period of growing financial difficulties, could hardly have been effected without personal negotiation between Urraca and Ponce. Just as in 1090 it was necessary for Hugh to travel to Burgos to consult with Alfonso VI on the perpetuation of the census, and in 1142 for Peter the Venerable to meet with Alfonso VII at Salamanca to arrange its final abolition, so it appears certain that a primary aim of Ponce's trip to Spain was inquiry into the queen's non-payment of the annual 2000 *mithkals*, resulting in the negotiation of an agreement in which Cluny, in view of prevailing conditions, agreed to accept property transfers in lieu of cash. Furthermore, since initiation of this new type of census settlement can logically be expected to commence immediately after the holding of such a conference, it seems to follow that queen and abbot met in the nearest preceding travel season for French visitors to the Peninsula. This is indirectly confirmed by several Spanish Cluniac charters. The diploma of 1 May 1112 by which Countess Aldonza and her daughter Elvira Moniz ceded Cluny and Abbot Ponce their monastery of San Salvador de Villaverde contains no overtones of a recent or immediately anticipated abbatial visit.[7] On the other hand, three later charters suggest something of the kind: (1) that of 14 December 1113, by which Urraca's chief Gallegan supporter Count Pedro Froílaz de Traba gave Cluny his great family abbey of San Martín de Jubia; (2) that of 26 December 1113, in which the count's wife, Doña Gontroda Rodriguez, granted this new Cluniac priory of San Martin her *villa* of 'Coina'; and (3) Urraca's own already cited grant of mid-January 1114, transferring to San Isidro de Dueñas the royal monastery of San Millán de Soto as the first of the new series of annual cessions by the queen. The importance of these donations, and their chronological conjunction with one another and with the adoption of the new census payments in kind, both point to a recent visit of the abbot of Cluny in the preceding summer of 1113.[8]

7. A.Bernard and A. Bruel, *Recueil des chartes de l'abbaye de Cluny* (Paris, 1876-1903), V, 3900.

8. Bernard-Bruel, V, 3906; Santiago Montero Díaz, « La colección diplomática de san Martín de Jubia », *Boletín de la Universidad de Santiago de Compostela,* VII (1935), no. 25, pp. 69-70; Colec. Velázquez, *loc. cit.*, no. 1396.

But the chronological question, as well as our whole understanding of the purpose of Ponce de Melgueil's Spanish journey, is further complicated by the probability that the abbot ol Cluny also served on this occasion as the apostolic legate of Paschal II. That the pope intervened in the prolonged war between Urraca and Alfonso *el Batallador* in the hope of securing a negotiated peace settlement has long been known, chiefly through the pages of the *Historia Compostellana*. This remarkable work, composed in the first half of the twelfth century by four (or possibly five) canons of the cathedral church of Santiago, and published in 1765 by Padre Henrique Flórez as Tomo XX of *España Sagrada*, twice refers to papal peace missions to the Peninsula under Paschal II.

The first passage, Book I, chapter 79, describes the activities of a papal envoy in Spain designated only (in Flórez' text) as *abbas Clusensis*. This abbot-legate visits in turn King Alfonso and Queen Urraca; he summons the bishops of Leon and Castile,[9] as well as representatives of the warring *reyes*, to a peace council to be held in mid-August in the pope's presence; and at Compostella he consults with Bishop Diego Gelmírez on the solution of the political crisis.[10] Flórez placed this legation in the year 1112 and identified the apostolic envoy as the abbot (Helmengaud) of the Italian Benedictine abbey of San Michele della Chiusa, insisting (p. 139, n. 1) that the manuscript reading was « Clusensem, non Cluniacensem. Est autem *Clusa* Abbatia Taurinensis Dioecesis ». Flórez' identification has been repeated by López Ferreiro, Säbekow, Kehr, Ballesteros, Biggs, and other authorities,[11] but the case against accepting this reading of the text and recognizing a minor Piedmontese abbot, relatively unknown in western Spain, as Paschal II's agent for resolving a major political and military crisis, is very strong. Flórez does not indicate whether the adjective *Clusensis* appears written out or abbreviated, or from which manuscript he obtained it. He used three inferior manuscripts for his edition, not the best and earliest at Santiago, and strongly emphasizes in his preface (paragraphs 17-18) that these must have been written by scribes ignorant of Latin, so teeming were they in errors of abbreviation and orthography. Under such conditions, confusion of abbreviated forms of *Cluniacensis* with *Clusensis* could easily occur. Throughout Book I of the *Compostellana*

9. For understanding the papal and other documents of this period, it is essential to recognize that *Hispania* commonly designates only the kingdom of Leon and Castile; where Aragon is included the term *Hispaniae* is employed.

10. H. Flórez and M. Risco, *España Sagrada* (Madrid, 1747-1879), XX, 138-142.

11. López Ferreiro, III, 387-389; Gerhard Säbekow, *Die päpstlichen Legationen nach Spanien und Portugal bis zum Ausgang des XII. Jahrhunderts* (Berlin, 1931), pp. 34-5; Paul Kehr, « El papado y los reinos de Navarra y Aragón hasta mediados del siglo XII », *Estudios de edad media de la Corona de Aragón*, II (1946), 149-150; Ballesteros, II, 343; Biggs, 89-90.

the only other references to the abbots of Cluny (cc. 16, 17) also omit the proper name and use the form *abbas Cluniacensis*. In view of this practice, it is difficult to believe that Pedro Anaya, the author of this portion of the work, would mention an Italian abbot without sufficient geographical information to distinguish him from the already mentioned abbot of Cluny.

Even more decisive are the general circumstances of the papal peace mission, which strongly suggest Ponce was the legate. Given the seriousness of the ecclesiastical no less than the political situation — Alfonso I's destruction of churches and monasteries and his violent expulsion from their sees of Archbishop Bernard of Toledo and the bishops of Palencia, Osma, Burgos and Leon — it is not likely that the papacy, which had hitherto on much less momentous occasions always employed cardinals or bishops as its peninsular envoys, would send an unknown legate, lacking acquaintance with, or prestige in, the Leonese-Castilian realm. It should be remembered further that this envoy superseded the permanent papal legate in Spain, the primate and archbishop of Toledo, and needed to be of high rank. Diego Gelmirez' petitions for papal aid, to which the *Compostellana* (c. 79), with doubtless some justice, attributes Paschal II's decision to intervene in Spain, had called for a cardinal or churchman of comparable station. Anaya's warm approval of the legate sent is implicit, and his references to the abbot's long-standing knowledge of, and admiration for, that stout Cluniophile, the bishop of Compostella, once more suggest Ponce of Cluny. Finally, it should be recognized that the war between Urraca and her husband was regarded by the pope, the Leonese-Castilian hierarchy and the nobles as fundamentally a question of the legitimate succession to the throne, involving the hereditary rights of Urraca, Alfonso VI's daughter, and her young son by her first marriage, Alfonso Raimúndez, as against those that Alfonso of Aragon claimed to have acquired by his marriage with the queen. Leon-Castile, and especially Leon, was a state with which, under Ferdinand I, Alfonso VI and Urraca, Cluny had strong personal and political ties; and on two previous occasions the abbot of Cluny had been called upon to settle dynastic disputes. The first occasion was in 1072, when Abbot Hugh intervened to secure the liberation of Alfonso VI after his defeat and imprisonment by his brother Sancho II of Castile[12]. Again in 1105-1107, the succession crisis involving Alfonso VI's two Burgundian sons-in-law, Count Raymond of Galicia and Count Henry of Portugal, was steered to a successful compromise by the same abbot, acting in this case through his able chamberlain in Spain, Dalmace Geret[13]. Thus Abbot Ponce was the natural, not to say the inevitable, papal choice for the task of restoring peace to a troubled Spain.

12. This episode is fully treated in my above-mentioned study.
13. David, *op. cit.*, pp. 275-290.

Yet, if the abbot-legate of the *Historia Compostellana*, Book I, c. 79, is admitted to have been Ponce de Melgueil, a chronological difficulty immediately arises, since according to Flórez Paschal II's legation fell in 1112, whereas on other grounds, as we have seen, the summer of 1113 is indicated for Ponce's visit. Flórez' chronology, indeed, has won general acceptance — Ballesteros alone dissents, although without stating his reasons — so that it is now assumed that the envoy left Rome after the Lateran Council of March 1112 and, after reaching Spain, conferred with Alfonso and Urraca in the midst of the latter's siege of her husband at Carrión that same summer. But this seems quite unlikely. The very fact that Ponce met first with Alfonso proves the contrary, for at the siege of Carrión the prior interview would necessarily have been with the besieger, Urraca. It is true that at the start of c. 79, we hear of two years' having elapsed since Alfonso I's expulsion (in 1110) of Archbishop Bernard from his see of Toledo; but this is patently a quotation or paraphrase from Gelmírez' letter to the Pope, which must have been written before April 1113, and probably in the summer or fall of 1112. Certainly, it is suggestive that in the almost identical passage at the end of the chapter, where Gelmírez tells the legate at Santiago of the abuses committed by the *tyrannus Aragonensis*, the term *biennium* is omitted, undoubtedly because it was by that time more than two years since Bernard's loss of his see. The fact is, c. 79 of the *Compostellana* belongs to a group of chapters, cc. 74-82, on local Gallegan affairs, with which Anaya interrupts his main narrative, carried down to 1112 at c. 73, and resumed again at c. 83 *sub anno* 1113. Chapter 79 is one of several chapters in this Gallegan excursus vaguely dated *interea* and *eodem tempore*, and the internal evidence shows that it belongs in 1113.

The date of c. 79, however, cannot be satisfactorily determined without also relating the problem to a succeeding chapter of the *Compostellana*, c. 89 of Book I. Here there occurs the text of a letter of Paschal II quoted by Bishop Diego Gelmírez in the course of a sermon he delivered to the Urracan forces besieging Alfonso's troops at Burgos in late June of 1113. In this letter, dated only as of 14 April, and directed to Archbishop Bernard and the bishops and magnates of Leon-Castile, the pope urges those addressed to assemble together for consultation on the restoration of peace and declares that, at the earliest opportunity, he is sending an apostolic legate to Spain. The modern authorities regard this legate of c. 89 (who is never subsequently mentioned in the *Compostellana*) as a second peace envoy who was sent to the Peninsula after the failure of the *abbas Clusensis* [14]. But the whole tone of the epistle is one of initial, not renewed, papal action: nothing is said of a failure of a proceding mission or of collapse of the plans for an Italian synod in mid-August. There is thus

14. López Ferreiro, III, 397-8; Säbekow, pp. 35-6; Biggs, pp. 95-6.

good reason to believe that — whether Anaya realized it or not — this is in fact the preliminary announcement of the abbot-legate's mission described out of chronological order in c. 79. This conclusion provides further confirmation of 1113 as the year of Paschal II's intervention.

To be sure, Diego Gelmírez might conceivably have quoted in June 1113 a papal missive of earlier date in order to strengthen his attack upon the royal marriage and the threat of a possible reconciliation of Alfonso and Urraca; but two facts prove the letter was actually written and received in 1113. First, Diego's strong pressure upon the primate to convoke immediately, even in the midst of the siege, the assembly of bishops and nobles ordered by the pope, shows that arrival of the promised legate was then regarded as imminent. Second, after the failure of this attempt at an immediate council, Bernard's summons of prelates and nobles to a council at Palencia on 25 October indicates by that late date alone that it was at that point thought necessary to postpone fulfilment of the pope's instructions until after the legate had completed his mission[15].

On the basis of the foregoing reasoning, it now becomes possible to attempt a reconstruction of the general circumstances of Ponce's Spanish journey. It would appear that the assumption, based upon the St Bertin chronicle, that the trip occurred in 1110 or 1111, is to be rejected, unless we posit two crossings into the Peninsula, in 1110 or 1111 and in 1113. This is altogether unlikely. Either the chronicle of St Bertin erred in its chronology, as it certainly did in assuming visitation of his priories was the abbot's chief objective; or, very possibly, the phrase « peragratis superioribus monasteriis etc. » must be taken to mean broadly that Abbeville was reached not at the conclusion of, but in the course of, Ponce's extended travels in Spain, Burgundy and France. The year 1112 is ruled out as well, since we know Ponce was at Cluny on 28 July of that year. It was then that he received the fragment of the True Cross that Archbishop Maurice of Braga sent to Cluny in the custody of the chamberlain Dalmace Geret. This precious relic would surely have been entrusted to Ponce himself if he had visited Spain that summer[16].

With the Alfonsine census in default from at least 1111, the abbot of Cluny, we can be sure, envisaged, if he did not actually plan, a Spanish visit before 1113. It is however impossible to determine whether Paschal II, who, as his letter of 14 April shows, was then still undecided as to his choice of a Spanish envoy, took advantage of an announced abbatial visit to employ Ponce's services, or whether

15. *Hist, Compost.,* I, 88.
16. M. Marrier, *Bibliotheca Cluniacensis* (Mâcon, 1915), p. 564.

he precipitated Ponce's decision to go to the Peninsula that year by naming him legate. In any case, it must be clear that the journey had a double purpose, on the one hand papal and diplomatic, on the other, Cluniac and financial; to these larger aims inspection of the peninsular dependencies and a pilgrimage to Compostella were largely incidental.

Ponce's route in Spain undoubtedly followed the line of the *camín francés* to Galicia. Since, as the *Compostellana* informs us, the abbot entered western Spain, he presumably crossed the Pyrenees at Roncesvalles and advanced towards Castile along the Navarro-Castilian stretch of the great highway, via Pamplona and Logroño. A halt can certainly be allowed for at Santa María de Nájera, below Logroño, Cluny's great Riojan priory at which Peter the Venerable also stopped in 1142. The meeting with *el Batallador*, who was doubtless in Castile, belongs somewhere between Nájera and Burgos, perhaps even at the latter city, where Cluny's Castilian dependency of Santa Coloma was located, and where, with the siege of Burgos ended, Alfonso could again find entrance. The parallel conference with the queen can be set in Leon, either at Carrión de los Condes, site of the Cluniac priory of San Zoil, or at Astorga, another pilgrimage road center serving Urraca in this period as a major base of operations. Since the queen's ambulatory court then regularly included a number of the Leonese-Castilian bishops (especially those expelled from their sees by the king of Aragon), the papal summons to the Italian council of mid-August must have been published by the legate in the same place where he met the queen, although it must have been apparent, in view of the late date and Alfonso's hostile reception of the papal proposals, that this assembly would never meet.

Within the year 1113 the time of the trip can be fixed with some precision. The publication of the papal epistle of 14 April to the prelates and nobles at the siege of Burgos places Ponce's arrival, then regarded as imminent, after the last week of June. The suggestion here that the abbot-legate actually appeared in Castile-Leon in July finds support in the description of his meeting with Alfonso, Urraca and Gelmírez, where emphasis is placed upon breaking up the reconciliation plans adopted by the two monarchs soon after the termination of the siege of Burgos in early July. Finally, Ponce would hardly publish the papal call to the Italian council after, or even too close to, mid-August. Thus July,and perhaps part of August also, the normal travel season for tourists in Spain, seems indicated as the period in which the abbatial journey occurred.

This is not the place to discuss the precise aims of papal policy as regards the settlement of the war in Leon and Castile, or the way in which the abbot- legate of 1113 carried out his diplomatic mission.

Obviously enough, the visit was a failure from the papal side, a relative success — with the resumption of census payments on the new basis in kind — from the standpoint of Cluny's financial interests. Much still remains to be done with the diplomatic aspects of Ponce's journey, but it will suffice for the moment if we have established the date, aims and approximate itinerary of what has been the most obscure of the three memorable crossings of the Pyrenees by the Cluniac abbots of the eleventh and twelfth centuries.

Charlottesville, Va., University of Virginia.

ADDITIONAL NOTE

Of the two principal mysteries surrounding Paschal II's mission to the warring spouses Urraca and Alfonso *el Batallador*, that of its timing is less crucial than the determination of the abbot-legate's identity. Due to the limited circulation, as Segl correctly observes,[1] of the little paper above, my brief on behalf of Abbot Ponce (Pontius, Pons) has enjoyed relatively scant notice, particularly among Spanish historians. Despite several objections made against it, I still deem it the only satisfactory resolution of the enigma.

Nothing further has been discovered which would support the still widely held belief that the papal emissary was Helmengaud of the Turinese abbey of San Michele della Chiusa, the view so successfully propagated in 1765 by Flórez (although it was not original with him since it had already appeared by 1721 in Berganza's *Antigüedades*).[2] That there was a link between this Piedmontese house and Spain is clear from Hadrian IV's confirmation of San Michele's possessions on 9 April 1156, where two Catalan monastic dependencies are named: Santa María de Cervia (dioc. Gerona) and a "monasterium de Cruzillis".[3] This however throws no light whatever upon why the unknown Helmengaud, rather than the customary prominent figure of cardinalitial or episcopal rank, was selected to head a highly important mission to the reigning monarchs of Leon-Castile and Aragon-Navarre. Such a choice, if ever made, remains almost inexplicable.

In contrast, the signs favoring Ponce can be further expanded. To the testimony of the Saint-Bertin chronicle concerning the Spanish visit, Urraca's resort from 1114 to cessions of monasteries and lands to Cluny in commutation of her father's promised annual census of 2000 gold dinars, the cluster of private benefactions made to the abbey in these same years, and the virtual certainty that for Leonese-Castilian scribes and their readers of the 12th century *Clusensis* could only have passed as a contraction for *Cluniacensis* and not for an Italian toponym unfamiliar in the Hispanic West—should now be added two other considerations. Cowdrey, in his careful biographical study, remarks on this Cluniac administrator's known capabilities as a skilful diplomat; and allowance can be made for the natural reluctance in Cluniac-influenced circles to mention Ponce's name after he was deposed in disgrace in 1122, which would explain why it was omitted from *Historia Compostellana*, I, 79.

[1] Peter Segl, *Königtum und Klosterreform in Spanien* (Kallmünz, 1974), 86.

[2] Francisco de Berganza, *Antigüedades de España* (Madrid, 1719–21), II, 28, col. 1. Note that J. Zurita simply follows without comment the manuscript reading: "el abad Clusense": *Anales de la Corona de Aragón*, I (Zaragoza, 1562), lib. I, xxxix (ed. A. Canellas López, Zaragoza, 1967, I, 126:48).

[3] P. Kehr, *Papsturkunden in Spanien. I. Catalanien*, II (Göttingen, 1926), 354–8.

The general case for Ponce's legateship in 1113 has been favorably received by two able students of Hispano-Cluniac relations: Segl, who accepts it without reservation; and Cowdrey, who finds it "attractive" although not conclusive, and prefers to suspend judgment pending preparation of the needed critical edition of *H. C.*[4] In contrast, B. F. Reilly's recent reconstruction of Urraca's troubled reign retains Helmengaud of Chiusa as Paschal II's envoy, and, pronouncing the year 1113 "impossible", espouses the mission's traditional ascription to 1112.[5] In view of Reilly's earlier close studies of the MSS and multiple authorship of *H. C.*,[6] it is regrettable—not to say surprising—that in this connection he silently passes over the key question of the paleographical validity of *Clusensis-Cluniacensis* in *H. C.* On chronological grounds, he objects to 1113 because Urraca and Alfonso were then at war—but this is precisely the situation which Pascal II, and I, allowed for. He declares that in 1113 there would have been no necessity for the legate's going on to Compostela after interviewing Urraca, since Gelmírez was then at the queen's side; but does this contradict my statement (318) that this interview took place at or near Carrión or Astorga? Without doubt, Cowdrey's deduction from two later letters of Gelmírez to Ponce that the two had never met should be given due consideration; I would not however regard this alone as sufficiently weighty to offset the generally strong indications supporting a Pontian legateship to Spain in the summer of 1113.

---

[4] Segl, *loc. cit.*; H. E. J. Cowdrey, "Two Studies in Cluniac History, 1049–1126," *Studi Gregoriani*, XI (1978), 200–3. See also R. A. Fletcher, *The Episcopate in the Kingdom of León in the Twelfth Century* (Oxford, 1978), 204: "possibly by the abbot of Cluny".

[5] B. F. Reilly, *The Kingdom of León-Castilla under Queen Urraca, 1109–1126* (Princeton, 1982), 83 and note 121.

[6] "The 'Historia Compostelana': The Genesis and Composition of a Twelfth-Century Spanish 'Gesta'," *Speculum*, XLIV (1969), 78–85; "Existing Manuscripts of the 'Historia Compostelana': Notes toward a Critical Edition," *Manuscripta*, XV (1971), 131–52.

XI

THE CLUNIAC PRIORIES OF GALICIA AND PORTUGAL: THEIR ACQUISITION AND ADMINISTRATION

1075-ca. 1230

One major consequence of the numerous errors and confusions that still impede valid assessment of the nature and historical significance of Cluniac expansion in the Iberian Peninsula has been the common failure to recognize the sharply regional distribution of the Burgundian abbey's trans-Pyrenean possessions. When we eventually possess a trustworthy geography of the Luso-Hispanic priories, subpriories, patrimonies and *cotos,* it is bound to become even more apparent than it is at present that the great majority of these lay in three principal areas — the Rioja Alta, the Tierra de Campos (i. e., the diocese of Palencia) and the Galaico-Portuguese West. The reasons for this neglected but unmistakable pattern of Cluniac territorial concentration in medieval Iberia have yet to be seriously investigated; but in the first two instances it is reasonably clear that they derive in large part from the intimate alliance forged between Cluny and the Leonese Empire of Hispania under the king-emperors Fernando I and Alfonso VI,[1] as the key initial cessions demonstrate: Santa María de Ná-

[This study was presented in abstract at the V Semana de Estudios Monásticos, held at the Monastery of El Paular, Spain, 23-28 September 1962, where Dom García M. Colombás, O. S. B., very kindly read it in his own Castilian version. For support in the preparation of this paper I am indebted to the Institute for Research in the Social Sciences, University of Virginia.]

1. Cf. R. Menéndez Pidal, *El imperio hispánico y los cinco reinos,* Madrid, 1950, 86-133; and my *Liturgical Intercession at Cluny for the King-Emperors of Leon* in *Studia monastica,* t. 3, 1961, 53-76.

jera (1079), the nucleus of the far-flung Riojan network of holdings, and San Isidro de Dueñas (1073), which played a somewhat similar role in the Tierra de Campos prior to the rise of San Zoil de Carrión de los Condes.

The third case is at once more obscure and more complex. For one thing, none of the abbey's Gallegan or Portuguese acquisitions was given by a reigning Leonese monarch, although that of San Vicente de Pombeiro (1109) can be linked to the imminent accession of Alfonso VI's daughter, the Infanta Urraca. For another, the documentation for most of the Luso-Gallegan priories is quite fragmentary;[2] and on such basic question as the origins, development and impact of each community upon its locale; the numbers, national origin and recruitment of monks; liturgical and customary practices; expansion and exploitation of patrimonies; control by abbatial and provincial administrators; and relations with episcopate, crown and aristocracy; almost everything remains to be done. Furthermore, neither the circumstances of the original Burgundian establishment in this zone nor the subsequent historical evolution of the houses annexed have ever been closely examined as a distinctive chapter in Hispano-Cluniac annals.

It goes without saying that two topics are central to progress on all the rest, and it is to these that the present paper will address itself. First, the problem of acquisition, with the aim of discovering precisely what cessions of monasteries in Galiçia and Portugal were made to the abbey, and when; the identity and connections of the donors; whether the grants were primarily due to Cluniac expansionism or to specifically peninsular initiative; and if the latter, whether in addition to spiritual motives the benefactions can be related to identifiable conjunctures in the history of the Leonese-Cluniac alliance. Secondly, the problem of administration, where interest centers principally upon the separation ca. 1170 of the Luso-Gallegan priories from the vast Pro-

2. Of the nine Luso-Gallegan priories, only for S. Martín de Jubia (cf. *infra*, n. 46) do we have cartularies and a relatively full diplomatic collection; for S. Vicente de Pombeiro a fair number of rent contracts survive (cf. *infra*, n. 38) but these commence in some number only in the 13th century. Otherwise, we are largely dependent upon the donation acts; scattered later charters; occasional references in secular, episcopal and papal texts; and from 1259, the extant visitation reports and acts of the chapters general for Spain, which have been published by Ulysse Robert, *État des monastères espagnols de l'Ordre de Cluny, aux XIIIe-XVe siècles, d'après les actes des visites et des chapitres généraux* in *Bol. de la R. Academia de la historia*, t. 20, 1892, 321-431. For the Portuguese sources, see Avelino de Jesus da Costa, *A Ordem de Cluny em Portugal* in *Cenáculo,* t. 4, 1948 (also, separately, Braga, 1948).

vince of Hispania and their inclusion for some half-century in a second Iberian *cameraria,* the Province of Galicia, that has remained virtually unknown to students of the Burgundian federation.

I

The first step is to decide just which monastic communities fall within the scope of the inquiry, and here it is essential to take into account ephemeral as well as permanent acquisitions. Failure to do this, along with other errors of omission and commission, renders unreliable the Galaico-Portuguese entries in catalogues of Hispano-Cluniac priories such as those provided by Berlière, Pérez de Urbel, Valous, Evans or Schmitz.[3] The Great List of all Cluny's daughter-houses throughout medieval Europe, which Marrier published in 1614 and upon which all modern authorities have depended, assigns the following eight dependencies of the *Prouincia Hispaniae* to our zone: [4]

Prioratus S. Saluatoris de Villa-viridi in Galicia, Austericensis diocesis [San Salvador de Villaverde].

Prioratus B. Mariae de Cluniaco, de Villa-francha, alias de Valle-Carceris, in Gallicia, Asturicensis diocesis [Santa María de Villafranca].

Prioratus de Valle-viridi, in Gallicia, Lucensis diocesis [San Pedro de Valverde].

Prioratus S. Vincentii de Palumberiis, in Galicia, Lucensis diocesis [San Vicente de Pombeiro].

Prioratus S. Saluatoris de Bondino, in Gallicia, Tudensis diocesis [San Salvador de Budiño] .

Prioratus S. Martini de Iuina, in Gallicia, Mindoniensis diocesis [San Martín de Jubia].

3. U. Berlière, *Les monastères de l'Ordre de Cluny du XIIIe au XVe siècle,* in *R. bén.*, t. 10, 1893, 107-112; Justo Pérez de Urbel, *Los monjes españoles en la Edad Media,* 2nd ed., Madrid, 1954, II, chap. 6; Guy de Valous, *Le monachisme clunisien des origines au XVe siècle,* Ligugé-Paris, 1935, II, 263-266 (fails to perceive identity of Vimieiro and Ombres while omitting Villafrío, Santa Justa de Coimbra and Santa María de Ferreira); Joan Evans, *The Romanesque Architecture of the Order of Cluny,* Cambridge, 1938, 46-47, 174-175 (wrongly includes as separate houses the toponymic doublets Jubia-Nebda, Budiño-Rodinum, Vimieiro-Ombres while omitting Santa Justa and Ferreira); Philibert Schmitz, *Histoire de l'Ordre de Saint Benoît,* 2nd ed., Maredsous, 1948, I, 238-246 and *D.H.G.E.,* t. 7, 1933, 1082-1083 (weak on Galicia, no treatment of Portugal).

4. M. Marrier, *Bibliotheca Cluniacensis,* Paris, 1614, 1746-1747.

Prioratus de Vmbreriis in Portugalia, Bracarensis diocesis [Santa María de Vimieiro].
Prioratus B. Mariae de Ratis, in Portugalia, Bracarensis diocesis, immediate subditus Prioratui de Charitate [São Pedro de Rates].

But of these eight houses two, San Salvador de Villaverde and Santa María (later San Nicolás) de Villafranca, must be discarded as in the diocese of Astorga and hence not in Galicia but León. On the other hand, three Luso-Gallegan cessions for which acts of donation survive — San Salvador de Villafrío, Santa Justa de Coimbra and Santa María de Ferreira — are not mentioned at all in this roll, clearly because they had been lost to Cluny by the late 13th century, the earliest date Dom A. Wilmart suggests for the materials used when the Great List was compiled (sometime after 1350).[5] Thus the correct number of priories in Galicia and Portugal can be set at nine, of which six — Villafrío, Pombeiro, Jubia, Ferreira, Valverde and Budiño were in Galicia; and three — Rates, Santa Justa de Coimbra and Vimieiro — in Portugal.

For each of these nine houses it is necessary to determine the date of its transfer to Cluny, its location (approximately at least), the donor or donors, and the motives for and immediate circumstances of the grant.

A. *The Cessions under Abbot Hugh the Great*

1. 31 August 1075: San Salvador de Villafrío: Galicia, dioc. and prov. Lugo, p. j. Lugo, ayunt. Castroverde, in the parish of San Juan de Barredo, between Labio and Castroverde, some dozen kms. NE of the city of Lugo.[6] This little-known monastery in the ancient *territorium* of Chamoso, given to Abbot Hugh and the monks of Cluny by the *conuersus* Enego Bermundo, i. e, Eneco Vermudo, with its villas, churches, *heredades,* meadows, vineyards, mills and cultivated and uncultivated lands, rarely appears in lists of Cluniac holdings in Spain

5. A. Wilmart, *Les établissements de l'Ordre de Cluny à la fin du Moyen Age,* in *Annales de l'Académie de Mâcon,* t. 23, 1922-23, 375-405.
6. Mapa Militar Itinerario de España, hoja 12; Sebastián de Miñano, *Diccionario geográfico-estadístico de España y Portugal,* Madrid, 1826-1828, II, 4, s. v. Barredo; *Nomenclator general de España,* Madrid, 1933 ff., XVI, 31.

and its identity has not hitherto been established.[7] The subscriptions of Bishop Vistruario and Counts Vela, Sancho and Froila in the donation charter connect the house with the Lugo region;[8] and the locative phrase "inter duos montes unus dicitur Cirius et alter Lapidus et iuxta riuulum quod dicitur Emeneda" can be paralleled in a diploma of 1130 by which Count Gutierre Vermúdez and his wife Toda give two parts of this monastery, obviously not by then in Cluniac hands, to Bishop Pedro III of Lugo;[9] and in royal confirmations of the patrimonies of this see issued by Fernando II (1178), Alfonso IX (1189) and Fernando III (1231).[10] These texts establish San Salvador de Villafrío as a *monasterio propio* possessing a substantial *abadengo* and royal *cotización,* and with a somewhat checkered career of royal and aristocratic ownership before finally passing in 1130 to the Church of Lugo. The Cluniac phase, commencing in 1075 was certainly over before 1126, the latest year in which Queen Urraca could have ceded the house to Count Gutierre,[11] and most likely well before this date since Villafrío is not mentioned among the Hispano-Cluniac dependencies listed in papal confirmations from 1076 on.[12]

7. Donation act: A. Bernard and A. Bruel, eds., *Recueil des chartes de l'abbaye de Cluny* (Paris, 1876-1903), IV, 3481.

8. On the bishop, M. Risco, *España Sagrada,* Madrid, 1747-1879, XL, 166 ff.; for the counts, cf., for example: Vela in L. Sánchez Belda, *Documentos reales de la Edad Media referentes a Galicia,* Madrid, 1953, no. 164; *E.S.,* XL, 180, 188 and Apénd. xxviii; Sancho in Sánchez Belda, op. cit., no. 159; Tumbo de Samos, esc. 133, 176, as cited by Plácido Arias, *Historia del real monasterio de Samos,* Compostela, 1950, 105, 107; Froila or Fruela Díaz, *E.S.,* XL, 228; R. Menéndez Pidal, *El Cantar de mío Cid,* 2nd ed., Madrid, 1944, II, 696-7. The same three counts appear in R. Escalona, *Historia del Real Monasterio de Sahagún,* Madrid, 1782, esc. 114 (p. 478, col. 2).

9. *E.S.,* XLI, 14 and 304-306 (Apénd. iv): "...duas partes monasterii sancti Saluatoris quod uulgo Villarfrigidum nuncupatur... in territorio Flamosi et capite montis quem Cirium uocant super riuulum aquae Recamundi nuncupatae discurrente ad aquam de Ameneda et inter alios duos maximos montes suis nominibus dignos quorum alter Cuperius alter uero Lapideus uocatur".

10. Fernando II, 7 Oct. 1178: "ex parte alia aduersus orientem Texero, Ameneda cum Villari frigido, Berreda, Vandalar et Rimiam" (*E.S.,* XLI, 332; cf. Julio González, *Regesta de Fernando II,* Madrid, 1943, 460-1); Alfonso IX, 18 Oct. 1189: "ecclesias de Framoso, cum Caabogi et Texeiro, et Ameneda et Uillarifrigido cum cauto suo" (J. González, *Alfonso IX,* Madrid, 1944, II, no. 30 (p. 53); M.ª del Pilar R. Laguzzi, *Cinco documentos lucenses* in *Cuadernos de historia de España,* t. 3, 1945, 18, no. 2); Fernando III, 1231: "ecclesias de Flamoso cum Caabogi et Texeiro et Ameneda et Villare frigido cum cauto suo" (*E.S.* XLI, 363).

11. Cf. the count's grant of 1130 to Lugo: "quod uidelicet monasterium habuimus ex datione bonae memoriae reginae dominae Urrachae, quae nobis contulit illud per scripturam firmam et authenticam concedente postmodum filio eius rege domino Adefonso ut omnibus notum est" (*E.S.* XLI, 304-5).

12. Cf. the bulls of Gregory VII (9 Dec. 1076), Urban II (1 Nov. 1088), Pascal

The donor Eneco Vermudo, son of Vermudo and Gerbira (Elvira), probably belonged to the family of the Count Vermudo whose ties with the Lugo region are discernible in diplomas of the late tenth and early eleventh centuries, and whose widow, Elvira Pinioliz, after making various gifts to the see of Lugo and becoming a *Christi ancilla,* lived on to at least 1034.[13] He may also be conected, perhaps as a brother, with Count Fernando Vermúdez, a leading Gallegan magnate of Alfonso VI's court ca. 1068-1080, whose Cluniac sympathies are suggested by his subscription to Countess Teresa's second donation charter to Cluny for the Leonese monastery of San Zoil de Carrión 29 January 1077).[14] In any event, like virtually all non-royal peninsular benefactors of Cluny in the eleventh century, Eneco must have been of noble origin, while the charter itself, drawn up in Spanish style and with Spanish subscriptions but claiming to be validated "in presentia domni Hugonis abbatis similiter et cuncte congregationis", must have been designed to be carried by him to Cluny for presentation at the time of his profession there.[15]

Two similar instances can be cited for this same period of aristocratic Leonese conversions to Cluny followed by migration to Burgundy: the *nobilissima femina* Fronildi or Fronilda Guterriz, daughter of a count and probably at the time widow of a Leonese noble, who "exiuit de locum suum et de auitacione suam et conuertit se ad Sancti Petri Cluniacensum" and Justa, *comitissa de terra spanensis,* widow of the powerful Beni Gómez chieftain Asur Díaz and stepmother of the famous Count Pedro Ansúrez, who — no doubt like Fronildi also a *Deo uota* — entered the Cluniac convent of Saint-Pierre-de-Marcigny-sur-Loire.[16] In the latter case donations of property accompanied

II (20 Nov. 1100, 16 Oct. 1109, 7 Nov. 1114) and Honorius II (2 Apr. 1125) in *Bullarium sacri ordinis Cluniacensis* (ed. P. Simon, Lyons, 1680), 18-20, 22-23, 32-33, 36-37, 37, 42-43.

13. Sánchez Belda, *Docs. Reales Gal.,* nos. 112 (982-999), 138 (1027); Tumbo Nuevo de Lugo, Madrid, Arch. Hist. Nac., Clero, No. 363, fols. 63-64 (1034).

14. *Chartes de Cluny,* IV, 3507; *real privilegio* to Sahagún of Alfonso VI, 22 Nov. 1068 (Escalona, *Hist. Sahagún,* esc. 103); R. Menéndez Pidal, *La España del Cid,* 4td ed., Madrid, 1947, II, 857, on Fernando's presence at the Council of Burgos, 1080.

15. Note also the preservation at Cluny of the original *pergamino,* which is unknown in peninsular archives.

16. Diploma of 9 Feb. 1078 in *Indice de los documentos del monasterio de Sahagún de la Orden de San Benito* (ed. V. Vignau, Madrid, 1874), no. 1138; J. A. Serrano Redonnet, *Ovetensis monete* in *Cuad. hist. Esp.,* t. 1-2, 1944, 185-187 (to be added to Jean Richard's admirable reconstitution, *Le cartulaire de Marcigny-sur-Loire (1045-1144),* Dijon, 1957).

profession; but the fact that at Justa's death this was immediately sold by Abbot Hugh to Pedro Ansúrez suggests that Eneco's heirs may have been allowed to redeem Villafrío shortly after 1075. But it is also possible that for reasons that escape us the cession was never carried through.

San Salvador de Villafrío, then, should not properly be included in a roll-call of permanent Cluniac subject-house in Galicia and Portugal, yet for several reasons this ephemeral donation has importance for understanding Burgundian establishment in the western zone. It ranks as the very first peninsular abbey to be granted Cluny beyond the boundaries of the Leonese *reino;* and as a monastic cession it is remarkably early for the whole Leonese-Castilian area, being preceded only by King Alfonso's gift on 29 Dec. 1073 of San Isidro de Dueñas.[17] It provides striking testimony to the still unstudied wave of Cluniac piety and enthusiasm that, in the last years of Fernando I and especially after Alfonso VI's restoration with Abbot Hugh's aid in late 1072, swept the Leonese royal family and high aristocracy. Lastly, its speedy disappearance, reflecting Cluny's indifference or lack of success means that not until the acquisition of San Vicente de Pombeiro in 1108, thirty-four years after the Villafrío charter and eight years after the first Portuguese cession, does Cluny gain a permanent outpost in Galicia.

2. — March 1100: São Pedro de Rates: Portugal, dioc. Braga, distr. Porto, conc. Póvoa de Varzim, at or near the surviving 12th century Romanesque church of this title ca. 28 kms. SW of Braga in the present *freguesia* of São Pedro de Rates.[18] This allegedly previously derelict *ecclesia* or *eremita,* having been rebuilt, was given with its *termini* and *ius* to the Cluniac dependency of Sainte-Marie-de-la-Charité-sur-Loire by Count Henry of Portugal and his wife the Infanta Teresa, daughter of Alfonso VI.[19] Since the Termo de São Pe-

17. *Chartes de Cluny,* IV, 3452, under date of 29 May; but a superior (though less complete) version in Acad. de la Hist., Colección Velázquez, t. IV, leg. 4, no. 1388, to be included in my forthcoming edition of the charters of San Isidro de Dueñas, reads "iiii kls Januarias", i. e., 29 December. For the significance of this date, the anniversary of Fernando I's death in 1065, see my "The Liturgical Context of Fernando I's Last Days according to the So-called *Historia Silense*", in the special number of *Hispania Sacra* dedicated to Dom Marius Férotin.

18. *Grande enciclopédia portuguesa e brasileira,* Lisbon-Rio de Janeiro, 1950-60, t. 24, 434.

19. *Documentos medievais portugueses. Documentos régios* (ed. Rui Pinto de Azevedo, Lisbon, 1958), I, 1, n. 6, from René de Lespinasse, *Cartulaire du prieuré*

dro, with the church of the same patronage, had existed since at least the reign of Fernando I;[20] since sometime between 1078 and 1091 the *ecclesia* received a small legacy from one Froila Crescones;[21] and since the *jantar* or purveyance *de sancto Petro de Ratis* is listed in the primitive Censual of the Church of Braga (1085-1091);[22] the donation act's allusions to ruin and long abandonment cannot be taken literally. No doubt extensive reconstruction was necessary to convert the parish church into the domicile of a monastic community.

It is evident that a substantial endowment of lands and juridical privileges accompanied this plantation of the first Cluniac priory on Portuguese soil. Henry and Teresa refer to *termini* and *ius;* these seem to have been the subject of a second, now lost, charter which fixed the boundaries of the Termo, extended various rights of *cotizacão,* and defined the monks' relations with the chief local population center, the Vila de Rates. For the Inquirições of 1258 under King Alfonso III preserve testimony by an ex-prior of Rates, Stephen, whose deposition is supported by two of the monks, the *juizes* of the Vila de Rates and Faria, and other witnesses, that at that time the priory still possessed authentic charters (*bonae cartae*) of Count Henry and Queen (as she came to style herself) Teresa, by which these patrons gave the district of Rates to La Charité *cautatum et demarcatum.*[23] Stephen also asserts that the priory was accustomed to pay the crown one-half the *colheita,* or purveyance to the king, owed by the Termo; that the men of the Vila owed military service to the king and for offenses committed outside the *couto* were subject to his *domo-mor,* which proves the priory possessed powers of justice within the *couto* even over the Vila; and

de la Charité-sur-Loire, Nevers-Paris, 1887, no. xl. The scribe *Regnerius presbiter* is certainly French and probably from La Charité. History: J. Augusto Ferreira, *Origens do christianismo na península hispánica. A Villa de Rates, sua igreja e seu mosteiro,* Póvoa de Varzim, 1912, 63-74; da Costa, *Ordem de Cluny em Portugal,* 27-35; *Grande enc. port. e bras.,* t. 24, 434-437.

20. Cf. *real privilegio* of Afonso Henriques, 15 June 1128: "en nos tenpos delrei don Fernando pelo termho de San Pedro de Rates" (*Docs. med. port. Régios,* I, 1, no. 90; Avelino de Jesus da Costa, *O bispo D. Pedro e a organização da diocese de Braga,* Coimbra, 1959, II, 21).

21. Da Costa, op. cit., II, 381 (no. 26); ibid., 17, no. 38.

22. Da Costa, II, 17; and cf. his scepticism regarding both the duration and extent of ruin, I, 23-4; but his assumption that São Pedro before 1100 was already a *mosteiro* is rightly rejected as without documentary proof by Dom José Mattoso in his important review of *O Bispo D. Pedro* in *R. d'hist. ecclés.,* t. 57, 1962, 170-176. Mattoso also questions the dating of the Censual.

23. Ferreira, *Origens,* 93-4; on Stephen as prior ca. 1227, cf. *Chartes de Cluny,* V, 4554.

that the monks avoided acquiring lands or *foreiros* involving loss to the crown. We learn also that the prior of Rates was barred from entering the Vila. In the absence of both the act of *cotização* and the royal foral of the Vila we cannot be sure that all these stipulations go back to 1100, and the references to Teresa as queen may favor a date subsequent to her husband's death in 1112; but everything suggests that in São Pedro de Rates the Cluniacs received a fairly impressive benefaction.

More difficult to perceive is why São Pedro was subjected not to Cluny herself, as normally with the earlier cessions in León and Castile, but to her great Nivernais daughter-house of La Charité, which had not previously obtained any peninsular affiliate. It should be noted that the gift was a double one, including not alone the priory and its temporalities but also an annual subsidy of all the *dízimos* or lay tithes due the *condes* from their domains (*reguengos*) between the Douro and Mondego rivers, i. e. a good part of the modern region of Beira.[24] The choice of beneficiary does not seem satisfactorily accounted for by ascribing it to one or both of the ex-Cluniac bishops, Gerald of Braga and Maurice Bourdin of Coimbra, who were Henry's principal agents in his reorganization of the Portuguese church. The saintly Gerald, bishop from 1096 and metropolitan after Pope Paschal II's restoration of the metropolitical rights of Braga on 28 December 1099, just three months before the Rates cession, does not subscribe the donation charter and, more significant, his original monastic ties were with the Cluniac community of Moissac, not La Charité.[25] Maurice Bourdin, to be sure, on 4 February 1102 gave La Charité the suburban church of Santa Justa de Coimbra; but Maurice had come to Spain from Limoges, and neither as archdeacon of Toledo, bishop of Coimbra, metropolitan of Braga nor anti-pope Gregory VIII, displays any other visible interest in the Nivernais community.[26] It is therefore much more likely

24. By the time of Afonso III (1248-1279) these *dízimos* are known to have been paid to São Pedro itself, and this may have been true from the beginning; cf. FERREIRA, *Origens*, 100; DA COSTA, *Cluny em Portugal*, 34.

25. BERNARD, *Vita beati Geraldi archiepiscopi Bracarensis*, cap. 1, in *Port. Mon. Hist., Scriptores*, Lisbon, 1856, 53, col. 2-54, col. 1; J. A. FERREIRA, *Fastos episcopais da Igreja Primacial de Braga*, I, 205-228, as cited in *Grande enc. port. e bras.*, XII, 336-7.

26. Pierre DAVID, *L'énigme de Maurice Bourdin* in *Études historiques sur la Galice et le Portugal*, Lisbon-Paris, 1947, 441-501, and references there cited; but on Maurice's Cluniac ties DAVID fails to consider his possible connection with the Rates cession or his known gift to La Charité in 1102 of Santa Justa de Coimbra.

that his generosity to La Charité was determined by that of Henry and Teresa two years before than the reverse.

As for Henry himself, family ties may well have been influential. He was a grandson of Hélie de Semur, and we know that the counts of Semur became patrons of La Charité, although unfortunately we cannot document this before 1162.[27] But behind the gift to what was then probably Cluny's most flourishing dependency there almost certainly lies a more decisive political factor, connected with the whole program of ecclesiastical and political autonomy then being vigorously pursued by the ambitious Count of Portugal.[28] By 1100 the intimate association, paternalistic and quasi-feudal, of Hugh of Cluny with Alfonso VI had given the abbey a powerful influence in dynastic and imperial affairs. We may be sure that Henry was fully aware of the secular as well as spiritual advantages in Burgundian gratitude and friendship. But the gift of a monastery and of annual revenues directly to Cluny, with the accompanying entry of the donor or donors into the abbey's *societas,* entailed from this standpoint certain drawbacks. It was likely to be overshadowed by, even worse, confused with, the king-emperor's own much greater beneficences, his string of monastic cessions and famous doubled census of 2000 gold *metcales* a year. The abbatial chamberlain sent annually to Spain by Hugh to collect the census and visit the peninsular priories could be expected to champion in Portugal the interests of Alfonso VI. And the priory itself, as may already have been happening with the older houses in León, would tend to fall into administrative dependence upon Cluny's chief western Hispanic center, San Isidro de Dueñas, a natural stronghold of Leonese imperialism. It is then as a counterpart to the steps Henry is known to have been taking before and after 1100 to strengthen comital power and independence in Portugal that his gift to La Charité, not the mother abbey, is most logically explained. From 1100 on he had a firm line

27. On Henry's still imperfectly known genealogy, see M. Chaume, *Les premières croisades bourguignonnes au-delà des Pyrénées* in *Annales de Bourgogne,* t. 18, 1946, 161-5; Jean Richard, *Sur les alliances familiales des ducs de Bourgogne aux XIIe et XIIIe siècles,* ibid., t. 30, 1958, 37-46; S. de Vajay, *Bourgogne, Lorraine et Espagne au XIe siècle: Étiennette, dite de Vienne, comtesse de Bourgogne,* ibid., t. 32, 1960, 233-261.

28. Luiz Gonzaga de Azevedo, *História de Portugal,* Lisbon, 1935-42, III, chap. 9; T. Brochado de Sousa Soares, *Autonomia e organização* in *História da expansão portuguesa no mundo* (ed. Antonio Baião, H. Cidade and M. Múrias, Lisbon, 1937-40), I, 65-8; Damião Peres, *Como nasceu Portugal,* 51-68; Demetrio Mansilla, *Formación de la provincia bracarense después de la invasión árabe* in *Hispania sacra,* t. 14, 1961, 5-21.

of connection with the Cluniacs that Abbot Hugh would recognize, a distinctly Portuguese line quite separate from that of the monarch of imperial León.

3. 4 February 1102: SANTA JUSTA DE COIMBRA: Portugal, Beira Litoral, in the parish of this name adjoining that of the celebrated monastery of Santa Cruz, in the *suburbium* of Coimbra to the N or NW of the city.[29] This second of Cluny's Portuguese acquisitions was presented to La Charité by Bishop Maurice Bourdin and the cathedral chapter of Coimbra through a mediator, Gaufredus, who is probably to be identified with the Compostelan archdeacon of this name, a close associate of Bishop Diego Gelmírez.[30]. This is the only dependency the Cluniacs came to possess in trans-Douro Portugal, and it was evidently of modest size: we hear of the *ecclesia sancte Iuste* and its conversion into a hospice before the transfer, but not of appurtenances.

29. The precise location remains uncertain but the parish of this title adjoined the well-known one of Santa Cruz: see the boundary delimitation charter of the latter (June 1137 or 1139?) in E. A. REUTER, *Chancelarias medievais portuguesas*, Coimbra, 1938, no. 90; E. Austin O'MALLEY, *Tello and Theotonio, the Twelfthcentury Founders of the Monastery of Santa Cruz in Coimbra*, Washington, 1954 (Catholic University of America, Studies in Mediaeval History, N. S., XIV), 90-1. On the priory's history, cf. DA COSTA, *Cluny em Portugal*, 15, 21, 23, 39-40; P. DAVID, *Coïmbre in D.H.G.E.*, t. 13, 1956, 207, and *Études*, 235; Miguel DE OLIVEIRA, *História eclesiástica de Portugal*, 3rd. ed., Lisbon, 1958, 141.

30. Donation act, from the Livro Preto of the see of Coimbra, in *Docs. med. port., Particulares*, III, Lisbon, 1940, no. 523; T. DE SOUSA SOARES, *Alguns diplomas particulares dos séculos XI-XIII*, Coimbra, 1942, no. 13. The text is not included in LESPINASSE, *Cart. de la Charité* or *Chartes de Cluny*. The date, given by its editors as '1102(?)' or elsewhere as '1102-1103' because of uncertainty whether the year of the Incarnation should be reckoned from 1 January or 25 March in a Portuguese document of this period, can be fixed with some confidence as 1102. A diploma of 5 April 1102, by which Bishop Maurice of Coimbra grants one Seguin "unam terram pro almunia que est sub monasterio Sancte Iuste" (*Docs. med. port. Partic.*, III, no. 64), proves the church of Santa Justa then already belonged to a monastic house; and other Coimbran charters establish that by 18 August 1102 the capitular prior Martin of the Santa Justa donation charter had been supplanted by his successor Gonçalo, who in the Cluniac act of 4 February appears as still archdeacon. Compare, ibid., nos. 67 (23 April 1102), 72 (1 May 1102), and possibly 79 (31 July 1102), with no. 81 (18 August 1102: "Gunsaluo Menendiz prior sancte Marie"). DAVID, *Études*, 362, n. 1, assumes the intermediary Gaufredus was an otherwise unknown abbatial chamberlain of Cluny herself, but like Count Henry Maurice Bourdin would not have found *persona grata* a Cluniac envoy "accredité auprès du souverain" [i. e., Alfonso VI]. On Archdeacon Gaufredus (Gaufridus), cf. *Hist. Compost.*, I, 16,20; alternatively, even if not the "Gaufredus filius Rainaudi Gaudet" found in a late 11th-century La Charité charter (LESPINASSE, no. 38), this intermediary may have been sent from La Charité directly and may have come to Coimbra in connection with the collection of the *dizimos* of Entre Minho e Mondego.

As an episcopal cession Santa Justa is unique among grants of monasteries to Cluny anywhere in the Leonese-Castilian state; and its exemptive rights were narrowly restricted since the monks owed the bishop of Coimbra fidelity, obedience and respect for his *ius episcopale totum*, even though in return they were to be protected against attacks by *pagani* (Muslims) and lawless Christians. Presumably the expectation was that the monastic *ecclesia* would also serve as a parish church; by 1137 and ca. 1155 we have specific references to the *parochia sanctae Iuste*;[31] and this helps explain why the house has left no traces in the La Charité documents or the confirmation of her possessions in 1144 by Pope Lucius II.[32]

Nevertheless, small as Santa Justa de Coimbra may have been, it remains a Cluniac center until at least the last quarter of the 12th century; and the few texts that survive for its history, bearing as they do on resistance to the see of Coimbra in matters of boundaries and tithes,[33] warn against underestimating the degree of independence and vitality of this house.

4. 22 February 1109: San Vicente de Pombeiro: Galicia, dioc. and prov. Lugo, p. j. Monforte, ayunt. Pantón, ca. 17 kms. SW of Monforte de Lemos, at the confluence of the rivers Sil and Miño.[34] This ancient *monasterio propio* of the Leonese crown, originally a double house, while not in a class with such ranking Gallegan abbeys as Celanova or San Martín de Jubia, was nevertheless of distinct size and wealth at the time it was ceded to Cluny by the Infanta Urraca, daughter of Alfonso VI and *totius Galletie domina*.[35] The original *abadengo* of lands, churches and the subject-house of San Víctor *in sauto Papelli*[36] dated largely from munificent endowments by the nun-

31. Reuter, *Chancelarias*, no. 90; da Costa, *Cluny em Portugal*, no. 18.
32. Lespinasse, no. 167.
33. Reuter, loc. cit.; da Costa, nos, 18, 19.
34. Mapa Militar Itinerario de España, hoja 12; M. Amor Meilán, *Provincia de Lugo* in *Geografía general del Reino de Galicia*, ed. Francisco Carreras y Candi, III, 1929, 601 ff.; Pascual Madoz, *Diccionario geográfico-estadístico-histórico de España y sus posesiones de ultramar*, Madrid, 1845-50, t. 13, s. v. Pombeiro.
35. Donation act: *Chartes de Cluny*, IV, 3533 (wrongly dated '1079?'); Antonio de Yepes, *Corónica general de la Orden de San Benito*, Irache, 1609-21, V, 136-7; *E.S.*, XVII, 20-1. Both these authors are ignorant of the donation act.
36. Near the Miño and Villamirón; cf. the *privilegio* of 1 March 964, cited in the following note.

queen Goto (964) and King Vermudo II (997);[37] and included, as its confirmation in 1139 by Alfonso VII to Prior Hugh of Dôle makes clear, a broad *coto* primarily on the north side of the Sil where the two great rivers of Galicia join.[38]

Uncertainty regarding the true date of the donation charter, which the *Chartes de Cluny* incorrectly redates from 1079 to 1117,[39] has long obscured the historical setting of San Vicente's passage to Cluny; but David's restoration of the original *x aspada*, as demanded by the subscriptions, fixes it firmly in 1109[40] and makes it possible to relate Urraca's benefaction to the climactic events in the imperial Leonese succession crisis during the last months of Alfonso VI's reign, particularly as these relate to Galicia. It will be recalled that after the death of Count Raymond of Galicia in November 1107 the king-emperor had recognized as co-rulers of the county his daughter Urraca, Raymond's widow, and her infant son, Alfonso Raimúndez, the future Alfonso VII; and had provided that in the event of his mother's remarriage young Alfonso would receive exclusive power over Galicia.[41] But in the summer of 1108, following the unexpected death of his son and heir-designate Sancho at Uclés on 30 May, the grief-stricken, mortally ill monarch adopted a new plan of succession to the imperial throne. At a great assembly in Toledo of prelates and nobles Alfonso formally designated Urraca as the future ruler of the entire empire, her *dominium* to become effective from the moment of his death; at the same time he opened negotiations for her marriage to King Alfonso *el Batallador* of Aragón.[42]

As seen from Galicia this meant complete abandonment of the settlement of December 1107 and denial of Alfonso Raimúndez' right

37. Emilio SÁEZ, *Notas y documentos sobre Sancho Ordóñez, rey de Galicia* in *Cuad. hist. España*, no. 11, 1949, 91-2, and cf. 61-3; SÁNCHEZ BELDA, *Docs. reales Gal.*, no. 82; YEPES, *Corónica*, V, 438v-439.

38. YEPES, V, Apénd., 439v-440. Very few 12th-century Pombeiro charters are know but the more ample number from the 13th-14th centuries registered in E. LEIRÓS FERNÁNDEZ, *Catálogo de los pergaminos monacales del Archivo de la S. I. Catedral de Orense*, Santiago, 1951, could be used in mapping the patrimonies.

39. V, 3925.

40. DAVID, *Études*, 454, n. 4. The thirty year error still misleads H. DIENER, *Das Verhältnis Clunys zu den Bischöfen* in *Neue Forschungen über Cluny*, ed. G. TELLENBACH, Freiburg i, B., 1959, 312, n. 634.

41. J. M. RAMOS Y LOSCERTALES, *La sucesión del rey Alfonso VI* in *Anuario de historia del derecho español*, t. 13, 1936-41, 38-40; Claudio SÁNCHEZ ALBORNOZ, *La sucesión al trono en los reinos de León y Castilla*, Buenos Aires, 1945, 43-45 (*separata from Boletín de la Academia Argentina de Letras*, t. 14).

42. RAMOS, 76-88.

to full sovereignty over Galicia despite his mother's imminent second marriage, and the Alfonsine formula is known to have aroused violent opposition on the part of the great majority of the county's nobles under the leadership of the powerful Pedro Froílaz de Traba, Count of Galicia. Even before the authentic timing of the Pombeiro diploma was determined, Gallegan hostility was patent in the fact that upon the king-emperor's demise on 30 June or 1 July 1109 Froílaz immediately proclaimed the three-year-old Alfonso Raimúndez king of Galicia; and over the next few years, as readers of the *Historia Compostellana* well know, he and his followers fought indefatigably to defend the child-monarch's cause against Urraca and the imperialists, to say nothing of the pro-Aragonese and pro-Portuguese factions, in the wars and political disorders to which Galicia fell prey.[43]

With San Vicente's transfer to Cluny now known to have occurred in February 1109, midway between the summer convocation of 1108 at Toledo and the open rebellion of the Alfonsoraimundists in July 1109, we can see that the origins of the grant lie in the months just before Alfonso VI's death when he and his daughter must have been seeking ways to counteract the rising threat of Gallegan separatism. In the donation act Urraca declares she makes the gift acting upon her father's advice (*consilio patris mei*). While styling herself Lady of All Galicia, she ignores the fact that she was legally sharing her power with her son, who is never mentioned explicitly in the charter, even in the *pro remedio* clause where his father Count Raymond, the Infanta herself and her *parentes* appear. On the contrary, when in the eschatacol Urraca cites her descent *ex omni gente regali* through her parents, the Emperor Alfonso and Queen Constance, she is deliberately excluding Alfonso Raimúndez as of only partially royal ancestry. This neo-Gothicist deprecation of her son was a theme popular at the time with the high Leonese clergy and undoubtedly propagated, if not inspired, by Alfonso VI himself.[44] The charter of 22 February, thoroughly Gallegan in content, contains only Gallegan subscriptions but these are significantly few in number: beside the Infanta's own notary, only four, all ecclesiastics, confirm — Bishops Diego Gelmírez

43. *Hist. Compost.*, I, 46-48 (*E.S.*, XX, 94-99; P.L., t. 170, 935-8); Antonio López Ferreiro, *Historia de la S. A. M. Iglesia de Santiago de Compostela*, Santiago, 1898-1909, III, 317-331.

44. Ramos, 46-48, 58-9. Due to the erroneous date attached to the Pombeiro donation charter, Ramos fails to discuss this text; and in general his otherwise brilliant monograph omits all attention to Cluny's role in the succession crisis. I hope to examine this subject at an early date.

of Santiago, Maurice Bourdin of Braga, Diego III of Orense, and Abbot Pedro of Celanova. Not a single supporter from the county's aristocracy, least of all Pedro Froílaz, whose name appears so regularly in previous pergaminos of Raymond and Urraca!

The Pombeiro cession, under these circumstances, takes on a distinctly pro-imperial and anti-Alfonsoraimundist significance. If from Cluny's standpoint — and here again peninsular initiative, not Burgundian expansionism, underlies acquisition of a new priory — the Infanta acted out of piety to create a major dependency in Galicia (the very first since the abortive transfer of San Salvador de Villafrío over three decades earlier), for Urraca as for her aged father the motives were as much political as spiritual. In peninsular eyes the grant constituted an affirmation of her independent authority in Galicia, apart from her son's; it extended to the county Cluny's influence as a loyal champion of the imperial crown as an ecclesiastical countermove to the recalcitrance and threatened revolt of the Alfonsoraimundists. Never before, during the many years that Urraca and Count Raymond had ruled Galicia, had either found it desirable to become a formal benefactor of the Burgundian abbey. Now, Pombeiro forged a quite new personal bond between the empress-designate and Cluny, in effect giving assurance to Abbot Hugh that the ties of *societas* and *coniunctio* existing since Fernando I's reign between him and the Leonese sovereigns would be maintained, along with the annual census, by Alfonso VI's daughter and successor. And, no less important, Cluny's acceptance of a Gallegan monastery, San Vicente de Pombeiro, entailed, as I see it, her commitment to support Alfonso's final succession scheme and Urraca's legitimate right, not only to the imperial title, but to supremacy over Galicia, in the face of all opponents, including her son.

B. *The Cessions under Abbot Ponce de Melgueil*

5. 14 December 1113: SAN MARTÍN DE JUBIA: Galicia, dioc. Mondoñedo, prov. La Coruña, p. j. Ferrol, 6 kms. from El Ferrol, near the mouth of the Jubia river, in the rainy coastal district of extreme NW Galicia.[45] Granted to Abbot Ponce of Cluny and his successors, with the approval of bishops Diego Gelmírez of Compostela

45. Mapa Milit. Itin., hoja 2; José PÍA ANDRADE, *La iglesia románica de San Martín de Jubia* in *Cuadernos de estudios gallegos*, t. 1, 1944-5, 227-236; Eugenio CARRÉ ALDAO, *Provincia de La Coruña* in CARRERAS Y CANDI, *Geog. gen. Gal.*, II, 324-329.

and Munio of Mondoñedo, by Count Pedro Froílaz of Galicia, his brother Rodrigo and sisters Munia and Visclavara, both nuns, and all other heirs.[46] From its foundation, orginally as a double monastery sometime before 977 (the date of the oldest extant charter), this house had been the familial *monasterio propio* of the Counts of Traba, the ancestors of Pedro Froílaz and his co-donors, who — as the diplomatic collection, the most complete surviving for any Hispano-Cluniac priory, shows — endowed it generously with lands, *villas* and at least one subject monastery, San Julián de Mondego, near Miraflores.[47] The primacy of the abbey in this whole *comarca* of Galicia is apparent from the section of the *Historia Compostellana* possibly written by the same Canon Pedro Anaya or Anáiz of Santiago who subscribes the donation charter to Cluny;[48] this tells how in 1110 during Gelmírez' controversy with the see of Mondoñedo over the archpresbyterates of Besoucos, Seaya and Trasancos (in the last of which Jubia stood), the bishop forced all nobles, rectors of churches and abbots of the disputed districts to swear fealty to him in writing.[49] In reproducing these oaths the chronicler gives first and in full the special one taken by Abbot Nuño, who also reappears among the oath-takers of the Froílaz family, to which he must have belonged; but all other abbots, patently of minor houses, are thrown indiscriminately with the clergy and nobles into a common declaration. This confirms the impression gained from the *pergaminos:* that in San Martín de Jubia Cluny acquired a large, well-endowed abbey, one of the great foundations of contemporary Galicia.

The cession act for San Martín contains the names of four don-

46. Donation act: *Chartes de Cluny,* V, 3906. This text is omitted from the edition of the Jubia charters by Santiago MONTERO DÍAZ, *La colección diplomática de San Martín de Jubia* in *Boletín de la Universidad de Santiago de Compostela,* t. 7, 1935, n. 25, pp. 1-159 (also separatly); hence his superfluous speculation, p. 15, regarding the date of annexation to Cluny. On San Martín's history, see FLÓREZ, *E.S.,* XVIII, 61-2 and, above all, MONTERO DÍAZ, 3-41.

47. MONTERO DÍAZ, 57-117 (130 *pergaminos,* 15 May 977 to 8 November 1199); no diplomas are given for the 13th century but pp. 146-156 contain a register of documents dating after 1300. For San Martín's acquisition of San Julián de Mondego, see ibid., no. 9 (9 November 1086).

48. See the discussion of the *Historia*'s multiple authorship in Dom Anselm G. BIGGS, *Diego Gelmirez, First Archbishop of Compostela,* Washington, 1949 (Cath. Univ. of Amer., Stud. Med. Hist., N. S., XII), xiii-xxxiv; on Pedro Anáiz, xxvi, xxxii-xxxiii. Biggs ascribes much more of Book I to Pedro than does L. SALA BALUST, *Los autores de la "Historia Compostellana"* in *Hispania,* t. 3, 1943, 16-69.

49. *Hist. Compost.,* I, 35 (*E.S.* XX, 79-84; *P.L.,* t. 170, 930-3). On Gelmírez' struggles to capture the archpresbyterates, LÓPEZ FERREIRO, III, 258-67.

ors, but there can be little doubt that Count Pedro Froílaz himself was chiefly responsible. This would naturally follow from his position as family head, but it is corroborated by the fact that in the first nine months following the gift, the other three co-donors each made a supplementary grant to the new priory. On 31 July 1114 the *Deo uota* Munia gave various properties belonging to her;[50] on 11 August her sister, the *Deo uota* Visclavara Froílaz, did likewise;[51] and ten days later on 21 August Pedro's brother Rodrigo followed suit.[52] These three charters bear subscriptions of other members of the family; they seek assurance for the donors of rights of Cluniac *societas*, burial in the priory's church and liturgical intercession by its monks; and they all clearly reflect the outburst of pious enthusiasm that must have attended the arrival from Burgundy of Peter, the first prior. Count Pedro himself, it should be observed, makes no such further supplementary donation, never again ceding properties to Jubia until shortly before his death, on 27 February 1125:[53] clearly, his share in the cession of 1113 outweighed that of his kin.

There is, moreover, good reason to think that Pedro's decision to cede San Martín was a sudden one. In a diploma dated 26 December 1113, i. e. ,twelve days after the Jubia cession, Count Pedro's second wife, Countess Gontroda Rodríguez (often styled Mayor) gave the abbey, as she still assumed it to be, the *villa* 'Coina' for the soul of Sancho Petriz, her son by a previous marriage, and this document seems unaware of the house's imminent conversion into a Cluniac priory and specifically alludes to its continuing governance by abbots.[54] The fact that neither the countess nor Abbot Nuño, who confirms the charter, anticipated the change of status indicates that the cession to Cluny was almost certainly decided upon during the time when, as we know, Count Pedro and his brother Rodrigo were away from home, perhaps at Compostela.[55]

50. Montero Díaz, no. 21.
51. Montero Díaz, no. 22.
52. Montero Díaz, no. 23. On all three donations, see ibid., p. 16.
53. Montero Díaz, n. 30.
54. Montero Díaz, no. 19.
55. We cannot be sure where the Jubia donation act was drawn up but the presence of Bishops Bernard of Toledo, Gelmírez and Munio of Mondoñedo, and of three canons of Santiago, points to Compostela; the *Hist. Compost.* leaves obscure the itineraries of these prelates and of Pedro Froílaz during the last months of 1113 (cf. López Ferreiro, III, 404-7; Biggs, *Diego Gelmírez*, 97-9) but it would have been natural for the archbishop, after attending at the end of October the Council of Palencia from which Diego had absented himself, to visit the shrine of the Apostle.

The question then arises: since neither Froílaz nor his kinsmen had previously shown Cluny the slightest favor, and since from 1108 the abbey's adherence to the Urracan cause as manifest in its possession of San Vicente de Pombeiro had placed it in open opposition to the Alfonsoraimundist party, what happened to persuade the Count of Galicia to turn over to the Burgundian monks the monastery so long revered and patronized by his ancestors? The full story is much too long and complicated for presentation here, but the three central reasons must be noted. First, there is by this time Diego Gelmírez' radical change of front in dynastic politics. As the Pombeiro diploma, which he confirmed, discloses, the Compostelan prelate was originally a collaborator in the Alfonsine program for Galicia of setting aside Alfonso Raimúndez and subjecting the county to the rule of Urraca alone. But well before 1113, partly because like other Leonese-Castilian churchmen Diego could no longer accept the canonical validity of the Aragonese marriage, he had changed sides and was indeed responsible, along with Count Pedro, for the coronation of Alfonso Raimúndez at Santiago on 17 September 1111.[56] This association with the Alfonsoraimundist party was reinforced in August 1113 by the *convenio* drawn up at Compostela in which Pedro Froílaz and his principal supporters swore fealty to the Church of Santiago;[57] and in the same period both the count and other members of his family bestowed upon the apostolic see lands and churches that present a suggestive counterpart to the approaching Jubia donation to Cluny.[58] Diego thus became one of the two leaders of the Alfonsoraimundists; and a striking feature of the San Martín charter is the prominence given this prelate's approval of the cession, which represents a complete reversal of his stand just three years previous, when in his quarrel with Bishop Munio of Mondoñedo he had exacted, with Rome's backing, an oath of fidelity from Abbot Nuño of Jubia and insisted that the house, as belonging to his diocese, owed obedience to the see of Santiago.[59]

Second, the year 1113 sees renewed efforts by Pope Paschal II, who had already in 1110 condemned the Aragonese marriage, and by Archbishop Bernard of Toledo, to rally the Leonese-Castilian hierarchy for a restoration of peace on the basis of Urraca's permanent separation

56. López Ferreiro, III, 346-367; Biggs, 65-84.
57. López Ferreiro, III, 405-7; Biggs, 97-8.
58. *Hist. Compost.*, I, 93-4, 100; López Ferreiro, 404-5; Biggs, 274-5.
59. Cf. n. 49, *supra*.

from Alfonso I.[60] This represented the definitive abandonment of Alfonso VI's succession plan by the Spanish bishops.

And, lastly, but most immediately decisive for the Jubia donation, there is the dramatic reversal of Cluny's previous policy towards Alfonso Raimúndez. Since Alfonso VI's death and down to 1113, Cluny under Ponce de Melgueil had remained loyal to the king-emperor's final succession plan despite Urraca's chronic estrangements from her impossible spouse, her continuing childlessness, and El Batallador's characteristically Aragonese coolness towards the abbey. But by 1113 this position had become completely untenable: no child had been born or was likely to be born of the disastrous marriage; Urraca's own short-lived alliance in the spring of that year with the Alfonsoraimundists against her husband and his Castilian supporters disclosed her own growing conviction that her son by Count Raymond was destined to be her heir; and papal and episcopal condemnations made the Aragonese marriage impossible to accept even during the intervals when the volatile queen-empress temporarily returned to her consort. The papal pronouncement in effect returned the dynastic situation to what it would have been without the marriage and restored Alfonso Raimúndez as the successor to the throne.

The abbot who came to Spain as papal legate in the summer of 1113, I have contended elsewhere against Flórez whom all scholars have followed, was not the unknown Italian Helmengaud of San Michele della Chiusa but Ponce of Cluny.[61] In my opinion, one of the chief accomplishments of this journey, which took the abbot all the way to Compostela, was his meeting there with the two leaders of the Alfonsoraimundist party: Diego Gelmírez, the old friend and *socius* of Cluny, and Count Pedro Froílaz. Although we have no direct testimony, the strong friendship now established between the Burgundian abbey and the Froílaz clan has left clear signs in the donation soon after of San Martín de Jubia and the henceforth close ties between this powerful family and the Cluniacs. This does not mean that Cluny abandoned support of Urraca, with whom indeed her relations are close for the remainder of the reign. But it does mean Burgundian acceptance of Alfonso Raimúndez as her successor, and explains why Pedro Froílaz, having gained with Gelmírez' aid, the abbey's influential backing for

60. López Ferreiro, III, 397-9, 424-5; Biggs, 95-99.

61. See my *The Spanish Journey of Abbot Ponce of Cluny* in *Ricerche di storia religiosa,* t. 1, 1957, 311-319; for the long-established view, which also places the visit in 1112, cf. López Ferreiro, III, 386-96; Biggs, 89-90.

his protégé, must have been eager to seal his new alliance with Abbot Ponce through entry into Cluny's privileged *societas* on the basis of a major monastic benefaction.

6. 8 July 1117: SANTA MARÍA DE FERREIRA: Galicia, dioc. and prov. Lugo, p. j. Monforte, ayunt. Pantón, ca. 10 kms. W of Monforte de Lemos.[62] The donation charter, by which Count Fernán Fernándiz and his wife, the Infanta Elvira, daughter of Alfonso VI, granted Cluny and Abbot Ponce one-quarter of this familial monastery, with its appurtenant houses, churches, vineyards and lands, is the only charter extant for the Cluniac period of this house, which by 1175 was in the possession of Cistercian nuns.[63]

The Gallegan count Fernán Fernándiz appears frequently among the foremost magnates at Urraca's court. Whether he is the same man who between 1108 and 1112 was in Count Henry of Portugal's service and can be found ruling Lamego in 1111, and who from 1112, the year of Henry's death, disappears from the Portuguese *pergaminhos*,[64] is uncertain but probable enough on chronological grounds and in view of Fernán's later connection with Toro, an area of much interest to Henrician expansionist schemes. There can, however, be no doubt that he is the count of this name who discloses pro-Cluniac leanings in his confirmation on 1 May 1112 of the diploma by which Countess Aldonza, daughter of Count Gómez Díaz and widow of Count Munio Fernándiz (possibly Fernán's brother) gave the Burgundian abbey her house of San Salvador de Villaverde in the diocese of Astorga.[65] It would be helpful to know the precise date of Fernán's marriage to the illegitimate daughter of Alfonso VI by Jimena Muñoz, but all we can be sure of is that soon after the death of her first husband, the celebrated Count Raymond IV de St-Gilles in 1105 in Syria,[66] Elvira must have returned to Spain. By 1115 both Fernán himself, then governing Toro as its count, and Elvira can be found among Urraca's loyal supporters in the dynastic conflict: both attend in that

62. Mapa Milit. Itin., hoja 12; MADOZ, *Diccionario,* VIII, 47. This house should not be confused with the nearby Santa María de Pallarés (YEPES, *Corónica,* IV, 302-303v), which never belonged to Cluny.

63. *Chartes de Cluny,* V, 3927.

64. *Docs. med. port. Régios,* I, 1, nos. 13, 21, 24, 28, 32, 36. Gonzaga DE AZEVEDO, *História de Portugal,* III, 108.

65. ESCALONA, *Hist. Sahagún,* no. 149; *Chartes de Cluny,* V, 3900.

66. *L'art de vérifier les dates,* Paris, 1770, 742; Laurita and John HILL, *Raymond IV de St-Gilles,* Toulouse, 1959, 20-21, 140.

year the extraordinary assembly of the imperialists at Oviedo, where Fernán was one of the three counts coming *de campis Zamorae et Tauri.*[67] In 1116 he was in the queen-empress's company when on 20 January she granted San Isidro de Dueñas the *aldea* of "Vellosiello de cebico de la torre" (Cevico de la Torre) and the monastery of San Torcaz;[68] and again on 15 October when she gave Sahagún a charter confirming its immunities and granting its abbot the right of coinage.[69] Most pertinent of all, on 4 July 1117, just four days before transferring his quarter-share of Ferreira, Fernán subscribes Urraca's donation charter giving San Isidro de Dueñas the *villa* of Baños.[70]

Whether both Urraca's and Fernán's July donations should be taken as more than related expressions of gratitude for Cluniac support in general or ought to be linked more specifically to possible Cluniac intervention in bringing about the truce then prevailing between Urraquists and Alfonsoraimundists, we have no means of determining. Certainly, the count's friendship with the abbey can be understood also in terms of his friendship, if not relationship by marriage, with the Beni Gómez — the most fervently pro-Cluniac of all the great Leonese noble families; and of his wife's probable attachment to the abbey not only through her imperial father but also through her mother Jimena Muñoz, who in 1120 gave Abbot Ponce the Asturian abbey of Santa Cruz de Castañeda.[71] In short, everything places the Count of Toro in the narrow circle of Leonese and Gallegan aristocratic families upon which, along with the imperial dynasty itself, Cluny was dependent for her expansion in Hispania.

The causes for the failure of the Ferreira donation remain obscure. In spite of his giving a quarter share, Fernán assumes the right to place the monastery as a whole under the authority of the Cluniac abbot. Presumably he expected the other three-quarters to pass into Burgundian hands, and it may be that other members of the family, possibly including the Rodrigo Fernándiz whose name follows his own in the 1115 list of magnates at Oviedo from Zamora and Toro, did not fulfill his expectations.[72] Whatever the reason, something went

67. J. D. Mansi, *Sacrorum conciliorum nova et amplissima collectio,* Florence-Venice, 1759-1798, XXI, 134.
68. Madrid, Acad. Hist., Colección Velázquez, t. IV, no. 1397.
69. Escalona, no. 149.
70. Col. Velázquez, t. IV, no. 1395.
71. *Chartes de Cluny,* V, 3948. Note also Fernán's subscription to Urraca's *real privilegio* of 4 January 1118 giving the monastery of San Martín de Frómista to the Cluniac priory of San Zoil de Carrión (Yepes, VI, esc. xviii).
72. Mansi, loc. cit.

wrong: eight years later Honorius II's bull of 1125 confirming a long list of Cluniac possessions, omits Ferreira from among those in Spain;[73] and a similar silence marks all subsequent papal confirmations, medieval lists of dependencies, and the visitation and general-chapter records. After 1117 Santa María is not heard of again until 1175 when it has become a Cistercian nunnery subject to Meira.[74]

C. *The Cessions under Abbot Peter the Venerable*

7. 20 February 1125: SAN PEDRO DE VALVERDE: Galicia, dioc. and prov. Lugo, p. j. Monforte, ayunt. Monforte de Lemos, 6 kms. N of the town.[75] This *monasterium s. Petri de Valle Viridi,* so often confused by both medieval and modern writers with the Cluniac priory in the diocese of Astorga of San Salvador de Villaverde (*de Villa Viridi in Valle Vidriale*),[76] was given to Cluny by Munio Romániz and his wife María Pérez.[77] The house can be traced back to at least 1115 when the same principals with their children gave it and its abbot Gudesteo the church of San Pedro de Canabal in the Tierra de Lemos.[78] This was a church Queen Urraca had previously bestowed upon

73. P. JAFFÉ, *Regesta pontificum romanorum,* Leipzig, 1885-88, I, no. 7193; *P.L.,* t. 166, 1225.

74. RISCO, *E. S.,* XLI, 31-2; M. COCHERIL, *L'Ordre de Cîteaux au Portugal* in *Studia monastica,* t. I, 1959, 53.

75. Mapa Milit. Itin., hoja 12; MADOZ, *Dicc.,* XV, 499; AMOR MEILÁN, *Geog. gen. Gal.,* III, 561-3, 577; *Enciclopedia universal ilustrada europeo-americana,* Barcelona, 1907-30, t. 66, 858, col. 1.

76. *Chartes de Cluny,* V, 3900, p. 251. Examples of this confusion can be found in the printed text of Paschal II's bull *Apostolicae sedis auctoritate* of 7 November 1114 *(Bull. Clun.,* 37; *P.L.* t. 163, 358); Fr. DE BERGANZA, *Antigüedades de España,* Madrid, 1719-21, I, 13; A. HERCULANO, *História de Portugal,* Lisbon, 1914-16, II, 245; F. FITA, *El concilio nacional de Burgos en 1080* in *Bol. r. Acad. hist.,* t. 49, 1906, 363, miscaptions 'Villaveza de Valverde' Alfonso VI's donation of San Salvador de Villaverde to Sahagún on 25 January 1100 (ESCALONA, *Hist. Sahagún,* no. 133; *Chartes de Cluny,* V, 3725); EVANS, *Romanesque Architecture of the Order of Cluny,* 47, omits Valverde while listing a non-existent 'Villaverde Palomar' and confusing San Salvador de Villaverde with Villafrío. Other examples could be cited.

77. The donation charter, if still among the pergaminos of Valverde preserved with those of San Vicente de Monforte, where Risco saw it (*E.S.,* XLI, 12), remains unedited; but my search some years ago did not locate it in A. H. N. Clero, legs. 778-9 (San Vicente de Monforte). For this house alone of the Gallegan group the donor's text did not survive in Cluny's archives, which explains its absence from the *Chartes de Cluny.* My knowledge of it depends upon Risco's all too brief résumé, which says nothing about intercessional provisions or the possibly illuminating subscriptions.

78. *E.S.,* XLI, 5-6.

Munio Romániz for his *buenos servicios* in her cause,[79] which proves that he must have been one of the few Gallegans loyal to her in these years. Munio's name occurs also in an Urracan diploma issued to the abbey of Samos on 31 May 1112.[80]

Munio Romániz must therefore have been a good *urraquista* and likely to be a friend of Cluny. He was not a count or even, so far as we can tell, a magnate of high rank; and he was so little connected with the imperial court that I have not found his subscription in any other *real pergamino* than that of 1112. By 1125 the civil wars were long over and Alfonso VII, ruling jointly with his mother, was little more than a year away from her death and his imperial coronation at León. Lifelong adherence to the imperial house, the possible example of nearby San Vicente de Pombeiro, perhaps above all the pervasive influence of Cluny in this corner of Galicia, evident also in the Villafrío and Ferreira donations — these exhaust the discernible motives other than the usual ones of piety. Munio's cession of San Pedro de Valverde received prompt papal recognition, for as the *obedientia de Valvert* it is already listed among the peninsular priories Honorius II confirmed to Cluny by his bull of 2 April 1125;[81] henceforth, for the rest of the Middle Ages, it appears regularly among the Luso-Gallegan dependencies.

8. 26 July 1126: SAN SALVADOR DE BUDIÑO: Galicia, dioc. Tuy, prov. Pontevedra, p. j. Tuy, mun. Porriño, ca. 9 kms. N of the city of Tuy and the Miño, close to its tributary the Louro and not far from the present Portuguese frontier.[82] Ceded by Count Gómez Núñez and his brother Fernando, this abbey had been from its foundation (at an unknown date) in the family of the donors; but on the death without direct heir of their uncle, Count Fernando, one-half of it had escheated by judicial decision to the crown.[83] It was after Alfonso VII's restoration of this lost portion to Count Gómez in a lost *real privilegio* that the two brothers acted to give Cluny the entire monastery, with its ancient *coto*, and all churches and lands within and without these limits.

79. Ibid.
80. Plácido ARIAS, *Historia del real monasterio de Samos*, Santiago de Compostela, 1950, 110-111.
81. *Bull. Clun.*, 42-3; *P.L.*, t. 166, 1225.
82. Mapa Milit. Itin., hoja 22; MADOZ, *Dicc.*, IV, 472.
83. *Chartes de Cluny*, V, 3993. History and bibliography in M. ALAMO, I. *Budiño, San Salvador de* in *D.H.G.E.*, t. 10, 1938, 1045-6.

Count Gómez Núñez, the principal agent of this extensive grant, since at the time he was in possession of three-quarters of San Salvador, is well-known as the count of Toroño, a district lying immediately north of Tuy, and as principal Gallegan protagonist in the dynastic wars under Urraca.[84] The *Historia Compostellana* describes him as one "qui fauebat regi puero et rebellabat reginae, potens situ et munimine castellorum et multitudine equitum atque peditum";[85] and most historians class him with Count Pedro Froílaz and Bishop Diego Gelmírez as a chief of the Alfonsoraimundists.[86] But the diplomatic sources reveal that in fact this mighty lord of the Gallegan marchlands of the Miño skilfully maintained ties with the rulers of Portugal no less than with the partisans of young Alfonso, and shifted his allegiance from one side to the other of the river as his own interests and survival dictated. This makes it necessary to define narrowly his exact political orientation in July 1126 so as to determine whether Gómez Núñez' donation of Budiño should be linked to Alfonso VII's imperial coronation at León some five months previous; or whether, in view of Queen Teresa's grant of Santa María de Vimieiro the very next year, we are dealing with a concerted Luso-Gallegan Teresist attempt to secure Cluniac support against both the Leonese king-emperor and the rising power of Alfonso Henriques in Portugal.

The first testimony we have to the political oscillations of the Count of Toroño comes from the diplomas of Count Henry of Portugal where he appears as a prominent *mesnadeiro:* in 1110-1111 as governor of the fortress of São Cristóvão, near Cerveira,[87] and in 1112 as holder of the high office of *mordomo-mor* (*maiordomus palatii ipsius comitis*).[88] Not long after Henry's death in the latter year Gómez clearly abandoned Teresa and the Portuguese court, for by 1115 he turns up among the select group of leading Gallegan barons whom Diego Gelmírez selected as his sworn defenders in the event of Ur-

84. López Ferreiro, *Hist. iglesia de Santiago,* III, chaps. 14-17; IV, chaps. 2, 6; Gonzaga de Azevedo, *Hist. Portugal,* III, 106-108; *Chronica Adefonsi imperatoris,* ed. Luis Sánchez Belda, Madrid, 1950, 234-5.

85. I, 111.

86. E. g., López Ferreiro, loc. cit.

87. *Docs. med. port. Régios,* I. 1, nos. 17, 18, 20, 24; cf. Gonzaga de Azevedo, III, 107.

88. *Docs. med. port. Régios,* I, 1, no. 30, reproduced in facsimile in *História de Portugal,* ed. Damião Peres, Barcelos, 1928-35, I, 495. Gómez Núñez also confirms nos. 19, 25, 26 and 32 (if this last document is of 10 May 1112 and not, as Rui de Azevedo now argues in op. cit., I, 2, 1962, 570-6, of 1117).

raca's violation of her latest pact with the Compostelan prelate.[89] In 1116, when Urraca came to Galicia to suppress the Alfonsoraimundists, she launched a major campaign against the Count of Toroño, only to be frustrated by the intervention in his behalf of Pedro Froílaz and — significantly — Queen Teresa of Portugal.[90] Gómez Núñez participated in the suppression of the communal revolt of 1117 at Compostela;[91] and in 1118, when the queen-empress and her son's partisans had joined in a campaign to drive Alfonso of Aragon from Castile, he fought in the allied army and doubtless accompanied its victorious march to Toledo, where it acclaimed Alfonso Raimúndez emperor: *rex Hispaniae*.[92] But in 1120 a very different picture emerges. In April of that year Teresa's diplomas suddenly begin to carry the subscription of Count Gómez,[93] and despite his presence at Compostela in 1121, when Gelmírez convoked the oath-takers of 1115,[94] his political attachments were clearly with Portugal and so continued to 1125 during the time when Teresa was successfully occupying the territories of Tuy and Orense.[95]

This might be taken to indicate a Portuguese background for the transfer of San Salvador de Budiño; but in fact the signs are unmistakable that shortly before his benefaction of 26 July 1126 Gómez had once more changed camps and aligned himself with the newly crowned Alfonso VII of Leon. The count's last appearance in a Teresan *pergaminho* falls on 2 September 1125.[96] By the spring of 1126, when shortly after his mother's death Alfonso VII faced a serious revolt in Galicia under the leadership of the noble Arias Pérez, the *Historia Compostellana* tells us that the king-emperor entrusted Bishop Gelmírez and Count Gómez Núñez of Toroño with its suppression. Both men discharged this mission with success, besieging Lobeira and other

89. *Hist. Compost.*, I, 104 (*E.S.*, XX, 100; *P.L.*, t. 170, 1000 C, with error 'Vermiz' for 'Gómez'); López Ferreiro, III, 371-2. 'Gómez' name occurs as late as 1 August 1112 in Teresa's *carta de couto* to the monastery of Santa Maria de Pombeiro, conc. Felgueiras (not to be confused with the Cluniac priory of San Vicente): *Docs. med. port. Régios*, I, 1, no. 35; António da Assunção Meireles, *Memórias do mosteiro de Pombeiro*, Lisbon, 1942, 121-2.

90. *Hist. Compost.*, I, 111 (*E.S.*, XX, 217; *P.L.*, t. 170, 1009 B); López Ferreiro, III, 458.

91. *Hist. Compost.*, I, 116 (*E.S.*, XX, 245-6; *P.L.*, t. 170, 1027 D).

92. *Hist. Compost.*, I, 117 (*E.S.*, XX, 249-250; *P.L.*, t. 170, 1030 A); López Ferreiro III, 496.

93. *Docs. med. port. Régios*, I, 1, nos. 53, 58, 60, 69, 70.

94. *Hist. Compost.*, II, 42; López Ferreiro, IV, 45-6.

95. Peres, *Como nasceu Portugal*, 74-5.

96. *Docs. med. port. Régios*, I, 1, no. 70.

strongholds of Arias, and forcing the obstreperous magnate into surrender.[97] Two other episodes of the same year confirm this imperial allegiance. Gómez was present in the great assembly of Gallegan bishops and nobles at Zamora, which offered loyal submission to Alfonso VII.[98] He may or may not have been present at the conference nearby at Ricobayo where Teresa, her consort Count Fernando Pérez de Traba (Pedro Froílaz' son and successor) and other Portuguese leaders agreed to a peace pact of limited duration with Alfonso VII; but in any case his alignment with Alfonso must have been strengthened by the resultant Portuguese evacuation at this time of Toroño, Tuy and other districts north of the Miño.[99]

Uncertain as the precise chronology of events in 1125-1126 remains, the general sequence is clear enough to show that when Count Gómez Núñez gave Cluny his family monastery of Budiño he was an adherent of Alfonso VII and thus of the Leonese-Cluniac alliance associated with the emperors since the time of Fernando I. It must have been in the spring or early summer of 1126, following his abandonment in September of Teresa, and after having given proof by the suppression of the Arias Pérez revolt of his loyalty to the newly crowned Alfonso VII, that the Count of Toroño received from his grateful sovereign the lost half of the familial monastery of San Salvador de Budiño, as recounted in the donation act. The now lost diploma effecting this restoration contained also, at Gómez' petition, a royal *cotización* of the house's ancient bounds, as we learn from the confirmation of these in Alfonso VII's *real privilegio* of August 1142, issued at Peter the Venerable's request in the course of the abbot's Spanish tour.[100] Then, at the end of July, Gómez Núñez, once more back in Toroño from the northern wars and the great assembly at Zamora, acted with his brother Fernando to give the entire house and *abadengo* to the monks of Cluny. In this chronological context the desire to confirm the new allegiance to Alfonso VII by simultaneously cultivitating the friendship of his Burgundian protector appears decisive.

97. *Hist. Compost.*, II, 84; López Ferreiro, IV, 126 (where Gómez González is wrongly given instead of Gómez Núñez, an error shared by Biggs, *Diego Gelmírez*, 195).

98. *Chron. Adef. imp.*, I, 5 (p. 9): "comes Gomez Munici".

99. Luis G. de Valdeavellano, *Historia de España*, 2nd ed., Madrid, 1955, I, 2, 427-8.

100. *Chartes de Cluny*, V, 4073: "per eosdem terminos quibus rogatu comitis Gomes, quando illud possidebat, cautaui".

The ties of benefactorial *societas,* once thus established, outlived the political alignment. For when, ca. 1138-1140, King Alfonso Henriques invaded Galicia in an effort to realize his mother's cherished dream of a Portuguese Alem-Minho, Count Gómez broke with Alfonso VII and once again took up arms under a Portuguese banner; [101] but this time to the ruin of his fortunes, for after the king-emperor had defeated Alfonso and his Gallegan allies, he dispossessed Gómez Núñez of the County of Toroño and all his lands. The old warrior fled for his life, not to Portugal but to Burgundy, there to end his days in the habit of St. Benedict as a monk of Cluny.[102]

9. 23 May 1127: SANTA MARÍA DE VIMIEIRO: Portugal, dioc. Braga, prov. Minho, distr. and conc. Braga, freg. Vimieiro, some 6 kms. to the SW of the Minhotan metropolis.[103] The monastery, then undergoing *restauratio,* was given with all its lands, churches and *couto* to Abbot Peter the Venerable and Cluny by Queen Teresa, daughter of the Emperor Alfonso VI, acting through the abbot's intermediary, the chamberlain Stephen.[104] This cession certainly sprang in part from the Portuguese queen's long-standing devotion to the Burgundian congregation, inherited from her father and confirmed by her late husband, Count Henry. One can sense also the shadows cast by her half-sister Urraca's death some fourteen months before and her own advancing years, in the detailed stipulations regarding intercession and commemoration. But it is necessary also to understand the political conditions under which this donation, the first of a monastic

101. *Chron. Adef. imp.,* I, 74, 77.

102. Ibid., I, 87: "...et rex abiecit a se comitem Rodericum et comitem Gomez Nunnii, pro eo quod ipsi inmiserant discordiam inter imperatorem et regem. Comes Gomez Nunii, ut cognovit se esse reum, verecundatus est, et transiens fugiendo montes Pirineos, vellet nollet, quia non erat ei locus ad habitandum, fecit se monachus in monasterio Cluniacensi." SÁNCHEZ BELDA, xli, n. 27, thinks the documentary sources do not support a collaboration of Gómez Núñez with Afonso Henriques but the reported flight to Cluny rings too true to be without foundation: probably the chronology of the count's rebellion against Alfonso VII requires further study.

103. *Grande enc. port. e bras.,* t. 36, 150-1.

104. Donation act: *Docs. med. port. Régios,* I, 1, no. 75; *Chartes de Cluny* V, 3995. The version [B], a 12th-century copy, found by Rui de Azevedo in Arch. Hist. Nac., Madrid, and unknown to Bruel, whose copy was no older than [B], preserves a fuller text: see now *Régios,* I, 2, 1962, 590-2. Cf. also the confirmation by Afonso Henriques, 23 May 1146: op. cit., I, 1, no. 24. The chamberlain Stephen is probably the same man as the prior of San Zoil de Carrión whom Queen Urraca calls "fidelissimo amico meo" (4 January 1118: YEPES, *Corónica,* VI, no xviii). On the history of the priory, cf. DA COSTA, *Ordem de Cluny,* 16-17, 35-39; idem, *Bispo D. Pedro,* II, 96.

house in Portugal since Santa Justa in 1102, and the only one given directly to the mother-house, was made.

In the long story of Teresa's ultimately frustrated effort to annex at least southern Galicia to the nascent Portuguese kingdom, the year 1127 set in motion a fateful series of events that leads straight to the battle of São Mamede (1128) and the queen's definitive elimination from the Portuguese scene by her son Afonso Henriques and his backers.[105] In spite of her pact with Alfonso VII at Ricobayo in 1126 — and perhaps because the *tempus marcatum* of this agreement had expired — Teresa made war upon the king-emperor in 1127, sending her troops across the Miño, seizing Tuy and other districts, including presumably the county of Toroño with its new Cluniac priory at Budiño, and in general re-establishing the control over the area she had exercised during the last half-dozen years of Urraca's reign.[106] Alfonso VII, however, once he was free to leave Castile after concluding the Peace of Támara with Alfonso el Batallador, moved swiftly westward and in a lightning campaign of six weeks expelled Teresa's armies from Galicia, invaded Entre Minho e Douro, and forced the chagrined Portuguese queen into renewed submission to his authority.[107]

Once again precise chronology is difficult to achieve; but the six weeks war can safely be set in the second half of the summer of 1127, since until July Alfonso was detained in the East fighting the Aragonese. What remains unclear is, first, how long before midsummer the Portuguese forces crossed the Miño, and, secondly, how long even before this Teresa had decided upon war with Leon. The best we can now say is that on 23 May, the date of the Vimieiro charter, the queen must have been either actively preparing for, or actually in the midst of, her occupation of Galicia. It is even possible that the presence of the chamberlain Stephen in her company at this time is to be accounted for by his having entered Portuguese-held territory while making a visitation of the new priory of Budiño, acquired the previous year.

Thus, the donation of Santa María de Vimieiro, made directly to Cluny, and not to La Charité, might seem to find its natural explanat-

105. A. Herculano, *História de Portugal,* Lisbon, 1914-16, II, 116-120; Peres, *Como nasceu Portugal,* 75-82; Valdeavellano, I, 2, 423-8.

106. *Hist. Compost.*, II, 85; *Chron. Adef. imp.*, I, 5; Biggs, *Diego Gelmirez,* 195-6.

107. Valdeavellano, I, 2, 427-8.

ion in Teresa's break with Alfonso VII in 1127 and her hope of securing Cluniac sympathy in her defense of Portuguese autonomy from Leon, the same hope that had inspired her husband Count Henry and herself a quarter-century before in their transfer of Rates to La Charité. But on reflection this seems improbable, for the abbey's interests and tradition were far too closely bound to the imperial Leonese house to encourage Portuguese secessionist hopes. Indeed, Teresa's grant makes so little political sense in this period of open warfare with Alfonso VII, that it seems necessary to suppose her original promise of the Minhotan *real mosteiro* was made some time before the formal drawing up of the donation act on 23 May 1127, which indeed mentions the *restauratio* already under way. The logical moment for the pledge would seem to be during the period of reconciliation between queen and emperor after their meeting in 1126 at Ricobayo where they arranged the peace pact.

On this assumption, the donation to Cluny was promised during the latter half of the year 1126, partly perhaps out of gratitude for the chamberlain Stephen's possible aid in the negotiations, but also as a visible token of Teresa's submission to the imperial authority with which Cluny was aligned. By the spring of 1127, with Portuguese troops across the Miño, circumstances were very different, and when in May Stephen arrived to take formal possession of Vimieiro, Cluny's third and last Portuguese acquisition, the political situation was the reverse of that prevailing when the house may have been promised. It can then be concluded that Queen Teresa, faithful to her word and mindful also of the intercessional benefits so strongly emphasized in her diploma, carried out her earlier commitment.

If this reasoning is sound, the grants of Vimieiro and Budiño have much the same background. Both would have originated in mid-1126 during the honeymoon months just after Alfonso VII's coronation, with their promise of restored peace and unity in the Leonese empire. And both would have rewarded Cluny for friendly assistance in promoting good relations with the king-emperor while publicly proclaiming the donors' association with the paramount ecclesiastical protector of Leonese imperialism.

II

In the light of the foregoing survey, and more specifically on the basis of the nine donation charters, which are historically illuminating even where in the cases of San Salvador de Villafrío and Santa

María de Ferreira the cession may have been only briefly, if ever, actually realized, certain conclusions may now be essayed regarding the chronology, geographical distribution, origins, and principal characteristics of Cluny's expansion in medieval Galicia and Portugal.

(1) With the exception of the early, ephemeral Villafrío grant of 1075, which properly belongs to the abbey's Leonese rather than Luso-Gallegan penetration, the establishment of Cluniac dependencies in westernmost Iberia falls within a single quarter-century between 1100 and 1127. In Cluniac terms, this covers the last decade of Hugh I, the abbatiate of Ponce de Melgueil, and the initial years of Peter the Venerable. In Leonese-Castilian annals, it embraces Alfonso VI's declining years, the reign of Urraca, and the initial biennium of Alfonso VII. We are therefore dealing with a significantly narrow span of time.

(2) The geographical pattern of the Galaico-Portuguese acquisitions differs perceptibly from that found in the other two chief areas of Cluniac concentration below the Pyrenees, the Tierra de Campos and the Rioja Alta. In contrast with the clustering in these regions of numerous large and small priories and sub-priories, dominated by the great centers of San Isidro de Dueñas, San Zoil de Carrión and Santa María de Nájera, the houses of Portugal and Galicia are dispersed — despite the admitted concentration near Monforte de Lemos of Pombeiro, Valverde and the lost Ferreira. No Portuguese sub-priories of Rates, Santa Justa or Vimieiro have turned up, while those of San Víctor *in sauto Papelli,* the only one known for Pombeiro, and such minor houses under Jubia as San Julián de Mondego San Salvador de Mugía, Santiago de Franza and others, were quite insignificant.[108] As regards diocesan distribution, the bishoprics involved are, in Portugal, Braga (Rates, Vimieiro) and Coimbra (Santa Justa) but not Porto; and in Galicia, Tuy (Budiño), Mondoñedo (Jubia) and Lugo (Pombeiro, Valverde, and the evanescent Villafrío and Ferreira) but not Orense or Compostela. In view of frequent generalizations regarding Cluniac influence at Santiago and the alleged deliberate planting of priories along the pilgrimage road, it should be observed (i) that no bishop of Compostela, including the notorious Cluniophile Diego Gelmírez, however generous in other respects to

108. Jubia acquired after passing into Cluniac hands, Mugía (1114), Franci (1114), San Andrés de Teijido and San Pelayo de Ortigueira (1162), and San Juliá de Narón (1163): Montero Díaz, *Colección diplomática de Jubia*, nos. 22, 23, 58,6

the abbey, ever bestowed upon the Burgundian congregation a single monastery or even lands within the diocese; and (ii) that of the Gallegan cessions, including the four in the Lugo area, not one was actually located on the great highway or even close to it. None, therefore, find mention in Uría's detailed reconstruction of the Gallegan stations.[109]

(3) While the donors of the nine cessions include Queen Teresa of Portugal, and the hand of Alfonso VI is undeniable in the Pombeiro grant of 1109, it is significant that neither Alfonso VI in his own name, Urraca after her accession, Alfonso VII nor Afonso Henriques appears among them. Four members of the imperial Leonese house are, however, present: Teresa as infanta (Rates) and queen (Vimieiro), Henry of Portugal (Rates), Urraca as *señora de Galicia* (Pombeiro) and the Infanta Elvira (Ferreira). Several counts or members of comital families are prominent: Eņeco Vermudo, son of Count Vermudo (Villafrío), Count Pedro Froílaz, his brother Rodrigo and sisters Munia and Visclavara (Jubia) Count Gómez Núñez and his brother Fernando (Budiño). Munio Romániz, who gave Valverde, was a humbler baron in Urraca's service; Bishop Maurice Bourdin of Coimbra (Santa Justa), the unique episcopal benefactor, a close confidant of Count Henry. The donations then can be ascribed to a quite small circle consisting mostly of non-reigning members of the royal house and a few comital families, although subsequent grants to the priories disclose a much broader range of fervor for Cluny on less exalted levels.[110].

(4) Of all the Luso-Gallegan acquisitions only Rates and Santa Justa were not already monastic communities at the time of transfer to Cluny. Although Henry and Teresa claim to have built the former from the ground up, the church was an ancient one; and Santa Justa had been an *ecclesia* before Maurice Bourdin converted it into a *hospicium* and gave it to La Charité. Teresa reconstructed but does not claim to have founded Vimieiro; and all six Gallegan donations were of existing *monasterios propios*. Except for San Martín de Jubia and (much less fully) San Vicente de Pombeiro, documented details of the *abadengo* each priory possessed are largely lacking, but the donors' allusions to *heredades, terrae* (*cultae, populatae, incultae, non popula-*

109. L. Vázquez de Parga, J. M. Lacarra, and J. Uría Ríu, *Las peregrinaciones a Santiago de Compostela*, Madrid, 1948-49, II, chaps. 14-17.

110. This last point comes out very strongly from an examination of Montero Díaz' edition of the Jubia *pergaminos*.

tae), meadows, vineyards, villages, churches, *cotos* and rights prove temporal endowments of some amplitude.

A little light upon relative size and wealth is shed by (i) the incomplete surviving statistics for the amount of annual census each priory came to pay the mother abbey from the time of Peter the Venerable; and (ii) what came to be the fixed norm for the number of monks in each chapter. The donation acts of Valverde, Budiño and Vimieiro specify a rate of one-half mark a year for the first two, and a full mark for Vimieiro, this last to be increased (to judge by other cases, perhaps doubled) following completion of its rebuilding. Such figures, running well below the 4 marks contemplated in 1132 for Sahagún, the 10 gold florins paid by Carrión or the 5 marks of Nájera, can be compared with the standard size assigned each community, although these quotas must be used with caution since they have not yet been shown to date earlier than the middle 13th century.[111] Valverde at this time was supposed to maintain 4 monks, Budiño 6, Vimeiro 3, Pombeiro 8 (or 12), and Jubia 6, in contrast with the 25 of Carrión and Nájera's 30.[112] Correlation of these two types of data can be only approximate, since Vimieiro, for example, with only 3 monks, paid a higher census than Valverde or Budiño, with 4 and 6 respectively. But these figures agree with deductions based on the diplomatic sources and on statistical comparisons with the abbey's other peninsular holdings, in presenting the Luso-Gallegan priories as by Hispano-Cluniac standards well-established communities of substantial wealth and importance. None of them, even the larger, like Rates, Budiño, Jubia, Valverde, Vimieiro or Pombeiro, ranked with Carrión Dueñas or Nájera but they manifestly belonged to an intermediate class, well above the many communities of the Tierra de Campos and Rioja Alta that tended to become subpriories of the three foremost Hispanic daughters of Cluny.

(5) In making their grants none of the donors mentions propagation of monastic reform as a motive, but esteem for Cluny's discipline and spirituality is implicit, and comes out strongly in Pedro

111. Cf. the 2 marks paid by San Salvador de Cornellana (*Chartes de Cluny*, V 3958) and Villafranca (Guy de Valous, *Le temporel et la situation financière des établissements de l'Ordre de Cluny du XIIe au XIVe siècle*, Ligugé-Paris, 1935 118): on the other cases cited, *Chartes de Cluny*, V, 4038 (Sahagún); Yepes, *Coronica*, VI, 87 (Carrión); Valous, *Temporel*, 118 (Nájera).

112. U. Robert summarizes the statistics drawn from official documents in his *État des monastères espagnols de l'Ordre de Cluny, aux XIIIe-XVe siècles, d'après les actes des visites et des chapitres généraux* in *Bol. Acad. Hist.*, t. 20, 1892, 332-3

Froílaz' insistence that Jubia's prior always be a senior monk from the mother house, trained in her customs and learned in the Scriptures, although the subprior might be drawn from an *obedientia*.[113] But it is of course the note of liturgical intercession that is most frequently sounded, and obviously not merely as a commonplace of medieval ecclesiastical donations but out of a deep regard for Cluny's renown as a center of such intercessory prayer. Henry and Teresa expect to be remembered in the orisons of the *religiosi uiri* inhabiting Rates, while Maurice Bourdin looks to the *monachorum orationes* at both La Charité and Cluny. Counts Pedro Froílaz and Gómez Núñez expect that the Cluniacs placed in their erstwhile familial monasteries of Jubia and Budiño will continue to pray for their souls and their kinsmen's.[114] And Queen Teresa, in the most detailed of such provisions, stipulates when ceding Vimieiro that she is to be associated henceforth with the merits and prayers of all Cluniac *obedientiae* as well as of the abbey herself, and after death to receive a *tricenarium* of Masses and perpetual commemoration of her obit.[115]

But central as are the spiritual motives, it is no less true that for understanding eight of the nine Luso-Gallegan cessions, all those which fall between 1100 and 1127, the political and military situation in the Leonese empire and Cluny's special relationship with the imperial dynasty, are as much or even more significant. Under Alfonso VI Rates and Santa Justa form part of Count Henry's drive for Portuguese autonomy just as Pombeiro is a crucial gambit in the preparation for Urraca's accession and the defense of her sovereignty in Galicia. In 1113, Pedro Froílaz' gift of Jubia coincides with Abbot Ponce's Spanish visit and the abbey's first formal acceptance of Alfonso Raimúndez as Urraca's rightful heir and future ruler of the Leonese state. Ferreira shows one of the queen-empress's prominent followers emulating her own example of donations to Cluny in Leon and Castile by a Gallegan grant similarly intended to confirm the ties between the imperial party and the Burgundian abbey; and Valverde comes from another such loyal *urraquista*. Budiño and Vimieiro, clos-

113. Cf. *Reg. Ben.*, cap. LXIV, on the abbot: "doctum lege diuina".

114. The Jubia charters demonstrate how after cession of a familial monastery to Cluny the donors and their descendants continued as generous patrons.

115. Version [B] of the donation act, *Docs. med. port. Régios*, I, 1, p. 97, presents a more complete text than [A] on this point. Here Teresa, in addition to requesting intercession "in obediencialibus ecclesiis" also asks as a member of the Cluniac *familia* for the "speciacilis et familiaris oracio pro me". On this special prayer for *familiares* cf. my *Liturgical Intercession*, 56.

ely following Alfonso VII's accession as emperor, are most convincingly understood in connection with their donors' recently achieved reconciliation with the new monarch and as a politically meaningful gesture of friendship towards his monastic ally. In short it is not too much to say that all but one, and that the earliest, of Cluny's acquisitions in Galicia and Portugal require for the full explanation of their timing and motivation the closest attention to the protagonists and factions involved in this period of the Leonese empire's desperate confrontation with the twin problems of unity and succession.

III

In tracing the evolution of the Galaico-Portuguese priories subsequent to their acquisition, particular interest attaches to the fact that for some half-century between ca. 1170 and ca. 1220 the seven surviving communities appear to have been placed outside the well-known Cluniac Province of Hispania and administered in a separate *cameraria* or province of Galicia under the rule of the priors of Santa María de Nájera. Except for that learned 17th century Benedictine. Fray Antonio de Yepes, historians have ignored this second trans-Pyrenean province, and the circumstances under which it was created and eventually abolished have never been investigated.[116] Yet an attempt to explore the subject, meagre and indirect as the evidence is, seems worth making, especially since the history of this unknown Iberian circumscription can be related to Cluny's little studied efforts in the later 12th and 13th centuries to defend her peninsular holdings against the growing forces of decline and despoliation.

Down to about the year 1170 the abbey's administrative connections with its remote subject-houses in Galicia and Portugal were little different, except for the La Charité subjection of São Pedro de Rates and Santa Justa de Coimbra, from those maintained elsewhere in Spain.[117] Each priory received from Burgundy its governor, a religious versed in Cluniac customs, discipline and spirituality, and for long most, if not all, of its monks. Abbatial visitation was rare: before 1200 only three abbots crossed the Pyrenees — Hugh I (1090), Ponce de Melgueil (1113), Peter the Venerable (1142), and of these only Ponce reached Galicia. From at least the time of Hugh V's *Statute*

116. *Corónica de San Benito,* IV, 327.
117. On Cluniac administration of dependencies, see VALOUS, *Monachisme clunisien,* I, chaps. 1-4; II, chaps. 2-4.

1200) all Cluniac priors were supposed to attend the annual meetings ›f the chapter-general in Burgundy,[118] but we have no evidence that ;he heads of the Luso-Gallegan houses complied with this requirement.

In practice, the true link between the mother church and the ’eninsula was the abbot's personal representative, the *camerarius ab- atis* or abbatial chamberlain, who travelled back and forth from 3urgundy to Spain.[119] Primarily, as his title implies, a financial agent, his confidential official negotiated donations of monasteries and lands, ollected installments of the Alfonsine census, and exercised authority ver the growing chain of dependencies. Around the middle of the 2th century the Cluniac itinerant abbatial chamberlain developed into resident administrator, stationed below the Pyrenees and serving lso as prior of either Santa María de Nájera or San Zoil de Carrión, 'ith his house the headquarters of what was now emerging as a Iispanic *cameraria* or province, stretching from the Najeran sub- riories in Navarre westward across Castile and Leon to the com- ıunities of Portugal and Galicia.

For the present inquiry the most pertinent fact is that after some venty years the Province of Hispania was subdivided and a second bero-Cluniac circumscription, that of Galicia, came into being. The xistence of this new *cameraria,* which had disappeared well before 250 and therefore receives no mention in our late medieval descript- ›ns of the Burgundian federation, can be proved from four different 'itnesses:

(a) an undated letter of Abbot Radulfus (Raoul de Sully, 1173- 176), directed to all the Cluniac priors of Hispania. This text, one f three found in a small register or *cuaderno* of the late 12th or early 3th century preserved among the *pergaminos* of San Zoil de Carrión, ›nfirms the authority of a Prior Humbert of San Zoil as *camerarius 'ispaniae* in these words: "Volumus autem uobis omnibus esse mani- stum quod omnium rerum que per Hispaniam preter Galiciam pos- demus, ipsum toto tempore uite sue camerarium et ordinatorem ex tegro constituimus".[120]

118. HUGH V, *Statuta,* cap. 58 (*P.L.,* t. 209, 894-5); A. BRUEL, *Les chapitres néraux de l'Ordre de Cluny depuis le XIIe jusqu'au XVIIIe siècle in Bibliothèque l'École des Chartes,* t. 34, 1873, 542-579; VALOUS, *Monachisme,* II, chap. 3.

119. VALOUS, op. cit., II, cap. 2; P. DAVID, *Le pacte successoral entre Raymond Galice et Henri de Portugal* in *Bulletin hispanique,* t. 50, 1948, 281-4.

120. Arch. Hist. Nac., Clero, leg. 1164, no. 2 p bis. My analysis in detail of this ıaderno Carrionense, which appears to have been brought together as a dossier of portant juridical acts for the use of Prior Humbert of San Zoil between 1174 and

(b) a diploma of Santa María la Real de Nájera, issued in 118[3] by its prior Guido, who styles himself "ego Guido prior de Naier[a] et camerarius Gallecie".[121]

(c) a letter of Pope Innocent III dated 28 Juanuary 1205, requesting archbishop of Toledo and his suffragans to assist Abbot Hugh V of Cluny in his projected visitation "ad partes Hispaniae et Galicia[e] pro reformatione ordinis circa domos quas in partibus illis haber[e] dignoscitur".[122] This geographical terminology, which must echo tha[t] supplied the papal chancery in the abbot's earlier request, shows Clun[y] still possessing two peninsular *camerariae*.

(d) the appearance by at least 11 July 1225 of a new formula fo[r] the Hispanic chamberlain: "camerarius totius Hispanie" or, in Romance, "camerero de toda España de la Orden de Crunego".[123] Thi[s] subsumes the abolition of the Gallegan province and the restoratio[n] of its constituent houses to the original Hispania.

These four texts confirm the existence of a *cameraria Gallecie* i[n] the later 12th and first quarter of the 13th centuries. But when, an[d] why, was this second Iberian province created? How is the strang[e] link with Santa María to be explained? Did Cluniac 'Galicia' includ[e] the three priories in Portugal as well as the four of Galicia proper[?] None of these question can now, or perhaps ever, be answered wit[h] finality but some progress towards their solution can be made, particularly since the role of Nájera as camerarial capital allows us to dra[w] not only upon the limited Gallegan and Cluniac evidence but also upo[n] Santa María's fuller documentation.

1190, along with the complete text of this and the two other letters of Radulfu[s] dating in or around 1174, will be found under the title "El abad Radulfo de Clun[y] y el prior Humberto de Carrión, 'Camerario' de España: Tres cartas inéditas d[e] hacia 1174" in *Anuario de estudios medievales,* Barcelona, t. 1, 1964, 197-216.

121. Arch. Hist. Nac., Clero, MS 258, Cartulario de Nájera, I, 218-9; Juliá[n] CANTERA ORIVE, *Un cartulario de Santa María la Real de Nájera del año 1209* i[n] *Berceo,* t. 12, 1957, no. 86, p. 496. Guido appears earlier as the Nájeran prior o[n] 19 April and 13 October 1179: GONZÁLEZ, *Alfonso VIII,* II, nos. 323, 329 (in th[e] latter of which GONZÁLEZ, p. 552, corrects 'Haimoni' to 'Guidoni'). The Santa Mar[ía] charter, ibid., no. 221, dated 14 March 1175 (also *Bibl. Clun.,* 1433-6, with date 117[?]; YEPES, VI, esc. xxv; *Chartes de Cluny,* V, 4258, with date 1177; CANTERA ORIV[E] in *Berceo,* t. 15, 1960, 201-218, no. 5, also with date 1177) which contains in versio[n] [C], p. 371, n. 17, the phrase "Guidone priore in Nazera existente" is considered b[y] GONZÁLEZ, p. 366, a falsification.

122. A. POTTHAST, *Regesta Pontificum Romanorum,* Berlin, 1874, I, no. 239[?] *Bull. Clun.,* 99-100.

123. Pamplona, Arch. de Navarra, Cámara de Comptos, cajón 1, no. 97 (11 Ju[ly] 1225); Arch. Hist. Nac., Clero, leg. 1165, no. P-28 (1240); *Chartes de Cluny,* V[,] 5259 (1279).

1. *The establishment of the Cameraria Gallecie.* The subtraction from the Hispanic chamberlaincy of certain priories placed under a *camerarius Gallecie* must already have occurred before the dispatch of Radulfus' epistle to the priors of Hispania, for the phrase *preter Galiciam* here is too casual, too devoid of juridical formality to have effected the actual institution of the new administrative district. Furthermore, the two other letters of Radulfus also contained in the *Cuaderno Carrionense* and of the same date, of which one is addressed to the prior-chamberlain himself while the other is directed to Gerald, *custos ordinis,* and the chapter of San Zoil, are silent regarding Galicia. The assumption must be that the recipients already knew the territorial limits of Humbert's authority. All three texts cannot date later than 1176; actually their content and purpose place them early in Radulfus' abbatiate, which began in late 1173, so that they are most likely to have been written soon after his election, probably in 1174.[124]

But how long before late 1173 or 1174 can the division into two provinces be placed, and under what abbot? Humbert must have been appointed to his double office of prior of Carrión and Hispanic chamberlain by Radulfus' predecessor Stephen (1161-1173) some time between 13 January 1167, when he was still serving as prior of San Isidro de Dueñas,[125] and before 28 March 1169, when Fernando II's *real privilegio* ceding Cluny as a new priory the church of Santa Agueda de Ciudad Rodrigo names him as prior-chamberlain at San Zoil.[126] This same diploma offers a *terminus post quem* for the carving out of the Gallegan circumscription, since the Leonese monarch, acting as he says "in manu domini Aumberti prioris de Carrione et camerarii Cluniacensis" uses this occasion to confirm to Cluny a select list of five priories in Leon and Galicia: San Salvador de Palaz de Rey in the city of Leon, San Salvador de Budiño, Santa María de Villafranca, San Vicente de Pombeiro and San Pedro de Valverde.[127] The inclusion of three of the four Gallegan dependencies in this list shows that as late as March 1169 the houses of the area were still under the jurisdiction of the provincial chamberlain of Hispania.

124. See note 120, *supra.*

125. Luciano Serrano, *El obispado de Burgos y Castilla primitiva,* Madrid, 1935, III, no. 137.

126. Fidel Fita, *Los cluniacenses en Ciudad Rodrigo* in *Bol. Acad. hist.,* t. 62, 1913, 355-7; cf. Julio González, *Regesta de Fernando II,* Madrid, 1943, 407.

127. Fita, loc. cit., p. 356 reads 'Vall(eolet)i' but Cluny had no priory at Valladolid, and the contraction should be expanded as 'Vall(e Virid)i'.

This narrows the interval for the emergence of the second Iberian *cameraria* to the some five years between the end of March 1169 and the promulgation of the three Radulfan epistles in late 1173 or 1174. These chronological limits could be further narrowed if we were sure which one of the immediate predecessors at Nájera of Guido, who in 1183, as we have seen, calls himself *prior de Naiera et camerarius Gallecie,* ought to be recognized as the first such Riojan administrator of the westernmost dependencies. Santa María's pergaminos supply the names of four different priors commencing in 1169: Raymond, Humbert, Achard and Hugh. Of these, the first two can confidently be ruled out. Raymond, whose stormy career terminated in 1169 with his expulsion from Spain by command of both Pope Alexander III and Alfonso VIII of Castile, clearly exercised authority over all the Hispanic houses.[128] His successor, Humbert of Carrión, who by at least March 1169 had become prior of San Zoil and chamberlain of Hispania, can be found also in *pergaminos* of 1170 and 1171 using the title of *prior Naierensis.*[129] This means that for several years following Raymond's departure, doubtless during a period of recovery from the latter's disastrous régime, Humbert acted as *locum tenens* at Santa María; and that all the peninsular houses of the Leonese-Castilian area were still in one province under his jurisdiction. With Achard and Hugh the picture changes, for these men became priors of Nájera while Humbert retained only the post of prior-chamberlain at Carrión.[130] Hugh, who does not appear in the Rioja before 1175, and therefore presumably after the composition of Radulfus' epistle mentioning Galicia, is too late to be a serious contender.[131] This leaves Achard who, we know, had been prior of San Román de Entrepeñas, the important Leonese neighbor of San Zoil de Carrión, as late as

128. F. Fita, *El concilio de Lérida en 1193 y Santa María la Real de Nájera* in *Bol. Acad. hist.,* t. 26, 1895, 332-383.

129. Julio González, *El reino de Castilla en la época de Alfonso VIII,* Madrid, 1960, II, no. 149; Ildefonso M. Rodríguez de Lama, *Colección diplomática riojana* in *Berceo,* t. 9, 1954, no. 5, pp. 103-4.

130. Arch. Hist. Nac., Clero, leg. 1164 (San Zoil de Carrión), no. 91. Note that the prior Humbert found at San Isidro de Dueñas in 1174-5 (Col. Velázquez, IV, nos. 1416, 1408) is not the Carrión chamberlain, but the Humbert who succeeded his namesake at Dueñas by May 11, 1169 (ibid., no. 1417; published by Antonio Suárez de Alarcón, *Relaciones genealógicas de la Casa de los marqueses de Trocifal,* Madrid, 1656, Apénd., esc. xxv). The two Humberts can be found together confirming the document of 13 January 1167 cited in note 125, *supra,* where one appears as prior, the other as sacrist.

131. González, *Alfonso VIII,* no. 229; Arch. Hist. Nac., MS 258, Cartulario de Nájera, 206-7.

1172 before being transferred to Nájera, where he can be found as prior in 1174.[132]

The uncertainties here are many but it looks very much as if the creation of the Gallegan province falls most naturally at the crucial point when Humbert, after temporarily holding the three highest Cluniac offices in the Peninsula, surrendered Nájera and confined himself henceforth to San Zoil's prioracy-chamberlainship. The installation at this time in the restored Riojan house of Prior Achard, whom Humbert would have known during both his Dueñas and Carrión periods as the experienced ruler of Entrepeñas, must have been on the chamberlain's recommendation. We can go even further and posit that it was Humbert also who must have persuaded the abbot of Cluny of the desirability of a separate *cameraria* under the headship of Santa María. In this light, the establishment of the new Province of Galicia can be assigned to the biennium 1172-1173, in which Achard replaced Humbert at Nájera, and to the abbacy of Stephen, Radulfus' predecessor, who abdicated in 1173.

This hypothesis of Humbert's primary responsibility for the Gallegan *cameraria* finds further support from what we know of this able administrator's vigorous steps, dating from the commencement of his chamberlaincy, to overcome the critical problems of internal discipline, financial stability, and external attack by laymen and bishops that ca. 1170 confronted the Hispano-Cluniac communities, and especially those of Galicia and the Rioja. We have cited Fernando II's donation charter of 28 March 1169 for Santa Agueda de Ciudad Rodrigo, with its unique clause confirming to Cluny five of her priories and warning off violators of their rights and properties.[133] In another diploma issued on 23 March 1169, five days before, the Leonese monarch had extended royal protection to Prior Constantine and the monks of San Martín de Jubia against *milites et satellites et rustici* who were invading the priory's *coto,* seizing its lands and carrying off into marriage elsewhere women from its *aldeas*.[134] Thus all four of Cluny's Gallegan houses were under attack and in need of the king's assistance.

Such threats to stability were not unknown in Leon, as the mention of San Salvador de Palaz de Rey and Villafranca in the

132. On Achard's prioracy of Entrepeñas, see Arch. Hist. Nac., Clero, leg. 1183, no. 16 bis (1153), unnumbered perg. (1164), no. 21 (1172); and on the shift to Nájera, Rodríguez de Lama, *Col. dipl. riojana,* no. 6, pp. 105-6: "prior Acchardus ste Marie de Nazara" (dated *mense Septembrio,* 1174).
(dated *mense Septembrio,* 1174).
133. See n. 126, supra.

charter of 28 March disclose; but it is in the Rioja that dangers even more serious than the Gallegan troubles can be found. Here the prior-chamberlain Raymond of Nájera had been engaged for over a decade in a bitter conflict with the see of Calahorra, whose bishops had urged the cardinal-legate Jacinthus during his Spanish tour of 1155 to annul Alfonso VI's donation of Santa María to Cluny on the grounds that it was really the Burgundian queen Constance who had connived at this alienation.[135] Calahorra also challenged the priory's title to the tenth of the portazgo of Logroño, granted it in 1149 by Alfonso VII,[136] disputed her possession of churches, tithes and lands, and the monks' right to perform parochial duties; and episcopal agents (according to Raymond) invaded the monastery, flogged the monks, stole their library, despoiled the altars, and caused damage amounting to over 500 *aurei.*[137] By 1169 Raymond had personally suffered defeat, for on 31 August Alexander III ordered him sent back to Cluny as a simoniac for having purchased a forged document declaring him abbot of San Millán de la Cogolla, and for having hoodwinked Alfonso VIII into believing that this incredible fantasy had the approval of the monks there as well as of Count Lope Díaz and the Calahorran bishop.[138] The king banished the unhappy prior-chamberlain from the realm on grounds of simony and illegal alienation of Nájera's patrimonies;[139] and Santa María was left demoralized and pilotless, to be rescued by the labors of Humbert of Carrión.

For Humbert, occupied down to at least 1171 in restoring stability to the Riojan priory, and more cognizant than any other Cluniac official of the multiple difficulties harassing the abbey's dependencies elsewhere, the creation of another province must have seemed urgent, not primarily because of conditions in Galicia, but in order to avert the threatened ruin of Santa María de Nájera. A second *cameraria* would provide the once flourishing priory, with its complex of subpriories, churches and domains extending beyond the Rioja into Na-

134. Montero Díaz, *Col. dipl. S. Martín de Jubia,* no. 81; González, *Fernando II,* no. 18.

135. P. Kehr, *Papsturkunden in Spanien, II. Navarra und Aragon* in *Abhandlungen der Gesellschaft der Wissenschaften zu Göttingen,* phil.-hist. Kl., N. F., t. 22, 1928, Heft 50, no. 77.

136. Kehr, no. 89.

137. Fita, *Concilio de Lérida,* no. 3; Rodríguez de Lama, *Col. dipl. riojana,* in *Berceo,* t. 12, 1957, no. 80.

138. Kehr, no. 109.

139. Fita, *Concilio de Lérida,* no. 4; González, *Alfonso VIII,* III, n. 937 ('sin fecha').

varre and the Castilian Bureba, with a governing official of far greater authority than a mere prior, who would be permanently resident in the house to guide its course as no intermittently present Carrión chamberlain could do. Furthermore, its establishment would diminish the danger that the Nájeran chapter, resentful of the inevitably austere measures required for its recovery, and mindful of Nájera's former position as camerarial seat of Hispania, might defy an authority imposed upon it from its rival San Zoil.

But why choose the priories of Galicia to provide the subordinate dependencies for a Riojan *cameraria*? Not certainly out of regard for contemporary provincial organization in the secular church, or the political boundary lines of the Iberian kingdoms. The diocese of Calahorra, in which Santa María lay, faced east as a suffraganate of Tarragona; and the division does not correspond to the then separated kingdoms of Castile and Leon. To be sure, ca. 1170 both Galicia and the Rioja were areas of intense inter-state conflict. From late in Alfonso VII's reign and on into that of Fernando II — at least until the latter's victory at Badajoz in 1169 — much of southern Galicia, and specifically the Toroño district with San Salvador de Budiño, was controlled by the armies of King Alfonso Henriques of Portugal.[140] In the same period the Rioja witnessed attempts by Sancho VI and Sancho VII of Navarre to annex this fertile region to Pamplona, although by 1179 Alfonso VIII of Castile had regained control of most of the area.[141] But no Cluniac plan to avoid enmeshment in these struggles or to appease Portugal and Navarre by placing the priories of the contested zones outside the Leonese-Castilian sphere of Hispania can be discerned; this could only have antagonized Fernando II and Alfonso VIII, with whom the abbey had far more intimate ties of friendship than with any other peninsular ruler.

A more likely explanation lies in the peculiar geographical and juridical structure of the Cluniac holdings below the Pyrenees. In Castile beyond the Rioja, as far as the former boundary with Leon at the Pisuerga river, there was only one authentic major dependency, the house of Santa Coloma de Burgos, acquired in 1081 from Alfonso VI;[142] a Castilian province contiguous with the Riojan cluster under Nájera was therefore impossible. Across the Pisuerga, which

140. Valdeavellano, *Historia de España,* I, 2, 560-1; González, *Fernando II,* 22-4, 32-3, 36-8, 41-4, 58-9, 67-9, 78-86.
141. González, *Alfonso VIII,* I, 774-820.
142. *Chartes de Cluny,* IV, 3582.

with Alfonso VII's partition between his sons Sancho III and Fernando II had ceased to be the frontier between Castile and Leon, there began the tightly knit complex of Cluniac possessions in the Tierra de Campos centering around Carrión and Dueñas. These formed the heartland of the Province of Hispania and a dichotomy along political lines would have placed Carrión in the same circumscription as Nájera. In Galicia, on the other hand, the four surviving congregations of Jubia, Pombeiro, Valverde and Budiño had all been originally ceded not to Dueñas or Carrión but directly to the abbot; and such communities could be readily separated from Hispania and placed in another *cameraria*.

As for the question whether the three Portuguese priories were included along with those of Galicia in the new province, this can not be proved from the scanty documentation, but seems very likely. The limited number of houses in both Galicia (four) and Portugal (three), the already noted disregard of political frontiers, the fact that the route of camerarial visitations to Portugal would naturally run through Galicia, not Leon, all favor this assumption. Vimieiro, like the Gallegan quartet, had been placed directly under the abbot by Queen Teresa and on geographical grounds would most naturally be grouped with them. Rates and Santa Justa were subpriories of La Charité, but even if these were visited from the Nivernais house (and we hear nothing of this until 1292, when São Pedro claimed to be exempt on this ground from intervention by the *camerarius* and the prior of Pombeiro acting as *uisitatores*),[143] it is probable that on all important matters they looked to the provincial chamberlain. Certainly from 1259, when the surviving capitular acta and visitation reports commence, these make no distinction between Rates and Vimieiro.[144] Once again certainty is impossible, but the impression is strong that Cluniac 'Galicia' embraced Portugal as well as the county proper, and that all seven Luso-Gallegan priories were placed under the governance of the prior-camerarius of Nájera.

2. *The suppression of the Cameraria Gallecie.* The history of the Province of Galicia from its foundation in 1172-3 is extremely obscure, and what data we have bear chiefly upon the problems of its abolition. The earliest date that suggests itself for the event is 1205, the year of Innocent III's already mentioned letter of 28 January

143. Robert, *État des monastères espagnols,* 352, 378.
144. Ibid., *passim.*

asking the archbishop of Toledo and his suffragans to welcome Abbot Hugh V of Cluny on his journey "ad partes Hispaniae et Galliciae pro reformatione ordinis circa domos quas in partibus illis habere dignoscitur".[145] The urgent reasons for such abbatial *reformatio* of the peninsular dependencies can be discerned in three papal bulls, also of January 1205. On the 20th, in response to the petition of the archbishop of Braga, the pope orders the bishop, dean and precentor of the Church of Tuy to enforce sentences of excommunication and interdict already imposed upon the Cluniac monasteries of São Pedro de Rates and Vimieiro and upon the persons there who dare to engage in sacerdotal functions in defiance of the archbishop.[146] On 29 January — the very next day after the letter to the Spanish bishops on Hugh's tour — two other bulls of general tenor, but obviously intended for early use in Spain, were dispatched: one instructs all bishops in whose dioceses Cluny had possessions to aid the abbey in recovering any of these that had fallen into lay hands;[147] the other confirms the Cluniac abbot's right to exercise full powers of disciplinary correction over his subject-houses.[148] All four texts illumine the grave situation confronting Cluny below the Pyrenees: breakdown of order within the priories; lay confiscations of their temporal; conflict with the episcopate over parochial activities of the monks under the abbey's privilege of exemption, this last applying specifically to the two Portuguese houses in the diocese of Braga.[149]

We might hypothesize therefore that in the course of a traverse of the Peninsula in 1205 Abbot Hugh V, personally witnessing the troubled conditions there, and the ostensible failure of the dual provincial system, ordered a return to the original single Iberian Province of Hispania; and that this explains why no explicit reference to the *cameraria Gallecie* or its chamberlain occurs after 1205. There are however two objections to dating the extinction of the Luso-Gallegan circumscription this early. The first is that we have absolutely no evidence, Burgundian or peninsular, that Hugh's trip was ever made; even with our fragmentary documentation some reflection of this first abbatial crossing of the Pyrenees since Peter the Venerable's visit of

145. Potthast, 2395; *Bull. Clun.*, 99-100.
146. Da Costa, *Ordem de Cluny em Portugal*, no. 3, p. 29.
147. Potthast, 2396; *Bull. Clun.*, 100.
148. Potthast, 2397; *Bull. Clun.*, 100.
149. The other Portuguese house, Santa Justa de Coimbra, if not already lost by this time, was doubtles so effectively subjected to episcopal control under the terms of Maurice Bourdin's charter as not to raise the question.

1142 might be expected. The second is that Santa María de Nájera, the seat of the Gallegan *camerarius,* seems to be in a relatively stable state ca. 1205, and hence unlikely to attract the abbot's unfavorable attention. From the turn of the century the priory had been under the capable rule of a native Riojan, Semeno (Romance: Xemeno, Jimeno), apparently the very first Hispano-Cluniac prior of peninsular birth, under whom it recovered or first acquired a number of revenue-producing patrimonies, as we learn from Semeno's lengthy report on his administration of the Nájeran temporal.[150] To be sure, this is a statement implying recovery from earlier troubles; however, between the end of 1202, by which time Semeno had retired to be replaced by a Frenchman, Girard,[151] and 1205, Santa María could hardly have declined so speedily as to discredit her capacity to govern Provincial communities. Thus, unless we argue that her priors, however effective in Riojan affairs, failed badly in meeting their responsibilities in the Galaico-Portuguese west, the necessity for suppressing the second *cameraria* at this time is difficult to discover.

But if the *cameraria Gallecie* survived, as in the absence of testimony to the contrary we may suppose it did, Hugh V's projected journey, its life cannot have extended beyond the abbatiate of Gerard of Flanders (1215-1220). The evidence for this, indirect and intricate, comes almost wholly not from Galicia and Portugal, but from Santa María de Nájera, which in the first half of the 13th century constitutes our principal key to the fate of the Galaico-Portuguese *cameraria.* Here three unstudied episodes, all of which can be linked to the Spanish policies of Abbot Gerard as regards Hispano-Cluniac administrative reorganization, require close examination. These are (i) the intervention at Nájera of the Cluniac *uisitatores* Eustorgius and Aymeric; (ii) the abbot's own journey to the Peninsula; and (iii) the activities at Nájera and Villafranca of the monk John, Gerard's appointee as *camerarius Hispanie.*

150. *Chartes de Cluny,* V, 4403, with date '1201 (?)'. On this document and its correct dating, see further, *infra.* On various topics in the history of Santa María de Nájera in the late 12 th and 13th centuries, see González, *Alfonso VIII,* I, 483-493; but a comprehensive study, monastic, administrative, economic and cultural, of this great priory is an imperative need.

151. Semeno's prioracy can be traced between 1197 (González, *Alfonso VIII,* III, no. 661), by which time he had succeeded Durandus (last attested for 1194: Fita, *Concilio de Lérida,* no. 11; Kehr, *Papsturkunden Nav. u. Arag.,* no. 208), and 1201 (*Chartes de Cluny,* V, 4402). Girard appears first in 1202 and down to 1205 in the Nájeran charters published by Rodríguez de Lama, *Col. dipl. riojana* in *Berceo,* t. 10, 1955, nos. 12a, 12b, 13a, 13b.

(i) *The Eustorgius-Aymeric visitation.* The sudden appearance at Nájera of two French Cluniac priors, Eustorgius of Saint-Flour in Auvergne, who also bears the title of *camerarius in Hispania,* and Aymeric of Saint-Germain,[152] is the first example I know for Spain of the abbey's later practice of sending pairs of annual visitors to inspect the dependencies. Since the exercise of authority at Nájera by a chamberlain acting *in Hispania* implies the absence of a resident prior-chamberlain there, and Santa María's re-incorporation into Hispania, it is essential to extract what information we can regarding the date and circumstances of this visit.

Virtually all the evidence consists of two marginal annotations in Semeno of Nájera's just mentioned account of his patrimonial administration while prior. First published by Havet in 1883 from the British Museum original,[153] and again in the *Chartes de Cluny,*[154] this relatively lengthy document consists of (a) a detailed account of all properties recovered or gained, buildings constructed (particularly after a great fire swept the town) and new *collazos* acquired, as a result of Semeno's own purchases or gifts secured by him; and (b) a statistical survey by individual domains showing progress made in agricultural equipment, livestock and crop output between the beginning and end of Semeno's prioracy. Two annotations have been added in this document's margins at some time subsequent to its composition, by another hand.[155] The first, placed near the close of the domanial survey, reads thus: "Hec omnia probata fuerunt sicut suprascripta sunt coram priore Sancti Flori, camerario in Hispania, domino Eustorgio et fratre Aymerico, priore Sancti Germani, et magistro Alano et omni conuentu Najarensi". The other, opposite a passage on the domain of San Jorge de Logroño, runs as follows: "Status domus Sancti Georgii apud Lucronium probatus fuit coram domino E., priore Sancti Flori et camerario in Hispania, et fratre Aimerico, priore Sancti Germani, per juramentum prepositi Stephani de Sancto Georgio et

152. The lamentably few documents between 1186 (no. 19) and 1223 (no. 22) in Marcellin BOUDET's massive *Cartulaire du prieuré de Saint-Flour,* Monaco, 1910, do not name the prior; the index makes plain that Eustorgius was a fairly common appellative in noble families of this part of Auvergne. Aymeric was presumably the prior of Saint-Germain-d'Auxerre in the time of Abbot William I, 1208-1220; cf. *Gallia Christiana,* XII, 385-6.

153. Julien HAVET, *Rapport adressé à l'abbé et au couvent de Cluny par Jimeno ex-prieur de Notre-Dame de Nájera (Espagne) sur sa gestion* in *Bibliothèque de l'École des Chartes,* t. 44, 1883, 169-178.

154. V, 4403.

155. HAVET, 177, n. 4; 178, n. 1; *Chartes de Cluny,* V, p. 771, n. 3; 772, n. 1.

Lupi Nauarri de Torrauento, clauigeri, qui dixerunt ita esse et si aliter inueniretur se emendaturos".[156]

From the action of the two extraordinary visitors from Cluny, one of whom is *camerarius in Hispania,* in inspecting the state of the patrimonies as here attested, and from the reference to Master Alan and the chapter, it is evident that the Nájeran prior is no longer a chamberlain and that Santa María's headship of the province of Galicia is either suspended or terminated. But where does the Semeno report, which is undated, really belong? Havet suggests 1201-1215;[157] Bruel the unacceptable '1201 (?)'.[158] The original text must have been drawn up some years after Semeno had ceased to hold the office of prior: not only does he style himself merely *frater* and consistently speak of his administrative measures in the past tense, but he specifically mentions the arrival at Nájera of the prior Master Alan.[159] Since Semeno's immediate successor was Girard (1202 to at least 1205),[160] we must locate after the latter date the term of Master Alan. This name and academic title are sufficiently distinctive in the Cluniac prosopography of the period to enable us to identify this prior with confidence as the "Magister Alanus Aglitus", the notary of Abbot William II of Cluny, who appears prominently among the high officials representing the Burgundian abbey in a settlement of a dispute with the abbot and monks of Moissac in October 1209.[161] This means he could not have been sent to Spain to become prior of Nájera before 1210 at the earliest; on the other hand, since a bull of Honorius III of 21 October 1216 names Guigo as prior of Nájera,[162] Master Alan must have either died or been relieved of his post by that time.

This places the Eustorgius-Aymeric visitation between 1210 and 1216, but the chronology can be still further narrowed. Among the San Román de Entrepeñas charters in the Archivo Histórico Nacional

156. I have followed here Havet's reading, based on the original, as against Bruel's conflation of this with Lambert de Barive.

157. P. 169.

158. P. 768.

159. Cf. *Chartes de Cluny,* V, p. 771: "modo dicimus de statu domorum quae sub potestate nostra erant, quomodo dimisi illas" and similar passages, *passim;* p. 772: "Ego frater S. dimisi in domum de Najera, quand domnus Alanus recepit prioratum de Najara". Of the transactions catalogued in the report, the latest that can be dated is of 1201 *(Chartes de Cluny,* V, 4402); since Don Diego Lope de Haro, who at the end of the report affirms its accuracy, died 16 September 1214 (González, *Alfonso VIII,* I, 310), the text falls between 1206 and 1214.

160. Cf. n. 151, *supra.*

161. *Chartes de Cluny,* V, 4451, p. 825.

162. Fita, *Concilio de Lérida,* no. 15.

is one by which a certain Dom Nichola transfers to this Cluniac house and its prior Hugh several *solares,* on condition that he hold these for life *in prestimonio* and enjoy the right of burial in the priory church.[163] This contract Hugh negotiates "assensu et uolumtate circe cluniacensis domni Eustorgii" The charter, which contains the sole Spanish reference I have discovered to Eustorgius other than the Semeno annotations, bears no date, but another San Román *pergamino* of 1215 also names Hugh as prior. This is not conclusive, however, since he may have been in office since 1206; but the naming of the *priorem Sancti Flori* in connection with the enforcement of the settlement of a dispute between Cluny and the see of Mâcon in April 1213 implies it was only after this date that Eustorgius was sent to Spain.[164] The Nichola agreement does establish one decisive point: that as *camerarius in Hispania* Eustorgius exercised jurisdiction not only over Nájera and therefore by implication over the Luso-Gallegan houses, but also in the rival province of Hispania, which included Entrepeñas. Such authority over the circumscription ruled from Carrión [165] in turn allows us to perceive that the prior of Saint-Flour's mission to the peninsula must have followed the death of the Hispanic prior-chamberlain Peter of Carrión, whose term of office reached back to at least 1196.[166] In February 1213, Peter, describing himself as *debilis et infirmus,* prepared a detailed list of all the patrimonies and revenues of San Zoil, obviously as a final report on his two decades of administration there; [167] he must have died not long thereafter.

All this makes it probable that Eustorgius as *camerarius in Hispania,* accompanied by his colleague from Saint-Germain, was sent to the Peninsula some time after the spring of 1213, when the double office of the Carrión prioracy and the resident Hispanic chamberlainship had become vacant, and while at Nájera Master Alan was still prior. In short, the Eustorgius-Aymeric mission has to be put bet-

163. Leg. 1184, no. 33-P. On *circa* as synonymous with *uisitator,* see Du Cange, II, s. v. *circa, circator,* and references there cited; also *Chartes de Cluny,* V, 4083, p. 437, on Ponce, Cluny's *circa* in Italy, 1144. Cf. the Premonstratensian *circatores* and *circariae:* H. M. Colvin, *The White Canons of England,* Oxford, 1951, 197-200.

164. Entrepeñas, leg. 1184, no. 53-P; cf. nos 34-P (1204) and 36-P (1206) on Hugh's predecessor William. For the prior of Saint-Flour in April 1215, *Chartes de Cluny,* VI, 4471, p. 25.

165. On recent interventions of the prior-chamberlain Peter of Carrión in the affairs of Entrepeñas, cf. leg. 1184, nos. 29-P (1196), 30-P (1196), 35-P (1206).

166. Cf. preceding note, and González, *Alfonso VIII,* III, no. 651.

167. *Chartes de Cluny,* VI, 4469 bis, pp. 934-940.

ween 1213 and 1216, which places it either in the last two years of Abbot Wilham II of Cluny (1207-15 April 1215) or the incumbency of his successor Gerard of Flanders (15 April 1215-1220). Between the weak, faltering William, whose incapacity to avert the abbey's threatened spiritual and financial collapse led his monks to depose him, and the able, experienced reformer and administrator Gerard, who after a successful career as the Cistercian abbot of Molesmes was elected to succeed William on the very day of his abdication, we need not hesitate to opt for Gerard, particularly in view of his display of special interest in Spain.[168] On this basis, therefore, I believe the *terminus post quem* of the Eustorgius-Aymeric episode should be set at April 1215; and since the *ante quem* has already been established by Honorius III's mention of Prior Guigo as October 1216, the visitation must have occurred in 1215 or 1216.

(ii) *Abbot Gerard in Spain, 1217-1218.* The intervention at Nájera in 1215-1216 of the two French *uisitatores,* with its implications for the collapse or suppression of the Gallegan province, can hardly be separated from Abbot Gerard's own trip to the Peninsula very shortly thereafter. Of the three sources for this extraordinary abbatial visit, two are *reales privilegios* of January 1218: one, of the 6th, issued at Benevente by King Alfonso IX of Leon;[169] the other, of the 13th, drawn up at Burgos in the name of the young Fernando III and his mother Berenguela.[170] Both charters assign Cluny certain royal revenues intended to defray the annual expenses of holding the chapter-general. The third text is a letter-patent of Gerard himself, composed at Nájera on 18 January, in which he declares that during his visitation of the "domos et prioratus in Hispaniis nobis subiectos" he has witnessed Najera's "magnam et intolerabilem uestium penuriam" under prior Guigo, and therefore bestows certain newly constructed dwellings near the priory gate upon the monks to provide additional income for their clothing.[171]

All three documents can be taken as charting the homeward leg of a trip across Spain that must have been begun in the preceding year 1217, during which in the fortnight 6-18 January 1218 the abbot

168. On Gerard, cf. *Bibl. Clun.*, 1664; Valous, in *D.H.G.E.*, XIII, 1956, 79-80.
169. *Chartes de Cluny*, VI, 4513; Julio González, *Alfonso IX*, Madrid, 1944, II, no. 353.
170. *Chartes de Cluny,* VI, 4514.
171. Fita, *Concilio de Lérida,* no. 16.

halted at the Leonese and Castilian royal courts, then in Benevente and Burgos, and at Santa María. This must have been a return visit to Nájera; whether the trip had taken him all the way to Galicia, we do not know. What is certain is that Gerard's activities reflect concern for Cluny's increasingly serious fiscal state and that he saw for himself the poverty at the traditional capital of the Gallegan *cameraria*. The chances are thus extremely good that it was in the course of this journey that the abbot convinced himself of the urgent necessity of reuniting all the Iberian priories in a single province under the headship of the stronger and stabler San Zoil de Carrión. This hypothesis is further supported by what we know of the provincial chamberlain John, Gerard's appointee to the post of administrator over all Spain.

(iii) *The Hispanic chamberlain John at Nájera and Villafranca.* We first hear of this new chamberlain in Fernando III's *real privilegio* of 6 January 1220, in which after affirming his reverence for his venerable friend, Abbot Gerard of Cluny — a palpable allusion to the visit of two years before — the Castilian monarch speaks of the service done him by "uos Johannes prior carrionensis et hyspanie camerarius eundo in Alamanniam pro karissima uxore mea regine Beatrice filia Philippi quondam regis romanorum".[172] Since the company of Castilian envoys was entertained in Germany for almost four months before escorting Duke Philip of Swabia's daughter Beatrice to Spain, where the wedding took place at Burgos on 30 November, 1219,[173] it follows that John must either have accompanied Gerard across the Pyrenees or have been sent out on the abbot's return to Burgundy; he was therefore in Spain by 1218 or early 1219, and clearly a Gerardian appointee.

Now it can be firmly established that John, unlike his predecessor at Carrión, the chamberlain Peter, but like Eustorgius, although not an itinerant official, exercised authority over Santa María de Nájera. A lengthy *pergamino* of the priory survives, entitled *Hee sunt distractiones seu alienationes Nazarensis ecclesie facte per Johannem came-*

172. Arch. Hist. Nac., Clero, leg. 1165 (San Zoil de Carrión), no. 4-R (orig.).
173. On this Castilian embassy to Germany, which also included Bishop Maurice of Braga, the Prior of the Hospitallers, the abbot of San Pedro de Arlanza, and a former Master of the Order of Santiago, see the *Chronique latine des rois de Castille*, ed. G. Cirot in *Bulletin hispanique*, t. 15, 1913, 35. Cirot, n. 40.4, confesses his inability to identify in this passage the *comarium carrionen*, who was unquestionably our *camerarius Carrionensis* John. On the date of the marriage, L. Vázquez de Parga, in *Diccionario de historia de España*, Madrid, 1952, I, 1121.

rarium Ispanie, which must have been drawn up by the senior monks of the chapter not long after John left the Peninsula for good ca. 1230.[174] This document bitterly assails him as "iste bonus camerarius" who out of sheer goodness of heart has outrageously despoiled Santa María in the interests of the see of Calahorra and various laymen. It accuses him of having alienated tithing and parochial rights and various itemized properties; of reducing the monks — with the aid of his nefarious English famulus Raolin (Rawlin) and despite Prior Guigo's opposition — to such straits that by the end of his chamberlaincy they were dependent for their very daily bread upon the charity of the Riojan magnate, Don Lope Díaz de Haro; and of having proclaimed the priory's indebtedness as 8600 *aurei,* instead of the 1600 Prior Guigo had previously sworn to in an assembly of the monks, the burghers of Nájera and the magnates of Castile, with King Fernando himself present. Whatever the justice of these charges — and the chamberlain's desperate measures to ward off Santa María's bankruptcy and threatened collapse might well have seemed intolerable to the monks affected — the crucial point here is that the *Distractiones* never deny John's constitutional right to intervene in the priory as *camerarius Hispanie.* Furthermore, by the autumn of 1222, if not before, John has replaced Guigo as Najeran prior,[175] and thus revived under similar emergency conditions the union in the same hands of the three great Cluniac posts in the Peninsula, just as Humbert of Carrión had temporarily done on the eve of the establishment of the *cameraria Gallecie.*

In this same period John appears in a Najeran diploma of 1225, preserved only in Romance translation, as not merely chamberlain of Hispania but as "camerero de toda España de la Orden de Gruniego".[176] This earliest example of a formula subsequently employed by later *camerarii* strongly implies the recent extinction of the dual provincial system and the restoration of the old large Hispania. It is interesting also that two years later we hear of the camerarial capital of All Spain's being fixed not at Carrión or Nájera but at

174. *Chartes de Cluny,* VI, 4596.

175. Fita, *Concilio de Lérida,* 376, cites a document he fails to identify of 7 September 1222 in which John appears as prior of Carrión and Nájera. A second pergamino of 8 October 1222 *(Chartes de Cluny,* VI, 4539) speaks of "domno abbate ac conuentu Cluniacense uolentibus predictas sententias inpugnare per domnum J. priorem Najarensem procuratorem suum ad hoc specialiter constitutum".

176. Arch. de Navarra, Cámera de Comptos, Cajón 1, no. 97; and cf. n. 123, *supra.*

the house of Santa María de Villafranca. An agreement between Cluny and the see of Braga, defining in November 1227 their respective rights in the Portuguese priory of Santa Maria de Vimieiro, depicts the abbey as represented by two *uisitatores et legati,* the sacrist Thomas and Martin, and also by "Johannem camerarium Villefrance"; [177] and the text goes on to declare that the prior of this house is to be named by "abbas Cluniacensis uel camerarius de Villafranca uel uisitator qui ex parte Cluniacensis monasterii uenerit ad partes illas uisitandas" and may be removed by the *camerarius Villefrance.* This is unmistakably official language since after receipt of the agreement at Cluny, presumably in 1228, Abbot Roland de Hainault issued a formal confirmation of this settlement likewise designating John as *camerarius* of Villafranca.[178] This shift of administrative base westward to Villafranca may possibly reflect troubles facing John at Carrión [179] as well as at Nájera; but the choice of a priory located in the northwestern corner of the diocese of Astorga at the point where the pilgrimage road clears the mountain pass leading to Galicia, suggests even more a deliberate plan to govern the all-inclusive Tota Hispania from a strategic and neutral site at the junction of the two older *camerariae.* The fact that this experiment can hardly have outlasted John's own incumbency, since by 1235 his successor Guy has returned to the traditional headquarters at Carrión,[180] does not alter the fact that it must have followed close on the recent amalgamation of Hispania and Galicia.

To summarize, finally, this discussion of the abolition of the province of Galicia, I would conclude (i) that the second Iberian *cameraria* survived the 1205 trip, whether made or not, of Abbot Hugh; (ii) that under Priors Girard, Master Alan and Guigo between 1202 and 1217 Santa María de Nájera, rapidly descending into *penuria* from its stability under Semeno, became increasingly impotent as an administrative center for the Galaico-Portuguese priories; (iii) that the Gallegan *cameraria* was in a state of *de facto* collapse at the time of the extraordinary intervention by Eustorgius and Aymeric; (iv) that Abbot Gerard, speedily following up this mission's alarming report, hastened to Spain in 1217-18 and then ordered the suppression of

177. *Chartes de Cluny,* VI, 4554.
178. Ibid., 4555.
179. Note that in a 1228 Carrión charter the *uisitator* Thomas acts "pro priore sancti Zoili" which hints at trouble at Carrión (leg. 1165, no. 2-E).
180. Leg. 1164, no. 26-P: "Yo don Gui camerero de Sant Zoyl...".

the moribund chamberlaincy; and (v) that from 1218-19 on, Gerard's agent, the chamberlain John, despite opposition at Nájera and Carrión, and probably also in Galicia and Portugal, as the Villafranca experiment suggests, labored to re-unite all the peninsular priories in a single Province of Hispania.

The Cluniac Province of Galicia can thus be assigned to the years between 1172-1173 and 1218. Behind the reasons for its abandonment — a definitive one, as by their silence the capitular acta and visitation reports make clear — lies not only Santa María de Nájera's failure as a camerarial seat but the general deterioration of Cluny's vitality and prestige everywhere, in which her peninsular daughters shared, a decline that goes back to the 12th century and becomes increasingly acute in the 13th. The capitular and visitation materials underscore repeatedly how after 1250 the six surviving Luso-Gallegan houses were inextricably enmeshed in the apparently insoluble problems having to do with recruitment of monks, incapable or dishonest priors, widespread immorality in the shrunken chapters, and mismanagement or permanent loss of revenues and lands.[181] From without, as the same sources reveal, these internal evils had their counterpart in ever more aggressive attacks by bishops upon the exemptive rights and parochial activities of the monks, and in the insatiable hunger for their lands evinced by the Leonese-Castilian nobility. This is, however, but one chapter, which cannot properly be detached, in the painful history of the decline of all Cluny's Hispanic houses in the later Middle Ages — a large and complex subject that requires investigation on some other occasion. Meanwhile, it must suffice to have explored here the chronology and circumstances of acquisition of the Cluniac dependencies of the Galaico-Portuguese zone, and to have resurrected, however tentatively, the forgotten Cluniac Province of Galicia.

University of Virginia — August, 1964

181. Robert, *État des monastères espagnols,* passim.

ADDITIONAL NOTE

The cessions to Cluny of the six Gallegan and three Portuguese monasteries which came to be included in the abbey's Province of Galicia can now be viewed in the light of further studies bearing on their motivation, political setting and proto-history. Peter Segl's substantial monograph on the Cluniac connection with the Leonese-Castilian dynasty to ca. 1150 re-examines thoroughly for the entire kingdom the circumstances and implications of the transfers made from Alfonso VI to Alfonso VII. It also provides the most complete bibliography of the sources and secondary literature.[1] As regards the Luso-Gallegan houses and their donors, Segl's conclusions do not differ significantly from my own, a few minor points excepted; nor, despite the emphasis given monastic reform in his title, has he succeeded in demonstrating that this was a prominent factor in any of the nine known cases.

On the priories in Galicia limited data will be found in the historical sketch by Arias of all the Benedictine communities of this province.[2] Linage Conde's massive study of Ibero-Benedictine origins does not deal directly with the priories of Galicia and Portugal, but has brief notices on their pre-Cluniac phase in the "Monasticon Hispanum" constituting the third volume.[3] Mattoso's concern with the Cluniac impulse toward Benedictinization in Minho and Beira, and the spread in northern Portugal of Cluniac customs from an assumed propagation center at Leonese Sahagún, does not pose these questions with specific reference to Rates, Santa Justa de Coimbra or Vimieiro.[4] The same is true of Feige, whose approach, basically political and oriented towards the secular church, is helpful chiefly on the general background of the three Luso-Cluniac dependencies.[5]

Bernard Reilly's masterly critique of the entire diplomatic documentation for Urraca's reign makes it possible now to relate the Galaico-Portuguese cessions more accurately to their political and prosopographic context.[6] At the same time, despite Reilly's focus upon the queen-empress' shifting alignments in the complex party struggles of the years after 1109, he does not seem to me to make sufficient allowance

---

[1] P. Segl, *Königtum und Klosterreform in Spanien: Untersuchungen über die Cluniacenserklöster in Kastilien-León vom Beginn des 11. bis zur Mitte des 12. Jahrhunderts* (Kallmünz, 1974), 128–9, 79–83, 151–8, 167–74.

[2] M. Arias, "Los monasterios benedictinos de Galicia," *Stud. monastica*, VIII (1966), 35–69, especially 61–4.

[3] A. Linage Conde, *Los origenes del monacato benedictino en la Peninsula Iberica* (León, 1973).

[4] J. Mattoso, *Le monachisme ibérique et Cluny* (Louvain, 1968).

[5] P. Feige, "Die Anfänge des portugiesischen Königtums und seiner Landeskirche," *Gesammelte Aufsätze zur Kulturgeschichte Spaniens*, XXIX (1978), 85–436.

[6] B. F. Reilly, *The Kingdom of León-Castilla under Queen Urraca, 1109–1126* (Princeton, 1982).

for Cluniac influence upon her policies as reflected in the benefactions of monasteries and lands in the Gallegan cases and throughout the Leonese-Castilian realm—a factor operative of course in other directions, and stemming from the imperial dynasty's special para-feudal bond with the Burgundian abbey. Thus, he neither mentions nor explains why in a *pergamino* of 1118—five years after (according to my dating) the 1113 visit of Abbot Ponce to Spain (Study X in this volume), and four after Urraca's initiation of her new censive policy, almost certainly a result thereof—she eulogizes, surely significantly, the Cluniac provincial chamberlain Stephen (who was also prior of San Zoil de Carrión de los Condes in León) as "fidelissimus amicus meus".[7] In short, there is still much to learn before the cessions under Abbot Ponce have been utilized to their full testimonial value for Hispano-Cluniac affairs.

Like my own paper, the above works leave untouched topics that also merit exploration: the domanial economy, relations with the local population and seigneurial administration of Cluny's Luso-Gallegan *abadengos*.[8]

[7] Yepes, *Corónica*, VI, no. 18.

[8] On the administrative side, see my "El abad Radulfo de Cluny y el prior Humberto de Carrión, 'camerario' de España," *Anuario de estud. med.*, I (1964), 197–215.

XII

PETER THE VENERABLE'S JOURNEY TO SPAIN

Students of Cluniac history, the twelfth-century translations from the Arabic and medieval Franco-Hispanic relations commonly affirm the importance of Peter the Venerable's sole visit to the Iberian peninsula. Yet their references to it, frequently incidental to discussion of other themes, abound in error and confusion; and it is hard to see how a satisfactory assessment of the broader implications of this celebrated journey can be achieved without more precise determination of its motives, date and itinerary. It is to these basic questions that this reconstruction of Peter's Spanish tour addresses itself.

It is essential, first of all, to recognize that the abbots of Cluny rarely crossed the Pyrenees: in 1090 Hugh the Great went as far as Burgos; and in 1113, as I hope shortly to demonstrate, Ponce de Melgueil travelled all the way to Compostella. But these were the only precedents; hence Peter's reasons for undertaking this arduous journey must have been substantial. Two he names himself: *uisitatio locorum nostrorum* and the pilgrimage to Santiago [1]. A third, the procurement of translations from the Arabic, might be inferred from his statement in the preface to the *Liber contra sectam siue haeresim Saracenorum* that this project sprang from his conviction that without accurate knowledge of Islamic teaching Western scholars could not successfully refute its errors [2]. But, pending more precise dating of Peter's anti-Islamic interests in connection with his whole scheme of combatting heretical Christian, Jewish and Muslim doctrine, this motive must remain uncertain. Peter could easily have

[1] 'Cum in Hispaniis pro uisitatione locorum nostrorum quae ibi sunt demorarer', *Ep.* 4.17 (*Bibliotheca Cluniacensis*, ed. M. Marrier, Mâcon 1915, 1115; *PL* 189, 657-658); 'ad remotas Hispaniarum partes et uelut ad peregrina tendentis', *Ep.* 4.12 (*Bibl. Clun.* 824-825; *PL* 189, 318; for the application of this text to Peter's journey, cf. n. 10, below). [To the editors of this volume, Drs. G. Constable and J. Kritzeck, I am indebted for various valuable corrections and suggestions].

[2] *PL* 189, 671.

understood, prior to the Spanish journey, the importance of securing a Latin version of the Koran, but the fact remains that, despite the abundant opportunity afforded by Cluny's peninsular priories and the numerous French-born prelates of Cluniac background in the Spanish hierarchy, no steps to this end were taken until the abbot was himself in the Peninsula. Furthermore, his list of the translated works as 'perditi hominis originem uitam doctrinam legemque ipsam que Alchoran uocatur' corresponds too exactly with what was actually done to be a trustworthy record of original planning [3]. Thus the question whether the translation project, as, e. g., d'Alverny thinks, antedated, or was not in fact, as others like Mandonnet and Monneret de Villard believe, a byproduct of, the Iberian visit, would seem to be an open one, although in my opinion the latter view is more probable [4].

In any case, such motives as these must be ruled secondary to a more compelling reason, one which Peter himself nowhere specifically mentions but which his itinerary and other evidence reveal, namely, the invitation extended by the Emperor Alfonso VII of Leon-Castile to meet with him on Spanish soil [5]. This invitation fairly clearly originated in the monarch's urgent need of Cluniac support at Rome for the imperial candidate in the politically crucial, disputed election to the archbishopric of Compostella. Peter accepted it, we may legitimately conclude from a principal accomplishment of his trip, as the opportunity to secure from Alfonso, in the midst of Cluny's extreme financial distress, a settlement of the unpaid annual subsidy granted the Burgundian abbey in perpetuity by the Emperor's grandfather, Alfonso VI.

The date of the journey is variously given in modern accounts as 1141, 1141-1142, 1142 or 1143 [6]; but the documentation establishes

---

[3] *PL* 189, 671.

[4] See M. Th. d'ALVERNY, *Deux traductions latines du Coran au moyen âge*, in *Archives d'histoire doctrinale et littéraire du moyen âge* 22-23 (1947-1948) 70 and n. 4; P. MANDONNET, *Pierre le Vénérable et son activité littéraire contre l'Islam*, in *Revue Thomiste* 1 (1893) 329; Ugo MONNERET DE VILLARD, *Lo studio dell'Islām in Europa nel XII e nel XIII secolo* (Vatican City 1944) 9.

[5] *Recueil des chartes de l'abbaye de Cluny* (ed. A. BERNARD and A. BRUEL, Paris 1876-1903) 5, 423-426.

[6] The date 1141, found in *PL* 189, 671 (PETR. VEN., *Prologus in Libro contra sectam siue haeresim Saracenorum*) and which (according to Dr. Kritzeck) occurs in Douai MS 381 fol. 180r dex, has been followed by many historians; but Peter's simultaneous assertion that this was the year when 'cum

1142 for the commencement of the trip and the abbot's sojourn in the Peninsula. The first definite chronological notice we have is of 29 July 1142, when Peter was at Salamanca with Alfonso VII [7]; but since he tells us himself that he was still at Cluny until after Christmas, and that by Pentecost he was in Spain [8], it follows that he must have left Cluny early in 1142 and have crossed the Pyrenees in the spring of that year. On the other hand, he disappears completely from the Spanish sources after 7 September 1142, and is next discovered, if we can trust the notice in the Rodolfus *uita*, at Le Puy, on his homeward march from Spain, on Ascension Day, which in 1143 fell on 13 May [9]. In that case the correct date for the entire journey would be 1142-1143.

From *Ep.* 4.12 it appears that at Peter's request his friend Archbishop Geoffrey of Bordeaux undertook to serve as general protector (*conseruator*) of all the Cluniac houses during the abbot's absence [10]. Of the company of monks, clerics and other companions, to whom Peter several times refers as comprising his escort, at least four can be identified with some confidence: Peter's own learned secretary, Peter of Poitiers [11]; the monk Master Thomas, mentioned as

---

domno Adefonso uictorioso Hispaniarum imperatore colloquium habui ', indisputably refers to Alfonso VII of Leon-Castile's siege of Coria in May-June, 1142 and Peter's conference with him at Salamanca ca. 29 July that same year.

7 BERNARD-BRUEL, *Chartes de Cluny, loc. cit.*

8 A miracle occurring in the archdiocese of Lyon after Christmas and reported to Peter at Cluny before he set out for Spain was ordered written down ' eodem anno in Hispaniis ante Pentecosten ' (*PL* 189, 899).

9 RODOLFUS, *Vita Petr. uen.* c. 16 (*PL* 189, 26-27).

10 The entire passage, which merits citation in view of possible conflicting interpretations, runs as follows: ' Ago quas possum gratias quia non imparem in mutui amoris constantia uos inueni, quem de amici ad remotas Hispaniarum partes et uelut ad peregrina tendentis mandatis et precibus tam deuotum conseruatorem habui. Commendaui ei monasteria nostra abbatias prioratus et cellas; et ecce non eius tantum sed et omnium nostrum uoce attestante fidissimum etiam in hoc commisso reperi '. I take this to mean that Peter is expressing gratitude to his devoted friend, the archbishop of Bordeaux, who served as Cluny's protector during the Spanish journey, and to whom Peter entrusted all Cluny's houses, an office Geoffrey discharged with great fidelity according to his own account and the witness of the monks of Cluny.

11 *PL* 189, 339, 649, 661; also, assuming the identity of Peter of Poitiers with Peter of St. John, 26-27.

present at Le Puy on the return journey [12]; Bishop Amatus of Oloron, who doubtless joined the party in southern France and soon left it, presumably to go on to Compostella in advance of the abbot [13]; and Bishop Stephen of Osma in Castile, who can be traced as far as the conference with Alfonso VII at Salamanca and who, it may be guessed, had previously carried to Cluny the imperial invitation that resulted in Peter's visit [14].

Which of the roads across southern France to the Pyrenees was taken, we cannot be sure, since the abbot's passage seems to have left no traces in the published cartularies of the Cluniac houses along the way. Probably it was the direct Cluny-Lyon-Le Puy-Conques-Cahors-Moissac route, which led through Ostabat to Roncesvalles and Pamplona; this was the shortest route and the one by which Peter appears to have returned. In Spain, he unquestionably moved westward along the *camino francés*, the great pilgrimage road to the shrine of Santiago; and it seems clear that he early stopped at two regular stations on the road, Estella in southern Navarre, and Nájera in the Castilian Rioja below the Ebro [15]. At Nájera the abbot apparently stayed some little time at the priory of Santa María de Nájera, the first Cluniac possession of significance he would encounter and one of the two chief Cluniac centers in all Spain.

Here, as Lacarra has rightly suggested [16], should doubtless be placed the well-known episode that Peter himself locates simply *circa Iberum* [17] — the commissioning of the four translators from the Arabic, Robert of ' Ketton ', Hermann of Dalmatia, Master Peter of

---

[12] *PL* 189, 26-27.

[13] Petr. Ven., *Liber de miraculis*, 1.28 (*PL* 189, 904); but Amatus does not subscribe the Salamanca charter of 29 July. The presence of this bishop from southern France might imply that Peter had come into Spain via Oloron-Somport-Jaca rather than the Roncesvalles route; but the bishop could easily have taken the crossroad from Oloron to the Roncesvalles route or have joined Peter west of Puente la Reina, where the two highways from France met. See map in Luis Vázquez de Parga, J. M. Lacarra and J. Uría Ríu, *Las peregrinaciones a Santiago de Compostela* (Madrid 1948-1949) 2,63.

[14] *Lib. de mirac.* 1.28; Bernard-Bruel 5, 425.

[15] *Lib. de mirac.* 1.28. For maps of the pilgrimage road stations in Spain, see Vázquez de Parga, Lacarra and Uría, *op. cit.* vol. 2.

[16] José M. Lacarra, *Una aparición de ultratumba en Estella*, in *Príncipe de Viana* 5 (1944) 173-184.

[17] *PL* 189, 650.

Toledo and the Moor Mohammed. This whole subject has been ably clarified in a recent study of M. Th. d'Alverny [18], but three additional points bearing directly upon the journey may be submitted. First, since Robert, Hermann and Master Peter were not Cluniacs and had no known ties with Santa María de Nájera, Peter's encountering at least the first two, and probably all four, scholars in the Ebro region, may indicate that they were in the vicinity because they were travelling with manuscripts from Toledo, with which city Master Peter and doubtless Mohammed can be linked, northward to Pamplona, where Robert's connections were intimate enough to secure for him an archdeaconate the following year [19].

Second, whether or not Peter the Venerable's purpose of securing Latin versions of the Koran and other Islamic doctrinal texts antedates 1142, it may be deduced that this interest was whetted, if not originally inspired, by the theological interests and manuscripts of the learned Mozarab Master Peter of Toledo. Neither Robert nor Hermann of Dalmatia, who under Chartrain influence devoted themselves almost exclusively to Arabic astronomy, mathematics and philosophy, and who had to be liberally subsidized by the unscientifically-minded abbot, is likely to have transported religious writings or to have pressed their translation upon him [20]. But Master Peter, who without complaint (and therefore, we may surmise, with less reward) put into his rough Latin — which Peter of Poitiers was assigned to polish to literary standards — the one polemic of the five works translated, the *Risālatān* of al-Hāshimi and al-Kindi, thus stands out as the probable link between the first translation of the Koran into a western language and Peter's anti-Islamic *croisade intellectuelle*, on the one hand, and the Toletan translators clustered about the cathedral school of Archbishop Raymond, on the other [21].

---

[18] *Deux traductions latines du Coran au moyen âge*, in *Arch. d'hist. doctr. et litt. du m. â.* 22-23 (1947-1948) 69-131; cf. also her *Pierre le Vénérable et la légende de Mahomet*, in *À Cluny: Congrès scientifique, travaux du Congrès* (Dijon 1950) 160-171, which I have not seen.

[19] *Bibl. Clun.* 1109; cf. Charles H. HASKINS, *Studies in the History of Mediaeval Science* (2nd ed. Cambridge, Mass. 1927) 120.

[20] *PL* 189, 650, 657, 671.

[21] *PL* 189, 339; D'ALVERNY 87-96. Neither Angel GONZÁLEZ PALENCIA in his biographical sketch *Noticias sobre D. Raimundo, arzobispo de Toledo* in *Moros y cristianos en España medieval* (Madrid 1945) 101-176 nor José María MILLÁS VALLICROSA, *Las traducciones orientales en los manuscritos de*

Finally, certain signs suggest that some, if not all, of the quartet accompanied the abbot of Cluny westward beyond Nájera and that the work of translating may have proceeded *en route*: the mention of *sapientes* in Peter's company when he heard the Peter Engelbert story recorded in *Liber de miraculis*, 1.28 [22]; the completion of Hermann of Dalmatia's version of the *De generatione Mahumet* at Leon [23], through which city Peter must have twice passed on his way to and from Astorga, the junction point for Salamanca; and the need for continuing collaboration between the Peters of Toledo and Poitiers. That literary activity was possible during the slow abbatial crossing of Castile and Leon is attested by the fact that Peter himself was collecting and writing down several stories subsequently incorporated into the *Liber de miraculis* [24].

Beyond Nájera, Peter's first known stop to the west was at one of the small dependencies that Santa María possessed near the pilgrimage road — perhaps San Pedro de Torrecilla or San Andrés de Cirueña, both *satis contigua* to Nájera — where he heard from the lips of Peter Engelbert the dramatic story of the rescue of King Alfonso VI's soul from torment through the agency of the monks of

---

la Biblioteca Catedral de Toledo (Madrid 1942) 10 throws any light upon the otherwise unknown Master Peter, who requires to be checked in the cartularies and *pergaminos* of the cathedrals of Toledo and Pamplona. The suggestion of GONZÁLEZ PALENCIA 167-168 and Marcelin DEFOURNEAUX, *Les Français en Espagne aux XIe et XIIe siècles* (Paris 1949) 46 that the archbishop influenced the translation project has little to be said for it: Raymond and Peter did meet at Salamanca in late July (BERNARD-BRUEL 5, 425 for the prelate's subscription to the charter of 29 July), but this was long after the commissioning of the translators at Nájera. A related problem to the translations from the Arabic that still awaits investigation is the Latin version of, or extracts from, the Talmud, which Peter used in his *Tractatus aduersus Judaeorum inueteratam duritiem* (*PL* 189, 507-650); if, as SÉJOURNÉ asserts (*DThC* 12.2, 2073-6), this tract appeared ca 1140, it may have suggested the Koran translation later. But if this date is correct, it would not be possible to link mention in the *Tractatus* of Jewish paper manuscripts (*PL* 189, 606: *ex rasuris ueterum pannorum*) to Peter's having discovered this novel writing material for the first time in Spain, as is asserted by Ramón MENÉNDEZ PIDAL in *Historia de la nación argentina* (ed. Ricardo Levene, Buenos Aires 1939) 2, 117 and André BLUM, *Les origines du papier*, in *Rev. historique* 170 (1932) 441-442.

[22] *PL* 189, 904.

[23] HASKINS 47; D'ALVERNY 80-81.

[24] 1.27-28.

Cluny [25]. Exactly when the journey was resumed we cannot be sure, but since by 29 July the abbot was in distant Salamanca, he must have been on the march in June or, at the latest, early July. For this stage of the tour, between the Nájeran dependency and Salamanca, there is no direct information, but visitation of at least two important Cluniac houses on the pilgrimage road can safely be assumed. These were, in Castile proper, the priory of Santa Coloma de Burgos, Cluny's one extra-Riojan daughter-house in that kingdom; and, in Leon, the great flourishing monastery of San Zoil at Carrión de los Condes, the principal Cluniac center for all western Spain [26]. From Carrión Peter would have to proceed west again on the *camino francés* to Astorga, the junction for the southern highway that crossed the Duero at Zamora and ran to Salamanca and the Extremaduran frontier zone. Both the selection of Salamanca, well off the pilgrimage road and as yet outside the sphere of Cluniac penetration in Spain [27], and the timing of what Peter calls his *colloquium* with Alfonso VII, were manifestly determined by the Emperor's military operations that summer against the Almoravid stronghold of Coria, to the south of Salamanca [28]. When the siege of this Muslim town, begun in early May, ended victoriously in June, Alfonso VII marched north with his army to Salamanca, and there Peter, who had probably tarried at San Zoil de Carrión until apprised of this by courier, joined him at the end of July.

The colloquium of Salamanca between the Leonese-Castilian emperor and the Cluniac abbot is in my opinion our chief key to the understanding of the whole *iter Hispanicum*. It is often erroneously

---

[25] *Lib. de Mirac.* 1.28.

[26] Peter's use of *moraver, demoraver* (*Bibl. Clun.* 1115; *PL* 189, 339) with reference to his Spanish stay suggests, as does the necessity of his waiting upon the termination of the Coria siege before joining Alfonso VII, a somewhat leisurely traverse of northern Spain in June and July, possibly punctuated by stop-overs of some length at Nájera and Carrión.

[27] The following year, however, on 29 October 1143, Alfonso VII ceded Peter and Cluny the church of San Vicente de Salamanca for conversion into a Cluniac priory (BERNARD-BRUEL 5, 428-430).

[28] *Chronicon Adefonsi imperatoris* (ed. H. FLÓREZ and M. RISCO, Madrid 1747-1879) 21, 380-381; I have not had access to the new edition by LUIS SÁNCHEZ BELDA (Madrid 1950). See also A. BALLESTEROS Y BERETTA, *Historia de España* (2nd ed. Madrid 1944) 2, 355 (with wrong date); LUIS GARCÍA DE VALDEAVELLANO, *Historia de España* (Madrid 1952) 1,913.

interpreted as the scene of an act of pure generosity towards Cluny on the part of Alfonso VII, because in the well-known diploma of 29 July 1142 emanating from the conference, that ruler refers to the annual census of 2000 gold *metcales* (mithqāls) conferred upon Cluny by his grandfather, Alfonso VI, and then formally cedes to Cluny the great Castilian abbey of San Pedro de Cardeña near Burgos, certain minor properties in Burgos, and an annual stipend of 200 maravedís from the royal revenues of that city's public baths [29]. Serrano has correctly interpreted this donation by a ruler notorious for lack of funds and for coolness towards Cluny, as embodying in fact an agreement reached at Salamanca between Peter and Alfonso to wind up the arrears of, and abolish for good, the Cluniac census of Alfonso VI [30]. Given the desperate state of Cluny's finances in this period, there can be little doubt that it was to secure some such measure of compensation for what had once been one of the Burgundian abbey's major sources of revenue, that Peter the Venerable went to Spain.

But the Salamanca charter cannot be attributed solely to the Leonese-Castilian emperor's sudden remorseful desire to discharge by a single stroke his legal indebtedness to Cluny, nor can it be correctly understood except as part of an agreement by which abbot Peter in turn undertook to attempt to persuade Pope Innocent II to approve the election and translation to the archiepiscopal see of Compostella of Alfonso's candidate, Bishop Berengarius of Salamanca. This is not the place to examine this hotly contested election or Alfonso VII's determination to obtain a friendly, financially generous metropolitan in a Galicia threatened by the rising power of the new Portuguese monarchy and torn ecclesiastically, as well as politically, by pro-Portuguese, pro-Castilian and pro-independence factions. It should be remembered also that Compostella's suffragan sees, located in the Luso-Hispanic borderlands of the old Visigothic ecclesiastical province of Mérida, added to the political importance of the Gallegan

---

[29] BERNARD-BRUEL 5, 423-426. I have in an advanced state of preparation a study of Cluny's Spanish census in which the act of 1142 is examined with reference to the story of Alfonso VII's financial relations with Cluny from the time of his accession.

[30] Luciano SERRANO, *El obispado de Burgos y Castilla primitiva* (Madrid 1935) 2, 23-24; also GONZÁLEZ PALENCIA, *Moros y cristianos* 167 and DEFOURNEAUX, *Les Français en Espagne* 47-48.

metropolitanate [31]. From an extant letter written soon after his return to Cluny, we know that Peter sent a carefully chosen envoy to Innocent II, the Cluniac monk Natalis, former royal chancellor of France and ex-abbot of Saint-Pierre de Rebais, to press the emperor's case. And in the letter itself, after praising Alfonso VII as a generous benefactor of Cluny, Peter assures the pope of the canonicity of Berengarius' election, warns him against the lies and bribes of the contesting claimant (presumably the successful Pedro Helías, the next archbishop of Santiago) and strongly urges the immediate recognition of Berengarius [32].

This Compostellan side of the Salamanca colloquium is important also for its bearing upon the difficult question of whether Peter's Spanish itinerary included a visit to Santiago and Cluny's Gallegan priories. That the crossing of Galicia, if it did occur, belongs in this stage of the journey rather than, as might alternatively be conjectured, in June or July prior to the meeting with Alfonso VII, seems strongly indicated not only by the lack of any pre-Salamanca clues, but also by the virtual certainty that before leaving Cluny Peter was made well aware of the Emperor's anxiety over the archiepiscopal election and would naturally consult with him before going on to Compostella. Particularly indicative of a Gallegan visit are the sudden importance Galicia and the abbot of Cluny jointly assume in certain imperial charters, presently to be detailed, for August and September of 1142; Peter's assurances to Pope Innocent II of his having collected testimony from scholars, magnates, clergy, prelates and monks in support of the canonicity of Berengarius' election [33]; and Alfonso VII's confirmation, issued at Peter's specific request, of the *cotización* or grant of immunities to the Cluniac Gallegan priory of San Salvador de Budiño and its *abadengo* [34].

Yet the evidence against an abbatial traverse of Galicia is also impressive. In neither Peter's writings nor the Spanish documenta-

---

[31] Cf. Antonio LÓPEZ FERREIRO, *Historia de la santa a. m. iglesia de Santiago de Compostela* (Santiago 1898-1909), 4, 224-227; Anselm G. BIGGS, *Diego Gelmírez, First Archbishop of Compostela, The Catholic University of America Studies in Mediaeval History*, N. S. 12 (Washington 1949) 185-186.

[32] *Ep.* 4.9; 3.5. Note St. Bernard of Clairvaux, after being visited by Berengarius on his way back from Rome to Spain, also urged Innocent II to confirm his translation (S. BERN., *Ep.* 212).

[33] *Ep.* 4.9.

[34] BERNARD-BRUEL 5, 426-427.

tion is there any express statement of a visit to Compostella. Peter does not say that he collected the information concerning Berengarius' election in Galicia, even though his language might suggest that only there could he have found so great a cloud of witnesses; nor do the known diplomas of any Gallegan dependency of Cluny, including Budiño, attest his actual presence. Thus it seems possible to contend that Peter may have remained at Carrión and that the Gallegan notables, and perhaps also the priors of the Gallegan houses, were summoned there to meet with him. This would dispose of the necessity of assuming a rather hurried trip of considerable length between late July and late August, and would support the hypothesis that the Emperor's involvement during May, June and July in the affairs of Coria explains Peter's leisurely movements before Salamanca and the lack of time for a Gallegan trip following the conference. There is also the possibly significant *uelut* in Peter's reference to himself in *Ep.* 4.12 as 'uelut ad peregrina tendentis', which may point to an original, but unfulfilled, intention of proceeding all the way to the Apostle's tomb. At the moment, on the basis of the evidence presently available, it seems difficult to be certain one way or the other, but on the whole the indications against Peter's having gone on beyond Carrión and Astorga to Compostella seem to carry greater weight.

Whatever the truth about the Gallegan traverse, it is clear that for Peter's movements from Carrión eastward the diplomas of Alfonso VII for August and September 1142 constitute an invaluable guide if arranged chronologically and geographically in the context of the homeward passage. There are five of these *pergaminos*: 1) the already-cited confirmation of the *cotización* to San Salvador de Budiño, issued at Peter's request at Carrión, August, no day [35]; 2) the confirmation of its properties and privileges to the cathedral church of Tuy, also issued at Carrión, in Peter's presence, August no day [36]; 3) the grant of a crown estate to the *mayordomo* Diego Muñoz, issued at Abia de las Torres, August, no day [37]; 4) the con-

---

[35] *Ibid.* The best but by no means complete guide to Alfonso VII's charters is Peter RASSOW, *Die Urkunden Kaiser Alfons' VII. von Spanien*, in *Archiv für Urkundenforschung* 10 (1928) 327-468.

[36] *España Sagrada* 22, 266-268.

[37] Peter RASSOW, *Urkunden Kaiser Alfons' VII. von Castilien* 1126-1155, in *Arch. f. Urkundenforsch.* 11 (1929-1930) 87-88.

firmation of its *fueros* to the *burgo* of San Zoil de Carrión, issued at Burgos in Peter's presence, 7 September [38]; and 5) the grant of a crown estate at Villagómez to Rodrigo Muñoz Lavegio, same place, same date, in which Peter is also mentioned [39].

These diplomas I have listed in what, from study of their subscriptions and other internal clues, appears to be the correct chronological sequence. What do they tell us? The two Carrión diplomas surely belong together: they mention Peter; deal with Gallegan matters; and carry the subscriptions of at least three prominent Gallegans, Bishop Pelayo of Tuy, Count Rodrigo Vélez and Pelayo Curvo, who do not appear in the other *pergaminos* of the group. If during August Peter did visit Galicia, it seems likely these three men, all key figures in Gallegan and Compostellan affairs, accompanied him back from Galicia and, after consultation with the Emperor, returned thither. The alternative would be to assume that Alfonso VII had previously summoned them to Carrión to give Peter testimony regarding the Compostellan election, in which case we might assume they brought with them other clerics and nobles, as mentioned in *Ep.* 4.9. Again, the charter issued at Abia de las Torres, which is located northeast of Carrión in the direction of Burgos, must postdate the Carrión charters, since it shows Alfonso VII, and therefore Peter, moving towards Burgos; and all three diplomas must belong at the end of August, since by 7 September abbot and emperor were in the Castilian capital, as the two September documents affirm.

Thus the evidence shows that on the return journey Peter and Alfonso VII travelled together from Carrion eastward to Burgos. This whole curious business of the Emperor's tarryng near Carrión in late August and accompanying the Cluniac abbot to the Castilian

---

[38] *Ibid.* 88-89.

[39] Fray Francisco de Berganza, *Antigüedades de España propugnadas en las noticias de sus reyes y condes de Castilla la Vieja* (Madrid 1719-21) 2,76: 'Facta carta Burgis tempore quo domnus Petrus Cluniacensis abbas Hispaniam intrauit'. Berganza refers to the text of this document as printed *in extenso* in his appendix (*escritura* 142), but *no consta*. L. Serrano, *Fuero de Cuevacardiel y Villalmundar*, in *Revista de Archivos, Bibliotecas y Museos*, 3ª época 16 (1907) 419-420, has published a diploma of Alfonso which he dates 28 July 1142, but the persons mentioned in the text and subscriptions demonstrate that this document actually belongs in 1150-1155. In Juan del Alamo, *Colección diplomática de San Salvador de Oña* (Madrid 1950) 1, 220-221, is a charter of 1142 showing the Emperor at Burgos, but unfortunately neither month nor day is given and there are few signatures.

capital, can, I think, only be explained in the light of the Salamanca colloquium and the cession to Cluny of San Pedro de Cardeña. This astonishing surrender into foreign hands of the great historic abbey of Castile, located close to Burgos, and connected in the national mind with the Cid and the exploits of ancient Castilian counts and kings, was certain to arouse strong opposition. Only by a solemn transfer of Cardeña by the Emperor in person, it may be conjectured, could the cession to Cluny, already effected on parchment, be carried out in fact. That Cardeña's annexation to Cluny did occur in September seems certain, but it is no less significant that Cluny was able to hold her new acquisition for less than four years. This was, however, sufficient time, as the *Chronicon de Cardeña* laments, for the Cluniacs to strip the abbey of its great movable wealth [40]. Given Alfonso's notoriety as a ruthless despoiler of monastic communities, and Cluny's pressing need, in 1142, for cash rather than another remote dependency, we may legitimately infer that this sequence of events had been foreseen at Salamanca.

From Burgos Peter would pass through Nájera and Pamplona again, moving towards Roncesvalles before the snows of winter blocked entry into France. At Pamplona, if we adopt d'Alverny's hypothesis, he may have left Peter of Poitiers, and the secretary and Robert of ' Ketton ' (who did not complete his translation of the Koran until sometime between 16 June and 16 July, 1143) may have collaborated in the assembling of the codex of translations from the Arabic which still survives, according to d'Alverny, in the Paris Arsenal MS 1162 [41].

Somewhere in Spain, on the return to France, the abbot possibly received reports of serious conditions at Cluny requiring an early return and resulting in a change of route north of the Pyrenees. For, in letters addressed to the archbishops Geoffrey of Bordeaux and Arnaldus of Narbonne, he declares that his intended visit to these prelates on his way home from Spain has had to be abandoned for reasons vaguely described as *fortuitus rerum euentus* and *multiplex curarum distractio* [42]. But whether we are to take one or both of these letters at face value is hard to say. If at the time both archbishops were residing in their sees, which is by no means certain,

---

[40] *España Sagrada* 23, 372.

[41] D'ALVERNY 96-103.

[42] *Ep.* 4.11, 12.

visits to both would have entailed a very long and circuitous route home. In any event, if we accept the testimony of Rodolfus that on Ascension Day (which would have to be 13 May 1143) Peter, returning from Spain, celebrated mass at Le Puy [43], he would seem to have returned to Cluny by the shortest route from Roncesvalles. Yet the possibility that he spent the winter and spring of 1142-1143 in southern France, where we have no trace of his movements, would indicate no great hurry to reach his abbey, an attitude at variance with not only the letters to the two archbishops but also with the financial crisis at Cluny. The best hope for a satisfactory determination of the date of his return is more intensive chronological scrutiny of Peter's activities connected with the Spanish visit once he was back home: the date of the epistle urging St. Bernard of Clairvaux to undertake the doctrinal refutation of Islam on the basis of the translations; the possible correspondence with Peter of Poitiers over the publication of the new versions; the dispatch of Natalis with the letter to Pope Innocent II; and the writing of Peter's own anti-Islamic *Summula breuis*. But the dating and analysis of these important matters fall outside the scope of the present paper.

---

[43] RODOLFUS, *Vita Petr. Ven.* c. 16; *Vita altera ex Chronico Cluniacensi BIBL. CLUN.* 648; *PL* 189, 26-27).

XIII

PETER THE VENERABLE'S TRAVERSE OF SPAIN: SOME FURTHER OBSERVATIONS

In the years since the commemoration in 1956 of the eighth centenary of Peter the Venerable's death, the Spanish journey of 1142 has continued to attract scholarly attention, both as a notable episode in the abbot's own career and as marking the commencement, at least above the Pyrenees, of serious Western study of the Islamic faith. Three important contributions appearing in this interval devote particular attention to the peninsular visit: (i) the new fully annotated edition of the Petrine correspondence prepared by Professor Giles Constable;[1] (ii) Father D. Van den Eynde's meticulous charting of all of Peter's principal travels;[2] and (iii) the Islamicist James Kritzeck's investigation of the various translations from the Arabic and of the anti-Islamic polemical tracts preserved in the so-called *Collectio Toletana*, the mid-12th-century codex intimately connected with the abbot's "croisade intellectuelle" that follows his return from Spain.[3]

In addition, studies by Martín Duque, Lemay, Sánchez Albornoz, Southern and Daniel, addressed to the whole movement of translation in 12th- and 13th-century Spain and to the rise of Christian apologetic against Islam, take due note of Peter's projects in the Peninsula.[4] Lemay indeed ascribes to the abbatial presence (which he erroneously retains in 1141) a decisive influence as for the first time linking the peninsular translators with the cathedral schools of France, and as carrying the whole work of translation from the Arabic beyond its hitherto narrowly scientific limits into the philosophical and apologetic spheres, with far-reaching consequences for the orientation of the so-called Toledan School under the patronage of Archbishop

---

[1] Giles Constable, ed., *The Letters of Peter the Venerable* (Cambridge, Massachusetts, 1967; *Harvard Historical Studies*, LXVIII), especially II, 262.

[2] Damien Van den Eynde, O. F. M., "Les principaux voyages de Pierre le Vénérable," *Benedictina*, XV, no. 1 (January–June 1968), 58–110 (especially 95–100). Cf. also, *idem*, "Remarques sur la chronologie du cartulaire de Cluny au temps de Pierre le Vénérable," *Antonianum*, XLIII (1968), 217–59.

[3] James Kritzeck, *Peter the Venerable and Islam* (Princeton, 1964), especially chap. 1: "The Journey to Spain" (3–14); *idem*, "Peter the Venerable and the Toledan Collection,' *Petrus Venerabilis, 1156–1956* (Rome, 1956; *Studia Anselmiana*, XL), 176–201; also M. T. d'Alverny, "Quelques manuscrits de la 'Collectio Toletana'," *ibid.*, 202–18.

[4] Angel J. Martín Duque, "El inglés Roberto, traductor del Corán. Estancia y actividades en España a mediados del siglo XII," *Hispania*, XXII (1962), 483–506; Richard Lemay, "Dans l'Espagne du XIIe siècle: les traductions de l'arabe au latin," *Annales: Economies-Sociétés-Civilisations*, XVIII (1963), 639–65; Claudio Sánchez Albornoz, "Observaciones a unas páginas de Lemay sobre los traductores toledanos," *Cuadernos de historia de España*, XLI–XLII (1965), 313–24; Richard W. Southern, *Western Views of Islam in the Middle Ages* (Cambridge, 1962), 37–9; Norman Daniel, *Islam and the West: The Making of an Image* (Edinburgh, 1960), *passim*.

Raimundo of Toledo.[5] There is, however, much exaggeration in this claim, and Sánchez Albornoz, more judiciously, refuses to regard this contemporary extension of focus as the "obra exclusiva" of the Petrine visit.[6]

It has been proposed that still another effect of the tour of 1142 should be acknowledged in the field of Hispanic historiography. Luis Sánchez Belda, when editing in 1950 the *Chronica Adefonsi imperatoris*, had suggested that this important work might be of Hispano-Cluniac provenance, the composition of Bishop Arnaldo of Astorga (1144–1152/3).[7] In 1963 Angel Ferrari, without discussing this ascription, argued that both the *Chronica* and the appended *Poema de Almeria* were the work of Peter of Poitiers, the learned French Cluniac who was Peter the Venerable's secretary and close companion during the journey through Spain.[8] The objections to such a hypothesis appear insuperable: Peter of Poiters was only briefly in the Peninsula, i.e. during 1142, and totally unpossessed of the mastery of Iberian inter-state political complexities or the deep-seated pro-Leonese bias displayed by the *Chronica*. This narrative indeed and the *Poema* appear to be by different hands; the *Poema* reveals no Cluniac interest whatever; and the *Chronica* passes over in complete silence the abbot's presumably widely known presence below the Pyrenees and his conference with Alfonso VII at Salamanca. Its solitary mention of the Burgundian abbey is in fact an incidental notice that it served as a place of refuge for the Emperor's defeated opponent Count Gómez Núñez of Toroño, a magnate who (as we have to learn from other sources) had previously been the donor to Cluny of the Gallegan priory of San Salvador de Budiño.[9] As for Sánchez Belda's earlier Asturico-Cluniac conjecture, this rests exclusively upon the anonymous statement to this effect preserved in an appendix of 1727 to the final volume of the *Sinopsis histórico-cronológica de España* of Juan Ferreras,[10] and requires to be received with extreme caution. Further investigation is needed of the activities from 1121 of the Cluniac priory of San Salvador de Astorga and the possible Cluniac influences in the cathedral chapter of the Asturican see dating from the episcopate of the French-born Bishop Alo (1123–1131), the poet and scholar who had previously served as Alfonso VI's chancellor.[11] In any case no connection whatever with the tour of 1142 is visible.

While the pertinent literature since 1956 continues to debate the question whether Abbot Peter's translation project preceded or coincided with the Spanish visit, the crucial contribution made by the Mozarab scholar Master Peter of Toledo, which I

[5] Lemay, 659. Lemay's paper, "L'apologétique contre l'Islam chez Pierre le Vénérable et Dante," in *Mélanges offerts à René Crozet*, ed. P. Gallais (Poitiers, 1966), II, 755–64, offers nothing further on the journey of 1142.

[6] Sánchez Albornoz, 314.

[7] *Cronica Adefonsi imperatoris*, edición y estudio por Luis Sánchez Belda (Madrid, 1950), xvii–xxi.

[8] Angel Ferrari, "El Cluniacense Pedro de Poitiers y la *Chronica Adefonsi Imperatoris* y la Poema de Almería," *Bol. R. Acad. Hist.*, CLIII (1963), 153–204. Cf. also his preceding article, "Artificios septenarios en la *Chronica Adefonsi Imperatoris* y Poema de Almería," *ibid.*, 19–67. On Peter of Poitiers, see especially Constable, *Letters*, II, 331–43, and references there cited.

[9] Cf. *Cron.*, ed. Sánchez Belda, cap. 87 (p. 67); *Chartes de Cluny*, V, no. 3993; Bishko, "The Cluniac Priories of Galicia and Portugal: Their Acquisition and Administration," *Studia monastica*, VII (1965), 327–31 (Study XI in this volume).

[10] Sánchez Belda, xvii, citing Juan Ferreras, *Sinopsis histórico-cronológica de España* (Madrid, 1700–1727), XVI, Apéndice, 10.

[11] On San Salvador de Astorga, see *Chartes de Cluny*, V, no. 3885; on bishop Alo, *ibid.*, no. 3884; E. Flórez and M. Risco, *España Sagrada* (Madrid, 1747–1879), XVI (1762), 198–210; J. Amador de los Ríos, *Hist. crítica de la literatura española* (Madrid, 1861–1865; reprinted, 1969), II, 341–42; A. Lambert, "Astorga," *Dictionnaire d'histoire et de géographie ecclésiastiques* (=*DHGE*), IV, cols. 1199–1226.

stressed, is becoming generally acknowledged, although it still merits closer scrutiny.[12] Kritzeck, emphasizing the need for further investigation in still another direction, calls attention to the impress of the abbot's Spanish contacts upon the composition or final revision of his *Liber aduersus iudeorum inueteratam duritiem;*[13] and in this light the journey of 1142, affecting Peter's Jewish in addition to his Islamic studies, assumes even greater importance as the first true trans-Pyrenean intellectual confrontation not only with Islam but with the full range of the medieval Iberian tri-fideistic *convivencia.*

As for my reconstruction of the abbatial itinerary, this has received general agreement except on one point, the date of El Venerable's return to Cluny, where Van den Eynde makes a sound correction which I am happy to adopt.[14] On page 175, in accordance with what I took to be the intent of the notice by Rodulfus in his *Vita* c. 16, that while on his way home from the Peninsula Peter celebrated at Le Puy the *missa de Ascensione*, I dated the abbot's presence in that town on Ascension Day, 13 May 1143, although not without calling attention to the apparent contradiction between this evidence for an unhurried movement across Southern France and the abbot's two extant epistles stating his imperative need to reach Burgundy as speedily as possible. Van den Eynde has now resolved this difficulty by explaining that at Le Puy, when called upon to cure a man into whose body a serpent had entered, Peter appropriately chose to offer as a votive mass that of the Ascension, the Gospel of which contains—as Rodulfus had noted—the words *serpentes tollent*. Since this Mass could be celebrated at any time, it in no sense fixes the halt at Le Puy on Ascension Day itself. This removes all objection to believing in a relatively rapid progress beyond Burgos (which the abbot must have left by mid-September 1142), so that even allowing for time spent at Le Puy to attend a formal *curia ecclesiastica*,[15] Van den Eynde's conclusion that Peter reached Cluny during October is convincing, although November would probably fit as well. At any rate, the necessity for extending the trip into 1143 is thus completely removed. The abbot's Spanish sojourn can now be taken as falling entirely within the single calendar year 1142.

A more difficult question is whether to expand Peter's peninsular itinerary so as to allow for a penetration of Catalonia, Aragon and eastern Navarre preceding his march through western Navarre, the Rioja, Castile and Leon, as reconstructed in my article. Although the data supporting this, much less firm or documentable than that for the western stages, has been ignored or little studied, a positive answer is strongly indicated. It has often been noted that in his polemical treatise *Contra Petrobrusianos hereticos* the abbot cites the personal visit he has made *in orientalibus Hyspanie partibus*, a phrase that presumably includes all northeastern Iberia. Conjecture relating to the chronology of this trip has almost always placed it well before that of 1142; but this frequently encountered assumption of an earlier Hispanic tour is in my judgment untenable. On the other hand, certain diplomatic evidence from the years 1133–1145 concerning the foundation of what became the Cluniac priory of San Adrián de Vadoluengo near Sangüesa seems to point to a now unknown Petrine visitation of this house in the spring or early summer of 1142. A review of these

[12] José Muñoz y Sendino had already made this point much earlier in his "La Apología del cristianismo de al-Kindi," *Miscelánea Comillas*, XI-XII (1949), 363–70. See also now Kritzeck, *Peter the Venerable and Islam*, 56–8; Daniel, 230 (and cf. 399–400, where Daniel strangely overlooks the possibility that Peter is the Mozarab whom he posits as annotator of Robert of Ketton's Koran in the *Collectio Toletana*).

[13] Kritzeck, "Peter the Venerable and the Toletan Collection," 192–5.

[14] "Peter the Venerable's Journey to Spain," *Petrus Venerabilis, 1156–1956* (Rome, 1956; *Studia Anselmiana*, XL), 163–75 (=Study XII in this volume). Van den Eynde, "Voyages," 98–9.

[15] Rodulfus, *Vita*, c. 16: "cum in Podio solemniter curiam celebraret" (*Bibl. Clun.* 648; J. P. Migne, *Patrologiae cursus completus. Series latina* [=*PL*], 189, col. 26).

questions will demonstrate that there are convincing grounds for placing at the start of Peter's traverse of Spain two now unrecognized stages: first, an entry into Catalonia; thereafter—though less certainly—a passage via the pilgrimage road through Aragon and across eastern Navarre to Puente la Reina.

I. *Sant Pere de Casserres and the Rock-Salt Mountain of Cardona*

In one of the more remarkable sections of the *Contra Petrobrusianos* Peter the Venerable describes at some length an extraordinary mountain of salt located in eastern Spain of which he had been told and subsequently saw with his own eyes: "... in orientalibus Hyspanie partibus ... miraculum quod prius audiens uix credidi, sed post quod audieram uidens, dubitare non potui."[16] The passage occurs in connection with the refutation of Petrobrusian disbelief in Eucharistic transubstantiation. Peter, in keeping with the new scientific materialism of his time, undertakes to demonstrate the validity of the Aristotelian formula of substantial without accidental change in physical things by noting how water can be transformed from a liquid into a solid substance, ice, and in the case of the Spanish mountain even more astonishingly, into salt. For this mountain in eastern Hispania, he writes, has rocks and cliffs not of stone but of hard shining-white rock salt (*sal gemma*), superior in purity to that recovered from the sea or springs, and which is the subject of a large-scale profitable trade on the part of the local inhabitants. Yet, despite the daily sinking of deep shafts into the mountainside, every year during the rainy season all such excavated places fill with water that hardens into salt, so that whatever has been removed is completely replenished, demonstrating that, as with the Eucharist, an element from heaven (water in this case) can be transformed on earth into a different physical substance.[17]

Now there can be little, if any, doubt as to the precise geographical location of Peter's montane miracle. Not only are major rock-salt deposits rare in northeastern or northern Spain, but at only one place do they take the extraordinary geologic form of an authentic hill of salt: the great rock-salt mountain of Cardona in Catalonia, to the west of Vich and between Solsona and Manresa.[18] Of the many modern descriptions of

[16] *Petri Venerabilis Contra Petrobrusianos hereticos*, ed. James Fearns (Turnhout, 1968; *Corpus Christianorum, Continuatio Mediaevalis*, X), 109–10 (c. 184); *PL* 189, cols. 805–6.

[17] "Extant in regionibus illis sallita, ut ita dicam, uel salsa montana, que pro saxis uel rupibus lapideum sal continent, sicque perlucidum, ut quia gemmeam preciosorum lapidum claritatem emulatur, salis gemma uocetur. Quod tam perspicuitate quam utilitate marino puteali omnique sali prepositum de montanis illis multo labore ab incolis eruitur et remotis quibusque pro magno munere datur aut pro magno lucro uenditur. De quibus montibus, cum diutinus rusticorum labor lucri auidus multam lucidi illius lapidis quantitatem eruerit et eruendo fossas multas eo sale inanes reliquerit, processu temporis pluuiali inundatione fossarum illa uacuitas repletur, ac repleta, post paululum in naturam illius cui admiscetur lapidis commutatur. Tali recompensatione effossus mons pene annuatim dampna illata restaurat, et quicquid de lapide amisit, aqua in lapidem conuersa compensat. Fit ergo celestis aqua lapis terrenus, que licet naturalem mollitiem in lapideam duritiam commutans, in alienam substantiam transeat, formam tamen priorem et speciem, sicut de christallo supra dixi, conseruat. Sed sicut nec de omni glacie nec de omni christallo hec dixi, sic nec de omni montis illius lapide hoc dico, sed de illo qui non de cenosa sed de limpidissima concretus aqua originis sue claritatem etiam in aliud mutatus non mutat" (ed. Fearns, *loc. cit.*).

[18] See Karl Baedeker, *Spain and Portugal*, 3rd ed. (Leipzig, 1908), 250; and the illustrated descriptions in *Enciclopedia universal ilustrada europeo-americana*, XI, 874–6; *Geografía de España y Portugal*, ed. Manuel Terán, IV, parte 2 (Barcelona, 1966), 273 and Lámina XLII; and cf. Miguel Gual Camarena, "Para un mapa de la sal hispana en la Edad Media," in *Homenaje a Jaime Vicens Vives* (Barcelona, 1965–), I, 490, 496, and map.

this still noteworthy spectacle, one of the last century may be cited in part, that of Sebastián de Miñano in his *Diccionario geográfico-estadístico* of 1826–1828—a description at points so reminiscent of Peter's own as to suggest a common source in local tradition or the propaganda of an unusually long-lived tourist bureau. At Cardona, says Miñano, "es muy célebre el mineral de sal gema de esta villa . . . un peñasco de sal maciza que se levanta encima de tierra, cosa de 400 á 500 pies . . . 1 legua de circuito, y su elevación no es menos que cualquiera de las otras montañas circunvecinas . . . Esta prodigiosa montaña de sal, desnuda de otra cualquiera materia, es única en Europa . . . y ni las aguas la disminuyen, ni ha podido agotarse con la continua extracción por espacio de tantos siglos; las lluvias no disminuyen la sal."[19]

This is firm proof that at some time in his travels Peter the Venerable reached central Catalonia, and it at once suggests that his presence here is to be accounted for in terms of a visitation to the nearby Cluniac priory of Sant Pere de Casserres (San Pedro de Caserras), a house lying to the south of Berga which had been given to the Burgundian monks in 1079 by Viscount Ramón Folch of Cardona.[20] In all probability it was at Casserres that the itinerant abbot first learned of the noteworthy saline mountain of the *comarca*; at any rate, it must have been from here that he made his excursion to behold the miraculous phenomenon for himself. Furthermore, it is to be recalled also that in 1142 Catalonia contained two other Cluniac dependencies in this vicinity which the abbot would surely have sought to visit at the same time—Sant Pere de Comprodon (San Pedro de Camprodón), 40 km. northwest of Gerona,[21] and Sant Pere de Clarà (San Pedro de Clarano), of uncertain location, but presumably near the village of this name not far from Ripoll and its venerable Benedictine abbey, and within reach from Comprodón.[22] We can posit with some confidence, therefore, an abbatial entry into Catalonia which may have touched at all three houses but very probably included Sant Pere de Casserres.

But when in fact are we to suppose that such a Catalan tour could have been carried out? Conjectures abound that the Venerable made one or more journeys into Spain previous to that of 1142 and the possibility continues to find support in the most recent literature. Constable admits that Peter may have been in Spain in either 1124 or 1127, although noting at the same time that "he is not known to have gone there before 1142–3";[23] and Van den Eynde, with particular reference to the Catalan visit attested by the saline passage of the *Contra Petrobrusianos*, warns against dismissing as "simplement fantaisiste" the thesis of an earlier peninsular trip than that of 1141–42 (*sic*).[24] Should we then regard the Catalan visitation as occurring in the course of such a hypothetical earlier crossing of the Pyrenees by Peter? Speculation on this point has ranged loosely over the years 1124, 1126, post-1126, 1127 and 1134, all but the last of these hypotheses apparently stemming from a false assumption of Rosseeuw Saint-Hilaire, who in the true spirit of 19th-century "pan-clunisme" had concluded that a reconciliation, which he placed in 1126, between the warring monarchs Alfonso VII of

---

[19] Sebastián de Miñano, *Diccionario geográfico-estadístico de España y Portugal* (Madrid, 1826–8), II, 381–2, s.v. *Cardona*.

[20] Donation act of 25 November 1079 in *Chartes de Cluny*, IV, 668–89 (no. 3541); cf. M. Alamo, "Caserras" in *DHGE*, XI, 1949, col. 1270, and bibliography there cited.

[21] Donation act of 1078 to Moissac by grant of Count Bernardo II de Besalú: *Chartes de Cluny*, IV, 645–7 (no. 3523); cf. J. Miret y Sans, *Relaciones entre los monasterios de Comprodón y Moissac* (Barcelona, 1898); M. Alamo, "Comprodón (San Pedro de)," *DHGE*, XI, cols. 664–71.

[22] The gift of Adalet Guadaldis on 3 (or 11) December 1080: *Chartes de Cluny*, IV, 682–3 (no. 3554).

[23] *Letters*, II, 287.

[24] "*Voyages*," 94–7, where however Van den Eynde concludes that "il n'y a plus de raison pour maintenir l'hypothèse d'un voyage dans la péninsule ibérique avant 1141–42" (p. 97).

León-Castile and Alfonso I *el Batallador* of Aragon-Navarre could only have been achieved by the abbot of Cluny while in the course of inspecting his peninsular dependencies.[25] But this surmise lacks all foundation. The circumstances surrounding the so-called Paces de Támara have now been given close scrutiny by two experts: R. Menéndez Pidal, who rejects the usual ascription of this treaty to 1127 as recorded in the *Chronica Adefonsi imperatoris* and favors a date of 1124; and J. Ma. Lacarra, who after exhaustive analysis of the diplomatic texts bearing on the itineraries of both rulers during the quadrennium 1124–1127 demonstrates—in my opinion, irrefutably—that the 1127 dating is correct.[26] More importantly, neither of these investigations disclosed the slightest trace of Petrine intervention, least of all in the form of the abbot's actual appearance in the Peninsula during the years in question. As for 1124, it is to be further noted that the donation act by which on 23 June in this year Alfonso VII's sister, the Infanta Sancha, gave Cluny the Leonese monastery of San Miguel de Escalada, although addressed to Peter, specifically declares that it is being placed in the hands of the *camerarius* Hugo de Crécy for transmission to the abbot, who must then patently not have been in Spain.[27] Similarly, Emperor Alfonso VII himself in 1132, when ceding the venerable abbey of Sahagún to the Burgundian monks, for identical reasons entrusted his *real pergamino* to this same abbatial intermediary.[28]

In short, all the hypotheses regarding Peter's supposed advent in Spain during the decade 1124–1134 remain without substantiation, and stand in flat contradiction to the fact that Cluniac affairs in Spain, including the annual inspection of the priories, were regularly administered by itinerant (eventually resident provincial) chamberlains (*camerarii*). Only for truly extraordinary reasons, therefore, did the Burgundian abbot himself ever undertake the arduous journey to Spain, as when in 1090 Hugo the Great came to Burgos to insure continuation of the Alfonsine *census duplicatus;* or Ponce de Melgueil, as the legate of Paschal II, sought in 1113 to resolve the catastrophic succession crisis arising from the ill-fated marriage of Alfonso VI's daughter Urraca and King Alfonso *el Batallador*. Peter's own trip in 1142, which followed receipt of an express *inuitatio* of Alfonso VII, and can be linked to the fate of the ever more indispensable Hispanic census and to a disputed election to the see of Compostela, was clearly another such exceptional venture.[29]

If the earlier dates can thus be eliminated as both inherently unlikely and without any support whatever from the known documentation, the question whether we can

[25] See E. Rosseeuw Saint-Hilaire, *Histoire de l'Espagne* (Paris, 1844–79), IV, 401; J.-H. Pignot, *Histoire de l'Ordre de Cluny* (Autun-Paris, 1868), III, 289: 1126; P. Séjourné, "Pierre le Vénérable," in *Dictionnaire de théologie catholique*, XII, 2 (Paris, 1934), col. 2067: "dès 1126;" Jean Leclercq, *Pierre le Vénérable* (Abbaye S. Wandrille, 1946), 12: 1126, 1134.

[26] R. Menéndez Pidal, "Sobre un tratado de paz entre Alfonso el Batallador y Alfonso VII," *Bol. R. Acad. Hist.*, CXI (1942), 115–31; J. Ma. Lacarra, "Alfonso el Batallador y las paces de Támara: cuestiones cronológicas (1124–1127)," *Estudios de Edad Media de la Corona de Aragón*, III (1947–48), 461–73; *idem*, *Vida de Alfonso el Batallador* (Zaragoza, 1971), 89–93.

[27] *Chartes de Cluny*, V, 327–8 (no. 3970): "per manum domni Hugonis camerarii." The attack upon the authenticity of this charter by Fidel Fita, "San Miguel de Escalada. Documento apócrifo del siglo XII. Auténticos del XIII," *Bol. R. Acad. Hist.*, XXXII (1898), 25–37, was made in ignorance of the full text as published by Bruel and is clearly unacceptable, although this is not the place to give this act the exegesis it merits. The biographical sketch of the chamberlain Hugo de Crécy in Constable, *Letters*, II, 311-5 (Appendix 0) does not cite the pertinent Spanish privilegios and requires revision at several points.

[28] *Chartes de Cluny*, V. 390–2 (no. 4038): "in manu domni Stephani eiusdem monasterii abbatis et Hugonis Cluniacensis camerarii."

[29] On all these points, see my article "Peter the Venerable's Journey" (Study XII in this volume).

validly accept the abbot's undoubted Catalan penetration as part of the journey of 1142 has to be confronted anew. The major objection, and at first sight a formidable one, is the universal agreement of scholars that the *Contra Petrobrusianos* was composed before this year, so that the narrative of the personal visit to the saline mountain must necessarily be attributed to some previous Spanish experience. To be sure, once again opinion has been widely divergent regarding the precise date of composition of this treatise. It was long customary to place it in the 1120s, usually at 1126–1127; then the 1130s, especially 1137, became favorites;[30] and, most recently, J. Fearns, the able editor of the new *Corpus Christianorum* edition, has decided in favour of 1139/40.[31] But none of these views precludes the possibility that, following his return from the Peninsula and before releasing the work for circulation, Peter could have revised or made interpolations in the text in the light of his visit to Spain in 1142. Constable, in fact, while assigning the first draft of the *Contra Petrobrusianos* to ca. 1137/8 and its subsequent revision and publication to 1140/1, nevertheless acknowledges "that some finishing touches were perhaps added after 1143", citing specifically the visit to the rock-salt mountain in eastern Spain as an example of these;[32] and Van den Eynde notes that the same may be true of the references in the treatise to the person and work of Muhammad.[33] In the latter regard I would suggest that this is particularly evident in Peter's brief summary of Islamic religious practices as against his usual concentration upon the doctrines. Here, in his comparative analysis of the role of sacrifice in the world's four theistic faiths—Christianity, Judaism, Islam and paganism—he characterizes Muslims as practising circumcision, given to frequent ablutions, prostrating themselves in prayer at fixed times of the day and night, allegedly (*ut fertur*) after taking food and drink, and [presumably, thereafter] allowing free rein to license.[34] This not altogether accurate assessment—note, for example, the usual western misunderstanding of post-abstinence consumption of food and drink during Ramadan—may owe something to the *Dialogus* of Petrus Alfonsi or the *Collectio Toletana;* this remains to be established. What is striking is that similar language regarding *circumcisio*, *gula* and *libido* appears in the *Summa totius haeresis Saracenorum* and Letter 111 (IV, 17), both of which belong in the biennium 1143–1144;[35] and that the allusions in the *Contra Petrobrusianos* passage to frequent ablution and the daily prayer cycle, which are not mentioned in these two texts, may well represent information collected in Spain in 1142. Another of Peter's major apologetic treatises, the *Liber aduersus iudeorum inueteratam duritiem*, the study of which has been unduly neglected but which has generally been attributed to an earlier point in the abbot's career, contains various passages Kritzeck identifies as drawn from the Toledan Collection and therefore interpolated into the work after the return from

---

[30] Constable, *Letters*, II, 285–8 (Appendix G) reviews previous conjectures.

[31] James Fearns, "Peter von Bruis und die religiöse Bewegung des 12. Jahrhunderts," *Archiv für Kulturgeschichte*, XLVIII (1966), 313–7.

[32] *Letters*, II, 288.

[33] "Voyages," 97.

[34] Sarraceni . . . circumcisionem suscipiunt, lauachris frequentibus utuntur, certis horis die certis nocte orationi maxime post cibum et potum, ut fertur, incumbunt, luxui omnino frena relaxant" (*Contra Petrobrus.*, ed. Fearns, 94, c. 161; *PL* 189, col. 793D).

[35] "Circumcisionem . . . tenendam esse decreuit [Mahumet], et super haec omnia, quo magis sibi allicere carnales mentes hominum posset, gulae ac libidini frena laxauit": *Summa*, ed. James Kritzeck, *Peter the Venerable and Islam* (Princeton, 1964), 207; *PL* 189, col. 654D. "Circumcisionem . . . tenendam esse decreuit, et super haec omnia quo magis sibi allicere carnales mentes hominum posset, gulae ac libidini fraena laxauit": Letter 111, ed. Constable, I, 297; *PL* 189, col. 342B. On the relationship between these two texts, cf. Constable, II, 275–84 (Appendix F).

Spain.[36] This further demonstrates the abbot's eagerness immediately to incorporate the fruits of his peninsular travels and his commissioning of translations into his apologetic writings.

These various indications make it altogether likely that shortly after 1142 Peter the Venerable inserted into the final redaction of the *Contra Petrobrusianos* an argument in favor of transubstantiation based upon his recent visit to the rock-salt mountain of Cardona and by implication to the priory of Sant Pere de Casserres. We can add further corroborative evidence from other sources. First, there is Peter's own flat statement in the *Liber de miraculis*, the completion of which falls after 1142, that he had travelled to Spain only once: *semel*, i.e., once and for all, not, be it noted, *olim*, *aliquando* or the like; and it is clear that throughout his works he uses *semel* in its strict classical sense.[37] This information of course agrees perfectly with what we have said above concerning the silence of the sources regarding any earlier Hispanic venture. Secondly, in view of the abbot's similarly explicit declaration of his intention on his journey to Spain to carry out a *uisitatio locorum nostrorum*,[38] we must assume in the absence of any indication to the contrary that he did in fact reach the Catalan dependencies of which Sant Pere de Casserres, not far from Cardona, was the most important.

Thirdly, there is an overlooked passage in Peter's Letter 111 (IV, 17) which offers a final compelling proof. This celebrated and lengthy epistle, written in 1143 or 1144 to St Bernard of Clairvaux, attempts to persuade the great Cistercian leader to undertake a refutation of Islam on the basis of the materials just gathered by the abbot of Cluny in connection with his recent trip to Spain—and indeed the letter was accompanied by a manuscript of one of the new translations, very likely that of the *Risāla* of al-Kindi.[39] But Peter had still another objective, one that takes up considerable space from the beginning of Letter 111—a plea for amity between Cluniacs and Cistercians. Here, in words that in the context of the abbatial visit to Cardona take on previously unenvisaged significance, Peter remarks that he is sending on to Bernard—no doubt along with the letter and the anti-Islamic manuscript—a personal gift of rock-salt (*sal gemma*), to be used for the seasoning of food but intended also to be the symbol of the brotherly love that in spite of all differences of dress or custom should prevail between the religious of the two Orders.[40] To be sure, the Cluniac abbot could have acquired this piece of rock-salt years before his trip of 1142 and from another source than a personal visit, but Peter's express statement in his account of the mountain of Cardona that it was the practice there to confer pieces of the valuable *sal gemma* upon visitors

---

[36] James Kritzeck, "Peter the Venerable and the Toledan Collection," in *Petrus Venerabilis, 1156–1956* (Rome, 1956; *Studia Anselmiana*, XL), 192–5. The possible connection of the Islamic data in the *Contra Petrobrusianos* with the *Collectio Toletana*, not here explored by Kritzeck, would doubtless repay investigation.

[37] *Lib. de mirac.*, I, c. 28: "Et quia semel Hispani [i]s ingressi sumus, quod in eisdem partibus de re simili contigisse ibidem constituti audiuimus, praetereundum non est" (*PL* 189, col. 903D). Cf. the similar use of *semel* in, for example, Letter 109 (IV, 15): "ut nunquam illum apud Cluniacum nisi semel uidere potuerim" (Constable, I, 272; *PL* 189, col. 320B); Letter 111 (IV, 17): "epistolam ... quam Cluniaci semel legi, sed nunquam postea ad relegendum habere potui" (Constable, I, 299; *PL* 189, col. 343D).

[38] *Summa totius haeresis Saracenorum*: "cum in Hispaniis pro uisitatione locorum nostrorum quae ibi sunt demorarer" (ed. Kritzeck, *Peter the Venerable*, 210; *PL* 189, col. 657A).

[39] Constable, I, 294; *PL* 189, col. 339C. Cf. Constable, II, 278.

[40] "Misi gemmeo amico salis gemmam, cuius corporalem usum uobis utilem olim audiui, et cuius spiritualem intellectum supra scriptis necessarium esse putaui" (Constable, I, 294; *PL* 189, 339B).

from distant parts, sounds like an allusion to an experience of his own.[41] At any rate, this saline present to Bernard and his fellow-monks at Clairvaux is so closely associated with a letter crowded with references to Spain, touching not only on the urgent need for anti-Muslim apologetics but even on socio-anthropological topics such as, for example, the peninsular use of black for mourning in contrast with that of white then current above the Pyrenees,[42] that it is difficult to believe that this salty symbol of Cluniac-Cistercian friendship can have any other provenance than Peter's trip of 1142.

Nor do we need to hesitate long as to just where to allocate the Catalan stage in the traverse of 1142. Everything we know regarding Peter's hurried homeward march that autumn from Burgos—his receipt of gloomy news regarding conditions at Cluny during his long absence, his cancellation of projected visits to Archbishops Geoffrey of Bordeaux and Arnaldo of Narbonne (both premising an intended homeward route far west of Catalonia), the urgency of transmitting to Pope Innocent II his promised endorsement of Alfonso VII's candidate in the disputed Compostelan election—rules out a halt, not to say sight-seeing at Cardona.[43] In contrast, at the start of the journey across Spain to distant Salamanca, the abbot's slow-paced movements during the spring and summer, indeed all the way to his meeting with Emperor Alfonso VII in late August, his extended stays at priories such as Nájera and Carrión, raise no chronological objections whatever. We conclude therefore that the travels in Catalonia of the as yet unwearied Burgundian compiler of natural and supernatural wonders can safely be assigned to the spring of 1142.

II. *Roncesvalles or Somport? San Adrián de Vadoluengo-Sangüesa and the Aragonese Route to Puente la Reina*

The testimony to Peter's presence in Catalonia at the commencement of his peninsular traverse raises in turn the question of his itinerary beyond Casserres and Cardona to that point on the main pilgrimage road near Estella where we again pick up the little company on its approach to the Rioja and Santa María de Nájera. Estella lies westward of Puente la Reina, the junction point of the Aragonese Somport and Navarrese Roncesvalles sections of the great highway, and to reach this station the abbot could conceivably have proceeded from Casserres across Urgel and Ribagorza, or else have dropped down south to strike the line of the Ebro. But he might also have returned from Catalonia into southern France, and, after taking the much travelled road above the Pyrenees via Arles, Montpellier, Narbonne and Carcassonne to Toulouse, re-entered Spain farther to the west.[44] If so, this would have been either at Roncesvalles, as has always been supposed with regard to his original entry, or by

[41] "... de montanis illis multo labore ab incolis eruitur et remotis quibusque pro magno munere datur aut pro magno lucro uenditur" (*Contra Petrobrusianos*, ed. Fearns, 109, c. 184; *PL* 189, col. 805D).

[42] Constable, I, 289; *PL* 189, col. 335A-B. Cf. R. Dozy, *Recherches sur l'histoire et la littérature de l'Espagne pendant le moyen âge*, 2nd ed. (Leiden, 1860), II, 98–9.

[43] *Lib. de mirac.*, I, c. 28 (*PL* 189, cols. 903D-904A). Peter does not specifically mention his stopping at Estella, as he does at Nájera, but this can legitimately be inferred from his admiring description of the castle there and its surroundings, and also from the phrase *ut aestimo* used to justify the toponym *Stella*.

[44] Consult the map of 'Los caminos de Santiago en Francia," in L. Vázquez de Parga, J. M.ª Lacarra and J. Uría Ríu, *Las peregrinaciones a Santiago de Compostela* (Madrid, 1948–1949), II, 45; and Lacarra, "Rutas de peregrinación. Los pasos del Pirineo y el camino de Santa Cristina a Puente la Reina," *Pirineos* I, no. 2 (1945), 5–27.

Somport, the Aragonese gateway through the mountains leading to Jaca, the Navarrese frontier near Sangüesa, and on to Puente la Reina. In the complete absence of direct documentary notices, the evidence on this point must remain purely circumstantial, but for what it is worth it would seem to favor the Somport-Sangüesa alternative, for the following reasons.

To assume an abbatial journey beyond Catalonia entirely within Spain raises formidable difficulties. Any east-west transverse route across the rugged mountain country of southern Ribagorza and the Cinca Valley would have imposed arduous, painfully slow passages in thinly settled lands, as yet imperfectly pacified outside the few larger towns. In later centuries, as indeed also in the Muslim epoch, the normal route would have been to move down the Segre River to its junction with the Ebro and then to follow up the valley of the latter stream past Zaragoza to the Rioja. If this route had been viable in 1142, we might even speculate that Peter was crossing the diocese of Tarazona at the very time when its French-born Bishop Michael and his learned canon Magister Hugo Sanctalliensis (of Santa Eulalia?) were preoccupied with the preparation of translations of Arabic works on astronomy, astrology, geomancy and mathematics;[45] and thus it would be tempting to place near Tarazona or Tudela the fateful meeting *iuxta Iberum* with the translators Hermann of Dalmatia and Robert of Ketton who shared these same scientific interests.[46] But in 1142, with Lérida still in Muslim hands (to 1149), this possibility can be eliminated. Furthermore, so famous a city as Zaragoza finds no mention in Peter's writings; it did not contain, as frequently alleged, a Cluniac priory;[47] most fatally of all, such an itinerary would have led straight to the Rioja and Santa María de Nájera well to the southwest of Estella, thus contradicting Peter's own declaration of the *itineris necessitas* that explains his presence in the latter area.

In this light, the alternative of a return from Catalonia to France and thereafter movement westward above the mountains to the trans-Pyrenean passes of Somport or Roncesvalles, offers the more probable solution; and of these two famous entry-ports into the Peninsula not Roncesvalles, as now believed and as supported in my original reconstruction of the abbatial journey, but Somport, has the stronger claim on at least three grounds. (i) If Peter did in fact recross the Pyrenees, he would be travelling on the pilgrim highway that ran from Toulouse, Auch and Oloron to Somport and Jaca, a much shorter route to Puente la Reina and Estella than by the pass of Roncesvalles farther to the west. (ii) Such an itinerary provides a logical explanation of why Bishop Amatus of Oloron, whose cathedral church lay directly north of Somport, turns up in Spain in the abbot's company.[48] (iii) Peter's program of a *uisitatio locorum nostrorum* creates a presumption of his having sought to visit the Cluniac priory of San Adrián de Vadoluengo in northeastern Navarre close to the Aragonese frontier and precisely on

[45] Cf. C. H. Haskins, *Studies in Mediaeval Science*, 2nd ed. (Cambridge, Mass., 1927), 43–66; J. M. Millás Vallicrosa, *Las traducciones orientales en los manuscritos de la Biblioteca Catedral de Toledo* (Madrid, 1942), 8–10, and *passim*; R. Lemay, "Dans l'Espagne du XIIe siècle, les traductions de l'arabe au latin,' *Annales: Economies-Sociétés-Civilisations*, XVIII (1963), 655–7.

[46] The study by J. M.ª Lacarra, "Una aparición de ultratumba en Estella (Pedro el Venerable, *De miraculis*, Lib. I, cap. 28)," identifying *iuxta Iberum* as a Riojan site in the neighborhood of Nájera, originally published in *Príncipe de Viana*, V (1944), 173–84, has been reprinted, with additional bibliographical data, in his *Estudios de historia navarra* (Pamplona, 1971), 139–52, 179–80. Cf. also Angel J. Martín Duque, "El inglés Roberto," 483–506, especially 483–90.

[47] The confusion by medieval Cluniac scribes of *Sangos(s)a* (Sangüesa) and *Saragossa* (Zaragoza), explains the appearance of a non-existent Caesaraugustan priory of San Adrián in the catalogues of Ibero-Cluniac houses compiled by Robert, Valous, Pérez de Urbel, Joan Evans and others.

[48] "Peter the Venerable's Journey" (Study XII), note 13.

the line of the Somport-Jaca-Puente la Reina highway at the point where this routeway to Compostela crossed the historic bridge over the River Aragón.[49] Peter had no such visitational reason for taking the Roncesvalles road, although a desire to pass through Pamplona cannot be altogether ruled out.[50] Moreover, in the years just before and after 1142 the canonical status of the Cluniac holdings at San Adrián de Vadoluengo was sufficiently controversial as to warrant, if not compel, the intervention of the Burgundian abbot while passing through Spain.

To explain this last factor calls for a summation of evidence I have presented elsewhere *in extenso*.[51] In 1133 a leading Aragonese nobleman, Fortún Garcés Caxal or Cajal, when terminating many years of service under Alfonso *el Batallador* as *señor* of Nájera, Viguera, Grañón and Belorado in the Aragonese-occupied territories of the Rioja and eastern Castile, gave Prior Peter and the Cluniacs of Santa María de Nájera a parting gift. This consisted of the church and *heredad* of San Adrián at Vadoluengo just below Sangüesa, two *heredades* more to the west near Aibar, and a valuable tract, the *soto* of Alcatén, well to the south at Tudela in the reconquered middle Ebro Valley.[52] The church of San Adrián then lay within the confines of the kingdom of Aragon, and from the terms of the donation charter, issued in the name of Cajal and his wife Toda and reserving to them vitalicial retention of all the ceded properties, it can be suspected that the intention was to prepare the way for eventual creation under Santa María's control of what would have been Cluny's first monastic dependency on Aragonese soil. Any such scheme however certainly foundered soon in the cataclysmic changes that transformed the political map of north-central Iberia following *el Batallador's* untimely death on 8 September 1134. Alfonso VII's swift conquest of the Rioja, the collapse of the Navarro-Aragonese federation and the emergence of an independent Pamplonese state under King García Ramírez, the latter's successful annexation of Sangüesa and Vadoluengo from Aragon, Aragon's fateful alliance in August 1137 with the County of Barcelona under Ramón Berenguer IV, and the long years of warfare between García Ramírez and his hostile neighbors on either side—such factors would have told heavily against the viability of a Burgundian subpriory located on the extreme eastern edge of Navarre yet attached to Nájera in the once again Leonese-Castilian Rioja.[53]

Furthermore, in this turbulent epoch Cajal himself, although at first enjoying high position as a chief counsellor of Alfonso I's fleeting successor Ramiro II *el Monje*, suffered a serious setback in both personal wealth and political influence in mid-1136.

---

[49] See Lacarra in *Peregrinaciones a Compostela*, II, 427, on the branch that diverged from the main road just beyond San Salvador de Leire and led to Sangüesa and the bridge over the Aragón.

[50] Sancho de Larrosa, bishop of Pamplona (1122–1142), perhaps mortally ill in the summer of 1142, died on 10 September, being immediately succeeded by Lope de Artajona (1142–1159). Sancho and Lope unquestionably continued this see's friendship with Cluny which was initiated under the French-born Pamplonese prelate Pedro de Anduque (1084–1115); note (see below) the part played by Sancho and Lope in the donation acts of 1141 and 1145 for San Adrián de Vadoluengo. On both prelates, see J. Goñi Gaztambide, "Los obispos de Pamplona en el siglo XII," *Anthologica annua*, XIII (1965), 134–358, at 204–78, where however their attitude towards Cluny is not examined.

[51] "A Hispano-Cluniac Benefactor in the Epoch of Navarro-Aragonese Separation: Fortún Garcés Cajal and the Founding of San Adrián de Vadoluengo (Sangüesa), 1133–1145," to be published in the forthcoming *Homenaje* to Prof. Claudio Sánchez Albornoz.

[52] Donation act in F. Fita, "Primer siglo de Santa María la Real, de Nájera," *Bol. R. Acad. de la Hist.*, XXVI (1895), 271–2 (no. 9); I. M. Rodríguez de Lama, "Colección diplomática Riojana," *Berceo*, XII (1957), 107–8 (no. 65).

[53] See J. M.ª Lacarra, *Historia política de Navarra* (Pamplona, 1972), I, 325–33; II, 11–27; Antonio Ubieto Arteta, *Historia de Aragón. La formación territorial* (Zaragoza, 1981), 203–12.

While travelling across Navarre as royal envoy to negotiate an anti-Navarrese alliance between Aragon and the Hispanic Empire of Alfonso VII, he had the misfortune to be taken prisoner by agents of King García Ramírez.[54] Only by paying the Pamplonese monarch an extremely high ransom was the magnate able to secure his liberation in 1137, and to raise this sum he had to turn over most of his numerous domains in Aragon, Navarre and the Ebro Valley to San Salvador de Leire in return for that wealthy abbey's provision of the necessary cash.[55] Although by Ramiro II's express order the lands Cajal had previously promised the Cluniacs of Nájera were excluded from this transaction,[56] those at Tudela and Aibar were in fact lost to them at this time.

It is however certain that although much impoverished and with visibly shrunken influence at a court that was now looking eastward to union with Barcelona, Cajal did not relinquish his commitment of 1133 to establish a Cluniac outpost near Sangüesa. In the course of the year 1137 he bestowed upon his recognizably French and very probably Cluniac chaplain Peter a *palacio* and *heredad* within the Sangüesan Burgo Nuevo, properties which he had succeeded in redeeming from Leire.[57] Once again, the language of the gift, made together with his wife Toda on behalf of themselves, their deceased son García Cajal (a casualty in late 1133 of Alfonso I's campaign against Mequinenza), and the magnate's own kinsmen (*parentes*) Kings Pedro and Alfonso of Aragon, implies the projected foundation of a monastic house capable of carrying out the donor's intercessional purpose.

This intention becomes plain in 1141, when, by a little known diploma, Cajal and Toda transfer directly to the abbey of Cluny not only the same church and *heredad* of San Adrián at Vadoluengo which in 1133 they had ceded to Santa María de Nájera, but also the *palacio* and *heredad* of the Burgo Nuevo given to the chaplain Peter just four years previously.[58] On this latest occasion Sancho de Larrosa, bishop of Pamplona, lent his formal sanction to the benefaction by consecrating the church of San Adrián to its changed function as the chapel of a new Cluniac community, no longer envisaged as a subpriory of Santa María de Nájera but a priory in its own right directly subordinate to the abbot of Cluny. From Cajal's subsequent diploma of 1145 we learn that from the date of the *dies consecrationis*, *monachi Cluniacenses* were in residence at Vadoluengo and in full possession of its temporal. The changed political boundary after 1135 meant however that instead of becoming, as foreseen in 1133, the first Burgundian outpost in Aragon, San Adrián de Vadoluengo, or as the Cluniac records designate it, San Adrián de Sangüesa (and often erroneously San Adrián de Zaragoza), now assumed a comparable role in Navarre, although, to be sure, in the latter kingdom Santa María de Nájera already possessed near Estella the subject-house of San Jorge de Azuelo at Berrueza.[59]

This substitution in 1141 of the mother abbey in Burgundy for the Riojan Santa María as the immediate superior of San Adrián can hardly have been effected without Peter the Venerable's knowledge and assent, and to his natural interest in visiting this latest peninsular dependency would have been added the circumstances of its disputable canonical status. This last factor becomes manifest in 1145 when it proved necessary for Cajal to repeat his cession of four years before by promulgating a second

[54] *Carta Pergamenea* in *Colección de documentos inéditos del Archivo General de la Corona de Aragón*, ed. P. de Bofarull y Mascaró (Barcelona, 1847–1910), IV, no. CL.

[55] *Chartes de Cluny*, V, no. 4046, where Bruel's reading of 'era MªCªLXXII' (1134) requires to be corrected to read 'era MªCªLXXV' (1137).

[56] *Carta Pergamenea, ad finem* (364).

[57] J. de Moret, *Anales del Reino de Navarra* (Tolosa, 1890), III, 319.

[58] See L. M. de Lojendio, *Navarre romane* (La-Pierre-qui-vire, 1967), 197.

[59] A. de Yepes, *Corónica de San Benito*, ed. J. Pérez de Urbel (Madrid, 1959–60), III, 110–1.

donation charter for San Adrián, the only one destined to be preserved by the mother abbey and eventually to find its way into Bruel's *Chartes de Cluny*.[60] In this text Cajal appears alone, Doña Toda evidently having died in the interval, but the *abadengo* attached to the church is identical, as is the list of persons for whom commemoration is sought: Cajal, Toda, their son García, the royal *parentes* Kings Pedro and Alfonso. No re-consecration was necessary but the bishop of Pamplona remains prominent, this time not Sancho de Larrosa but his successor Lope, to whose *interuentus et auctoritas* the diploma attributes itself. The fact that abbots from three major monasteries on both sides of the Navarro-Aragonese border also attend as witnesses—John of San Juan de la Peña, Peter of Leire, Peter of Santa María de Irache—further underscores a determination to remove all juridical clouds surrounding the grant.

In this context it is difficult not to speculate that the amicable relations the acts of 1141 and 1145 disclose between Cluny and the Church of Pamplona owe something to Peter's friendship with the erudite English cleric Robert of Ketton who headed his Koranic translation team of 1142 and with whom the abbot, after returning to Burgundy, remained in scholarly correspondence. Master Robert can be found in the 1140s as a particularly prominent archdeacon of the 'Iglesia Iruniense', a principal episcopal counsellor, and the stalwart defender in his archdeaconry of Valdonsella—the valley of the Onsella and middle Aragón rivers below Sangüesa—of Pamplona's rights to various churches there against the counter-claims of the bishops of Zaragoza and Calahorra.[61] Since this was a time when the prelates of the latter see were also seeking papal annulment of Alfonso VI's 1079 cession of Santa María de Nájera to Cluny and hoping to resume full episcopal authority over the great Riojan community, it is tempting to posit some degree of collaboration between Robert and Peter in the denial of jurisdiction over San Adrián to Nájera, which lay in the diocese of Calahorra no less than in the hostile kingdom of León-Castile. This relationship, however, doubtless developed too late to lend its strength to the case for a Petrine stopover at Vadoluengo in 1142.

Nothing the preceding paragraphs have adduced can be taken as definitely proving that in 1142 Peter the Venerable touched at the priory of San Adrián. Yet if we take into consideration the factors just presented, the presumption would seem reasonably strong that after leaving Catalonia Peter re-entered Spain by the Aragonese gateway of Somport and Canfranc rather than that of Roncesvalles, and visited San Adrián de Vadoluengo-Sangüesa in person.

---

60 *Chartes de Cluny*, V, no. 4104.

61 Martín Duque, "El inglés Roberto," 491–505; P. Kehr, *Papsturkunden in Spanien, II. Navarra und Aragon, in Abhandlungen der Gesellschaft der Wissenschaften zu Göttingen, phil.-hist. Kl.*, N. F., XXII (1928), Heft 50, pp. 58–9.

INDEX

Abadal i de Vinyals, Ramon: I 6,11-12
abbess, consecration of: I 14-15; III 534A-5A
abbots, at Toletan councils: V 140-151A
-as uicarii episcoporum: V 142-5
-iure proprio: V 146-50,151A-2A
abbots, Cluniac, in Spain: X 311-19; XI 338-9,347-8,352-3;XII 163-75
abbots, consecration of: III 534A-5A
-elections of: I 4,27,34-5
Absalom, abbot Búbal, pactum of: I 28;III 516,535A
Achard, prior of Nájera: XI 343
Adulfus, abbot Arcos de Furco: I 34
Afonso I Henriques, king of Portugal: IX 162;XI 331-2
Ailo, abbess Piasca, pactum of: III 522
Alan, Master, prior of Nájera: XI 350-1
Albelda, San Martín de: III 527-8,530, 535A-6A
Aldonza, countess: X 313,324
Alfonso I, king of Asturias: I 5,40; III 524
Alfonso III, Chronicle of: I 40;III 524
Alfonso VI, king-emperor of Leon-Castile: VII 54-5;VIII 54-5,61-6, 77A-8A,80A;IX 171-3,189A-90A; X 311,313,315;XI 317-8
Alfonso VII Raimúndez, king-emperor of Leon-Castile: VIII 75-6;IX 187; X 311-13;XI 317-19,327-33;XII 164-5,169-74;XIII 5-6,11-12
Alfonso I, king of Aragon-Navarre: VIII 78A-81A;X 312,314-16,318; XIII 6,11-12
alliance, Leonese-Cluniac: VIII 54-5, 75-6;IX 177-8
-Portuguese-Cluniac: IX 177-83
Alvaro, pactum of: III 521
Amatus, bishop of Oloron: XII 166; XIII 10,17
Arciselus (Arcisclus), abbot Sotovellanos, pactum of: I 39;III 519
Arcos de Furco, San Verísimo de: I 34
Argilegus, abbot Naroba, pactum of: I 14,26-8;III 521-2
Arias, Maximino: I 33
Astorga: IX 162-7,170-1,175,186; XII 168;XIII 2
Asturias, pactual monasticism in: I 40;III 522-3
Augustine, St., Regula Prima: II 377, 396A
Aymeric, Cluniac visitor in Spain: XI 349-52
'Azadina', SS. Pedro y Pablo de: I 11; III 525,536A
Azenarus, abbot Modúbar, pactum of: III 526-7,529
Azevedo, Luís Gonzaga de: IX 174
Azevedo, Rui de: IX 155,183-4,189A

Baixo Mondego, pactualism in: IV 144-5
Barion, Hans: V 140 n5
Basil, St., Regula: I 21;II 388-9, 397A-9A
Beatus, monk of Liébana: III 521
Beira: XI 313
-pactual monasticism in: IV 142-4
Benedict of Aniane: I 10;II 385,388; III 524,527-8
Benedict, St., Regula: I 10,14,41; III 529-30,533A-4A;VI 346
Benedictinism in Spain: I 1-2,14-15, 41-3;III 529
-Carolingian Reform: I 2,5,41-2; III 514,528-30,534A;VI 346,363-364
Berengarius, bishop of Salamanca: XII 170-1
Bernard of Clairvaux, St.: XII 175; XIII 8-9
Bernard of Cluny, Consuetudines: VII 52-4;VIIII 55-65,67
Bible, Hispano-Latin: II 384-5,394, 398A
Bobadilla, nunnery of: II 386;III 533A
Bourdin, Maurice, bishop of Coimbra: IX 180;X 315-6;XI 313-5,335,337
Braga, see of: I 22-3;IX 175,180
Britonia, see of: I 18
Brou, Louis: I 13
Búbal, Santa Eulalia de: I 28,31,34; III 516
Budiño, San Salvador de: XI 307,327-331,336;XII 171-2;XIII 2
Burgalese (Lérins) Formula: I 5-6,9-11,42;III 525-30
Burgos: I 11;III 520-1;VIII 70;IX 186-8

Burgos, Santa Coloma de: XI 345; XII 169

Cajal, Fortún Garcés: XIII 11-13
Calahorra, see of: XI 344;XIII 13
Calendar, Hispanic liturgical: VII 48-49,52-7
cameraria of Galicia: XI 341-56
camerarius abbatis, Hispano-Cluniac: IX 184;XI 339
Camprodón, San Pedro de: XIII 5
Cardeña, San Pedro de: I 11;III 536A; XII 170,174
Cardona: XIII 4-5,8-9
Carrión de los Condes, San Zoil de: IX 156,163,168-70;XI 310,339; XII 169,172-3
Carthaginensis provincia, councils of; V 142,146-9,152A
Casserres, Sant Pere de: XIII 4-5,8
Castañeda, Santa Leocadia de: I 33-4
Castile, county of: III 519-21
-pactualism in: I 40-1
-cult of St.Isidore of Chios in: VI 345-64
-Isidorian toponymy of: VI 360-1
Catalonia,Cluniac priories in: XIII 3-9
-pactual claims for: I 11-12
Celanova, San Salvador de: I 33,35-37;IV 152-3
census hispanicus to Cluny: VIII 60, 70-1,77A;IX 177-8,190A;X 311-313,320A;XI 314;XII 169-70
chamberlain, Hispano-Cluniac provincial: XI 339;XIII 6
Chiusa, San Michele della: X 314, 320A-21A
Chronica Adefonsi imperatoris: XIII 2
Ciudad Rodrigo, Santa Agueda de: XI 341,343
Clarà, Sant Pere de: XIII 5
Clunia, San Isidro de: VI 354-6
Cluny, abbots of, in Spain: X 311-19; XI 338-9,347-8,352-3;XII 163-75
-custumals of: VIII 55-72,78A
-expansion in Spain: VI 346;VIII 62-3,75-6;IX 156,178-82;X 312-13;XI 305-38;XII 169-70;XIII 5
-in the province of Galicia: XI 339-356
-in the province of Hispania: XI 338-40,345-6,353-6
-liturgical intercession at: VIII 53-56,67-70,79A-81A;XI 337
codices regularum: I 3,10;II 385-8; III 524,529,534A-5A
-Escorialensis a.I.13: I 38,40;II 381 381,385-6,398A;III 516,533A
-Escorialensis s.III.32: II 386; IV 150
-Lirinensis: I 10
-Trevirensis: II 385
Coimbra, county, pactualism in: IV 143-4
Coimbra, Santa Justa de: IX 181; XI 315-16
Compostela, pilgrimage road to: IX 163;XII 166-7;XIII 9-11
-see of: XII 170-3
coniunctio, Leonese-Cluniac: VIII 54-55,75-6;IX 177-8
-Portuguese-Cluniac: IX 177-83
Consensoria monachorum: I 7,9-10; II 377-95,396A-9A;III 516
consensorial monachism: I 21,25; II 393-4,398A
Constance of Burgundy, queen-empress of Leon-Castile: VIII 71-3;IX 178; XI 318,344
contractual monachism: I 20-5;II 377, 389-94,398A;III 514-30;IV 139-40
conversi: I 20-1,31-2
coronation oath, Visigothic: I 4,24
Cowdrey, H.E.J.: VIII 77A;X 320A-321A

Dalmace Geret, Cluniac chamberlain in Spain: IX 184-8;X 312,315, 317
David, Pierre: I 18;VIII 73;IX 189A; XI 317
Debruyne, Donatien: I 9;II 378-95, 396A
Díaz y Díaz, Manuel: I 10-11,38;II 397A;III 533A,535A
Diego Porcelos, count of Castile: III 520
doctor, *doctrina*: II 378,380-1,399A
Dueñas, San Isidro de: III 534A;VI 345-7,352-3,359-60,362-4;VII 54-5;VIII 76;IX 156-60,178,181-182;X 313;XI 314,325,341
-cession to Cluny: VI 346;VII 54-5
Dumio, monastery-see of: I 18-19; II 392

Elvira, daughter of Alfonso VI: XI 324-5,335
Eneco Vermudo: XI 308-11,335
episcopate, Galaico-Visigothic: I 17-18,22
episcopus saecularis: I 23;II 394
-*sub regula*: I 17-20,23;III 515
Escalada, San Miguel de: XIII 6
Estella: XII 166;XIII 10
Eufrasia, abbess Ura, pactum of:

I 14,29-30;III 518-20;IV 148
Eustorgius, Cluniac visitor in Spain: XI 349-52

Feige, Peter: IX 189A-90A;XI 357A
Fernán Fernández, count of Toro: XI 324-6
Fernán González, count of Castile: I 30;III 528;VI 354
Fernández Alonso, Justo: V 151A
Fernando I, king-emperor of Leon-Castile: VI 346,357-8;VII 47-59; VIII 54-5,57,60-1,64
Fernando II, king of Leon: XI 309,341, 343,345
Fernando III, king of Leon-Castile: XI 353
Férotin, Marius: I 12-13;VII 50
Ferrari, Angel: XIII 2
Ferreira, Santa María de: XI 324-6
Flórez, Enrique: X 314-6
Floriano, Antonio: I 28 n.95;III 532A-533A
Floritus, abbot of Vacariça: IV 147, 149
Florus, martyrology of: VI 348-50
Formula, Burgalese (or of Lérins): I 5-6,9-11,42;III 525-30
Franquila, abbot of Celanova: I 35,36
Froílaz, Pedro: XI 318,320-2,328,335
Fructuosus of Braga, St.: I 7,17-19, 22-23;II 392
-Regula monachorum: I 17,23
Fulgaredus, abbot Mezonzo, pactum of: I 28-9;III 516-17

Galicia, Cluniac province of: XI 338-356
-Cluniac priories in: XI 311-16, 331-8
-landowning classes in: I 20-4
-pactual monasticism in: I 32-7; III 513-7,533A;IV 140-3,153-4
García, king of Galicia: VIII 72
García III, king of Navarre: VIII 55
García Sanz, A.: I 12
gasalianes: III 523,531
Gelmírez, Diego, bishop of Compostela: X 314-17,321A;XI 315,319, 322-3,328-9,334-5
Gennadius, St., bishop of Astorga: I 33
Gerald, bishop of Braga: IX 180,189A; XI 313
Gerard of Flanders, abbot of Cluny: XI 348,352-3
German imperial rulers, relations with Cluny: VIII 57-9,74
Gómez Núñez, count of Toroño: XI 327-31,335;XIII 2
Gontroda Rodríguez: XI 321
Gonzalo Fernández, count of Castile: VI 355
Gregory of Tours, Lib. in gloria martyrum: VI 348-9,352
Guido, prior of Nájera: XI 342
Guimarães, São Salvador de: I 36; IV 152-3
Guisandus, abbot Orbañanos, pactum of: III 518,519
Gustioz, Rodrigo: VI 354-9
Gutierrez, Fronildi: XI 310

Hallinger, Kassius: VIII 78A
Helmengaud, abbot of Chiusa: X 314-15,320A-21A;XI 323
Henry II, German emperor: VIII 57-59,73-4
Henry I, king of England: VIII 73 n.69
Henry, count of Portugal: VIII 81A; IX 155-8,189A-90A;X 314;XI 311-15,328,331,335,337
Hermann of Dalmatia: XII 166-8; XIII 10
Herwegen, Ildefons: I 2-5,17-18,23-24,26,39-40;II 377-8;III 513-16, 525,535A;IV 140
Hispana canonical collections, Spanish MSS of: V 141 n.6
Hispania, Cluniac province of: XI 338-340,345-6,353-6
Hispanic Rite: I 4,12-16,31;III 534A-535A;VII 47-51
Historia Compostelana: X 314-16, 321A;XI 320,328
Historia Silense: VII 47-59
Hontoria de Riofranco, San Isidro de: VI 537-9
Hugh I, abbot of Cluny: VIII 61-4,70-71,79A-81A;IX 177-80,189A-90A
-Luso-Hispanic cessions under: XI 308-19
-Statuta of: VIII 72-4
-Vitae of: VIII 65-6
Hugh V, abbot of Cluny: XI 340,347-348
Hugh de Crécy, Cluniac chamberlain: XIII 6
Humbert, prior of Carrión, Cluniac chamberlain: XI 339,341-5

Ildephonse of Toledo, St., De virg. B. Mariae: VIII 77A
imperialism, Hispanic: VIII 54-5,58-59
incursio: II 382-3,398A

Indulfus, abbot Santillana, pactum of: III 522-3
Innocent II, pope: XII 171
Innocent III, pope: XI 340
invasio: II 382-3,398A
Isidore of Chios, St., Castilian cult of: III 534A;VI 345-54
-martyrdom: VI 345,347
-Passio: VI 351-3
Isidore of Seville, St.: VI 346-7
-death: VII 51-2
-Regula: I 8-9,21;II 388-9,394, 397A-8A;III 529,533A-4A
-translation: VI 346;VII 48,58-9
Isidorian toponomy, Castile: VI 360-361
iuramentum: I 16,21,30;II 393

John, Cluniac chamberlain in Spain: XI 353-6
Jorden, Willibald: VIII 53
Jubia, San Martín de: XI 307,319-24, 336,343
Julian, abbot Pinza, pactum of: I 35
Justa, countess, Cluniac nun: XI 310-311

King, P.D.: I 24;V 191A
Koran, Latin version of: XII 163-4; XIII 13

Lacarra, José María: XII 166;XIII 6
La Charité-sur-Loire, Cluniac priory: IX 178,180-1;XI 311-14
landowning classes, Galicia: I 20-4
Lara, infantes de: VI 355
Larrosa, Sancho de, bishop of Pamplona: XIII 12-13
Laturce, San Prudencio de: I 38;III 526-7,530,535A-6A
Leander, St., Regula: I 6,8
Leça, São Salvador de: I 38;IV 142-149,152-4
Leire, San Salvador de: XIII 12-13
Lemay, Richard: XIII 1-2
Leodegundia, abbess of Bobadilla: I 11,40;II 386;III 516,533A
León, San Isidro de: VII 47-51,55-9
Lérins (or Burgos), Formula of: I 6, 8-11;III 525,534A-6A
Lérins, St.-Honorat de, codex of: I 9-11
Libellus a RB subtractus: I 14,41-2; III 530
Liber ordinum: I 7,13-15,31,41;VI 350-1
liberti as monks: I 32
Liébana, pactual monachism in: III 521-2
Liébana, Santo Toribio (San Martín) de: III 521-1
Linage Conde, Antonio: I 2,7-8,12,38,41; II 397A-8A;V 191A;XI 357A
liturgy, Hispanic: see Hispanic Rite; Liber ordinum
Loyo, Santa María de: I 35-6

Mabillon, Jean: I 9-10;III 525,527
Martim Munoz: IX 165
Martin of Braga, St.: I 18;II 392;V 145 n.16
Mattoso, José: I 2,7,9,30,37-8;IV 142-143,152;XI 357A
Maurice, bishop of Braga: X 317
Mendes, Unisco: IV 145-6
Meyvaert, P.: I 10
Mezonzo, Santa María de: I 28-9,32-4,36; III 516-7
Michael, bishop of Tarazona: XIII 10
Minho, pactualism in: IV 145-7,152-3
Modúbar, San Martín de: I 11;III 526-7, 529
monastic traditions, Hispano-Benedictine: I 1-2,14-15,41-3;III 529
-Hispano-Celtic: I 18
-consensorial: I 21,25;II 393-4,398A
-Mozarabic: I 5,32;III 514,533A;V 148
-pactual: I 1-43;III 513-31;IV 139-54
'Mortalones', Santiago de: I 29,34
Mozarabic Rite: see Hispanic Rite
Mumadona Dias, countess: I 36;IV 152
Mundó, Anscari: I 6,9-10
Munio Romaniz: XI 307,326-7,335
Muñó, San Isidro de: VI 359-60

Nájera: XII 166
-Sts. Nunilo and Alodia, nunnery at: III 434A-5A
Nájera, Santa María de: VIII 75-6;XI 339-46,348-9,353-6;XII 166,168-9;XIII 11-13
Naroba, Santos Pedro y Pablo de: I 14,25-28;III 521-2;IV 148
Nonna Bella, abbot Pedroso, pactum of: III 518,520

Odilo, abbot of Cluny: VIII 55,74
Orbañanos, San Juan de: III 518
ordines, monastic: I 12-16;III 534A-5A
Orlandis, José: I 31;V 152A
Osanius, abbot Viñón, pactum of: III 522
Osoredo Trutesendes: IV 145-6
Oviedo, San Vicente de: III 532

Pacto Sucessório: IX 155-88,189A-90A
pactual monachism, Castile: I 4-5,7-11,

15-16,29-30,38-43;III 513-31
-Catalonia, claims for: I 11-12
-Galicia: I 5-8,15-25,28-38;III 514-17
-Liébana: I 25-8;III 521-2
-Portugal: I 4-5,30,32,36-8,42-3; IV 139-54
-Rioja: I 5,7-8,11,15,38,41-3;III 525-30
-Suevo-Visigothic: I 8-25,42-3
pactum: I 3-4,8-9,12-16,23-6;II 392-393;III 513-17;IV 139-40
-abbatial: I 25-32
-binary: I 25-32;IV 146-9
-Burgalese (or of Lérins): see Burgalese Formula;Lérins, Formula of
-of Reg. communis: I 6-7,17,19, 23-5,29-31,38-40;II 389-90,392-393,397A-8A;III 515-16,518,522-523;IV 139-40
Pamplona: XII 166,174;XIII 12-13
pan-pactual thesis: I 6-16,33
Paradela, Santa Marina de: I 36
Paschal II, pope: IX 186;X 314-15, 320A-1A;XI 322-3
Payo Erigis Botan, notary: IX 163, 171-2
Pedro I, king of Aragon-Navarre: VIII 78A-81A
Pedroso, San Miguel de: III 518
Pérez de Urbel, Justo: I 2,6-9,16, 32-3;III 536A
Peter (of Andouque), bishop of Pamplona: VIII 79A-80A
Peter of Poitiers: XII 165-7;XIII 2
Peter, monk-chaplain of Sangüesa: XIII 12
Peter of Toledo, Master: XII 166-7; XIII 2-3
Peter the Venerable. abbot of Cluny, Spanish visitation: XII 163-75; XIII 1-13
-cessions to Cluny under: XI 326-338;XII 174
-Hispanic notices in: VIII 74-5;XII 163-4;XIII 3-5,7-9
-Islamic interests: XII 163-4,167, 175;XIII 1-2,7-8
-Jewish interests: XII 168 n.21; XIII 3,7-8
-translation of Koran: XII 166-7; XIII 10
Petrus, abbot 'Azadina', pactum of: III 525,536A
Pinza, San Ciprián de: I 35
Poeck, D.: VIII 78A
Pombeiro, San Vicente de: XI 307-7, 316-19,336
Ponce (Pontius) de Melgueil, abbot of Cluny: X 311-19,320A-21A;XI 319,323-4,357A
-cessions to Cluny under: XI 319-326
Portugal, pactual monachism in: I 32-38;III 517;IV 139-54
Potes, Liébana, pactualism near: III 521-2
presbyteral monasticism: I 22
Priscillianism: II 378-82,392,396A
profession, monastic: I 3-4,16-17
provinces, Cluniac, in Spain: XI 306-307-338-56

Quintila, abbot Loyo, pactum of: I 35

Radulfus, abbot of Cluny: XI 339,341-342
Ramiro I, king of Aragon: VIII 55
Ramiro II, king of Aragon: XIII 11-12
Randulfus, presbyter of Leça: IV 142, 145,147
Rates, São Pedro de, Cluniac priory: IX 180-1;XI 308,311-15
Raymond, count of Galicia: VIII 81A; IX 165,172-3,175-88,189A-90A; X 314;XI 317
Raymond, prior of Nájera: XI 344
regina Hispaniae (-arum): VIII 57, 60,68-9,73-5
Regula communis: I 4 and n.9,17,20-24;II 398A;III 515-16
-pactum of: I 24-5,39-40;II 389; III 515-16;IV 140,150-1
Regula mixta: I 2
Regula ss. Pauli et Stephani: II 380, 399A
Reilly, Bernard: IX 189A-90A;X 321A; XI 357A-8A
rex-imperator Hispaniae (-arum): VIII 54,58-60,64,67-70,77A; IX 185
Ribas de Sil, San Esteban de: I 35
Rioja: XI 344-5
-pactual monachism in: I 5-8,11, 15,38,41-3
Robert of Ketton: XII 166-7,174;XIII 10,13
Rodanius, abbot Tejada, pactum of: I 39;III 517-18,520;IV 150-1
Rodrigo, count of Castile: III 520
Roncesvalles: XII 166;XIII 9-11,13
Rosende, San Martín de: I 34
Rosendo, St., bishop of Mondoñedo: I 36-7;IV 152
Rules, monastic, in Spain: see Basil;

Isidore; Fructuosus; Regula Communis; Libellus a RB subtractus

Sabaricus, pactum of: I 14,38-40; III 516,533A-5A;IV 150-1
sacramentum: I 16,21,30
Sáez, Emilio: I 28
Sahagún: IX 163,167-9,176;XIII 6
Salamanca, conference of: XII 165, 169-71
Salvus, abbot of Albelda: I 42 n.140; III 530
Samos, San Julián de: I 35
Sanabria: IX 160-2
Sancha, queen-empress of Leon-Castile: VIII 60-1,64,68-70,78A; XIII 9-10
Sánchez Albornoz, C.: I 35 n.120, 40-1
Sánchez Belda, L.: XIII 2
Sancho III el Mayor, king of Navarre: VI 362-3;VIII 54-5,63
Sancho, son of Alfonso VI: IX 172-6, 180-2;XI 317
Sancho García, count of Castile: VI 356-60
Sangüesa: XIII 12-13
-San Adrián de: see Vadoluengo
Santillana del Mar: III 522-3
Segl, Peter: X 321A;XI 357A
Seguin, Cluniac chamberlain: VIII 70
Semeno, prior of Nájera: XI 349-51
Serrano, Luciano: III 518;VI 357
servi-monachi: I 20,31-2
Sisericus, abbot Santiago de 'Mortalones', pactum of: I 29
Smaragdus, Expositio (Explanatio): I 41;III 528,530
Sobrado, San Salvador de: I 33 n.112
societas, of Cluny: VIII 53-4
Somport: XIII 9-11,13
Sotovellanos, Santa María de: I 39-40;III 519
Sousa Soares, T. de: IX 189A-90A
Statuta, Hugh I of Cluny: VIII 72-4
Stefanus, abbot Tabladillo, pactum of: I 42;III 526-7
Stephen, bishop of Osma: XII 166
Stephen, prior of Rates: XI 312
Stephen, Cluniac chamberlain: XI 331-3,358A
Stutz, Ulrich: I 23
subditi: I 32
Sueves: I 18-19

Tabladillo, San Juan de: I 11,42;III 526-7,529
Talmud: XII 168 n.21
Támara, Peace of: XIII 5-6
Tejada, San Pedro de: I 39-40;III 517-18,520;IV 150
Teresa, infanta-queen of Portugal: IX 156,160;XI 311-13,328-33, 335
Thompson, E.A.: V 151A-2A
Tierra de Campos: VI 351,353,356, 359-63;IX 171-2,174;XI 346
Toledo, Mozarabic monasteries of: V 148
-translators of: XII 167;XIII 1-2
Toledo, Visigothic Councils of: II 390; V 139-50
traditio: I 3-4,31-2;III 518,523
Tudeildus, abbot Vacariça, pactum of: I 30,38-9;III 517;IV 140-4,148-150,153-4

Udalric of Cluny, Consuetudines: VIII 60,67-70
Ura, San Mamés de: I 14,29-30;III 518-21
Urraca, queen-empress of Leon-Castile: VIII 75-6;IX 176,179-80,185,189A;X 312-13,315-18, 320A;XI 316-19,324-7,357A-8A
Urraca, abbess Villagonzalo Pedernales, pactum of: I 14;III 526-7

Vacariça, São Salvador de: I 30,37-39;III 517;IV 141-9
Vadoluengo, San Adrián de: VIII 82A; XIII 3,10-13
Valerius, De genere monachorum: I 21-2,31;III 524
Valpuesta: I 40;III 519-20
Valverde, San Pedro de: XI 307,326-327,336
Van den Eynde, D.: XIII 1,3,5
Vega, A.C.: II 378
vicinal monasticism: I 20-2,24-5
'Villa domini Didaci', Santa Eulalia in: I 36
Villafranca, Santa María de: XI 307, 353-6
Villafrío, San Salvador de: XI 308-11
Villagonzalo Pedernales, San Julián de: I 11,14;III 526-7
Villaverde, San Salvador de: X 313; XI 307-8,324.326
Vimara, abbot Mezonzo, pactum of: I 29,36
Vimieiro, Santa María de: XI 308, 331-3,336
Viñón, San Pedro de: III 522
Visclafredus, abbot Rosende, pactum of: I 34

Vives, José: V 151A
Vogüé, Adalbert de: II 396A

Wamba, king: I 19;V 192A
Wollasch, Joachim: VIII 78A

women, monasticism of: I 11,13-15; 28-30,41-2;III 534A-5A

Zaragoza: XIII 10,13